CHILDREN IN
ENGLISH SOCIETY

STUDIES IN SOCIAL HISTORY

edited by

HAROLD PERKIN

Senior Lecturer in Social History, University of Lancaster

A catalogue of books available in the
Studies in Social History and new books
in preparation for the Library will be
found at the end of this volume

CHILDREN IN ENGLISH SOCIETY VOLUME I

*From Tudor Times
to the Eighteenth Century*

by

Ivy Pinchbeck and Margaret Hewitt

LONDON: Routledge & Kegan Paul
TORONTO: University of Toronto Press

*First published 1969
in Great Britain by
Routledge & Kegan Paul Ltd
and in Canada and the United States of America by
University of Toronto Press
Printed in Great Britain by
C. Tinling & Co Ltd, London & Prescot*
Reprinted in 2018

© *Ivy Pinchbeck and Margaret Hewitt
No part of this book may be reproduced
in any form without permission from
the publisher, except for the quotation
of brief passages in criticism*

*RKP SBN 7100 6499 3
UTP SBN 8020 1650 2*
ISBN 978-1-4875-8128-2 (paper)

Contents

	PREFACE		vii
	LIST OF ILLUSTRATIONS		xi
I	Introduction	page	1
II	Childhood and Family in Pre-Restoration England		4
III	Child Marriage		44
IV	The Royal Wards		58
V	Borough Orphans		75
VI	The Vagrant and Delinquent Child		91
VII	'The Succourless Poor Child'		
	1. *Tudor Policies for the Deprived Child*		126
	2. *The Children's Workhouse Movement*		146
	3. *'Workhouse Innocents'*		175
VIII	The Illegitimate Child		200
IX	The Twin Disciplines of Work and Worship		
	1. *Apprenticeship*		223
	2. *The Religious Training of Children*		259
X	The Schoolchild		276
XI	The Child in a Changing Society		298
	BIBLIOGRAPHY		313
	INDEX		331

Preface

This book is the first of two volumes dealing with changing social attitudes towards children in English society and the resulting influences on social policy and legislation. They cover the whole period from Elizabethan times to the mid-twentieth century. At one time, children were regarded simply as the young of the species and the chattels of parents, but today they form a special age group of the community with a newly-defined status based on legal rights safeguarded by the State. In tune with the changing pattern of society's aspirations for the rising generation and the future welfare of the nation, specific social services are now provided for children.

The research into the social factors which led to this fundamental change in the pattern of English society originated in a course of postgraduate lectures on *The Child in English Society* for students of London University who were preparing to enter the Child Care Services. In the preparation of these lectures it became apparent that there existed no adequate systematic study of children in English society, and of the development of legislation affecting them; nor any thorough analysis of the social and economic forces and influences which shaped it. In the attempt to fill this gap it seemed desirable to start the study in the sixteenth century since some aspects of Tudor social policy for children are surprisingly more akin to the ideas of the Welfare State than those of any intervening period.

The present volume deals with these early idealistic policies and their ultimate failure, and the subsequent alternating patterns of benevolence and enthusiasm, indifference and neglect throughout the seventeenth and eighteenth centuries. It reveals no record of consistent progress for the welfare of various categories of children, but its study gives perspective to present-day policies and has important lessons for present and future administrators.

The second volume will deal with the more important developments of the nineteenth and twentieth centuries. In the larger, more complex industrial society of the nineteenth century the failure of society to provide adequately for the care and welfare

PREFACE

of children and the future of the nation became an urgent national problem. Renewed efforts by reformers to deal with both old and new problems resulted in a spate of legislation and new social policies for children. The notable achievements of the period 1800-1950 will be assessed in this final volume, and it is hoped that these two books will provide a significant addition to the literature of historical sociology in which children and childhood have so far been very largely neglected.

Many years have elapsed since this study was begun, and I have received generous help from many quarters. My grateful acknowledgments are due first to the Council of Bedford College who generously provided me with research assistance for the early stages of the work. To Daphne Hall and Dr. Peter Brock I owe much for the zeal and enthusiasm with which they pursued their researches, and much of their work is incorporated in this volume. My then colleagues of the Department of Sociology at Bedford College, Baroness Wootton and Professor Lady Williams, have from the outset given me great encouragement and help, and to them I express my warm appreciation and thanks.

To the Nuffield Foundation I owe a great debt of gratitude for their generosity in providing a grant to enable me to retire from University duties and to devote my whole time to the completion of the work. Unfortunately a breakdown of health shortly afterwards brought the work to a standstill for several years. It was only when I was able to secure the collaboration of Dr. Margaret Hewitt, a former pupil, and now Senior Lecturer at Exeter University, that further progress became possible. Dr. Hewitt has not only undertaken the necessary Library visits which I am no longer sufficiently mobile to make, but has played a major part in the arrangement and writing up of the material already collected. I am deeply grateful for her invaluable help, for without her enthusiasm and devotion the work could not have been completed, and it is therefore now published in our joint names. I am also grateful to the Nuffield Foundation for their kindly patience when the work was delayed by several periods of ill health.

Passages in Chapters II, III, IV, VI, VII and VIII have already appeared in my articles in the *British Journal of Sociology* for December 1954, December 1956 and March 1957,

PREFACE

and I am grateful to the editor and publisher for permission to reprint this material here. Acknowledgments are also due to the authorities who have allowed me to quote from copyright sources.

Finally, I am glad to acknowledge a debt to Mr. Roger Ashley of Worcester College for the efficient way in which he carried out the tedious job of checking the documentation and references, and to Miss Pamela Ffooks for the speed and skill with which she typed and re-typed successive versions of the text.

Long Crendon   IVY PINCHBECK

Illustrations

facing page

1. Cornelia Burch, aged two months by an unknown artist, 1581 (The Marquess of Tweeddale)   20

2. The children of James I, 1613 by an unknown artist (Major-General Sir George Burns, from a photograph in the Courtauld Institute)   20

3. Elizabeth Bridges as a girl of 14 (Collection of the Duke of Bedford)   21

4. Unknown child aged nine months by an unknown artist, 1590 (Mrs. A. T. Carre)   36

5. Title-page of Richard Mulcaster's *Positions*, 1581. Mulcaster was headmaster of Merchant Taylors' School 1561–86, and St. Paul's 1596–1608. (The Folger Shakespeare Library, Washington)   37

6. Children's games in the sixteenth century (Radio Times Hulton Picture Library)   68

7. Elizabethan schoolroom: woodcut of 1592 (Radio Times Hulton Picture Library)   68

8. A Tudor law court in session: The court of wards and liveries with Sir William Cecil, Lord Burghley, as presiding judge. By an unknown artist engraved in the eighteenth century by Vertue (The Goodwood Trustees)   69

9. The original charter of Exeter Court of Orphans (City of Exeter Archives)   84

10. 'Dining Hall, Asylum', drawn by Rowlandson and Pugin. Published in 1808, by Ackermann's at London (Radio Times Hulton Picture Library)   85

ILLUSTRATIONS

facing page

11. (a) The Title-page of Vowell's *Book of Orders* (City of Exeter Archives) 100

    (b) An extract from Vowell's *Book of Orders* in which he warns of the dire consequences of neglecting the welfare of the orphans of the poor (City of Exeter Archives) 100

12. Title-page of *The Poore Orphans Court, or Orphans Cry*, 1636 (Trustees of the British Museum) 101

13. Thomas Coram 1668–1751 (Radio Times Hulton Picture Library) 116

14. *The Industrious 'Prentice*. William Hogarth 117

15. The London Charity School Children in St. Paul's on the occasion of the National Thanksgiving for the recovery of George III, 1787. From a drawing by E. Dayes (Trustees of the British Musuem) 212

16. *The Graham Children*. William Hogarth (The Tate Gallery) 213

17. From, *A Collection of Pretty Poems For The Amusement of Children Three Foot High* (The Osborne collection of early children's books, Toronto Public Library) 228

18. The Princess Sophia Matilda of Gloucester. Reynolds (Royal collection) 229

I

Introduction

ONE of the more remarkable features of mid-twentieth century English society is the considerable social concern and statutory provision for the care and welfare of children. It is equally remarkable that the easy acceptance that such a concern is the unique achievement of the present age has largely gone unchallenged. 'Of all the assets of which the State stands possessed', wrote Clarke Hall in 1917, 'none are more valuable than the children, but of all its assets, the State has been in the past of none so wasteful or heedless.' This summary generalisation was doubtless prompted by the awakening in England of the public conscience to the importance of the care and welfare of children which was one of the most striking developments of the later nineteenth century. In our own day, admiration for the legislative successes which ultimately attended the promptings of nineteenth-century reformers and led to an entirely new conception of the duty of the State towards the child has contributed to a distorted assessment of the sociological significance of their achievements – as indeed, Clarke Hall's assertion well illustrates. However true it may be that eighteenth and early nineteenth-century social attitudes demonstrate a conspicuous lack of concern for the welfare of the children in that age, children certainly loomed large in the paternalistic legislation of the sixteenth and early seventeenth centuries. They were regarded as an important part of the social structure and valuable assets of

INTRODUCTION

the commonwealth; the problems associated with their maintenance and training were matters of national concern. Ideas as to the kind of training were often vastly different from those of today, but similar emphasis was laid on the importance of training each child for his proper place in society. Amidst much that is alien to our own modes of thought, some few aspects of social policy seem nearer to the ideas of the Welfare State than those of any other period intervening. But in a mental climate essentially different from our own, benevolence and harshness, even ferocity, were often intermingled, and a review of the treatment of children in various social groups reveals many social attitudes that contrast sharply with those commonly held today.

The present volume represents the first half of a study of social concern for children in England from the Tudor paternalism of the mid-sixteenth century to the legislation of the Welfare State of the mid-twentieth century. In it we shall analyse the various aspects of Tudor policy concerning children and discuss the ways in which later generations deliberately or unconsciously modified these policies. As a result of changed social attitudes the failure to provide adequately for the welfare of children was again by the end of the eighteenth century becoming a matter of increasing concern among thinking people and prompted a renewal of local and voluntary efforts to solve what had clearly become urgent national problems. It is no reflection on the sincerity of the personal, religious and humanitarian motives of many of the reformers to say that, in many ways, their concern was prompted by the changing context of social and family life in a country where urbanisation and rapid increase in population were presenting old problems such as poverty, vagrancy and delinquency in a new light and posing new problems relating to health, education and training. The terms in which these tendencies were recognised and discussed, and the attempts made to remedy some of them by statutory action, will be the subject of a second and final volume. Together, it is hoped that these two books will prove a significant addition to the literature of historical sociology in which social attitudes to childhood and to children have so far been very largely neglected.

In many ways, the solutions to which nineteenth-century reformers carefully felt their way were a restatement in modern

INTRODUCTION

terms of concepts which Tudor legislators had tried to incorporate in their social provision for children. For example, the growing demand in the nineteenth century for a national system of education was based on the belief that an untrained labour force was a threat both to the economy and to political stability – a belief which had informed much of Tudor legislation relating to the children of the poor in the sixteenth century, as we shall see. Again, the more recent demands for children to be educated according to their aptitudes and abilities and not merely according to their parents' income or social status would have been well understood by the citizens of London in the sixteenth century, who themselves subscribed large sums of money to establish a system of institutions to achieve precisely this end. Similarly, it could be argued that the establishment of a system of family allowances in England is the twentieth-century recovery of the sixteenth-century belief that 'if a man in pittie will ease his beast which is oppressed with burden, he must in nature relieve his neighbour which is oppressed with charge'. On the other hand, it is certainly true that a great deal of what we most value in our own social provision for children is not merely a recognition of a general responsibility for the young but a direct consequence of particular developments in the fields of medicine and developmental psychology which give us an understanding of children and childhood denied to our forebears. It is precisely this understanding which very largely makes twentieth-century social provision for the child qualitatively different from the provision made by Tudor governments for children of their own day.

II

Childhood and Family in Pre-Restoration England

1

IN Tudor, as in Victorian society, children were emphatically to be seen, not to be heard. Indeed, a child was not even to be much in evidence to the eye. It was deemed neither courteous, decorous nor wise to make him appear of value or note in his own eyes or in the eyes of his seniors. Amongst the upper classes, bonfires were often built in celebration of a wife's pregnancy: the actual birth might cause a similar conflagration. But having arrived, the child's infant progress was deemed of too little interest or importance to his family to merit record. Hence we know very little about the sort of lives very young children led. Accustomed as we now are to the centrality of the child in the family and to exhaustive studies of the motives, thoughts and activities of children, the lack of importance attached to childhood in Tudor England seems on first acquaintance astonishing. It becomes less astonishing, however, when one remembers how brief the total span of life – particularly of infant life – could be in the sixteenth century. Overcrowded houses, with their lack of adequate sanitary provisions, were the breeding ground of the contagious diseases, especially 'plague', which ravaged the country year after year until the middle of the seventeenth century. With the existing level of medical knowledge, disease and pain had to be endured and early death was to be expected.

CHILDHOOD IN PRE-RESTORATION ENGLAND

The average life span was set perhaps at thirty years, sometimes a little more, but with a large number of people in their grave long before that. Not surprisingly in these conditions the rate of infant mortality was appallingly high, hence the common practice of administering baptism, the sacrament necessary for the salvation of souls, on the same day that the child was born. It was not unusual, as a second child was born to a mother, for her first-born of twelve months or so to die.

In *The Boke of Chyldren* (1544), the first book on paediatrics ever to have been written by an Englishman, Thomas Phaire listed 'the manye grevous and perilous diseases' which commonly afflicted children of his day. His list included:

> Apostume of the brayne.
> . . . .
> Terryble dreames.
> The fallyng evill.
> The Palsey.
> Styfness of limmes.
> Bloudshotten eyes.
> Scabbynesse and ytche.
> . . . .
> Neasing out of measure.
> Bredyng of teeth.
> . . . .
> Colyke and rumblyng in the guttes.[1]

Phaire, a practising physician as well as a Solicitor in the Court of the Welsh Marches and Member of Parliament for Cardigan for several years, wrote his books 'to doo them good that have moste nede, that is to saye, children: and to shewe the remedies that god hath created for the use of man, to distribute in englyshe to them that are unlearned, parts of the treasure that is in other languages . . .'[2] His book was evidently a commercial success as seven separate editions were called for. Whether his 'holesome remedies' did not prove more fearful than the original disease is rather less certain. The prescribed remedy for 'teething in infants', once associated with convulsions from which many children died, was as follows:

'There be divers thinges y^t are good to procure an easy breeding of

[1] op. cit., p. 22 (1957 reprint of 1553 edition).
[2] ibid., p. 113.

teeth, among whom the chiefest is to annoint the gummes with the braynes of an hare, myxt with as much capos grease and honey, or any of these thynges alone, in exceeding good to supply the gummes and the synewes.'

More familiar to the modern parent would be his recommendation of the use of teething rings:

'To cause an easy breedyng of teethe, many thinges are rehearsed of autours, besydes this premisses, as the first cast tooth of a colte, set in silver and borne, or redde coralle in lyke maner, hanged about the necke, where upon the chylde ofte-times labours his gummes . . .'

'Apostume of the brayne', which heads Phaire's list – probably what we would now call meningitis – was to be remedied by 'a bath of mallowes, camomylle, and lillies sodden with a shepes head, till the bones fall, and with a sponge or softe cloutes, all to bath the head of the childe in a apostume, with the broth as hote as may be suffered, but in a hote matter, wete the broth luke warme, in the cooling, and after the bath, set on a playster thus.'[1] Even the most sanguine believer in the efficacy of 'natural' remedies might doubt the success to be expected of such recipes and it is difficult not to suspect that the curtailment of many infant lives was as much the result of the 'remedies' as the 'innumerable passions and diseases' to which children were subject.

Occasionally, Phaire's diagnosis of the causes of some diseases provides an interesting comment on prevailing standards of child care. Many diseases, for example, he attributes to 'an evyll diete' given to children 'whom they fede upon metes that increase rotten humours . . . by kewyse excesse of eating and drinking and surfitte'. Some afflictions he traces to more specific causes. Ulceration of the heads of infants, he claims, was caused 'manye times by droppyngs of restye bacon and salte beefe on their bare headdes' from the sides of bacon and salt beef which commonly hung from hooks in the ceiling.[2] Others, according to Phaire, are not merely attributable to a carelessness bred of ignorance, but to the deliberate exposure of children 'cast away by a wycked mother' – a practice not only significant of contemporary standards of infant welfare but of contemporary evaluation of child life itself.[3]

[1] ibid., pp. 23, 39, 40,
[2] ibid., p. 31.
[3] ibid., p. 10.

The high rates of mortality prevailing amongst children inevitably militated against the individual child being the focus and principal object of parental interest and affection. Indeed, they sustained the centuries-old belief that many children were begotten that a few might be preserved and bred a curiously detached attitude to the deaths of children. 'I have lost two or three children at nurse', wrote Montaigne, 'not without regret but without grief.'[1]

The precariousness of child life also detracted from the importance of childhood as an age status. In a society where few lived to grow old, age was of less significance than survival. Today, when every child is taught not merely its name but its age as soon as it can speak, this indifference to the age of children is one of the more curious features of sixteenth-century life. Parish Registers of birth were introduced in 1538, but long after that date, registration was never kept with any exactitude. Not in fact till 1836, after the Registration of Births Act – and even then by no means in every case – was it possible in this country to ascertain a person's age with any precision. Only in lawsuits did this uncertainty about age present occasional difficulties. Where feudal inheritance was not the principal point at issue, the procedure for proving age was simple. The individual conconcerned would be called before the judges of the case who settled the matter *aspectu corporis* – by his physical appearance. If there was any doubt in the judges' minds, they could summon a jury, composed in part of relatives, from whom further information was sought. In the case of a feudal ward, where property in land, right to marry and sale of wardship might all turn on the exact month and year of the child's birth, uncertainty of age raised more serious questions which were dealt with by specially appointed Committees of Wards whose duty it was to call for very detailed evidence to establish the date of a child's birth. In the absence of official records, such evidence was inevitably a matter of personal recollection, the date of birth being 'proved' by associating it with another outstanding event which occurred at the same time and for which there might be corroboration from other witnesses. Climatic events – thunderstorms, earthquakes – death or accidents amongst the relatives such as

[1] Quoted P. Ariès, *Centuries of Childhood*. 1962. p. 29, from Montaigne's Essays, vol. II, p. 8.

the breaking of a leg loomed large in the evidence given before the Committee. In the fourth year of Elizabeth's reign, for example, an old woman of 72 'proved' the age of Charles Framlingham of Shelley, Suffolk, by her recollection that he was born 'in the same year that the extreme hot summer was in and this she knoweth to be true by the occasion that she was then servant with the same Francis at the time of the birth of the said Charles and did within a fortnight after his birth bear the said Charles in her arms from Shelley to Crowshall in Debenham to be nursed'.[1]

For the most part, however, fascinating though they might be, the involved processes of Tudor justice were irrelevant to the lives of the majority of children whose age was not anything to be remarked. Of far greater general importance was the consciousness that children could be used to advance family fortune. Conscious of the brevity of life and all too aware of the possibly disastrous consequences of leaving estates unsettled at their death, parents were eager to introduce their sons and daughters into the adult world at the earliest possible moment, usually between the ages of seven and nine. Infancy was but a biologically necessary prelude to the sociologically all important business of the adult world. Children were thus not indulged with special treatment – no storybooks appear to have been written specifically for children – and the incidents of their children's lives received little special attention in parents' letters and journals. When, in 1620, E. Chamberlayne first published his *Reflections on the Present State of England*, written so that 'the whole state of England might be seen at once', he thought it adequate to devote rather less than four of its five hundred and sixteen pages to a section 'Concerning Children in England' – a section which dealt not with children in general but exclusively with the legal rights of children in the holding and disposing of property.[2]

Since childhood was of so little importance in contemporary society, children themselves pushed forward with eager anticipation in the affairs of the outside world. At an age when upper-class boys are today leaving their preparatory schools, in the sixteenth and seventeenth centuries their forebears were

[1] See J. Hurstfield, *The Queen's Wards*. 1958. pp. 162-3.
[2] 1669 edn. (Reprint).

going up to University. Hugh Latimer (b. 1490), later Bishop of Worcester, went up to Cambridge in 1504 at the age of fourteen. John Holles, afterwards Earl of Clare, who was born some seventy years later, was only twelve years of age when he matriculated for Christ's College, Cambridge in 1579. It was recorded of this young man that 'From his childhood he expressed an extraordinary towardliness, . . . his understanding and apprehension being quicke, and his judgement sound and ripe even in the morning of his life; . . . To Cambridge he was sent very young (being not thirteene yeares of age) but so well fitted for the University that the Maister of the Colledge (of wch he was) posing him at his first comming both in grammer and Greeke, and receaving from those years unexpected satisfaction to every question, he caught him up in his armes, and kissing him, to those that were by, said "This childe (if he lives) will prove a singular honour and ornament to this kingdome" '[1] – a prediction fully validated by subsequent events. Cambridge was far from having the monopoly of these precocious children. In 1595, at the age of twelve years, Edward, Lord Herbert of Cherbury, entered University College, Oxford, 'where he remembered to have disputed at his first coming in logic, and to have made in Greek the exercises required in that College oftener than in Latin'.[2]

It was the common custom, in the case of a young boy being sent to University, to send him with a guide or superintendent who remained with him as long as he stayed at the University. Edward, however, was accompanied to Oxford by his widowed mother who, after finding her son a fit tutor to whom she commended her son, 'continued there with him, and still kept him in moderate awe of herself, and so much under her own eye as to see and converse with him daily, but she managed this power over him without any such rigid harshness as might make her company a torment to her child, but with such a sweetness and compliance with the recreations and the pleasures of youth, as did incline him willingly to spend much of his time in the company of his dear and careful mother; which was to her great content'.[3]

[1] Gervase Holles, *Memorials of the Holles Family, 1493–1656*. ed. A. C. Wood, *Camden 3rd Series*, vol. LV, pp. 88–9.
[2] *The Autobiography of Edward Lord Cherbury*, ed. Sidney L. Lee, p. 39.
[3] ibid., Appendix III, pp. 314–15, quoting Walton, Life of George Herbert.

CHILDHOOD IN PRE-RESTORATION ENGLAND

Writing early in the seventeenth century, John Brinsley puts the age of entering University at fifteen, solemnly arguing in favour of this higher age not merely on the ground that it was preferable academically but because 'it is desirable that University students should be such as have good discretion how to governe themselves there, and to moderate their expenses, which is seldome times before fifteen yeares of age'.[1]

Whilst fifteen was apparently becoming the age before which responsibility was not to be expected of scholars, it was still possible to bear responsibility and earn distinction on the field of battle, at a much earlier age. Tudor parents had a statutory duty to see that their sons over the age of seven practised shooting at the butts rather than spend their time at 'handball, football or hockey', so that by early practice English efficiency with the long bow should be maintained. Hugh Latimer described how, as a small boy, he was trained in archery by his yeoman father. 'I had my bows brought me according to my age and strength; as I increased in them, so my bows were made bigger and bigger. For men shall never shoot well unless they be brought up to it.' Upper-class children serving as pages frequently accompanied their lords to battle at an incredibly early age. Lord Herbert's youngest brother, Thomas, born posthumously in 1597, was brought up for a while at school, then sent as page to Sir Edward Cecil, lord general of his Majesty's auxiliary forces to the princes in Germany, 'and was particularly at the siege of Juliers [1610], when he showed such forwardness as no man in that great army before him was more adventurous on all occasions'.[2] Thomas was thirteen years old at the time. Similarly, Prince Charles – later Charles II – at the age of twelve was in attendance on his father at the battle of Edge Hill (1642).

Upper or lower class, this early entry upon an adult career typified pre-Restoration England. At the age when young gentlemen were going to the wars or up to the University, other boys had either been working in the fields for some years or had entered on their apprenticeship.

At the same time, young girls of the upper classes were embarking on service in noble households. Maids of honour in

[1] *The Grammar Schoole*, p. 307.
[2] *The Autobiography of Edward Lord Cherbury*, pp. 23–4.

both the sixteenth and seventeenth centuries frequently entered the Queen's service as children. Lady Bridget Manners, for example, went to the Court when she was thirteen as one of Queen Elizabeth's maids of honour. For a young girl, life in a great household was not without its hazards, and her own mother, the widowed Countess of Rutland, was not entirely easy in her mind about the appointment. But, on the death of Bridget's father when she was eleven years old, Bridget had been sent to be brought up in the household of her step-grandmother, the Countess of Bedford. So far the child had received practically no education; her one accomplishment, to play the lute; her great detriment, a tendency to stoop. The Countess of Bedford found her ward so charming and attractive a girl, however, that she decided not to bother about her neglected education, but to obtain for her the next vacancy in the Queen's privy chamber. Lady Rutland, none too enamoured of the prospect of a Crown appointment, hoped that 'it would not as yet fall so, for Bridget has no acquaintance in that place and is therefore most unfit for it'.

Her daughter's guardian thought otherwise and continued to make interest at Court to such good purpose that Lady Bridget received the next appointment. The Countess of Rutland reluctantly sent two hundred pounds to buy an outfit, coupled with the admonition that Bridget should 'behave herself as shall be pleasing' and not disgrace her family by stooping at Court. The girl's grand-uncle, Roger Manners, one of the Esquires of the Body, was brought to write her a letter advising her how to conduct herself – an interesting example of how, in this hierarchical society, children were formally instructed how to behave towards members of its different social classes:

'First and above all things that you forgott not to have daily prayers to the Almightie God to endue you with his grace; then that you applie yourself hollye to the service of her majestie with all meeknes, love and obediens; wherein you must be dyligent, secret and faythfull. To your elders and superiors, of reverent behaviour; to your equalles and fellow-servants, syvill and courteyse; to your inferiors you must show all favour and gentlenes. Generally, that you be no medeler in the cause of others. That you use moch sylens, for that becometh maydes, especially of your calling. That your speech and indevars ever

CHILDHOOD IN PRE-RESTORATION ENGLAND

tend to the good of all and to the hurt of none. Thus in breve madam have you thes rules; which, if you have grace to follow, you shall fynd the benefit and your friendes shall rejoyce of your well doying.'[1]

Sad to say, none of Bridget's relations entertained the slightest anticipation that she would bring them anything but discredit. In the event, she appears to have been quite a success. Among the duties of the maids of honour, when the Queen dined alone, were included the laying of her Majesty's table – a ceremony performed with much veneration – taking charge of dishes brought by the yeomen of the guard and carrying them into the Queen's apartment where, except on public festivals, she dined, waited upon by her ladies. Bridget's role on these occasions was to act as the Queen's carver – no mean responsibility.

It is worth noticing how very significant for this young girl's subsequent upbringing was the death of her father and equally worth remembering how insecure were the lives of all children in a society where prevailing mortality rates frequently resulted in the premature death of one or other parent. Subsequent remarriages, the realignment of family relationships and the birth of a second or third family must often have contributed to a domestic atmosphere where children, particularly those of the earlier marriage, were forced out into the adult world when still, by modern standards, very young.

The records of the Verney family provide more than one illustration of this point. Sir Ralph Verney, who died in 1543, during the reign of Henry VIII, left nine young children concerning whom he made an earnest appeal to the 'overseers' of his will to 'maintain them in erudition and learning and [to] advance their welfare by good marriages and other promotions'. His wife, their own mother, who subsequently remarried four times, appears to have been more than content to leave these affairs to others since 'she had other matters on hand than the care of her first husband's children'.[2] Similarly, Sir Francis Verney, born many years later and who lost his own mother when he was five years old, was brought up by his father, Sir Edmund Verney, who had frequently to be away attending to the business of his estates, and his father's third wife, Mary

---

[1] Quoted Violet A. Wilson, *Queen Elizabeth's Maids of Honour*. 1922. p. 189.
[2] *Memoirs of the Verney Family*, ed. F. P. Verney. 1892. vol. I, p. 52.

Balkeney, whose third marriage this was also. According to all accounts, Francis 'seems never to have been under any control either from affection or education'.[1]

2

Brevity of life of both parents and children, dramatic as it appears by contrast to the longevity of the twentieth century, is only a partial explanation of why children and childhood was of so little account in pre-Restoration England. Of profound significance also was the current conception of society in which the family, not the individual, was the essential unit of social organisation. In such a view, children were no different from the adult members of the family in that they were all conceived as component parts of a far larger unit, the extended family, to whose interest those of the interrelated nuclear families of parents and children were subordinated. The promotion of family ambition, the advancement of family interest, not the realisation of private ambition and the achievement of personal success were seen as the common, all-important social task. Hence, unlike modern society, where personal happiness and fulfilment are regarded as the *sine qua non* of a successful marriage and of family life, the personal affections of husband and wife, parents and children, were of minor concern in sixteenth- and seventeenth-century England. Love was not regarded as a sufficient reason for marriage; although, once married, a husband and wife had a duty to love one another. Time and again, this is one of the themes stressed in the very large number of treatises published at this time, the so-called Books of Domestic Relations, written for the education and edification of the middle classes into whose homes so many found their way.

Typical of these was Becon's *Boke of Matrimony* (1543), which stresses the excellence and dignity of marriage; what marriage is from different points of view; for what purposes it was instituted; and offers advice on the principles of conduct of a family. Touching on the duties of husband and wife, Becon presents them as being 'to love each other, to beget children, to live chaste'. The duties of a husband to his wife were 'to act as guide, philosopher and friend, to provide for, defend and help

[1] ibid., p. 60-1.

her', while the duties of a wife to her husband were 'to serve him in subjection, to be modest in speech and apparel, to have charge of the house and its management'.[1]

To the modern eye, the distinction Becon makes here between the respective duties of husband and wife reveals an unfamiliar relationship on which to found mutual love. Basic to Tudor ideas of family, however, was that of the husband as head and governor of his house, concerning which Biblical evidence was constantly adduced. Even after the break with Rome, when new opinion regarding women and marriage began to gain favour, the most *avant-garde* of the Books of Domestic Relations continued to lay stress on the necessity of the obedience of the wife, even where they advocated other methods than the traditional beating of wives to achieve it. Henry Smith, for example, published an expanded sermon in 1591, *A Preparation to Marriage* in which he commands husbands not to strike their wives, – 'Husbands must holde their hands and wives their tungs.'[2] Wife-beating, however, continued to have its advocates long after Smith's utterance on the subject, as the protestations of William Heale's *An Apologie for Women* (1609) and the anonymous *Anatomy of a Woman's Tongue* (1638) all too clearly show.

In a society where the romantic view of marriage was so heavily at a discount, it is hardly to be expected that the parent-child relationship would be sentimentalised. In Becon's treatise, in the section on 'the conduct of the family', the duties he outlines of the child to the parent are the almost exact counterpart of the duties of the wife to her husband as he had already stated them. Children were to be 'subject and obedient', since 'the word of God hath given parents great prerogatives over their children'.[3]

These prerogatives a father often upheld with his children or with his wife with ferocious determination. Sir Peter Carew, later in life to become a famous soldier but in his youth 'rather a troublesome boy', ran away from Exeter Grammar School and, climbing on to a turret of the city wall, threatened to throw himself down if a master tried to come after him. His father, hearing of this, had him coupled to a hound, led back home and

---
[1] See Chilton Latham Powell, *English Domestic Relations 1487–1563*. N. Y. 1917, p. 128.
[2] See L. B. Wright, *Middle-class Culture in Elizabethan England*. 1935. p. 208.
[3] See Powell, op. cit., p. 128.

chained in a dog-kennel, where he remained until he succeeded in escaping.¹ More commonly, however, a Biblical punishment for those who rebelled against Biblically inspired authority was employed – the rod. In one of the earliest handbooks on the upbringing of the young, parents were advised:

> If thy children be rebel and will not bow them low,
> If any of them misdo neither curse nor blow;
> But take a smart rod and beat them in a row
> Till they cry mercy and their guilt well know.²

Remarkable for the temperateness of its advice on the use of corporal punishment – which he considered 'as necessary for children as meat and drink' – was Thomas Becon's *Catechism*, published in the reign of Edward VI: 'Notwithstanding the correction ought to be gentle and favourable ... According to the fault and also according to the nature of the child that offendeth.' Before punishing their children, he adjures parents to explain the nature of their fault and the reason for punishing and call for amendment. 'The good will of the father toward his child ought to appear and shine even in the midst of his anger, and a moderation is to be had both in words and stripes; that the wits of the children be not dulled, nor they driven to such an hatred of their parents that they begin no more to love as parents, but to hate them as tyrants and hereof take an occasion to run away from them.' The over-indulgent father, he asserts, is to be condemned but 'even so are those parents to be discommended which furiously rage against their children, and without consideration beat them as stock fish'. Such parents he claims are 'rather butchers than fathers'.³

Rather more typical of the age was the tone taken by Becon's friend, Hugh Latimer, in the course of a sermon he preached in Lincolnshire in 1552:

'I exhort you, in God's behalf, to consider the matter, ye parents: suffer not your children to lie, or tell false tales. When you hear one of your children to make a lie, take him up, and give him three or four good stripes and tell him that it is naught; and when he maketh another lie, give him six or eight

---
¹ M. St. Claire Byrne, *Elizabethan Life in Town and Country*. 1947. p. 186.
² Quoted by Sylvia Lynd, *English Children*. 1942. p. 16.
³ *The Catechism of Thos. Becon.*, ed. John Ayre. 1844. p. 354.

stripes and I am sure when you serve him so, he will leave it . . .'[1]

Ministers, parents, teachers chanted in chorus 'foolishness is bound up in the heart of the child': in all children they detected 'a stubbornness and natural pride which must be broken and beaten down so that the foundation of their education being laid in humility and tractability, other virtues might in their turn be built thereon'.[2] Girls and boys alike were subjected to this brutal and brutalising discipline of physical violence which had long been the first resort of English parents. Furnivall, for example, quotes two incidents relating to Agnes Paston, which illustrate very clearly how deeply rooted in English practice such discipline was. In 1457, she wrote a letter to the tutor of her fifteen-year-old son saying that 'if the boy hath not done well nor will not amend, truly lash him till he will amend'. Of her daughter, Elizabeth, who had been so foolish as to advance wishes of her own as to the man she would marry, it was related that 'she was never in so great sorrow as she is nowadays, for she may not speak with no man, whosoever come . . . nor with servants of her mother's . . . and she hath since Easter the most part been beaten once in the week or twice and sometimes twice on a day, and her head broken in two or three places . . .'[3] Over a century later, young girls were being treated with an equal severity. Lady Jane Grey related to Roger Ascham when she was fifteen years old:

'When I am in the prescence of either father or mother, whether I speake, kepe silence, sit, stand or go, eate, drinke, be merrie or sad, be sewying, playing, dancing, or doing anie thing els, I must do it, as it were, in such weight, mesure and number, even so perfitelie as God made the world, or els I am so sharpely taunted, so cruellie threatened yea presentlie some tymes with pinches, and nippes and bobbes, and other waies which I will not name for the honour I bear them so without measure misordered that I think myself in hell till tyme cum that I must go to M. Elmer (Aylmer) who teacheth me so gentlie and so pleasantlie, with sach faire allirement to learning that I

---

[1] *The Works of Hugh Latimer*, ed. G. E. Corrie. 1844. vol. I, p. 501. (From Sermons preached in Lincolnshire, 1552.)

[2] A. M. Earle, *Child Life in Colonial Days*. 1899. pp. 191-2.

[3] Foreword of *Early English Meals and Manners.*, p. vii.

think all the time nothing whiles I am with him. And when I am called from him, I fall on weeping.'[1]

Queen Elizabeth herself did not scruple to use violence against her maids of honour when they displeased her. She is reputed to 'have used the fair Mistress Brydges (the daughter of Lord Chandos) with words and blows of anger'.[2] In a world where extreme pain was a commonplace of everyday existence, physical violence was taken for granted in all walks of life.

The acceptance of physical punishment was instilled into the children themselves by the custom of teaching them to 'kiss the rod' by the repetition of set phrases. In Richard Whitford's *A Worke for Householders*, first published in 1531 and reprinted in 1532, 1533 and 1537, is set out under the heading 'Discipline of Children' a litany of penitential verses to be given to children to repeat at the end of the day:

> Yf I lye/backebyte/or stele
> Yf I curse/scorne/mocke/or swere
> Yf I chyde/fyght/stryve/or threte
> Then I am worthy to be bete
> Good mother or maytresse myne
> Yf any of these nyne
> I trespace to your knowynge
> With a newe rodde and a fyne
> Erly naked before I dyne
> Amende me with a scourgynge.[3]

By the beginning of the seventeenth century, there is some evidence that for children as for wives, the infliction of severe physical punishment was becoming rather less socially acceptable and two divergent attitudes to the disciplining of children begin to emerge: the old, medieval, puritanical attitude and the other which preferred children in the Puritanical sense of the word 'spoilt'. Influential in this latter development were the *Essays* of Montaigne (b. 1533) in which he describes how he had been brought up by his own parents. These *Essays* had had a great vogue on the Continent and in England a generation before Florio's version appeared in 1603 and began to influence the

[1] From Roger Ascham, *The Scholemaster*. 1570. Ed. W. A. Wright, 1904. pp. 201–2.
[2] Quoted Wilson, op. cit., p. 223.
[3] Quoted Powell, op. cit., pp. 109–10.

upbringing of children from that time forward. In marked contrast to Lady Jane Grey's account of her own upbringing, Montaigne relates how he was never beaten and, in a well-known passage, suggests that schools should properly be places of delight, hung with green boughs rather than places of misery dedicated to the 'bloody twigs'.[1] Montaigne's immediate success was perhaps limited, but contemporary evidence shows it to have been far from ineffective. A letter written in 1639 from the two-year-old Edmund Verney's great-grandmother to his grandfather and father in London to whom he had been sent, is an indication that in some minds the idea that parents might profitably spare the rod had taken root:

'Let me beg of you and his mother that nobody whip him but Mr. Poerrye [his tutor]; Yf you doe goe a violent waye with him, you will be the first that will rue it, for i veryly beleve he will reserve ingery by it.'[2]

Nevertheless, it would be folly to suggest that such evidence implied a diminished insistence on the awful authority of parents. Children continued to be drilled into habits of obedience and reverence to their parents, habits which not only related to attitudes of mind but to overt behaviour. Elizabeth Tanfield, later Lady Falkland (1585–1639) as long as her mother lived always knelt when speaking to her mother 'sometimes for more than an hour together, though she was but an ill kneeler and a worse riser'.[3] Long after Lady Falkland's death, children were trained to adopt respectful postures when in the presence of their parents. The necessity for this is dealt with at some length in Thomas Cobbett's *A Fruitfull and Usefull Discourse touching on the Honor due from Children to Parents, and the duty of Parents towards their Children* (1656). Cobbett was a Puritan minister who emigrated to Lyn in New England and his *Discourse* – first published there in 1654 and subsequently widely read in England – is a book of two hundred and forty-three pages containing an exhortation to filial reverence and paternal duty based on innumerable references to Holy Writ. Like writers of the earlier Books of Domestic Relations, he combed the whole Bible for references and texts with which he interspersed every few lines of

---

[1] See Lynd, op. cit., p. 24.
[2] *Memoirs of the Verney Family*, vol. I, p. 217.
[3] Quoted Earle, op. cit., p. 193.

his work. In effect, the *Discourse* is a lengthy exposition of the fifth Commandment. Children were advised to 'Present your Parents so to your minds, as bearing the image of God's Father-hood, and that also will help your filiall awe and Reverence to them.' According to Cobbett, filial reverence consisted of a holy respect and fear both of a parent's person and of his words: a reverent child felt ashamed of his faults before his parents; he feared to lose their favour, feared to cross their just interests, feared to grieve them or to fall short of their expectations. Moreover, he displayed these fears in his outward actions. The Old Testament is quoted to show that God required children that 'they should rise up and stand bare before their Parents when they come to them, or speak to them ... It stands not with Parents' Honour for children to sit and speak, but rather they should stand up when they speak to Parents'. If a child saw his parents approaching him, he went to meet them and bowed to them; he spoke reverently to them and of them, and to express his sense of shame for his faults, he blushed and confessed his unworthiness when they corrected him.[1] Children's irreverence, Cobbett claims, is shown by their rudely sitting before their parents and 'in gabling, laughing and flouting, even in their parents' prescence'. Children, he argues, should not 'prevent or interupt their parents in speaking' and cites Job (29.9.10) where even 'Princes and Nobles' are said to have refrained from speaking in the presence of their elders.

Unhappily, Cobbett has to record that not all seventeenth-century children seem to have treated their parents with the respect due to them: 'Again, how over familiar do too many children make themselves with their parents? as if hail-fellow well met (as they say) and no difference twixt parent and child: too many there are who carry it proudly, disdainfully and scornfully towards parents, and its well their very parents escape their faults: but what the end of such graceless children will be', Cobbett grimly observes, 'we have shewed from Proverbs 30.17.'[2] ('The eye that mocketh his father, and despiseth to obey his mother, the ravens of the valley shall pick out, and the young eagles shall eat it.')

---

[1] Edmund Morgan, *The Puritan Family*. Boston, 1944. p. 59.
[2] Thomas Cobbett, *A Fruitfull and Usefull Discourse touching on the Honour due from Children to Parents and the Duty of Parents towards their Children*. 1656. p. 94.

It has sometimes been claimed that, with the growing ascendancy of Puritanism in England in the seventeenth century, a change for the worse appeared in the condition of English children. As far as their attitudes to the punishment of children is concerned, however, this would be a difficult case to substantiate. As E. S. Morgan remarks of Puritan praises of the rod, it is essential to remember that they regarded it as the last resort. They saved their highest approval for a much more intelligent discipline which depended for its efficacy both upon the development of a special attitude in the child and upon a thorough understanding by the parent of each child's personality.[1] 'Parents', wrote Cobbett, 'should observe the genius, bent and capacity of their children . . . then carry it wisely and suitably towards them as that their disposition requireth.' Children were to be admonished 'if they be strongly bent to some vice worse than others . . . after which course taken, then watch them more narrowly, and spare them not for it if they fall into lying again.' Earlier in his *Discourse*, Cobbett had written that parents should secure their children's respect, not by immediate and constant recourse to the rod, but by being themselves models of good behaviour. Thus, whilst parents are warned against undermining their authority 'by being too fond of your children and too familiar with them at sometimes at least, and not keeping constantly your due distance: such fondness and familiarity breed contempt and irreverency in children', they are also urged not to demesne themselves 'by reproachful and reviling speeches . . . in rashness of anger and fury or by any other uncivil, or unseemly expression of rage against them, as flinging things at them, which might endanger life or blind . . .'[2]

3

The seriousness with which parents were advised 'to keep their distance' with their children hints at changes that were beginning during the second half of the sixteenth century in the organisation of family life, which were to have far-reaching effects not merely on the family itself but on the whole of society. Traditionally, the size of a middle- or upper-class household

[1] Morgan, op. cit., p. 59.
[2] Cobbett, op. cit., pp. 96–7, 219–20.

1 (*top*) Cornelia Burch, aged two months by an unknown artist, 1581
2 (*bottom*) The children of James I, 1613 by an unknown artist

3 Elizabeth Bridges as a girl of 14

might be as many as thirty or forty, sometimes even more. This enormous size was a consequence of including in one's 'family' not merely one's own children, but their young brides, sometimes even first-born grandchildren; one's elderly relatives, cousins, sisters, unmarried aunts, as well as domestic servants and any apprentices of the head of the house. All these lived together as one household, eating and living in common, with no special part of the house set apart for the servants and apprentices. This arrangement was to some extent a reflection of a medieval application to household organisation of 'economy of scale'. Increasing affluence, however, was making it possible for some sections of the wealthy classes to discriminate domestically between family and servants' quarters, while the growth of the middle classes – the yeomen farmers, the small merchants and tradesmen – led to smaller homes in which a more personal family life became possible.

Although we have so far mostly referred to the Books of Domestic Relations to illustrate the advice they gave on the relation of husband and wife and the disciplining of children, these topics did not exhaust the advice they had to offer. Above all, it is important to recall that every one of them laid special emphasis on the parental duty to see that children were educated in some honest calling and to prepare girls for marriage and housekeeping. Becon admonished parents 'towards the end of their [children's] schooling ... to give thought to the most suitable career for them and their aptitudes'.[1] Just how, in practice, this was achieved depended on the social class of the parent. Writing of the social structure of Elizabethan England, A. L. Rowse remarks 'never can there have been more class-consciousness, one feels, in any age'[2] and draws attention to the great care taken by the upper classes, at a time when it was customary to dress children as diminutive adults, to dress their children according to their rank. Indeed, as Dr. Rowse points out, the authoritarianism which characterised the parent–child relationship at this time, was directly related to this consciousness of social hierarchy: 'The constant theme of Elizabethan thought and teaching on the subject of society is the necessity of order and degree and the consequent insistence upon authority

[1] Becon, *Catechism*, ed. Ayre, Parker Society, Cambridge 1844. p. 355.
[2] A. L. Rowse, *The England of Elizabeth*. 1951. p. 245.

and obedience. The lesson was enforced through all the institutions of society, through a thousand channels.'[1]

Elizabethan society was characterised by three major divisions. The nobility and the landed gentry; the unskilled labourers, illiterate peasantry, and the very small artisans whose trade required little training and whose rewards were meagre; and between these two extremes a group, already rapidly increasing, whose thought and interest centred in business profits, 'merchants, tradesfolk, skilled craftsmen and the host of small proprietors of town and countryside'. Of the poorer classes we must admit quite frankly that we know very little of how they educated their children to 'an honest calling'. A largely illiterate peasantry leaves few records for later generations to ponder. Parents whose homes had walls of mud or turves and roofs of reed thatch, the floors of bare earth, the furniture a trestle table and rough stools or forms and who lay at night on mattresses of plaited straw were scarcely in a position, however, to support their children through either a prolonged education or a long apprenticeship. Some of them were too poor to support their children at all and the parish records contain numerous entries concerning the desertion of unwanted children who were found dead on the roads from exposure and starvation – a practice which continued among the poorer classes up to the nineteenth century. Thus in December 1556, a woman named Morton was brought before the Mayor and Aldermen of London for having abandoned her child in Southwark Street. She was sentenced to be whipped in Bridewell and then put in pillory in Cheapside with a paper on her head reading 'Whipped in Bridewell for having foresaken her child in the streets'.

Children of the poor fortunate enough to survive an infancy parlous enough without these additional hazards must have been put out to work at the earliest possible opportunity. For the children of the agricultural labourer there could have been only slight chances of education and apprenticeship. Poverty and tradition alike ruled otherwise. Following on the great scarcity of agricultural labour after the Black Death, attempts had been made to tie the labourers and their children to the soil. A statute of 1388 ordained that any boy or girl 'which used to labour at the Plough or Cart, or other Labour or Service of Husbandry *till*

[1] ibid., p. 532.

they be of Age of Twelve Years, that from thenceforth they shall abide by the same Labour, without being put to any Mystery or Handicraft'. At the same time, the landowners begged the King to ordain that 'no bondman nor bondwoman shall place their children at schools, as has been done, so as to advance their children in the world by their going into the Church'. A subsequent statute of 1405–6 forbade workers in husbandry to 'put their Son or Daughter, of whatsoever Age he or she be, to Serve as Apprentices to no Craft nor other Labour within any City or Borough in the Realm, except he have Land or Rent to the Value of Twenty Shillings by the year at leest, but they shall be put to other labours as their Estates do require, upon Pain of one Year's Imprisonment, and to make Fine and Ransom at the King's Will'. A saving clause added, however, 'that every Man and Woman of what Estate and Condition that he be, shall be free to set their Son or Daughter to take learning at any manner of School that pleaseth them within the Realm.' Re-enactment of these regulations shows how difficult it was to enforce the law, but the assumption that labourers' children were 'used to labour at the Plough or Cart' under the age of twelve itself suggests that probably few of them had other opportunities.

Writing at a time when grammar schools were increasing in number, William Forrest was advocating the primary education of children in the reign of Henry VIII: 'Those too young to take employment to be trained up to handicrafts ... infantes, I mean Under Eight yeares of age; their tyme I wolde thus too be put in Usage'. At four, children should be put to school 'to lerne some literature' so that they can understand God's ways, 'to worke in that age their power is but small'. He continues:

> Leste some perhaps, at this might thus objecte,
> The poureman his child cannot so prefer:
> bycause hee hath not substance in effecte
> for so longe season to fynde his scholer,
> as (for his schoolinge) too paye his Maister;
> to which I answere, it must provyded bee;
> in eaveye towne the Scoole too go free.[1]

A similar idea was suggested by Thomas Starkey in his *Dialogue* where he advocated the establishment of parish schools

[1] F. J. Furnivall, *Early English Meals and Manners*. 1818. p. xcii.

for all children under seven years of age. An interesting illustration of how much this sort of suggestion was likely to impress contemporary society is quoted by Furnivall: '... the secular Cathedral Church of Canterbury was altered from monks to secular men of the clergy, viz. prebendaries, canons, petty canons, choristers and scholars. At this creation were present Thomas Cranmer, archbishop, with divers other commissioners ... it came to pass that, when they should elect the children of the Grammer School, there were of the commissioners more than one or two who would have none admitted than the sons or younger brethren of gentlemen. As for others, husbandmen's children, they were more meet, they said, for the plough, and to be artificers, than to occupy the places of the learned sort; so that they wished none else to be put to the school, but only gentlemen's children.' To Cranmer's objection that poor men's children were 'more apt to apply their study, than is the gentleman's son delicately educated', it was replied that 'it was meet for the ploughman's son to go to the plough and the artificer's son to apply the trades of his parent's vocation; and the gentleman's children are meet to have the knowledge of government and rule of commonwealth. For we have, they said, as much need of ploughmen as any other state; and all sorts of men need not go to school.' Cranmer refused to be taken in by this argument, not least because he saw it as a restriction on 'the freedom of God to distribute his good gifts of grace upon any person, nor nowhere else but as we and other men shall appoint them to be employed, according to our fancy, and not according to his most godly will and pleasure...' He did not scruple to add that, but for this freedom, 'none of us here being gentlemen born (as I think) but had our beginning that way from a low and base parentage' could have risen to their present pre-eminence.[1]

This story gains in point as an illustration of how class feeling was coming to influence educational provision when one remembers that schools such as the one at Canterbury had originally been designed for the lower ranks of society and open to the sons of the poorer gentry. Moreover, it is interesting that Cranmer, who had himself risen to eminence by education, was only disposed to argue: 'that if the gentleman's son be apt to learning, let him be admitted; if not, let the poor man's child

[1] ibid., p. li and p. lii.

that is apt enter in his course'. The scandalous way in which choristers and poor boys were eventually done out of their proportion of the endowments in the Cathedral schools, and even, as was the case with Christ's Hospital, in foundations of later origin which had been intended almost exclusively for the children of the poor, is too well known to need further documentation here. It certainly encourages the belief that, for the most part, the children of the poorer classes were excluded from education and set to work as soon as they were capable of scaring crows, tending a flock of sheep, holding a spindle, knitting, or any of the hundred and one things that the smallest, least educated child might do to contribute to his keep.

Whilst the details of the upbringing of poor children remain shrouded in the obscurity which was to typify the rest of their lives, the way in which the upper and middle classes prepared their children for the adult world is extensively documented, and in the differences in child-rearing practices which characterised these two social groups can be found both clues to the realignment of contemporary socio-economic forces and the key to the emergence of modern conceptions of childhood and family.

To the outside observer there seemed little to distinguish – or to choose – between upper- and middle-class practices:

'The want of affection in the English is strongly manifested toward their children,' wrote an Italian observer at the beginning of the sixteenth century, 'for having kept them at home till they arrive at the age of seven or nine years at the utmost, they put them out, both males and females, to hard service in the houses of other people, binding them generally for another seven or nine years. And these are called apprentices, and during that time they perform all the most menial offices; and few are born who are exempted from this fate, for everyone, however rich he may be, sends away his children to the houses of others, whilst he in return, receives those of strangers into his own. And on inquiring their reason for this severity, they answered that they did it in order that their children might have better manners. But I, for my part, believe that they do it because they like to enjoy all their comforts themselves, and that they are better served by strangers than they would be by their own children. Besides which, the English being great epicures, and very avaricious by nature, indulge in the most delicate fare themselves and give their household the coarsest bread, and beer, and cold meat baked on Sunday for the week, which, however, they allow them in great abundance. That if they had their own children at home, they would be obliged to give them the same food as they made use for themselves.'[1]

There was, of course, nothing new in this sending of children from their own home at an early age. In the Middle Ages, every aristocratic household had its nucleus of young pages, esquires and maids, themselves the offspring of noble households, and the practice of vicarious child-rearing had merely spread until it became a habit with the well-to-do to send their children away rather than complete their education at home. Amongst the merchant classes, where the whole problem of education was bound up with apprenticeship, many company regulations forbade the apprenticing of sons to fathers, so that where these families were concerned (and there were none more honourable or highly esteemed among the middle class) a similar custom had been established of necessity. In neither the upper nor the middle classes, however, was it altogether true that the children were invariably sent off to complete strangers. In many cases they were sent to friends or acquaintances or perhaps relatives. But in every case the purpose of sending the children away from home was the same: to ensure for them a quality of supervision and training unalloyed by the sentiment of family in a household whose own influence might, it was hoped, be used to the benefit of the children it accepted into its service.

The significance of the practice in pre-Restoration England is analysed by P. Ariès in *Centuries of Childhood* where he points out that this was 'an apprenticeship in a much wider sense of the word than its use today. Children were sent to another family, with or without contract, to live and assume their life, or to learn the manner of a knight, or a craft, or even to follow instruction in classical education. The "services" the children rendered were not those of the paid domestics – as the Italian diplomat, tricked by the ambiguity of language declares – but the kind of service linked with medieval chivalry; a personal attendance through which one learnt ways of behaviour and social manners. "Apprenticeship", seen in this broad sense, was thus a formalised system

[1] *A Relation, or rather a true account of the Island of England* . . . (translated by Charlotte Augusta Sneyd), *Camden Society*. 1847. No. 37, pp. 24–5.

of education stemming from medieval days when schools had been established for clerics only. There was nothing servile about such an apprenticeship: it was a carry over from the days when, for the nobility and gentry, accomplishments – manners and courtesy, music and singing, knowledge of orders of precedence, rank, heraldry and the ability to carve – were much more important than academic education. Such accomplishments could not be acquired in the Universities but in the houses of the nobility and gentry'.[1]

The Earl of Essex, in a letter to Lord Burghley, written in 1576, commends his son to him:

'Nevertheless, uppon the assured Confidence that your love to me shall dissend to my Childrenne, and that your Lordship will declare yourself a Friend to me, both alive and dead, I have willed *Mr Waterhouse* to shew unto you how you may with Honor and Equity do good to my Sonne *Hereford*, and how to bind him with perpetual Frendship to you and to your House. And to the Ende I would have his Love towardes those which are dissended from you spring up and increase with his Yeares, I have wished his Education to be in your Household, tho' the same had not bene allotted to your Lordship as Master of the Wardes; and that the whole Tyme, which he shold spend in *England* in his minority, might be devided in Attendance uppon my *Lord Chamberlayne* and you, to the End that as he might forme himself to the Example of my Lord of *Sussex* in all the Actions of his Life, so that he might also reverance your Lordship for your Wisdome and Gravity, and lay up your Counsells and Advises in the Treasury of his Hart.'[2]

Nearly half a century later, the nobility were continuing the same practice. In 1620, the Earl of Arundell wrote out instructions for his son whom he was sending to be brought up in the household of the Bishop of Norwich:

'You shall in all Things reverence, honour and obey my Lord Bishop of *Norwich* as you would do any of your Parents, esteeming whatsoever he shall tell or Command you, as if your Grandmother of *Arundel*, your Mother, or myself, should say it; and in all things esteem yourself as my Lord's Page; a breeding which youths of my house far superior to you were accustomed

[1] op. cit., 411.
[2] Furnivall, op. cit., p. xv.

unto, as my Grandfather of *Norfolk* and his Brother, my good Uncle of *Northampton* were both bred as Pages with Bishops . . .'[1]

A period spent in service was the usual method at this time of preparing upper-class girls to adorn the only vocation open to them – marriage. Moreover, since the one and only aim of most Tudor parents was to dispose of their daughters as speedily as might be by arranging an early and, if possible a wealthy, match for them, the household into which a girl was sent was usually chosen with this end in view.

Some households earned a considerable reputation for the way in which they raised the girls placed in their care, a reputation of which their mistresses were well aware and considerably proud. The Countess of Huntingdon, whose ability as an instructress of upper-class girls was as widely acknowledged as Lord Burghley's as an instructor of their brothers, writes of herself in 1618 in a letter: '. . . me, whoe though my self doe say it, I think ther will none meke questen, but j knoe how to breed and gouern yong gentlewomen.'[2] The Countess clearly also knew how to make suitable matches for them, as the early matrimonial history of the young heiress, Margaret Dakins (b. 1571) well illustrates. Margaret was received into the Countess's household at an early age and her first two marriages were both arranged for her by the Earl of Huntingdon. The first, when she was eighteen, to the son of the Earl of Essex who, with his two sisters, was being brought up in the Earl's house; and the second, after this young man's early death, to the Countess's own nephew, Thomas Sydney, 'whose preferment the same Earle sought'.[3]

It is worth noticing, incidentally, that the 'co-educational' nature of the household over which the Countess of Huntingdon presided was by no means unusual. Nor apparently were some of the consequences. The parents of the Lady Anne Clifford (b. 1590) were both reared in that 'very school of vertue', the household of the Earl of Bedford, to whom her father had become a ward at the age of eleven.[4]

Unlike their nineteenth-century descendants, these girls were not so much trained to attract husbands – their parents or guardians were as likely as not to do that for them – but to become

[1] ibid., p. ix.
[2] *Diary of Lady Margaret Hoby*, ed. D. M. Meads. 1930. p. 7.
[3] ibid., p. 9.
[4] ibid., p. 56.

CHILDHOOD IN PRE-RESTORATION ENGLAND

good wives. The lessons they had to learn in the 'schools' to which they were sent were as many and as complex as the duties of the state for which their education was a preparation. A mistress of a household such as they themselves might preside over, would be expected to manage a large number of servants, to supervise the working of estates of which they were often left in charge, to ensure a store of food and clothing for the needs of a numerous household which might be literally cut off from civilisation during the winter months, and to undertake the making of drugs and simples and the practice of surgery and midwifery. Thus Margaret Dakins had her education directed to writing, the keeping of accounts, to acquiring a knowledge of household and estate management, of surgery and salves, as well as to singing and playing the alpharion. Her personal diaries, written when Lady Hoby (after her third marriage), show how extensively she was required in later life to employ these skills:

'I went to a wiffe in trauill of child, about whom I was busey tell: I a Cloke, about which time, She bing deliuered and I hauing praised god, returned home and betook ny selfe to priuat praier ...'[1] There are numerous entries referring to her attending to the minor ailments and injuries of 'poore folkes': 'dressed apoore boies legge that came to me ... dressed the hand of one of our seruants that was verie sore Cutt',[2] she writes. No contemporary would have thought these activities in the least extraordinary for a woman in her position. To act as a midwife was frequently the benevolent duty of the lady of the manor, who usually knew more of simple surgery and medicine than anyone in the village. Acquirement of such knowledge was an essential and traditional part of the upbringing of girls of wealth and rank, since no doctor was, as a rule, available and the whole district depended on her ministrations or upon those of the local quack or herdswoman. Elsewhere, Lady Hoby notes that she has been engaged in 'stilling'[3] and preserving sweetmeats, and that she 'was busie to dye wooll tell allmost diner time',[4] or, again, that she has been occupied with the management of the estate.[5]

[1] ibid., p. 63.
[2] ibid., p. 100.
[3] ibid., p. 137.
[4] ibid., p. 81.
[5] ibid., p. 167.

Just as Lady Hoby had been trained by service in a large household, so she in turn trained numbers of women in her own service. 'I talked with Mistress Bell who Came to offer me the saruices of one of hir Daughters',[1] she records. In 1603, she writes that her Cousin Gates has brought his daughter Jane 'beinge of the age of 13 yeares auld, to me, who, as he saied, he freely gave me.'[2] Her frequent references to these young women throughout her diary – 'I wrought in the house with my maides all the afternone';[3] 'After prairs, I wrought as I was accustomed, with my maides,'[4] – give some indication both of how careful and how intimate was the supervision given to the training of girls by the lady of the house and also of how intimate was their relationship. That in such circumstances, the mistress whom they served could – and often did – come to take the place of a girl's own mother is scarcely surprising. The Italian diplomat, however, found it both surprising and horrifying: '... if the English sent their children away from home to learn virtue and good manners and took them back again when their apprenticeship was over, they might perhaps be excused; but they never return, for the girls are settled by their patron', as indeed, we have already seen was certainly the experience of the young Margaret Dakins and others.

Horrifying or not, the practice of sending upper-class girls to be educated continued well into the seventeenth century. Sir Hugh Cholmley, for example, wrote of his wife whom he had married in 1622: 'the people and the county about Whitby owe a perpetual obligation to her memory ... for as divers (and of the best in the country) desired to have their daughters in service with her; so being dismissed with many good qualities, they did communicate them to others ...' Sir Hugh then goes on to make special mention of a set of green cloth hangings with flowers made by her and her maids, for '... in her younger years, when first a housekeeper she employed herself and her maids much with their needles; but her chief delight was in her book, being addicted to read, being well versed in history ...'[5]

This last tribute to Lady Cholmley's virtues is an interesting

[1] ibid., p. 166.
[2] ibid., p. 202.
[3] ibid., p. 167.
[4] ibid., p. 182.
[5] ibid., pp. 267-8 (quoting Sir Hugh Cholmley – memoirs. 1870. pp. 49-51).

sidelight on contemporary women's education and is an important qualification to the general impression of its almost exclusively 'practical' nature. While reading, writing, music, needlework and housewifery were the essentials for the majority of girls, other more intellectual studies were considered appropriate for the daughters of the more scholarly families among the gentry and aristocracy. Queen Elizabeth came to be known as the 'learned princess' and after her accession continued to read Greek and Latin with Ascham until his death. She set high standards of education to her Court and Violet Wilson, in *Queen Elizabeth's Maids of Honour*, claims that these young women were 'highly educated girls, they were fitted both by birth and accomplishments to be the intimate companions of their royal mistress'.[1] Contemporaries were themselves considerably impressed by the gentlewomen of Elizabeth's Court. William Harrison comments in his *Description of England:*

'And to saie how many gentlewomen and ladies there are, that beside sound knowledge of the Greeke and Latine toongs, are thereto no lesse skilfull in the Spanish, Italian and French, or in some one of them, it resteth not in me; sith I am persuaded that as the noble men and gentlemen doo surmount in this behalfe, so these come verie little or nothing at all behind them for their parts; . . . [of the women of the Court] some [occupy their time] in continuall reading either of the holie scriptures, or histories of our owne or forren nations about vs (and diuerse in writing volumes of their owne, or translating of other mens into our Englishe and Latine toongs,) . . .'[2]

Accounts such as this call to mind the celebrated erudition of the daughters of Sir Thomas More and the perhaps less well documented but to contemporaries equally impressive learning of the daughters of Sir Antony Cooke, a scholar of some repute who had helped in the education of Edward VI, to each of whom their father, in his will, left the choice of some of his books, 'ten volumes à Latin and one à Greek'.[3]

It would be incautious to conclude from William Harrison's narrative that the Court of Queen Elizabeth was like the senior common room of a women's college. Nor would it be wise to

[1] op. cit., p. 3.
[2] op. cit., ed. Furnivall, New Shakespeare Society, Ser. 6. I. 1877. pp. 271-2.
[3] *Diary of Lady Margaret Hoby* (introd.), pp. 12-14.

assume that Sir Antony's daughters were 'typical' of the young women of their class. There is an abundance of evidence to qualify the first conclusion and far too little evidence to substantiate the second assumption. The very tone of contemporary accounts inclines the reader to believe that these were indeed exceptional women. Nevertheless, they serve as an important reminder that contemporary conviction that marriage was women's one career was not then, as it later came to be, necessarily associated with a firm belief in their intellectual incapacity. Whilst many parents were following the traditional practice of sending their daughters away to learn such useful skills as such as Lady Hoby and Lady Cholmley could teach them, there were a few, even in the sixteenth century – the Greys, Russells, Sydneys and Cookes among others – who were clearly anxious that their daughters should acquire intellectual skills. Not that they wanted to produce those abominations of the nineteenth century, 'blue stockings', but because, believing that 'sexes as well as souls are equal', they wished their daughters to be 'complete women'. Sir Antony Cooke's first anxiety, we are told, was to 'embue [his daughters'] infancy with a knowing, serious and sober religion, which went with them to their graves; and his next, to inure their youth to obedience and modesty . . .' He cultivated their talents till they were renowned for learning and yet taught them at the same time, to regard all study as a recreation and 'to place their real business in the needle in the closet, in housewifery in the kitchen and hall' in the hope that 'his daughters might have for their husbands complete or perfect men, and that their husbands might be happy in complete women'.[1]

One particularly interesting feature of the education of the daughters of this household is that not only was there this emphasis on intellectual development, but that, unlike the young women we have discussed earlier, they were educated at home. How common this was, as compared to the practice of sending girls away, it is impossible from the evidence available to assess with any degree of certainty. Whilst Anne Boleyn was sent away at the age of nine to learn manners at a foreign court, Lady Jane Grey was taught at home by a tutor as also, for a time, was Lady Anne Clifford. Whilst Margaret Dakins was educated

[1] ibid., pp. 13–14.

in the household of the Countess of Huntingdon, Grace Sherrington (b. 1552), the second of the three daughters and co-heiresses of Sir Henry Sherrington of Lacock Abbey, Wiltshire, was brought up with her sisters by her parents and a much loved governess, a poor relation in the household, one Mistress Hamblyn, her father's niece whom Grace's mother had herself brought up and trained to become a suitable governess for the children.

Probably Grace's upbringing, rather than that of the daughters of Sir Antony, is a more typical illustration of the 'home' education of most similarly placed girls in the sixteenth century. Recollecting her childhood, she wrote in her *Journal* of how her mother beat her severely in order to instill the precepts of virtue 'and never so much for lying'. Her governess, she records, 'scoffed at all dalliance, idle talk and wanton behaviour appertayning thereto, with a touch of conceit to the heed thereof. She counselled us when we were alone so to behave ourselves as yf all the worlde did looke upon us, and to doe nothing in secret whereof our conscience might accuse us, and by any means to avoyd the company of serving men, or any of lyke disposition, whose ribald talk and ydle gestures and evill suggestions were dangerous for our chaste ears and eyes to hear and behold ... And when she did see me ydly disposed she wold sett me to cypher with my pen, and to cast up and prove great sums and accompts, and sometimes to wryte a supposed letter to this or that body concerning such and such things, and other tymes let me read in Dr. Turner's Herball and Bartholomew Vigoe, and at other tymes sett me to sing psalmes, and other times sett me to some curious work; for she was an excellent workwoman in all kinds of needlework, and most curiously she would perform it ... '[1]

It thus appears, from these and many other accounts, that for most girls, the content of their education was much the same whether they were sent away to be instructed or were kept at home. And just as the nature and scope of domestic responsibility changed little over the years, so too this content showed little sign of modification. By contrast, however, the nature and scope of the social, political and economic responsibilities of their brothers were changing markedly in the course of the six-

[1] ibid., pp. 49-50.

teenth and early seventeenth centuries and by the mid-sixteenth century, the way in which these boys were being trained for these responsibilities had become the subject of increasing complaint.

Among Burghley's memoranda for the Parliament of 1559 at Elizabeth's accession, is the following:

'That an ordinance be made to bind the nobility to bring up their children at some university in England or beyond the sea from the age of 12 to 18 at the least ... The wanton bringing up and ignorance of the nobility forces the Prince to advance new men that can serve, which for the most part ... (through coveting to be hastily in wealth and honour) forget their duty and old estate and subvert the noble houses to have their rooms themselves ...'[1]

The old social order, sustained by physical prowess and gilded by the courtesies and services of chivalry was passing; subtler policies of state were demanding flexible minds, not the skills of the tilt yard. The continuance of a system of education in which, with few exceptions, the sons of the nobility were given little training for their position or for the management of their estates or academic training in any marked degree was a legacy of the colourful laws of heraldry but not the key to political success in the devious counsels of the Tudors.

Roger Ascham, perhaps one of the most famous of English tutors, pleads in *The Scholemaster* the need for blending the old with the new: that the nobility should be brought up to learning, although even he believed that this should be linked with pleasant pastimes:

'To ride comely, to run fair at the tilt or ring, to play at all weapons, to shoot fair in bow and straight in gun, to vault lustily; to run, to leap, to wrestle, to swim; to dress comely, to sing and play of instruments cunningly; to hawk to hunt to play at tennis, and all pastimes generally, which be joined with labour, used in open place, and in the daylight, containing either some fit exercise for war, or some pleasant pastime for peace, be not only comely and decent, but also very necessary for a courtly gentleman to use. ...'[2]

Ascham's own education was itself one of the notable exceptions to the general rule of neglect of academic training in the

[1] Quoted A. L. Rowse, op. cit., pp. 259–60.
[2] op. cit., p. 64.

first half of the sixteenth century. Born in 1515, he was sent very young to the family of Sir Anthony Wingfield, who placed Roger, together with his own sons, under a tutor named Bone – an arrangement very similar to the one made by Sir Thomas More and the Duke of Suffolk for their own children and one which, according to Furnivall, had grown considerably by 1570. The evidence on which he bases this claim is Mulcaster's *Elementaire*, published in that very year, in which Mulcaster complains greatly of 'the rich aping the custom of Princes' in having private tutors for their boys and withdrawing them from the public schools to which some of them had been sent.[1]

One particular group of children who were early influenced by the new feeling for formal education were the Royal Wards. These children, discussed in more detail in a subsequent chapter, were a group of fatherless children placed under the care of a specially constituted officer of the Crown – the Master of the Wards – and were orphans who by any technicality, however slight, might be said to be heir to lands held in fief from the Crown. In the reign of Elizabeth, they were defined as 'those whose landes, descending in possession and coming to the Queen's Majestie, shall amount to the cleare yearly value of $\bar{C}$ markes or above'. The education of these children had been just as much a subject of complaint as had that of the other children of the nobility and gentry, hence they were included in Humphrey Gilbert's idealistic scheme for an *Achademy* in London, which was to provide education for the leaders of society. Like most idealistic schemes, Gilbert's was never realised. This did not preclude others, however, from recommending more practical measures for the education of the Wards. Thus Sir Nicholas Bacon, later Lord Keeper, who was Attorney of the Court of Wards for a while, wrote in 1561 to the newly appointed Master of the Wards – Sir William Cecil – indicating to him how his charges were to be brought up. The wards were to attend divine service at 6 a.m. (nothing is said about breakfast!) after which they were to study Latin till 11 a.m.; to dine between 11 and 12; to study with the music master from 12 till 2; from 2 p.m. till 3 p.m. they were to study with the French master and from 3 p.m. till 5 p.m. they were to study with the Latin master again. At 5 o'clock they were to go to evening

[1] Furnivall, op. cit., p. xxv.

prayers after which they had supper. Until 8 o'clock they were to be allowed 'honest pastimes' and then to be sent to bed at 9 p.m. Children over the age of sixteen were to attend lectures upon 'temporal and civil law'.[1]

The advantages of this type of education over the traditional training by service were far greater than may appear at first sight. The practical relevance of a knowledge of the law to those who might be called upon to administer it and would certainly be expected to accept the heavy responsibilities imposed on them by it, is obvious enough. So too are the advantages of commanding both Latin and French at a time when both languages were the international vehicles of political and polite exchange. But more than this, was the importance of the study of the classics as a means of inculcating moral precepts and 'right' judgements. Above all, the classics were at that time the one body of organised knowledge, the one intellectual discipline in the study of which a child's mind might be sharpened into a more formidable instrument of politics than the best tempered sword could ever be. Differently though particular kinds of knowledge may be estimated in particular historical periods, in the sixteenth century as now, knowledge gave power. It was precisely because he understood this that Burghley was so anxious for the education of the sons of the upper classes. Equally, it was precisely because they saw its relevance to their own lives and aspirations that the middle classes were eager for the education of their sons.

More than in any other walk of life, good education was essential to the merchant's success. With the expansion in trade of the fifteenth and sixteenth centuries, the demand for apprentices who could read and write and keep accounts increased, and the knowledge that through the new grammar schools his sons might pass to great rewards urged every father to give his sons educational opportunity. Mulcaster, a progressive schoolmaster of the Ascham type who was to be the first headmaster of the new Merchant Taylors' School, remarked that 'everyone desireth to have his son learned'. When monastic and chantry schools were being suppressed, individual tradesmen and merchants, as well as the great Merchants' companies, gave

---

[1] Articles devised for the bringinge up in vertue and lerninge of the Queenes Majesties wardes being heires Males. Quoted Bell, *An Introduction to the History and Records of the Court of Wards*. 1953. p. 120.

4 Unknown child aged nine months by an unknown artist, 1590

POSITIONS
VVHERIN THOSE PRI-
MITIVE CIRCVMSTANCES
BE EXAMINED, WHICH ARE NE-
CESSARIE FOR THE TRAINING
vp of children, either for skill in their
booke, or health in their bodie.

VVRITTEN by RICHARD MVLCASTER, *master
of the schoole erected in London anno.* 1561. *in the parish of Sainct Laurence Povvntneie, by the vvorshipfull
companie of the merchaunt tailers of the said citie.*

Imprinted at London by Thomas Vautrollier
dvvelling in the blacke Friers by Ludgate
1581

5 Title-page of Richard Mulcaster's *Positions*, 1581. Mulcaster was headmaster of Merchant Taylors' School 1561–86 and St. Paul's 1596–1608

generously to education. In the thirty years previous to 1512 – the year St. Paul's School was founded – more grammar schools had been founded and endowed in England than had been established in the three previous centuries. By 1577, the work of school founding had proceeded so far that Harrison could observe: 'Besides these Vniversities, also there are a great number of Grammer schooles through out the realme, and those verie liberallie endued . . . so that there are not manie corporat townes now Vnder the queenes dominion, that hain not one Grammer school at the least, with a sufficient living for a maister and usher appointed to the same.'[1]

Children were not normally admitted to these schools till they were seven or eight years old, the age at which the upper-class boy was sent away to be a page. According to the schoolmaster John Brinsley: 'If any begin so early, they are rather sent to the school from troubling the house at home, and from danger, and shrewd turns, than from any great hope and desire that their friends have that they should learn anything in effect.' From Brinsley's account of a typical school timetable, one might also wonder whether younger children would have had the stamina to stay the course.

'The school-time should begin at six; all who write Latin to make their exercises which were given overnight, in that hour before seven.' Children had to be punctual or to be punished; 'to be noted in the black bill by a special mark, and feel the punishment thereof: and sometimes present correction to be used for terror'; (i.e. to frighten the rest). From six o'clock, the day was to be set out as follows: 'Thus they are to continue until nine [at work in class] . . . Then at nine . . . let them have a quarter of an hour at least, or more, for intermission, either for breakfast . . . or else for the necessity of every one, or for honest recreation, or to prepare their exercises against the master's comming in. After, each of them to be in his place in an instant, upon the knocking of the door or some other sign . . . so to continue until eleven of the clock, or somewhat after, to countervail the time of the intermission at nine', i.e. to make a full five-hour morning.

In the afternoon, all were to be in their places by one o'clock and to continue work till three or three-thirty, when there

---

[1] Quoted Furnivall, op. cit., p. lviii.

would be another intermission as in the morning at nine o'clock, after which they were to work on again until five-thirty. The day was then to end with a reading from the Bible and 'with the singing of two staves of a Psalm'. The typical school day, therefore, was exactly twelve hours all told! Even so, some people apparently objected to the two short intermissions on the grounds that the boys 'then do nothing but play', but Brinsley himself believed that the brief respites helped the boys to work harder, although he warned that the boys' games ought to be carefully supervised: 'clownish sports, or perilous, or yet playing for money, are in no way admitted'.[1]

The regimen Brinsley outlines was very much that followed in the grammar schools generally. At St. Paul's, for example, where in the winter the boys had to bring their own wax candles to light their books, teaching was from seven to eleven in the morning and from one o'clock till five o'clock in the afternoon, with prayers morning, noon and – if not night – certainly in the evening. No holidays or 'play days' were allowed under penalty of forty shillings from the High Master unless commanded by the King, the Archbishop or the Bishop.[2] At Lord Williams' school, Thame, a boarding-school (founded 1559), there was rather more regular provision for holidays; a weekly half-holiday in addition to festivals, and four holidays a year of rather over a fortnight each. Masters at this school were not to be absent for more than a month in the year since 'boys scarcely learn in three days what they easily forget in one, if owing to too much holiday, they get out of practice'.[3]

If the modern schoolchild would undoubtedly feel that these hours of work and provision for holidays compares very unfavourably with those to which he himself is accustomed, he would view the prevailing school discipline with equal disfavour. Since, however, as we have already seen, parental discipline was extremely severe by modern standards, accounts of school discipline can come hardly as a surprise. Beating and whipping were the normal methods of maintaining order and instilling knowledge. According to an account of Henry Peacham (a

[1] See W. J. Rolfe, *Shakespeare the Boy*. 1897. pp. 110–11.
[2] R. Ackermann, *History of the Colleges of Winchester, Eton and Westminster; with the Charterhouse, the Schools of St. Paul's, Merchant Taylors', Harrow and Rugby, and the Free-School of Christ's Hospital*. 1816. pp. 21–2.
[3] J. Howard Brown and William Guest, *A History of Thame*. 1935. pp. 92–3.

contemporary of Ascham) one schoolmaster was in the habit of beating his scholars to keep himself warm on cold mornings, and in the *Disobedient Child* Thomas Ingeland portrays a boy pleading not to be sent to school because of the cruelty practised on his companions:

> Their tender bodies both night and day
> are whipped and scourged and beat like a stone
> That from top to toe the skin is away.[1]

Birch rods were sold in the streets of London by pedlars crying: 'Buy my fine Jemmies; Buy my London Tartars!' By a grim humour, the cost of these rods was often charged to the boys' bills.

Since the main purpose in discussing changes in educational practice is to indicate their consequences for parent–child relationships and for prevailing concepts of childhood, detailed analysis of school syllabuses of the pre-Restoration period, fascinating though they may be, must not detain us. Nevertheless, one feature all these syllabuses had in common is highly relevant to our particular theme. It will already be quite clear that in these schools, a heavy emphasis comparable to that in Bacon's scheme of studies for the Royal Wards was placed on classical studies. As in Bacon's scheme, so here, the purpose of much of this classical teaching was to instil right ways of conduct. Even though a few hard thinking critics might believe that too many boys wasted their time in such classical discipline, the average middle-class parent did not think to question the practical quality of instruction that obviously sought to inculcate such good morality; in general he believed that even a boy who left the grammar school early to begin an apprenticeship would receive valuable training which would help him to become a godly and successful man. This emphasis on moral teaching, there can be no doubt, maintained the classical grammar school in popular favour throughout the sixteenth century with a group who might have been expected to demand utilitarian courses and who were, in fact, moving to more practical instruction.

In addition to references to classical authors, constant appeal to Scripture and to the ear of God Himself in their efforts to instil virtues in the young, the grammar schools made extensive

---

[1] W. J. Rolfe, op. cit., p. 115.

use of the courtesy books or books of good manners. These works, perhaps the best known guides to contemporary notions of good conduct, ranged from the little primer of behaviour illustrated by Erasmus, *De Civilitate Morem Puerilium* . . . *A lytell booke of goode manners for chyldren* (1532) to the philosophic treatises on education and cutlure exemplified in Castiglione's *The Courtyer*, translated by Sir Thomas Hoby in 1561. Others contained exhortations to youngsters to lead lives of piety, thrift and diligence. All of them were highly moralistic. Contemporary concern for moral virtues, strong in all classes, was nowhere stronger than amongst the middle classes into whose libraries so many of these books, like the Books of Domestic Relations, found their way. One such book, Seager's *Schoole of Vertue*, was used as a regular school-book as John Brinsley's *Grammar Schoole* (1612) testifies. Brinsley enumerates the 'Bookes to bee first learned of children: 1. their Abcie, and Primer. 2. The Psalms in metre, because children wil learne that booke with most readinesse and delight through the running of the metre, as it is found by experience. 3. Then the Testament. 4. If any require any other little booke meet to enter children; the Schoole of Vertue is one of the principall, and easiest for the first enterers being full of precepts of ciuilitie, and such as children will soone learne and take a delight in, throw the roundness of the metre, as was said before singing of the Psalmes . . .'[1] This particular book, first published in 1557 and reprinted as late as 1626, commended various prayers for use on rising and on going to bed and continued with general instruction for desirable behaviour in manners and morals on all occasions:

> Flye ever slouthe
> And over much slepe;
> . . . .
> Cast up thy bed.

There are special instructions on how to behave in the street; how to behave in waiting on parents at table; and how to behave at one's own meals. It advises on behaviour in Church and contains grave warnings against gambling, swearing, lying, anger, malice and commends the virtues of charity, love and patience. Significantly, the last lesson the *Schoole* had to teach was the list

[1] Furnivall, op. cit., p. lxxviii.

of duties of each degree in the hierarchical society in which the pupils found themselves. In Elizabethan society, status differences were to be as much learned from these little expositions of social theory as from the hazards of practical social experience and the children of the middle classes did not lack for guidance, both general and detailed, which would help them to cultivate the behaviour of a gentleman.[1]

The association in middle-class consciousness of moral rectitude with social and economic as well as spiritual salvation: their belief that a particular way of life must lead to business prosperity, social advancement and an eventual seat on the right-hand of God never waned throughout the sixteenth and seventeenth centuries. It was in their determination to acquire and promote knowledge that lay middle-class success and their gradual rise to power in the nation's affairs. And just as the development of organised education in the grammar schools was the *sine qua non* of this success so also was it the necessary condition of the emergence of a new concept of family and a new consciousness of childhood.

4

Elizabethan enthusiasm for educational provision was not limited to the grammar schools. According to Leach, a considerable number of elementary and free schools were founded in the latter part of the reign to teach the three 'R's' and in James's reign the number greatly increased.[2] There is little evidence to indicate what proportion of children were affected by these new developments, but Dr. Hoskins has expressed the view that 'England had more schools in Elizabeth's time than we know of. Many Leicestershire villages had these village schools . . . And if they existed in Leicestershire there is reason to suppose they were to be found all over England.'[3] In these elementary schools, both in the town and in the country, there is evidence to suggest that girls were taught as well as boys. Elizabethan educationalists were keen advocates of the education of girls as Mulcaster

[1] *The Schoole of Vertue, and booke of good nourture for chyldren, and youth to learne theyr dutie by.* 1557. (Seager), p. ii
[2] A. F. Leach, *English Schools at the Reformation*, vol. I, p. 105.
[3] Quoted Rowse, op. cit., p. 502.

testified – 'myself am for them tooth and nail'.[1] And their faith in feminine capacities was apparently not unjustified, for Dr. Rowse believes that in Elizabethan times, 'it will be seen that there was a higher level of literacy among women than at any other time until the later nineteenth century'.[2] The immediate and ultimate consequences of these new developments in both grammar and elementary education were to be of immeasurable importance. The modern schoolchild might pardonably wonder that the multiplication of schools in which the hours were so excessive and the discipline so severe should be hailed as marking a substantial advance towards the child-centred family. The real sociological significance of these schools, however, lay not so much in their methods of imparting knowledge as in their representing a system of education in which children were prepared in institutions created for their own special needs in contrast to the traditional system of education by service, or apprenticeship, whereby children acquired knowledge as little adults in an adult world. Whilst under the traditional system, 'childhood' effectively ended at the age of seven or at the latest, nine, the effect of organised formal education was to prolong the period during which children were withheld from the demands and responsibilities of the adult world. Childhood was, in fact, becoming far less a biological necessity of no more than fleeting importance: it was emerging for the first time as a formative period of increasing significance.

The enthusiasm of the middle class for the education of their children may have stemmed from motives of self-interest; it was to result in a new emphasis on the direct responsibility and concern of the parent for the welfare of his own child. This began to manifest itself in a variety of ways. Whereas, when a child had been sent away to be bound apprentice, the master of apprentices had been responsible for his food and clothing, when a child was sent to school, his parents had to provide and pay for these themselves. Not only had they to pay such fees as were required by his school but they now became directly involved in superintending their child's progress in the school and, when he attended a school in the same town, often rehearsed him in the lesson he had learned that day or in the exercise he was to pre-

[1] D. Gardiner, *English Girlhood at School.* 1929. p. 191–3.
[2] Rowse, op. cit., p. 503.

pare for the morrow. Even where, as was not uncommon for children whose parents lived in the country, a child went a long distance to school and was boarded there during the term, his return to his home at regular intervals for the holidays emphasised yet again the direct and abiding link between a child and his family and of the responsibility of the parent rather than the master of the household or of the apprentices for his upbringing. The increased emphasis on the responsibilities of a parent for his own child and the increased contact between parent and child which the new system of education inevitably implied made possible a consciousness of 'family' which was not so easily developed under the old system, where prolonged absence in the house of another whose life the child was expected to absorb had frequently resulted, as we have seen, in his interests and often his affections being bound up with those of the house in which he had been placed rather than with those of his own family. Roger Ascham, for example, was entered at St. John's College, Cambridge, 'by the advice and pecuniary aid of his patron, Sir Anthony Wingfield': many an apprentice was set up in trade by his master.

It is of immense importance, however, not to assume that the old system implied a general lack of affection of parents for their children. There are numerous references to fathers such as Sir William Holles (1507–1590) of whom it was recorded, 'His paternall love for his children and grandchildren was exemplary, bearing alwais a great and tender affection for them all . . .'[1] The sending of upper-class children away in their early years to be reared in other households did not mean that parents did not love their children, but that they were concerned less for themselves than for the assistance of these children towards the common work – the establishment of the family, the promotion of family ambition. Family honour and prosperity rather than family feeling and affection was the main concern of its individual members and nothing illustrates this so well as the circumstances in which many of these children were married.

[1] *Memorials of the Holles Family*, Camden, vol. LV, p. 45.

III

Child Marriage

THE age at which children were legally able to marry was no exception to the general rule of the early assumption of adult responsibility in the sixteenth and seventeenth centuries. By law, a boy was of age to contract a fully valid marriage at fourteen and a girl at twelve. Nevertheless, the ecclesiastical courts, which even after the breach with Rome continued to have virtually undisputed jurisdiction in matrimonial causes, had long recognised *'matrimonium per verba de futuro'* or 'espousal' as a legal precontract of marriage and one which could take place above the age of seven. The essential distinction between these espousals and those made at the later ages was that the former were voidable until the children 'came of age' and had, accordingly, to be ratified or reaffirmed when they were 'of ripe age': '. . . that which is made between two persons that are under age, is to bee holden and accounted unlawfull. And though it should be done by consent, or commandment of Parents, yet it is of no moment. This alwaies remembered; except it bee ratified by a new consent of the parties after they come to age; or that they in the meane time have had private and carnall copulation one with another. . .'[1]

In practice, this last proviso, as Furnivall's *Child Marriages* clearly shows, was by no means always an effective or absolute bar to a subsequent repudiation of a precontract of marriage.

[1] William Perkins, *Christian Oeconomie.* 1609. Pickering Trans., p. 55.

CHILD MARRIAGE

From the twelfth century onwards, there had been general agreement throughout the Roman Catholic Communion that consent, not consummation, established and validated Christian marriage. Hence, although consummation might be held to be evidence of consent, the ecclesiastical courts, as their records show, were by no means bound to accept it as conclusive proof of validity.

Current matrimonial practices were, however, a great deal more complex than this statement indicates. Despite the view of the canon lawyers that a valid espousal could not take place before a child was seven years of age, there is evidence to show that such espousals did take place, and in a Church with a priest as witness to the 'marriage'. In 1563, Brigitte Dutton and George Spurstowe were 'married' when he was six and she between four and five years old. A witness at the marriage recorded that 'Brigette coulde not perfectlie speake the words of matromonie after the priest, because she was at that tyme in yeares tender and younge.' The following year, John Somerford and Jane Brerton, he three and she two years old, were carried into Church for their 'marriage', an event which impressed even a contemporary as being 'the youngest Marriage that ever he was at'.[1] Other records, however, have references to equally youthful brides and grooms. Robert Parre, who was married to Elizabeth Rogerson at Backford in Cheshire at the age of three 'was hired for an apple bie his uncle to go to the Church' where his uncle had to hold the child in his arms during the ceremony.[2] John Rigmarden, also married at the age of three, was held in the arms of the priest who tried to coax him to repeat the words of matrimony. 'Before he had got thro' his lesson, the child declared that he would learn no more that day. The priest answered, "You must speak a little more, and then go play you".'[3]

Espousals of children continued for many years. Two of Brigitte Dutton's sisters and one of her brothers were all 'married' before they were eleven years of age. Occasionally, the children reacted strongly against parental pressures, like little John Bridge who 'would eat no meate at supper' after his wedding and 'did weep to go home with his father'. When put to bed with his child bride, John 'lay with his back to her all

[1] *Child Marriages, Divorces and Ratifications etc. in the Diocese of Chester, 1561-6*. E.E.T.S. ed. F. J. Furnivall, 1897. p. 39.
[2] ibid., p. 26.
[3] ibid., p. 22.

CHILD MARRIAGE

night'. Initiative in these cases, however, does not always seem to have rested with the children's parents, as the salutory experience of James Ballard illustrates. At the age of about ten, James was 'inticed with two Apples' by 'a bigge damsell and marriageable' – i.e. of at least twelve – 'to go with her to Colne and to marry her'. As a result, the curate who officiated at their nuptials was disciplined by the Archbishop of York, but the legality of the contract established by their escapade was undoubted, as the subsequent suit for divorce in the Bishop's court testifies.[1]

All the preceding illustrations relate to the gentry and upper classes, and it is important to note that recent evidence indicates that marriage of very young children was far from common either among the gentry or among the nobility. Lawrence Stone, for example, argues that only six per cent of the peerage actually married under fifteen years of age in the sixteenth century and only five per cent in the seventeenth century.[2]

If one asks how common child marriage was among the population as a whole, no very accurate answer can be given since all the necessary evidence on which one might be based is not available. A partial answer, however, may be found in Peter Laslett's *The World We Have Lost*, where the calculation is made that all the child marriages described by Furnivall constitute less than one per cent of all marriages in the Diocese of Chester for the period 1561–6.[3] This does not mean, of course, that if child marriages were unusual among the gentry and upper classes, they were non-existent among the poor. In his *Anatomie of Abuses* (1583) Phillip Stubbes refers to the practice of child marriage as being at the root of a great deal of contemporary poverty:

'And besydes this, you shall have euery sawcy boy . . . to catch up a woman and marie her, without any feare of God at all . . . or, which is more, without any respecte how they maye lyve together with sufficient maintenance for their callings and estat. No, no; it maketh no matter for these things: so he have his pretie pussie to nuzzle withal. . . . Than build they up a cotage, though but of elder poals, in euery lane end, almost, wher they lyue as beggers al their life. This filleth the land with such store

[1] ibid.
[2] L. Stone, Marriage Among the English Nobility. *Comparative Studies in Society and History*, vol. III, p. 186.
[3] Laslett, op. cit., p. 86.

of poore people, that in short tyme (except some caution be provided to prevent the same) it is lik eto growe to great pouertie and scarsnes, which, God forbid! . . .'

So urgent a problem did Stubbes feel this to be that he was moved to propose that 'a law should be made that none (except uppon speciall and urgente causes) should marie before they come to XX or XXIIIj or, at the least, before they be XIIIj or XVIII yeares old' on the grounds that this would diminish the number of beggars in the land. To the objection that this diminution would be more than counterbalanced by an increase in the number of illegitimate children born, he answers firmly: 'No! The occasion of begetting manye Bastards were soone cot off if stern punishment was meted out to offenders, instead of light as at present.' Reluctantly, Stubbes concedes that death, 'a meet punishment', would probably be thought too severe. His suggested remedy is thus the less final, though still quite drastic, punishment of branding the parents of illegitimate children with a hot iron.[1]

The vigour and colourfulness of Stubbes's account notwithstanding, one may well wonder just how reliable an observation on the habits of the poor it really was. Certainly there are reasons for supposing that the pressures towards early marriage bore less strongly on this particular section of the population. It is interesting that Stubbes himself implies this when he inveighs against 'little infants in swaddling clowts' (his 'sawcy boy' was anything from ten to twenty years of age) being married 'by their ambicious Parentes and friends, when they know neither good nor evill'. No hint here of poverty being the natural expectation of these child marriages; rather the reverse! Here at least Stubbes's view can be corroborated time and again. Thomas Becon, in his *Catechism*, wrote: 'Some parents greatly abuse their authority while they sell their children to others for to be married for worldly gain and lucre, even as the grazier selleth his oxen to the butcher to be slain, having no respect to the person, whether he be godly or ungodly, honest or dishonest, wise or foolish . . .'[2]

Whether they abused it or not, parental authority over the marriage of their children as over any other aspect of their

---

[1] Phillip Stubbes, *The Anatomie of Abuses*. 1583. ed. Furnivall, 1879. p. 97.
[2] op. cit., p. 372.

children's lives had long been accepted. The Books of Domestic Relations all contain a discourse on whether or not children should marry without their parents' consent and all were pretty well agreed that they should not, even though they were legally of age. Similarly, in his pamphlet *A Bartholomew Fairing for Parentes . . . shewing that children are not to marie without the consent of their parentes, in whose power and choice it lieth to provide wives and husbandes for their sonnes and daughters* (1589), John Stockwood, a Minister and preacher at Tunbridge, was unequivocal in his assertion: 'The question here is not, what children in regarde either of age or wit are able for to doo but what God hath thought meet & expedient . . . For there are many children found sometimes far to exceede their fathers in wit and wisedome, yea and in al other gifes both of mind & body, yet is this no good reason that they shold take vpon them their fathers authoritie . . .'[1] The grounds on which Stockwood bases his argument are equally unequivocal: 'the children are worthelie to be reckoned among the goodes and substance of their fathers, and that by a more especiall right than anything els, the which belongeth unto their possession'. Thus for children to arrange their own betrothal is quite wrong, 'for it standeth with great reason, that the owner dispose of the goodes, and not contrariwise the goodes of the owner, which were in deed a thing verie absurd and contrarie to all reason . . .'[2] In fact, after analysing the situation, Stockwood finds that the plague is a judgement sent by God on account of the prevalent disobedience of children!

We have already noticed that in Tudor England the prevailing conception of marriage was practical rather than romantic, and, if the insistence on the duty of children to obey their parents contributed to this conception, it is important to recall that so also did the reciprocal duty laid upon parents. The Books of Domestic Relations stressed the duty of parents to achieve a 'good Marriage' for their children. In practice, this duty was often honoured vicariously amongst the upper classes, since a child's patron commonly arranged these matches, as in the case of Margaret Dakins. A 'good match' was not necessarily or even primarily one in which the happiness of the two people most

[1] op. cit., p. 82.
[2] ibid., pp. 21–2.

nearly involved was achieved, but, certainly among the nobility and gentry, one in which family fortunes were advanced, the succession ensured and the family name and estate safeguarded. Love was not, or only rarely, considered a sufficient basis for marriage although, as we have seen, the Books constantly reiterated that it was a duty of the married state. 'The fashion amongst the gentility', as Clare told Scarborrow in Wilkins's *The Miseries of Enforced Marriage* (1607) 'is to marry first, and love after by leisure.'

It should be remembered that for the 'gentility' of Clare's day, there were very special reasons why the predilections of individuals should not be allowed free reign in the choice of marriage partners. In the twentieth century, the typical form of private property is the single transferable share, ownership of which is open to any who can afford to buy on the market, either individuals or groups which act as individuals. In the sixteenth and seventeenth centuries, stability and material advancement depended on property in land, ownership of which was associated with a family or household rather than an individual. Hence in the acquisition or disposal of property, the family not the individual was of chief importance and in a society where property ownership was associated with not merely economic but social and political status, the rights of the family relating to its property were jealously guarded. Not surprisingly, therefore, where marriage was concerned, it was the status of the family into which one married and the power of its connections which made a marriage desirable, not the personal characteristics of the two people involved. Despite her proposed husband's well-known difficult and undisciplined character, Margaret Dakins's third marriage was forced upon her by her family because of his equally well-known and more heavily weighted family connections.

If the businesslike manner in which the nobility of the period went about arranging the marriages of their children seems to us now rather strange, it does not strike so jarring a note as the equally businesslike arrangements made in later centuries whose true character was concealed under a veneer of cloying romanticism. With practical detail, Lady Russell, for example, writes to the Earl of Rutland concerning the dowry of her daughter Elizabeth, aged seven:

CHILD MARRIAGE

'My Lord and I do not doubt your plain dealing in this matter which touches us nearest of anything in the world, and therefore we are ready to inform you what revenue and portion will come to Bess. On these points my Lord says that if he have no son he will assure Studley to her after his and my decease, and that he will give her a lordship called Elton, immediately on her marriage, which will be worth £600 a year within eight years of the marriage. If my Lord have a son she shall have £4000 more which shall be charged upon Studley...' Negotiations for this match fell through, however, and Bess arrived at Whitehall aged fifteen, 'a very fine gentlewoman, very fayre, and a great rich marriage', as a Court gossip chronicled.[1]

Whilst the nobility used marriage as a method of securing and advancing their estates, the merchants used it as a method of advancing their business interests. The aim of the Tudor merchant was to live as comfortably and die as rich as he could. With its useful and ever-widening circle of friends, a prudent marriage would inevitably improve a man's prospects in life. It was unthinkable not to marry, not to found a family: love and happiness were anyway a matter of chance, and most sensible men were content to leave the arrangements in the hands of parents and go-betweens.

It is very easy to condemn these arranged marriages as being merely in the interests of the parents. There is much evidence, however, to show that, particularly as regards the marriage of their daughters, the interests of the child were not entirely absent when parents contrived a marriage. Elizabeth and George Hulse, for example, were married in 1561, when she was three or four and he but seven years of age: 'she was married to hym because her frendes thought she shuld have had a lyvinge bie hym'.[2] Similarly, Joan Leyland and Rafe Whittall were married in the following year, when they were both about eleven years old, 'because the said Rafe had about 40/- a year of land' or, as her father put it, 'because she should have had bie hym a prety bargane, yf they cold have lovid on the other...' Unfortunately, 'the one could not fancy the other... and she ever loved other boys' and Joan subsequently brought a suit for divorce in the ecclesiastical court at Chester.[3]

[1] Quoted Wilson, op. cit., pp. 219-20.
[2] Furnivall, op. cit., p. xv.
[3] ibid., pp. 4-12.

On the other hand, it would be ingenuous to imply that the anxiety of a parent for the early marriage of his child was always shot through with altruism. Sometimes the anxiety of a parent for the early marriage of his child was based primarily on the hope that the marriage settlement would rebound to his own benefit and extricate him from his debts. Thomas Fletcher, for example, aged ten was married to Anne Whitfield, aged nine, 'because the father of Thomas Fletcher was in debt, [so] he married his son to William Whitfield's daughter for a piece of money, for discharge of his debt with the marriage goods'.[1] Or again, Elizabeth Ramsbothom was married in 1561, at the age of thirteen or fourteen, to John Bridge, who was about eleven years old since, 'when the said John Bridge was but two years old, his grandfather and the father of the said Elizabeth Ramsbotham made a bargaine of marrige: and the marrige was paid bie the father of the said Elizabeth, to bie a pece of land; and therefore the said John was married under age, after the deathe of his grandfather, bie the Executours of his said grandfather, to the said Elizabeth to save the monie'.[2] (i.e. to save his father having to pay back the money given by Elizabeth's father, which would have ruined him). Few pieces of evidence so well illustrate the presumption of parents on the profitable marriage of their children to redeem their fortunes as the reaction of Sir Frenschville Holles, who had contracted 'some good round debts' when he discovered that his son, Gervase, had secretly contracted himself in marriage to one on whom he had 'placed an unalterable love:' '. . . do you know my condition?' his father demanded of him, 'Do you understand that I am indebted and have no hopes to winde my selfe out of that laborinth but by your marriage? . . .'[3]

From whatever motives child marriages were contracted, as the sixteenth century advanced, there was increasing debate not so much as to the right of parents to arrange such matches but as to their right to do so irrespective of their children's own feelings. Then as now, this debate on the 'current state of marriage' owed a great deal to the revelations of the contemporary equivalent of the 'sensational press' (ballads and broadsheets) and

---

[1] ibid., p. 4.
[2] ibid., pp. 6-8.
[3] Gervase Holles, *Memorials of the Holles Family*, p. 203.

to the popular playwrights as, for example, in the publicity all three gave at the end of the sixteenth century to the sordid details of the murder of old Mr. Page of Plymouth by his child-wife, Ulalia.[1] But the more serious-minded public had for some years been urged by puritan writers to consider whether or not parental authority used merely for parental gain would ultimately produce a Christian society based on secure family relationships. As we have already seen, Becon was highly critical of the way in which parents effectively 'sold' their children to the highest bidder; and even John Stockwood, who some years after Becon's indictment was vigorously upholding the traditional view that children were but the chattels of their parents, ultimately came down against parents 'who force marrige where there is no love for sake of material gain'; a practice he regarded as particularly prevalent amongst the nobility.[2] Similarly, Charles Gibbon, the author of a number of obscure pious works, urged well-to-do parents not to force a marriage on their unwilling children, lamenting the evils which result from marriages which 'bee brought together more for lucre than for loue, more for goods than good will, more by constraint than consent...' Gibbon was writing the year after Page's murder and it is interesting that he, like the sensationalists, draws particular attention to the grotesque inequalities of age between a man and his wife which was often a characteristic of the arranged marriage. 'Is there no difference betweene the withered Beech and the flourishing Bay tree?' he asks. 'Such an husband is an hell to a tender Virgine, and that such a marriage, is the beginng of al miserie, and no doubt he that bestows his daughter no better, shall abridge her griefe, by following her to the grave...'[3]

Technically, of course, it had always been true that no child could be married unwillingly since the ecclesiastical courts held consent of the contracting parties to be the *sine qua non* of a fully valid, technically non-voidable marriage. Indeed, the extremely literal way in which the courts were prepared to accept and uphold as fully valid a marriage contracted by an exchange of declarations of consent *per verbe de praesenti*, however irregular the circumstances in which they had been made, was

[1] G. B. Harrison, *Elizabethan Journals*. 1938. section I, p. 361.
[2] Stone, op. cit., p. 186.
[3] Charles Gibbon, *A Work Worth Reading*. 1591. p. 7.

a constant source of alarm. The mere exchange of declarations 'I take thee for my wife' and 'I take thee for my husband', if made by persons of age, was a fully valid marriage. All the property and legal rights consequent upon it were identical with those resulting from wedlock in Holy Church, a circumstance which in itself must have urged parents to follow Burghley's advice: 'marry thy children in haste lest they marry themselves'. No doubt Sir Frenschville Holles in his 'laborinth' of debt bitterly reproached himself for not having followed this course, but since Gervase and his bride were both of age when their secret espousal was effected there was nothing he could do about their marriage, much as he disapproved of it. It was the insistence on consent that also made it possible for Margaret Paston ultimately to marry the man of her own, not her mother's, choosing. Not many girls can have shown such resolution as Margaret, however, certainly not those who were taken into church in the arms of their parents; and the severity of parental discipline, even where children were aware of their rights in the matter, must have discouraged the majority of children from asserting themselves against their parents' declared wishes. After a few years of married life, however, the situation was different. Then, those who found their unions intolerable might feel more free to repudiate the espousals made for them by their parents. The number who ultimately exercised this right was sufficiently great for the ensuing separations and divorces to emerge as one of the principal objections to the practice of early marriage to satisfy family ambition rather than personal happiness.

As early as 1553, Strype was writing in his *Memorials:* 'The nation now became scandalous for the frequency of divorces; especially among the richer sort . . . That which gave occasion also to these divorces was, the covetousness of the nobility and gentry, who used often to marry their children when they were young, boys and girls; that they might join land with land, possession to possession, neither learning, nor virtuous education, nor suitableness of tempers and dispositions regarded; and so, when the married persons came afterwards to be grown up, they disliked many times each other, and then separation and divorce, and matching to others that better liked them, followed; to the break of espousals and the displeasure of God . . .'

Not least among the anxieties of critics of enforced or premature marriages, and certainly one which engaged the attention of Puritan writers, was the standard of morals which was the traditional and inevitable corollary of such matches. 'It is to be feared,' wrote one commentator, 'they that marry where they do not love, will love where they do not marry.' Strype himself argues this to be one of the significant contributory causes of divorce:

'Of this vice (of whoredom) cometh a great part of the divorces, which nowadays be so common, accustomed, and used by men's private authority, to the great displeasure of God, and the breach of the most holy knot and band of matrimony. For when this most detestable sin is once so crept into the breast of the adulterer, so that he is entangled with unlawful and unchaste love, straightway his true and lawful wife is despised, her presence is abhorred . . . Therefore, to make short work, she must away, for her husband can brook her no longer. Thus through whoredom is the honest and harmless wife put away and the harlot received in her stead.'[1]

Scandalous though the number of marriages ending in separation or divorce might be, Puritan writers placed equal stress on the hypocrisy and misery of the many marriages which endured. '. . . Yf it bee so, that they remayne styll together, what frowning, ouerwhasting, scolding, and chiding, is there between them, so that the whole house is filled up of those tragedies eue unto the toppe.'[2] Many saw such marriages not only as an inevitable temptation to adultery but, at a time when there was in any case a far more tolerant attitude towards adultery by men than by women, as directly responsible for the maintenance of a moral double standard. Since the double standard is essential to the arranged marriage, any attack on the one must necessarily lead to the undermining of the other, and on this score alone the criticisms of the Puritan moralists played a very significant part in modifying contemporary thinking about child marriages. Their constant pressure for a tightening up of moral standards made a forced marriage to an unloved partner, both in theory and in practice, less and less acceptable to men and was a powerful influence both in encouraging sons to assert themselves and, in the late sixteenth and early seventeenth centuries, in gradually

[1] John Strype, *Ecclesiastical Memorials*, 1822 edn, vol. II, pt. II, pp. 138–40.
[2] Thos. Fuller, *The Holy State*, Cambridge, 1642. p. 14.

softening the attitudes of parents to restricting the choice of marriage partners for their children.

Attitudes so deeply rooted not merely in tradition but in human avarice change only slowly, however, and where most was to be gained by marrying children off young, the practice still survived for many years, as for example in the case of the Duke of Bedford and his bride Elizabeth Newland, who were married in 1695, when their combined ages were twenty-seven. It is recorded of these two that, unimpressed by the importance and solemnity of the occasion, they both got into trouble for running away from the banquet to play in the garden.[1] Yet it is significant not merely that King James I should declare that 'parents may forbid their Children an unfitt Marriage, but they may not force their Consciences to a fitt' and that Lord North should write, in 1638, of the need to persuade parents to leave 'theer Children full freedome with theer consent in so important a case' but that a monarch and a nobleman should see fit to make such assertions.[2]

By the middle of the seventeenth century, most parents had, in practice, conceded to eldest sons the right of veto to being married off to a girl of their father's choice, although absolute discretion in their marriage was far from being conceded. When, in 1619, the widowed Lady Verney married, as her second husband, the son of Sir William Clark 'without his father's privity' (though they were both fully of age, she being about thirty-two and he forty-five) 'yet the old knight is so much offended that he threatens to disinherit him, and hath vowed they shall never come within his doors . . .'[3] The woman's right of veto was accepted far more slowly and only after bitter family struggles and scandals harmful alike to family pride and fortune. Naturally, conditions varied according to the temperament of the father, but on the whole, although it was becoming less common by the end of the century for girls to be married extremely young, daughters continued to be under heavy parental pressure as to whom they might marry. Among the aristocracy, there is some slight evidence of an advance in the allowing of their daughters' choice between 1540 and 1640, but even here there could be no legal

---

[1] Christina Hole, *The English Housewife in the Seventeenth Century*. 1953. p. 13.
[2] See Stone, op. cit., p. 186.
[3] *Memoirs of the Verney Family*, vol. I, p. 69.

freedom, since the revised Canons of 1603 made the marriage of children under twenty-one years of age dependent on the consent of parents or guardians.

It has been claimed that, at least among the aristocracy, by the beginning of the seventeenth century many daughters were allowed a right of veto as regards the man they were to marry, certainly with kind and affectionate parents,[1] but evidence suggests that most daughters seem to have fallen in with their parents' views willingly enough, and some parents would not be thwarted and tried to coerce their disobedient girls. The story of one such case is interesting not merely because it illustrates just how difficult it continued to be for a girl to exert her will as regards her marriage but also because it constitutes a salutary warning against judging the practices of another age by the standards of our own. Early in the seventeenth century Dorothy Osborne, daughter of Sir Peter Osborne, set her heart on marrying Sir William Temple, and immediately ran into the opposition both of her father and of her brothers. Until she could overcome their opposition, she would not marry Sir William but remained unshakeable in her choice through many years of constant lecturing on its impropriety. Only after the death of Sir Peter were the two at last married. Impressive as her behaviour was as a demonstration of filial respect and paternal domination, the remarkable thing was that this woman who had so faithfully followed the dictates of her own heart, had little opinion of love-matches: 'To marry for love were no reproachful thing if we did not see that of the thousand couples that do it, hardly one can be brought for an example that it may be done and not repented of afterwards'.[2]

It is, of course, possible to discount this remark as not untypical of the conservatism which sometimes overcomes the *avant-garde* when their conduct threatens to become acceptable. But it was also very typical of the way in which romantic love was regarded in pre-Restoration England. The Italian diplomat, to whom we have referred more than once already, remarked that he had never seen an Englishman really in love, 'whence one must conclude, either that the English are the most discreet lovers in the world, or that they are incapable of love'. Allowing

[1] See Godfrey, *Home Life under the Stuarts, 1603–1649.* 1925. p. 126.
[2] ibid., pp. 131–4 passim.

for his Latin lack of sympathy for the English temperament, his strictures were probably true enough. Tudor Englishmen were not of a remarkably romantic disposition. They were practical and prosaic, toughened by a harsh upbringing and the struggle to survive. In their world, romantic love played little part: the results, as in poetry, were usually tragic, and so not generally followed. Love and marriage were poles apart. Romantic marriages in sixteenth-century England were rarities and continued long to be so, as they still are in parts of Europe.

But not all arranged marriages were necessarily the breeding ground of unhappiness. Indeed there are some who would argue, not entirely without evidence, that the change from the arranged to the romantic marriage, although it can be taken as a sign of social progress, does not in our own age seem to have resulted in a marked increase in marital happiness. It is simple enough to produce from the records of the bishops' courts of the sixteenth and seventeenth centuries a mass of evidence indicating the miseries which ensued from these arranged marriages, but there was no court to which one applied for a certificate of contentment: happiness does not advertise itself.

In the last analysis, it is essential to remember that the bulk of the evidence critical of the effects, direct and indirect, of such marriages relates to the nobility and gentry and that if this evidence is sifted, a very large part relates to the marriages of one group of children in especial – the royal wards.

IV

The Royal Wards

THERE is an Elizabethan painting, familiar in reproductions, which depicts a session of the Court of Wards, where a high-hatted Lord Burghley blandly presides. It is a picture of an historical anachronism: of a strange resuscitation of a feudal custom fashioned into a government department to serve Tudor financial needs. Throughout the Middle Ages, land had commonly been held in return for military service, which itself involved a whole series of complicated feudal dues of which the obligation of a tenant to serve his lord for forty days in the year is probably now the best remembered. In feudal times it had seemed just when war, plague or mere accident resulted in the death of the tenant owing military service, leaving a minor as heir, that the overlord should have some control over the upbringing of the child in order to ensure his efficient and loyal service when he came of age. And that, in addition, the overlord should have some control over his ward's property so that he could temporarily use it to obtain military service from another. If the heir were female, the overlord went further and claimed a right of consent to her choice of husband, lest she should be so heedless as to choose a husband incapable of military service or worse, one who was not *persona grata* to the lord. From right to consent to a female ward's marriage, it was but a step to choosing whom she should marry and but another to the treatment of that right as a saleable article. Hence, by the thirteenth century, the sale of wardship and marriage had become a speculative traffic and wards themselves, chattels who could be bought and sold.[1]

Out of the debris of feudalism, the astute Tudors picked upon this old custom of wardship and marriage as a promising source of revenue. The establishment of the Court of Wards by Henry VIII was but the system's full development for, under his father, this 'antiquated and moribund institution', which had long lost its chief moral and political justification, had been called back to life for the special purpose of raising revenue. From the first year of Henry VII's reign, a sustained effort was made by the Crown to reveal descents and minor successions of land held in chief and to search out 'concealed' wardships. In 1503, Sir John Hussey was appointed Master of the Wards and made responsible for their supervision and, significantly, for the selling of their wardships. Thus, in creating by statute in 1540 the Court of Wards, Henry VIII was merely formalising a work already well in train.

The immediate cause of the new administrative machinery was the dissolution of monastries, with its subsequent sales of the vast monastic lands. The majority of the new owners were required to hold their lands by 'knight service', which now implied little or nothing but the right of the Crown over the wardship and marriage of heirs who inherited during their minority. The Court was thus created to meet these responsibilities but, more especially, to handle the revenues which these astute conditions of sale guaranteed to the Crown.

Writing of the Court, Hurstfield, in *The Royal Wards*, comments: 'By the act of 1540, the Crown established more firmly, and openly proclaimed, its control over the main items of its feudal revenue and stood ready to tap these sources more effectively than it had done for generations. In so doing it would make feudal marriage pay a dividend greater than ever before in its long history.'[2]

Whatever may be said of the morality of this ingenious device, administratively it was an undoubted success. From the year of its inauguration, the numbers of wards coming under its supervision rose annually; and so did the sale of wardships. There were nearly thirty per cent more royal wards at the end of

[1] Hurstfield, op. cit., p. 5.
[2] ibid., p. 17.

Elizabeth's reign than at the beginning since, in spite of growing resistance, Burghley and his officials had broken through the barriers of hostility, concealment and fraud to uncover, by the end of her reign, some ninety new wardships a year. Towards the end of Edward VI's reign, about fifty wardships were up for sale; by the second year of Elizabeth's reign, the number had risen to seventy-two and by the thirty-seventh, towards the end of Burghley's Mastership, they had risen to ninety-two. Large numbers of newly orphaned children came into 'protection' each year and many hundreds were under its jurisdiction from previous years.[1]

In terms of actual revenue to the Crown, the sale of wardships represented an annual average income of £14,677, the total net income for the whole of Elizabeth's reign being £645,807. In terms of other sources of income, or as a contribution to the national income, this amounted to very little. But greater harvests were being reaped elsewhere. The profits of intermediaries, the rewards of private suitors, were of immense significance and provide a major explanation for the survival of the system in the face of increasingly bitter criticism – a whole community of men were drawing all or part of their incomes from the unofficial profits of feudalism. Had the full profits been paid to the Court of Wards, and none gone to intermediaries, the Queen would have been provided with an unexpended two million pounds. In fact, she received one-fourth of that sum and a group of her subjects were, between them, making about two million pounds out of the business of wardships.[2] This was a fact of immense social and political significance. Fiscal feudalism was, in effect, being employed to bring an annual income to the Crown and, in lieu of salary, an annual income to those in the government service. Fees and stipends paid to officials were notoriously out of line with their responsibilities and their importance and their standard of living; unofficial fees bridged the gap.

When the Court of Wards sold a wardship, they tended to fix the price as a ratio of the annual value of the ward's land; taking into consideration the age of the heir, the number of brothers who might succeed him if he died young or, if the heirs were female, how many there were. In general, the official price was

[1] ibid., p. 262.
[2] ibid., pp. 339–46 passim.

fixed at a figure of anything up to fifty per cent above this annual value, although it might be considerably more. Thus, if lands were valued at ten pounds per annum, the wardship would probably be sold by Burghley for either ten, fifteen or twenty pounds; occasionally it might be as much as thirty pounds. 'Female wards', however, were proportionately very much dearer, not merely because there were literally fewer of these but because their marriage, which went with their wardship, was a much more valuable investment, carrying with it the land of the heiress, whereas a male ward took back his own land when he came out of wardship at the age of twenty-one.[1]

The official valuation of a wardship was, of course, far from being its real price. Coke, the Attorney General, for example, bought the wardship of Walter Aston from Burghley for a total sum of £1,300, of which £300 was the valuation and £1,000 a fee to Burghley himself for his 'services' in according the wardship. (Subsequently, Coke sold the wardship to the ward himself for £4,000; which represented an increase of 200 per cent on its original valuation.) Small wonder that Burghley was able to receive unofficially three times more than his official salary! Or that at the end of Elizabeth's reign, the Clerkship of the Court of Wards, whose holder was also able to benefit from similar 'negotiations' in fact received something like £400 a year, although his official salary came to a mere £10![2]

If the officers of the Court were the first to make a profit from such sales, they only stood at the head of what was sometimes a not inconsiderable queue of men who were anxious to speculate in the same market. Coke made a clear profit to himself of £2,700. The wardship of Elizabeth Long, however, proved a profitable speculation to a much larger number of men, passing from the ownership of Thomas Cecil – Burghley's son – who bought it for £250 and who, before having parted with one farthing of this sum, sold it to John Manners for more than five times the original price – for £1,350. Manners then himself sold the wardship some years later to a Charles Morison for £2,450, nearly ten times the original price.[3]

With such fat pickings to be made, small wonder that the

[1] ibid., pp. 275–6.
[2] ibid., pp. 343 et seq., pp. 274–5.
[3] ibid., pp. 274–5.

numbers who competed for the ownership of these orphans whose lands and marriages might be of such direct benefit to their guardians were swollen by many who merely speculated on the strength of a market which so shrewdly exploited human avarice sanctified by family ambition. All the evidence shows that competition for wardships was acute. What kind of people bought them? The proportion of widows was not high. Mothers, after the initial sale of their child's wardship, sometimes went into the open market to try to buy back the guardianship at second or third hand. Such evidence as we have, does not indicate that many transfers ultimately restored a child to its mother. Nor do we have more than scanty evidence of what these transfers must have cost the mother. What we do know is that they sometimes lamented the price as being beyond their reach. For the rest, guardians were drawn from almost all classes of men, but more especially from noblemen, courtiers and royal officials. The list of men to whom wardships were granted in Elizabeth's reign includes porters and footmen, clerks and stewards, feudaries and country gentlemen as well as nobility.

Under Cecil's Mastership, the practice was introduced, in 1611, of allowing the child's relatives a month's pre-emption on the wardship which, according to H. E. Bell, led to an appreciable increase in the granting of wardships to either the child's mother, his relatives or the ward himself:[1]

Date	Total number of wardships granted	To mother, kin or ward
Reign of Edward VI	232	46 ($\frac{1}{5}$)
Reign of Mary	258	83 ($\frac{1}{3}$)
1558–63	365	88 ($\frac{1}{4}$)
1587–90	225	73 ($\frac{1}{3}$)
1611–14	368	168 ($\frac{1}{2}$)
1628–30	222	128 ($\frac{1}{2}$)

Even so, the figures continued to indicate a disregard of family relationships which in modern society would be found intolerable and even to contemporaries was far from acceptable. The main demand of Stuart Parliaments was precisely that wardship should go to the closest kin.[2] But here, as always, it is important not to

---
[1] H. E. Bell, *An Introduction to the History and Records of the Court of Wards and Liveries.* 1953. p. 116.
[2] ibid., p. 116.

fall into the trap of reading into these protests motives which are more typical of the twentieth century than of the age in which they were made. Family interest, rather more than family feeling, seems very often to have been the spur of many of the critics who inveighed against a system which allowed rights of guardianship to be sold outside the immediate family circle. Moreover, Sir Henry Spelman's much quoted remark that such sales left a mother doubly bereaved: 'equally lamenting the death of her husband and the captivity of her child',[1] glosses over the undeniable fact that there were many cases where, at least as far as the child was concerned, the transfer of guardianship must have been a welcome release. More than one mother was found to be 'light and of ill behaviour';[2] and, in such cases, by transferring the care of the child to some more responsible person the Court of Wards was performing, in a primitive fashion, one of the duties of a twentieth-century magistrates' court. A Tudor widow did not mourn her deceased spouse for long. It was very common, before the year was out, for a stepfather to be installed. A lot, of course, depended on the mother and the stepfather, but some contemporaries seriously asked themselves whether a child might not be better treated by a guardian who had bought the wardship in order to marry the heir to his own child than by a stepfather who might be less concerned about the health and welfare of his charge. Some widows, it was said, 'usually upon second marriages, exchange the natural care of their children with the love of their second husbands (for the most part unthrifts or greedy cormorants), that usually make a prey of the children and their estates'.[3] Certainly there is evidence to support this view. Bridgett Molineaux, whose wardship her mother and stepfather attempted to conceal, was obviously dear to them more for her inheritance than for her person since 'by which negligence, the same warde of late fell into a cole pitt a verie greate depth and by that fall was so grievously brused that thereby she was in verie greate perill of her life . . .' There was also the case of Richard Rogers (1628) whose wardship was awarded to his mother and stepfather, Sir Robert Banister, who according to Richard's tutor, 'behaved with great inhumanity, refusing to let

---

[1] Quoted ibid., p. 117.
[2] Hurstfield, op. cit., p. 331.
[3] ibid., p. 332.

anyone sit up with the ward, turning his horse from the stable and his tutor from the house.'[1] Our stepfathers, though possibly less harsh, treated the upbringing of their wards equally casually. Gervase Holles's maternal grandfather, John Kingston, was only three when his father died in 1556. His wardship was granted to his mother, Margaret, and to Christopher Kelke who had married her. John 'had g^t disadvantages of education wch comonly young wardes have who are left to their owne will. And I have heard him say y^t he had proceeded at the schoole no further than Ovid's Metamorphoses before he threw away his booke and got him a kennell of houndes.'[2] When reading contemporary criticisms of the way in which guardians brought up their wards, it is as well to remember that kinship was no guarantee of quality in a ward's upbringing.

There is, indeed, a large amount of evidence highly critical of the guardians' conduct. 'That the proceedings hath been preposterous', Sir Nicholas Bacon told Burghley, in 1561, 'appeareth by this; the chief thing and most of price in wardship is the ward's mind, the next to that his body, and the last and meanest his land'. That was the theory, but the practice was utterly different. 'The buyer of a wardship', wrote Sir Thomas Smith, quoting contemporary opinion in his *De Republica Anglorum*, 'will not suffer his ward to take any great pains, either in study or any other hardness least he should be sick and die before he hath married his daughter, sister or cousin, for whose sake he bought him: and then all the money he paid for him should be lost.'[3] Sir Humphrey Gilbert's opinion was even more trenchant. He spoke of wards being brought up in 'idleness and lascivious pastimes, estranged from all serviceable virtues to their prince and country, obscurely drowned in education for sparing charges'. These poor standards of education were, he said, deliberate, 'of purpose to abase their minds lest, being better qualified, they should disdain to stoop to the marriage of such purchasers' daughters'.[4]

Hugh Latimer in Edward VI's reign, and Nicholas Bacon in Mary's reign and again under Elizabeth, and Gilbert a decade later, all proposed the establishment of a school for wards where

[1] Bell, op. cit., pp. 117–18.
[2] Gervase Holles, *Memorials of the Holles Family*, p. 215.
[3] op. cit., pp. 120–2.
[4] Hurstfield, op. cit. p. 120.

their educational needs would be far better satisfied than in the average private household. Their proposals came to nothing. The origin of the Court of Wards had nothing to do with contemporary educational theory and the significant and remarkable efflorescence of educational ideas which the century witnessed passed it by.

Against the mounting and increasingly bitter criticism of the effects of the Crown's traffic in wardships, by a sublime irony, one man, maligned by his enemies for the fortune he amassed by his manipulations of the Court of Wards, stands out also as a remarkable example of guardianship at its very best. This man was Burghley himself, to whom the mother of the Earl of Essex wrote, thanking him for his care of her son: 'who may say he hath happily met with a second father instead of a guardian'.[1]

John Clapham, one of Burghley's secretaries, wrote of him after his death, 'he was made Master of the Wards and Liveries by means of which he grew rich and oft-times gratified his friends and servants that depended and waited on him'. And Thomas Wilson, nephew of Elizabeth's Secretary of State, estimated that wardship brought in about twice as much to Burghley as to the Queen each year. These may well both have been subjective opinions; hearsay nurtured on jealousy and inflated into conviction, but Hurstfield, in his study of *Royal Wards*, gives a list of recipients of eleven wardships and the gifts they gave to Burghley for them. The official charge arranged by Burghley for nine of them was £906 13s.4d., while the unofficial charge was £3016 13s.4d., i.e. Burghley obtained from these transactions more than three times as much as the Queen. In the space of two and a half years, he received about three thousand pounds at a time when his official salary was less than four hundred pounds. That Burghley took gifts is beyond dispute, but so also did every other official great and small in Tudor England. Without them, officialdom would have withered and died away, for the salaries, even of men in the upper ranks of the government were small; the Lord Chief Justice of England himself only receiving two hundred and thirty pounds a year.[2] Equally beyond dispute was Burghley's care for the wards under his personal guardianship.

[1] ibid., p. 259.
[2] ibid., pp. 263–80 passim.

There can be no doubt that at Cecil House in the Strand there existed the best school for statesmen in Elizabethan England, perhaps in all Europe. Sir Nicholas Bacon's proposal for a school for wards, which he sent to Burghley, came to nothing.[1] Sir Humphrey Gilbert's proposal met a like fate.[2] The pragmatic mind of Burghley could no doubt see difficulties in the way. But the school for young men – not simply wards – which he set up in his own household surpassed anything that had gone before. Hence the competition for admission. The Duke of Norfolk, when preparing himself for the scaffold, bequeathed the upbringing of his sons to Burghley, his political enemy. The first Earl of Essex, when he lay dying in Ireland in 1576, asked – not for the first time – that his son should be brought up in Burghley's care. Lady Russell, his sister-in-law, asked him to admit her troublesome son, Edward Hoby, to his household, in the hope that he would there learn to mend his ways. The Countess of Lennox seems to have had exactly similar difficulties, and therefore asked Burghley to take her son into his home 'to be brought up and instructed as the wards be, so long as shall be needful'. The Bishop of Ely asked the same thing on behalf of his own son.

It was a highly selective school to which only very fortunate young men gained admission. 'Most of the principal gentlemen in England', his domestic biographer tells us, 'sought to prefer their sons and heirs to his service, in so much as I have numbered in his house, attending on the table, twenty gentlemen', each worth at least £1,000 a year in lands. Parents were well aware that entry into Cecil House meant not merely unique educational opportunities, but also attractive prospects in advancement in later life. The quality of the education – cultural and political – was beyond dispute.

On the purely academic side the education was intensive and, within the limits set by the age, conventional. Lord Oxford's day began before seven in the morning and, after exercise and dancing, there was an interval of half an hour for breakfast, from seven-thirty to eight o'clock. There followed French, Latin, writing, drawing, common prayers, and dinner. The afternoon

---

[1] Articles devised for the bringinge up in vertue and lerninge of the Queenes Majesties wardes beinge heires Males. Quoted Bell, op. cit., p. 120.
[2] *Queen Elizabethes Achademy.* 1570.

was devoted to cosmography, more Latin and French, then 'exercises with the pen', common prayers, and supper. Sunday was spent in prayer, reading the gospel, and 'riding, shooting, dancing, walking and other commendable exercises'. If Cecil House could attract the flower of England's youth, it could also attract some of the best scholars of the day. Lawrence Nowell, Dean of Lichfield, was a tutor there, so was Robert Ramsden, Archdeacon of York and chaplain to Burghley; the scholar Sylvius Frisius likewise joined the staff. John Harte, the Chester Herald, one of the earliest spelling reformers and a pioneer of shorthand in this country, exercised a general supervision of the wards and Roger Ascham came to stay with Burghley. But if the wards learned a good deal from their formal instructors, they must have learned a great deal else, about the art of politics from their guardian's guests, the greatest men in the land and from Burghley himself. None, in fact, could hope to rival the education that Burghley gave to the youths in his care and few attempted to follow his example.

If self-interest played so large a part in the kind of education most guardians bestowed upon their wards, the same approach marked the guardians' care of the estate. It is true that there were many warrants going out of the Court of Wards for special grants towards the upkeep of the property, preceded in important cases by a special survey made by the feodary. But the grant might be tardy and the need urgent. No less a person than the Earl of Leicester experienced difficulty in getting authority from Burghley for expenditure upon the estate of his ward, Edward Verney. For the child's sake, said Leicester, he was willing to do what was necessary out of his own pocket, but meanwhile, he warned Burghley, the house and lands were decaying.[1] More serious than any failure of the Court of Wards, was the failure on the part of the guardian, through neglect, cupidity or for other reasons. The lease of the Ward's lands could, by the nature of things, be only of limited duration. His death, or coming of age, would terminate it. Here were all the temptations to a lessee to force the land to yield a quick return. In theory the ward when he came of age, or his friends when he was a minor, could bring an action against the guardian for the damage suffered by the property; but it is unlikely that a ward would have been

[1] Hurstfield, op. cit., p. 121.

likely to call upon an already depleted estate to meet the heavy costs of a legal action. Sir Thomas Smith, who quoted some frank comments about the education of wards, had some even sharper things to say about the treatment of their estates. Their inheritance, he tells us, when they came of age, 'consisted of woods decayed, old houses, stock wasted, land ploughed to the bare'.[1] Years later, the same allegation was made in the course of a debate on wardship in the House of Commons in 1604. In the course of this debate too, prominence was given to the most dominant criticism of wardship.

Guardianship, as everyone then well knew, was a means to one end: marriage. The main reason for buying a wardship was either to marry the ward to a child of one's own, thus profiting from its estates; or to sell the marriage to another, thus making a profit on the original purchase of the wardship. To avoid their children's falling into wardship was one of the main concerns of fathers who owed knight service to the Crown. According to Furnivall, this anxiety was itself one of the strongest pressures towards the marriage of children at a very early age since such an espousal would save the child were he to be left an orphan from being exploited and married for the profit of a stranger even though it might not save his estates. 'There was never such marrying as in England as is now,' wrote Latimer. 'I hear of stealing of wards to marry their children to. This is a strange kind of stealing: but it is not the wards but the lands that they steal... And many parents constrain their sons and daughters to marry where they love not, and some are beaten and compulsed. And they that marry thus, marry in a forgetfulness and obliviousness of God's commandments.'[2] The pressure on parents to arrange the early marriage of an heir and so avoid the exploitation of his marriage in wardship is more readily understandable in view of the short expectation of life. Moreover, the Crown did not scruple to sell a wardship even before the death of the reputedly ailing parent; hence it is not surprising that the very threat that a child was likely to pass into the hands of another was sufficient to encourage a parent to arrange a child's marriage, even from his deathbed. When Sir Giles Strangeways, for example, was reported dying in 1546, the Crown granted the wardship of his heir, his

[1] op. cit., pp. 120–2.
[2] *The Works of Hugh Latimer*, edit. G. E. Corrie, vol. I, pp. 169–70.

6 (*top*) Children's Games in the sixteenth century
7 (*bottom*) Elizabethan schoolroom: Woodcut of 1592

8 A Tudor law court in session: The court of wards and liveries with Sir William Cecil, Lord Burghley, as presiding judge. By an unknown artist engraved in the eighteenth century by Vertue

grandson, to Sir Richard Rich. But Sir Giles lingered long enough to marry his grandson off, and thereby deprived Sir Richard of his ward.[1]

As the sixteenth century advanced there was unsparing criticism of the behaviour of unscrupulous guardians. 'Others, more dishonestly, force base and inconvenient matches upon them; either matching them to their owne children, and so raysing their owne estates thereby: or else, selling them for mony to others; (and which is worst of all) lest the orphan should suspect and shunne the offer propounded; what do they do? They marry them in their childhood at 10, 12 or 13 yeares of age, long before the time of meet cohabitation, sending the one to travaile, till he have fulfilled his yong wives yeares: who when they returne, come to them with a forced affection and that breeds disdaine, where there should be greatest affection.'[2]

In theory, a ward might not be married to a person of lesser rank, and the Court of Wards had the power to act in the ward's interests in cases of 'disparagement', but there is evidence to show that this power was by no means always used, as, for example, in the case of a schoolmaster, in the reign of James I, who married his young ward of fourteen to his daughter, 'a harlot', aged twenty-eight.[3] Indeed, at a time when the sale of wardships for the sake of their marriages was so common it could hardly be expected that their personal rights would account for very much in the calculations of the traders. Often, a wardship was bought to provide for an illegitimate son. In the will of the first Lord Rich, drawn up in 1567, among other provisions was one for his illegitimate son, Richard. Lord Rich's executors were to 'provide or buy one woman ward or summe other woman having Mannors, londes and tenements in possession of the yerely value of Two hundreth poundes by yere over all chardges at the leaste for mariage to be had and solempsised to the said Richard'. If Richard should refuse to marry the girl, the executors were 'to sell the saide warde... to the uttermost advantage'.[4] The possibility that the ward might refuse to marry Richard was not even thought worth considering. The reason for

[1] Hurstfield, Corruption and Reform under Edward VI and Mary: The Example of Wardship, *English Historical Review*, vol. LXVIII, No. 266, Jan. 1953. pp. 34–5.
[2] Daniel Rogers, *Matrimoniall Honour.* 1642. p. 94.
[3] Bell, op. cit., p. 126.
[4] Stone., op. cit., p. 185.

this was not merely that children's views were rarely of much moment; but that there were serious financial disincentives to wards rejecting the marriages offered to them since they would then be liable to a 'fine', payable when they came of age, of a sum equivalent to that which their guardians might have expected to gain from the sale of the marriage. Substantial amounts of money might be involved. Stories have survived, some of them possibly exaggerated, of wards being mulcted of thousands of pounds for refusing to comply with their guardians' request. It was rumoured that the refusal of one of Burghley's own wards, the Earl of Southampton, to marry one of his guardian's grand-daughters cost him very highly indeed.[1] On his own evidence, such a refusal cost Lord Sandys £2,000.[2] The number of heiresses who defied the wishes of their guardians was probably fewer, not least because their physical stamina made them more susceptible to crude methods of obtaining their 'consent'. Daniel Rogers, however, implies that as far as male wards were concerned, there was sufficient feeling for independence of choice in the matter of whom they should marry for the guardian to profit thereby: 'Instead of offering yea providing meet wives for them, such as might be in every way suitable to their place, birth and worth, what doe they? Surely they turne to the spoile and offer them such as they know will be unwelcome, and so thereby purchase a great fine unto themselves . . .'[3]

George Whetstone was one of many who, towards the end of the sixteenth century, declared these forced marriages of wards as one of the greatest evils of the sale of wardships.

'I crye out upon forcement in Marriage, as the extreamest bondage that is: for that the raunsome of libertie is ye death of the one or ye other of the married. The father thinkes he hath a happy purchase, if he get a riche young Warde to match with his daughter: But God he knowes, and the unfortunate couple often feele, that he byeth sorrow to his Childe, slaunder to himselfe, and perchance, the ruine of an auncient Gentlemans house, by the riot of the sonne in Lawe, not loving his wife . . .'[4]

---

[1] Hurstfield, Lord Burghley as Master of the Court of Wards, 1561-98, *Transactions of the Royal Historical Society*, 4th Series, vol. XXXI, 1949, p. 105.
[2] Hurstfield, *The Queen's Wards*, p. 142.
[3] Daniel Rogers, op. cit., p. 94.
[4] George Whetstone, *An Heptameron of Ciuill Discourses*. 1582. Section FI (the seconde dayes exercie).

Surely, sympathetic though the modern reader must be to cries such as these, they must hear in them an echo of similar indictments of the marriages not of wards by their guardians but of children by their own parents. Feudal guardians, while negotiating a marriage tended to think in terms of hard cash and the building up of an estate. But so, very often, did parents who, with the best will in the world, negotiated marriage contracts on behalf of their children.

Similarly, Brinkelow's complaint against 'the selling of wardys for mariage, whereof ensueth adultery . . .', also serves as a reminder that although the position of the wards was at law peculiar, as regards their marriages and the criticisms that could be made of them they were far from unique. 'Oh mercyful God,' cries Brinkelow, 'what innumerable inconuenyencys come by selling of wardys for lucre of goodys and landys, although the partyes neuer fauor the one the other after thei come to discrecyon, to the great encreasing of the abhomynable dyuorcement, which hath of late been moch used. Now God confound that wicked custome; for it is to abhomynable, and stynketh from the erth to heavyn, it is si vyle. What myschefe hath comme of it, it is too well known to many men, I nede to wryte no furder therein . . .'[1]

Nevertheless, despite impassioned appeals such as this and others, there is evidence that some arranged marriages of wards were a triumphant success despite all the hazards. Such was the marriage of Mary Blacknall to Ralph Verney. Mary, heiress to a substantial fortune left to her by her father John Blacknall, sometime Mayor and a wealthy citizen of Abingdon, was left an orphan at the age of nine. After several disputes among her guardians over her marriage, she was married at the age of thirteen to Ralph Verney, heir to Sir Edmund Verney, who was aged fifteen. The couple did not actually live together for another two years; Mary, as was often the custom, returning home to her relatives for the next two years. Their marriage, which lasted until Mary's death in 1650, was one of great happiness for them both. Sir Ralph was to speak of his wife's death as 'the greatest greife thet ever yet befell me' and to express the pious hope that, although in heaven none are married or given in

[1] Henry Brinkelow, *Complaynt of Roderyck Mors*, c. 1542, E.E.T.S. ed. J. M. Cooper, 1874, p. 18.

marriage, 'Wee, who ever from our very childhoods lived in soe much peace, and Christian accord heere on Earth, shall alsoe in our Elder yeares for the full compleating of our Joyes, at least be knowne to one another in Heaven...'[1]

Mary's story is in fact far more than a moving testimony to the possibility of achieving happiness in a world where so many obstacles seem to have been strewn in the path to its realisation; it is also a witness to the way in which the Court could, and on this occasion did, exercise its rights in the interests of the ward. One of her guardians, named Libb, tried in an underhand way to marry her to his own son before she was twelve; but another, her Uncle Wiseman, becoming aware of this, appealed to the Court and an order was made that the ward, 'unmarryed, unaffyed, and uncontracted', should, under a penalty of £5,000 be sent to Lady Denham of Boarstall in Buckinghamshire, to be brought up with her daughters.

In the last analysis, the Court of Wards was abolished in 1646 in response to the mounting fury of the criticism by the spokesmen of the land-owning classes who, understandably, saw wardship as a perpetual threat both to the stability and viability of their estates. Throughout the sixteenth century opposition to the royal prerogative of wardship was persistent both on moral and utilitarian grounds. In the 1530s, Starkey described it as 'a great error in our commonweal and policy', and denounced the practice of placing a ward with a stranger who cared nothing for 'his learning and virtue' but only for marrying him off and leasing his lands. In the next decade, radicals like Brinkelow and Latimer criticised in the strongest terms the abuses associated with the selling of the ward's marriage – 'to the great encreasing of the abhomynable vyce of adultery, and dyvetlyssh dyuorcement, which hath of late been moch used'. In his famous treatise, *De Republica Anglorum* of 1583 Sir Thomas Smith records the two contemporary conflicting viewpoints on the subject. On the one hand, there were the conservative upholders of traditional practices who still defended wardship as a method of educating 'good knights'. On the other, there were 'many men' who considered it 'verie unreasonable and unjust, and contrarie to nature, that a Freeman and Gentleman should be bought and solde like an horse or an oxe, . . . and then to marie at the will

---

[1] *Memoirs of the Verney Family*, vol. III, p. 30.

of him, . . . who hath bought him, to such as he like not peradventure, or else to pay so great a ransome'. When the heir came out of wardship, he found his estate gone to ruin: 'woods decayed, houses fallen downe, stocke wasted and gone, land let forth and plowed to the baren'. A few years later, the eminent lawyer, Swinburne, condemned the selling of the ward . . . to such as 'seek to make most advantage of him', and forced him into marriage with 'my master's daughter, sister, cousin', or some other unsuitable mate.[1] At Elizabeth's death, public opinion was sufficiently strong for an attempt to be made by Parliament to end the system and to persuade James I, on his accession, to accept 'a perpetual and certain revenue out of our lands' in exchange for surrendering his rights of wardship. In the debate in 1604, the Commons urged the natural claim of the mother and next of kin to the upbringing of the children and the arrangement of their marriages; 'the great hindrance and decay of men's houses and posterity' that resulted from the custom; the harm done to the children by 'forced and ill-suited marriages'; and even the damage done to England's standing abroad by what they rightly claimed to be an anachronism which had long lost its original justification. Negotiations, however, broke down. The King's demands for compensation were placed too high; and other vested interests proved too strong. There can be no doubt that the fury of the system's critics was exacerbated by the knowledge that large fortunes were being made by the officials of the Court from the sales of the rights of guardianship over those whom it was technically *in loco parentis*. The Court of Wards was clearly a corrupt institution, even allowing for financial arrangements common then, but which would not be tolerated today. The Queen's subjects were blackmailed and bullied into paying sums of money to escape the consequences of feudal wardship. The Crown itself was robbed of the greater part of its revenues from this source by the servants appointed to collect them. Nevertheless, those who defended the Court begged James I, when the wardship controversy was at its height, not to yield one jot of its social responsibility and influence. To abolish it, one of its defenders argued, would mean 'the overthrow of an honourable court, by which many orphans have received protection to oppression'. When we consider the evils

---

[1] *A Treatise of Testaments & Last Wills*, 7th edn. 1803. vol. I, pp. 286-7.

attributed to feudal wardship, it is worth recalling that in Jersey, where no Court existed, it was the custom for guardians 'to be chosen by those who call themselves kin, neighbours and friends of the said infants, which custom is often abused, because the kin, neighbours and friends choose men to serve their base ends, or strive by underhand means to put in other . . . guardians at their fancy to the prejudice of the orphans'.[1]

Under a great Master, like Burghley, the Court of Wards did concern itself with welfare matters, and more than once intervened decisively to protect the heir against intruders, an oppressive guardian, the waste of his lands, or other abuse. In a lawless age when intrigue and riot and sudden dispossession were the frequent accompaniment of disputes over land, a minor heir might well benefit, rather than suffer, from being under the shelter of so powerful an institution as the Court of Wards and so eminent a judge as Burghley. And behind him was the supreme executive and authority of the Privy Council, whose thunderbolts upon an erring guardian or a recalcitrant sheriff could, on occasion, be used with devastating results. The Court spoke with the conscience and voice of the Queen and, on many occasions, it acted without charge or favour, in the interests of some young orphan of mean estate. For this it had an honourable reputation and formed one aspect of that Tudor paternalism which anticipated to some degree the later ideas of the Welfare State.

[1] Quoted Hurstfield, *The Queen's Wards*, p. 332.

V

Borough Orphans

THE exploitation of the orphan child with means was not limited to the landed classes. It was a problem which also concerned merchants and tradesmen who wished to provide for their offspring. The guardianship of an orphan child with a considerable inheritance could be a profitable business for a guardian who, while providing for the child, made a handsome profit from investing his inheritance at interest during his minority. To prevent such abuses and to safeguard the property of orphans, the burgesses of the larger towns adopted the policy of appointing the Mayor or Chamberlain to act as the special guardians of orphans. Thus, in the sixteenth century, while Burghley presided over the Court of Wards, in some of the towns, the local burgesses, often confirmed in their authority by Royal Charter, exercised a municipal control over the welfare and property of the orphans and freemen of their borough. In such places as Leicester, Chester and Exeter, municipal responsibility for the welfare of such children appears only to have been made clear during Elizabeth's reign, although in others it can be traced back far earlier.

Historically, this municipal responsibility for the orphans of freemen of the borough rose in part from the townsmen's wish to free themselves in all respects from their feudal lord and thus to bring wardship of their freemen's children under their own jurisdiction. Thus by Charter or by prescription of the lord's right of wardship was substituted protection by the borough of burgesses' orphans' inheritance. Guardians had to be approved by the governing body of the borough and account to be rendered to it for their trust. With wardship went apprenticeship, and the enrolment of bonds of apprenticeship before the town council had its origin, perhaps, in the borough control of wardship.

In Bristol, the legal basis of borough control over the goods and persons of orphans born in Bristol, and children of freemen goes back to the Charter of Edward III (1331), which itself confirms the previous custom of the mayor's right to give control of such orphans into the hands of guardians who were to give surety and account for their guardianship.[1] There thus developed in many municipalities a borough court of orphans for the administration of this responsibility. It was the City of London 'where there hath been a Court of Orphans time out of mind' and where 'the custom hath been, that if any Freeman or Freewoman died, leaving Orphans within age unmarried, that they have had the custody of their bodies and goods, and that the Executors and Administrators have used and ought to exhibit true inventories before them . . .',[2] which provided the model for similar Courts – as for example that set up in Exeter in 1563, authorised by Charter and Letters Patent during Elizabeth's reign. In her Letters Patent to the City of Chester, 1574, 'desiring to provide for the safety, defence, and government of orphans and infants' and to avoid 'waste and destruction' of their goods, the Queen granted to the Mayor and citizens 'the custody and government of all and singular orphans of the citizens and their property during their childhood and (when of age) deliver it over to them with any profits accruing at that age and in that manner and form as it is in our city of London'.[3]

The purpose of providing for such Courts by Royal authority was not so much to introduce a wholly new concept of municipal responsibility – by the late sixteenth century, almost all the large towns had already made some attempt to establish the principle of municipal responsibility for the care and protection of the

[1] The Charter is given in full in Bristol Charters 1155–1373, ed. N. Dermott Harding, Bristol, 1930, *Bristol Records Society's Publications*, vol. I, p. 75.

[2] *The Reports of . . . Sir Henry Hobart*, 1641. p. 347.

[3] Rupert, H. Morris, *Chester in the Plantagenet and Tudor Reigns*. Chester, 1875. p. 547.

orphans of their freemen[1] – but rather to regularise and give formidable sanction to the Mayor's rights and responsibilities in this particular sphere. This was quite clearly recognised at the time. John Hooker, Chamberlain of Exeter from 1555, writing under the alias of John Vowell his *Orders enacted for Orphans and their portions within the Citie of Excester, with sundry other instructions incident to the same*, drew attention to the fact that under the terms both of the Charter granted to the city in 1561 and of the private Act of Parliament confirming the Charter under which the Exeter Court of Orphans was set up, the City Corporation had bound themselves 'by an Othe and a dutie to performe that which before was but voluntary and of curtisie'. This they had done, since 'if any one thing is above another to be respected and tendred in the publique weale: it is the care to be had of young Orphans and Fatherlesse children. Who being destituted of their owne naturall parents: are to be provided for, now by the common Fathers of the common weale, whose making and marring lyeth now in their hands and devotions . . .'[2]

Equally clear, if the system of borough orphanage were to work at all efficiently, was the desirability of associating the functions of the Courts with the authority of the Crown. In Northampton, for example, where the old use had been for the Mayor, in association with two Chamberlains, to preside over an Orphans' Court, it had not always proved easy or indeed possible to uphold the Court's right of guardianship. In 1557, 'there hath been established diverse good and godlye Orders for the Orphans as in the books of Records for Orphans at large appeareth', the Orders 'hath been by some misliked of and partly by some refused to be kept'. Hence, in 1582, the town assembly declared that . . . 'whosoever being free of the same towne and Refusinge the observation of the said Order at anye tyme hereafter shalbe by the mayor for the tyme being commytted to prison untill he or they shall and will observe the same'.[3] It can have been thus no small addition to the status of this Court to have behind it the authority of the Queen's Letters Patent,

---
[1] See *The Records of the Borough of Northampton*, London-Northants ed. by C. A. Markham and J. C. Cox. vol. II, 1898, p. 119.
[2] John Hooker, alias Vowell, *Orders enacted for Orphans and for their portions within the Citie of Excester, with sundry other instructions incident to the same.* 1575. p. 5v.
[3] *The Records of the Borough of Northampton*, pp. 119–20.

granted to the City in 1599, in which she gave the Mayor, Bailiffs and Burgesses the custody of the orphans of any Burgess and empowering them 'to collect and cause to be kept in the common treasury by the Chamberlain all goods and chattels belonging to the said orphans' which was to be returned to them with increase when they came of age or married 'as is done in the city of London.'[1] Moreover, as on at least one occasion in Bristol, the authority confirmed by Royal decree made it possible for the city fathers to appeal to the Privy Council to uphold the authority of the Court when they believed it was being flouted.[2]

Precisely why some citizens should wish to flout the Courts' authority only becomes clear when one understands the practical implications of the functions of such institutions and, since London became the model for many of them, it is worth analysing its activities in some detail. In medieval times if a citizen died leaving orphans under age and unmarried, then by custom, the custody of their person and property went to the Mayor and Aldermen of the City who, following the practice of guardianship in socage, handed over their care to the nearest friends of the deceased unable to inherit their property. Such guardians usually had to provide security at the Guildhall for the proper maintenance of their wards during their minority and for being able to hand over their inheritance in good order when they came of age. Proceedings could be taken against the guardians if they failed in their obligations. The Mayor and Aldermen exercised their jurisdiction over the children through a Court of Orphans, its chief officer being the Common Sergeant, and in practice the Court would only appoint a guardian for an orphan in the absence of a testamentary guardian. One of the main objects of the Court was to ensure that a child's inheritance was not wasted by the widow or by some adventurer who might marry her.

With certain refinements this was the nature and the function of the Court in the sixteenth century. It operated as a court of record, responsible to that of the Aldermen. At the death of a freeman, his executors were obliged to exhibit in the Court an inventory of his personal estate; a list of any debts owing to him; and a list of any debts owed by him. The value of the estate, together with the list of debts owing to him, were entered in the

---

[1] ibid., vol. I, p. 124.
[2] See John Latimer, *Sixteenth Century Bristol*. Bristol, 1908. pp. 96-7.

Common Sergeant's book and against these entries and deducted from their total value were set the man's personal debts; the expenses of his funeral; the expenses of administering his estate; and his widow's personal effects – at law, counted as her own property. What remained was then divided by the Court into three portions between the widow, other beneficiaries under the will (in the case of London, these necessarily excluded both the widow and the man's children) and his orphans. Between the orphans, this last portion of the man's estate was 'to bee equally shared ... notwithstanding any will made to the Contrary'.[1] Unless surety was given to the Court by the orphan's guardian, these 'orphans' portions' had to be lodged in the City Chamber (the City Treasury) at the Guildhall to be refunded to the children when they either came of age or married. By an ordinance of 1552, no girl orphan was allowed to marry without the consent of the Court, it being generally agreed that 'they do bestow themselves in ungodly marriages ... [and] ... do spend and consume their Patrimony and Portions in short time'. The Court thus could impose a fine of 2d. in the £1 of the orphan's portion if she married a freeman without their consent and of 3s. in the £1, of which 2s. had to go to the offended relatives and 1s. to the Chamber if she were so strong headed as to marry any other than a freeman.[2]

In practice, the Court's jurisdiction over the inheritances of minors was even more extensive than either its title or the foregoing description of its functions suggests. Since its principal object was to defend the right to property of the children of freemen against misappropriation, the Court also claimed authority over any lands or goods within the City which were left to a minor even where the child's father was still living, although in such cases the father was usually appointed to act on behalf of the child on his giving the Court some security for doing so.[3]

The requirement that, unless security be given, orphans' portions had to be deposited in the City Chamber was a distinctive feature of the London system. On these deposits, the City

---

[1] *The City-Law, or the course and practice in all manner of juridicall proceedings in the Hustings in Guild-Hall.* 1647, trans. of old Fr. MS., p. 7.

[2] John Stow, *A Survey of the cities of London and Westminster*, ed. John Strype, vol. II, pp. 322–3.

[3] *The City-Law* ... , pp. 6–7.

paid an annual interest varying from three to six per cent and from them the guardians were allowed 'orphans' findings' – the expenses incurred in caring for and educating their wards. In a period of doubtful accountancy, such an arrangement was not without its hazards as we shall see, but its substantial advantages as a device to protect orphans' interests can be seen from Sir James Whitelocke's account of his own family's experiences. His mother, being left a widow, married as her second husband 'a notable unthrift' who proved unkind to her and careless of the welfare of her four sons by her previous marriage and because of whom she had great difficulty in bringing them up properly and preserving their 'portions'. Nevertheless, with the protection of the Court of Orphans, to whom no acceptable security had been offered for their management by her present husband, 'by her extreordinarye providence and patience did effect it that she preserved in the hands of the city as orphans' goods 600 £. For her fower suns everye of them 150 £.'[1]

This then, in outline, was the 'model' Court of Orphans to which Elizabethan City Charters and Letters Patent referred and in the light of whose example provincial Courts were ordered. In Exeter, where the Court was presided over by the City Chamberlain, it was required that, within a month of a freeman's death his executors or administrators were to bring an inventory of the man's estate, together with the dead man's will, into the Court on pain of imprisonment. As in London, the estate was then divided into three portions, although here, the orphans seem to have been able to benefit directly from the will as well as from the 'orphans' portion' which was divided equally among them. The inheritance of the orphans was to be converted into ready money and if it so wished, the Court was empowered to require that the orphans' portions should be deposited in the City Chamber. As in London, the Exeter City Chamber allowed interest on these monies but ordered that 'nothing be allowed unto the Orphans towards their finding of that portion, because it is intended that their money lieth upon some good security consideration in their hands, and for their better sureiti, without any commodotie or profit to the Chamber'. Otherwise the Court might allow the guardians to hold the child-

---

[1] *Liber Famelicus of Sir James Whitelocke*, ed. John Bruce, *Camden Society*, 1858. p. 6.

ren's inheritance in which case they not only had to offer a proper security of their management but had to make proper financial arrangements for their wards' support out of their inheritance. This was to be calculated on the basis of 1s. in the first hundred pounds held; 8d. in the second; 4d. in the third; 'and if the orphanage do amount to any more, then shall Recognisances be taken reserving such severall allowances as according to the rate'. A general Court of Orphans was to be held annually on the Monday after Mid-Lent Sunday before the Mayor and Common Council 'at which all surities upon any recognisance shall be called' to see there was no default. In the meanwhile, 'if the Mayor and Councel shall suspect the Executor or any other person or persons to convey any such goods out of the libertye of the Citie, then the Mayor may cause and will the common Cryer which is Sergeant at armes in that case to sequester the same in safe keeping'.

It is important to remember that this Court, like similar Courts of Orphans elsewhere, was only concerned for the welfare of a particular group of fatherless children. In 1575, the City Chamberlain himself drew attention to this when he contrasted the care and protection given by the city governors to the orphans with property with 'such orphanes, who having nothing left unto them, and being destitute of all relief, are left to their own dispositions . . .' The fate of such children as these will be discussed later.

Since the Court of Orphans was supposed to be a defence against the misappropriation of the orphans' estates, it is perhaps not at all surprising that the Orders made by the Common Council at Exeter should stress the point that 'who soever hath the use of the Orphans portions and what soever gain, profit and commoditie groweth by the use thereof, no profit shall growe unto the Chamber of the Citie but all to the Orphan'.[1] Nevertheless, it is quite clear that there were real advantages for a City's holding the orphans' portions itself as the records of Beverley, a small town in Yorkshire well illustrates. In April 1668, consent was given for the corporation of Beverley to take over the responsibility of administering the estate of Leonard Allanson who had recently died and to 'enter upon and secure the estate for the payment of his debts and for the education of

[1] See Vowell, op. cit., pp. 35–9.

his four children'. In May, the Mayor was authorised to arrange with a Richard Meadley for the education of Mary Allanson for a period of three or four years and the Clerk wrote to 'one Skipton in Craven', who was the children's uncle, about the education of the two Allanson boys. All this is perfectly straightforward. But in November, £95 of Allanson's money was brought in of which £40 was used to pay off his debt to John Bevell and the rest put in the Town Chest 'until it can be made up to £150 to pay Mr. Heron', from whom the corporation had borrowed that sum in the April of the previous year.[1] In this instance the corporation were obviously using the orphans' portion – not necessarily misappropriating it – for their own purposes, no doubt intending to produce the money from some source or other when the time came for the children to claim their inheritance.

'Robbing Peter to pay Paul' has never been a policy which inexpert financiers have been well advised to follow. In London, where similar transactions took place, the highly complicated financial arrangements of the City must have provided many a pitfall for the unwary or unduly optimistic in a period of uncertain accountancy. In London, the most serious hazard was in fact the existence of several 'funds', one of the largest being 'the orphans' monies deposited in the Chamber', whose annual floating balances masked the true state of the City's income. Even in 1633, the manuscript accounts of the City of London Chamberlain relating to the orphans' monies make anxious reading for, whilst £16,842 5s. 7d. had been deposited in the Chamber, £28,539 0s.4d. had been paid out by it over the year.[2] Two years later, the Mayor and Citizens, in the course of a petition to the King concerning a £70,000 fine which had been imposed upon them by the Star Chamber, submitted: 'no personal estate appertains to the city but what belongs to the orphans, to whom more is owing by 40,000l, than is in the Chamber to satisfy'. Further, they claimed, because of their heavy expenses in maintaining public amenities, which used up the whole revenue and because of suits being brought against the City in the Exchequer 'many are unwilling to bring orphan's

[1] Beverley Borough Records, 1575–1821, ed. J. Dennett, *Yorks. Archeological Society Records Series*, vol. LXXXIV, 1933, pp. 143–5.

[2] Melvin C. Wren, The Chamber of London in 1633, *Economic History Review*, 2nd Series, vol. I. 1948, pp. 46–7.

money into the Chamber and merchants refuse to be free of the city . . .'[1] The imposition of the fine would thus make it quite impossible for the City to find the money due to the City's orphans. In 1638, due to non-payment of debts owing to it and to their 'loan' of £40,000 to Charles I, the City became indebted for £70,000 and the Chamber's credit, already suspect, very much impaired.[2]

During the next fifty years, the City sustained blow after calamitous blow to its finances. The Great Fire of London destroyed an immense amount of property which had been a source of revenue to the City and which could never be replaced; and this, together with the Irish wars and the Civil war, vastly reduced the 'Cities Ancient great Revenues' from which it had in the past been able to counterbalance its debts. Even worse, having borrowed large sums of money from the City, Charles II stopped the Exchequer in 1671, where £750,000 of the orphans' money was deposited. In 1683, the King finally seized the City's Charter 'which so ruined their Credit, that all payments into the Chamber ceased',[3] and the City could not now even hope to pay its debts. To some extent at least, the City's difficulties had been of their own making. An already difficult situation had only been exacerbated by injudicious spending, lending and beni-ficence. The pamphlet presenting *The Case of the Distressed Orphans of London*, issued on 22 October 1691, uncharitably asserted that the current financial difficulties of the City were due to 'the extravagence and fraud of its ologarchy' and its wasteful use of monies vested in the Chamber, an assertion not unnaturally resented by the City itself which claimed that the City's debt was 'Contracted only by the many great and unavoidable Calamities that have befallen the City, and by payment of Interest from time to time: And not (as hath been suggested) by the present government of the City, or in Expenses to Maintain the Mayor and Sherriffs, who serve the City at their own great Expence; And some of them have had their Estates greatly exhausted thereby.'[4] Be this as it may,

---

[1] *State Papers Domestic, 1635–36.* p. 56.
[2] *The Case of the City of London, In Reference to the Debt of the Orphans and Others.* 1693.
[3] ibid.
[4] *Reasons Humbly Offered, For Setling a Yearly Income from Hackney-Coachmen, and by a Duty on Coals, towards the Relief of the Orphans of the City of London.* 1691.

neither by their own account nor by those of their critics does the City's handling of the orphans' money appear to have been very sound. A tract, *Newes from Guild-hall* (1650), when the City was already indebted some thousands of pounds to the orphans, stated that 'the City Banks and Revenue is by undue means exhausted and the Orphans' money uncharitably and unconsciously embezzled', a situation which the author claimed was bound to arise and continue when the whole of the City's revenue was entered into one account, in which the expenditure was greater than the revenue, instead of the orphans' money being held and accounted for separately. The City's own explanation, *In Reference to the Debt of the Orphans and Others*, issued as a one-sided leaflet in 1693, though rather different in its details, only testifies on other grounds to their own ineptitude. They argue, for example, that since the City first got into serious financial difficulties in 1638, from which time they had had to pay interest on it, 'the then Gov^t of the City very improvidently allowed the Executors of the Citizens to bring into the Chamber Orphans Portions upon Interest, which ought to have been only deposited by such Executors as could not, or would not give the Chamber Security for them; And by that means a great Cash was kept in the Chamber, of which no profit was made; and out of the same, Interest was constantly paid for the said debt as also for the said Portions: So that by a true Account, Money being paid in at Interest to pay Interest, the said Debt of £70,000, in 54 years, hath increased to above 5 times that Sum; And the Interest paid also to the Orphans, contrary to the Custom of the City, hath made up the rest of the present debt.'

After Christmas 1683, although no more money was deposited on orphans' behalf in the City Chamber, 'there had been such Care to get in Debts owing to the City and to improve their Revenue, That they have paid to all Poor Orphans (whose Portions in the Chamber of London exceeded not £55) their whole debt'. This effort had cost the City £10,673 2s. 8d., and further payments they had made to Orphans and others for interest had amounted to a further £105,540. By 1693, however, when the City was indebted to the sum of £747,500 to the orphans, the City Aldermen, finding the burden of their debt too great to bear, applied to Parliament for assistance.

The previous year, a Bill had in fact been introduced into the

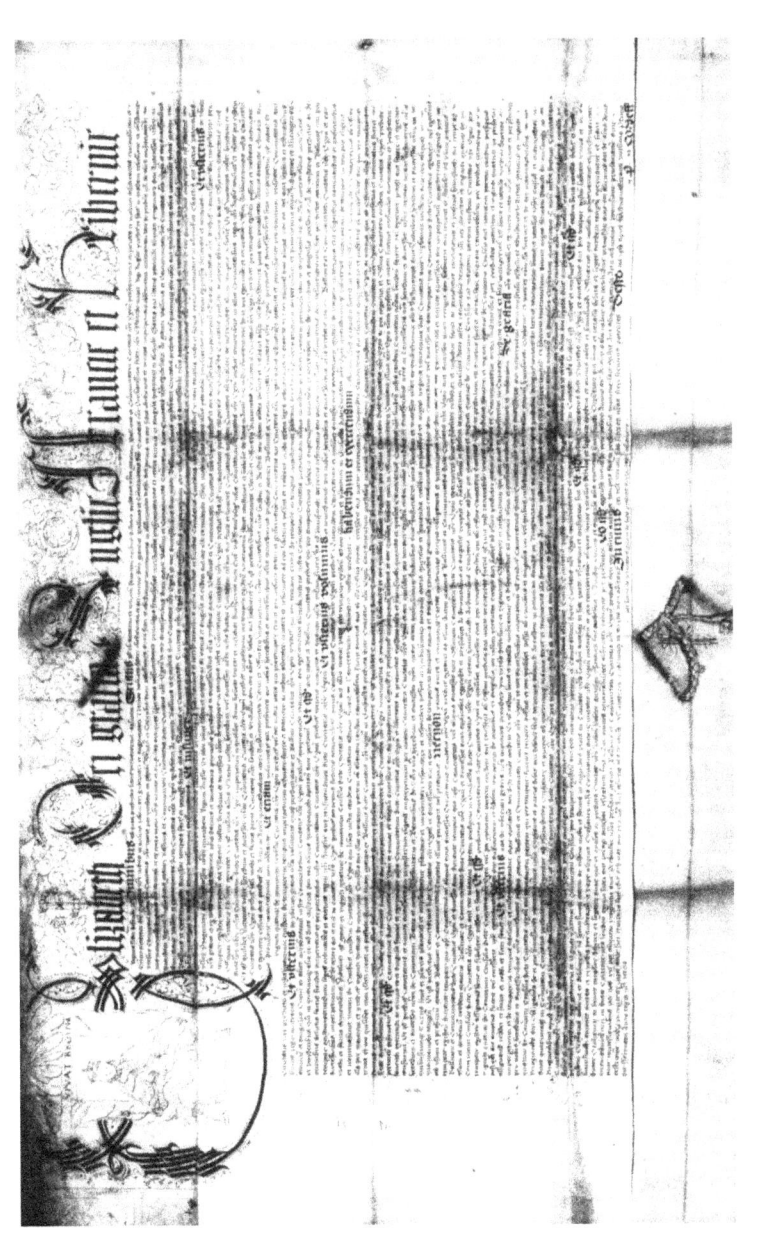

9 The original charter of Exeter Court of Orphans

10 "Dining Hall, Asylum" drawn by Rowlandson and Pugin. Published in 1808, by Ackermann's at London

House of Lords on behalf of the orphans' interest, which had been intended to provide some sort of remedy but, opposed by the City, it was dropped. A further attempt in 1692, though introduced and passed in the House of Lords failed in the House of Commons. The City had itself proposed in 1691 that money obtained by hackney coachmens' licenses, together with the receipts from a tax on coal entering London, should be devoted to paying off its debts to the orphans and the last proposal, with other provisions, did find part in the *Act for the Relief of the Orphans and other Creditors of the City of London*,[1] which eventually received the Royal Assent in 1694 and established an 'Orphans Fund' to allow the City to repay its debts to them. The Fund was to be recruited from a charge of £800 per annum laid on the City's lands: £2,000 per annum levied on the personal estates of the citizens (a tax which was withdrawn only in 1795); a duty which was to be levied upon wine and coal entering London; and a tax upon binding apprentices. Originally, the Fund was established to meet the interest and arrears of interest on the City's debts, but it proved sufficiently buoyant to support the gradual redemption of the principal debt to the orphans or their heirs and finally, when it was seen that the debt could be extinguished – which it finally was in 1820 – other liabilities were made chargeable to it.

Over and above every other provision the Act made, however, it ordered that: 'noe person or persons whatsoever shall att any time be compelled or obliged by vertue of any custome within the said City or by Order or Process of the Court of Orphans . . . to pay or deliver into the Chamber of the said City of London and sum or sums of money or personal estate due or to be due or belonging to any Orphan or Orphans of any Freeman of the said City any Law or Usage for inforcing the same notwithstanding'.[2] Anyone, father or executor, wishing to pay such money in voluntarily on a child's behalf might continue to do so and on the child's marriage, any interest which had accrued on such a deposit together with the principal was to be paid to the child or would be paid on his coming of age. In practice, although it was no longer compulsory to do so where no satisfactory security could be offered to the Court, it appears to have remained usual

[1] 5 & 6 Wm. & M., c. 10.
[2] ibid., Clause XVII.

to do so and the number of inventories does not noticeably fall off immediately after the passing of the Act. But gradually they become fewer and fewer until the middle of the eighteenth century, though no particular year showed a spectacular decline.

It is important to recognise that, although the Act of 1694 abolished any compulsion in the matter of depositing orphans' money in the Chamber, it did not suspend the need for the executors of a freeman's estate or the guardians of the orphans to give an account of the dead man's assets; nor did it withdraw the necessity for security to be given to the Court for their wards' inheritance. Thus the Court of Orphans came to exercise a similar control over the citizens' orphans as did the Court of Chancery for minors in general. William Maitland, writing in the mid-eighteenth century, records of the London Court of Orphans that 'This Court is occasionally held by the Lord Mayor and Aldermen, who are Guardians to the children that are under the Age of twenty-one years at the Decease of their Fathers; and who take upon them not only the Care and Management of their Goods and Chattels but likewise that of their Persons, by committing them to careful and faithful Tutors, to prevent disposing of themselves during their minority, without their Approbation.

'The Common Sergeant is authorised by the said Court, to take exact Accounts and Inventories of all deceased Freemen's Estates; and the youngest Attorney of the Mayor's Court, being Clerk to that of the Orphans, is appointed to take securities for their several Portions, in the name of the Chamberlain of London . . . for the Service of the said Orphans; and to whom a Recognisance or Bond, made upon the Account of an Orphan, shall by the Custom of London, descend to his Successor; which is hardly known elsewhere.

'When a Freeman of London dies, and leaves Children in their Minority, the Clerks of the several Parishes are to give in their names to the Common-Crier, who is thereupon immediately to summon the Widow or Executors to appear before the Court of the Lord Mayor and Aldermen, to bring in an Inventory of, and give Security for the Testator's Estate . . .' (within two months) 'And in case of non-Appearance, or Refusal of Security, the Lord Mayor may commit the contumacious Executor to Newgate . . .'[1]

[1] William Maitland, *The History of London from its Foundation to the Present Time*. 1756. vol. II, p. 121.

The real death-blow to the London Court of Orphans, however, was dealt in 1724 when at long last, London freemen were given the right of free disposition of their estates: 'And to the intent that persons of wealth and ability, who exercise the business of merchandise... within the said city, may not be discouraged from becoming freemen of the same, by reason of the custom restraining the citizens and freemen thereof from disposing of their personal estates by their last will and testaments, be it further enacted... That it shall and may be lawful to... give, devise and will and dispose of his and their personal estate and estates, to such... persons and to such... users, as he or they shall think fit; any custom or usage of or in the said city... to the contrary thereof in any wise notwithstanding.'[1] After this, although if a freeman so wished or if a freeman died intestate, the old custom was still enforceable, and although technically the Court still retained certain rights over city orphans such as the power to demand an inventory of an orphan's goods, together with a statement of any debts owing or owed from the executors, the control over the marriage and apprenticeship of orphans, and the right to demand the Court's assent to the person of the guardian, the activities of the Court very much diminished. New ideas of property ownership and of the rights of the individual citizen had finally contrived to reduce a medieval relic to an unimportant administrative irrelevance.[2]

Even in the sixteenth century the conflict between the property interest of the freemen and of the City had been recognised as one of the chief reasons why there was local opposition to the Courts of Orphans. In Bristol, as we have seen, this led to the Corporation soliciting a letter from the Privy Council – not to much effect, it should be said – which would uphold their authority over the disposition of the estates of freemen's orphans. In Northampton, the Mayor had had to threaten the imprisonment of executors for refusal to deal with the local Court of Orphans; and in London, the Mayor and Aldermen were obliged to defend their custom of enforcing the tripartite division of a freeman's estate and the equal division of the orphans' portion among all the man's children before the Privy Council itself.

[1] II Geo. I, c. 18. (1724), Clause XVII.
[2] Alexander Pulling, *A Practical treatise on the laws, customs, usages and regulations of the City and Port of London*, 1849 edn. pp. 196–7.

This last can be illustrated from the dispute which arose in 1583 between Sir James Harvey, himself an Alderman of the City and Alexander Avenon, son and heir of a prominent London citizen concerning 'the non-performance of certain promises made by the said Sir James in respect of a marriage, concluded chiefly by his own means, between his daughter Claire and Avenon'. Apparently unwilling to proceed with the marriage, Sir James had disinherited his daughter and left all his property among his other children, appointing his son, Sebastian, his sole executor, maintaining that a citizen should be free to dispose of his estate as he wished. In doing this, Harvey had not merely contravened the City custom of tripartite division of a freeman's estate, he had also attempted to set aside the traditional practice of the equal division of the orphans' inheritance between all surviving children. Apparently, Harvey had canvassed the support of the Privy Council and in a letter to them the Mayor and Aldermen of the City defend both customs on the grounds that they were both ancient and according to the common law; that they provided for the maintenance and education of the children during their minority; that it preserved the inheritance, 'should one die, for the rest of the brothers and sisters, where otherwise they [the orphans dying under age] might by Flattery or other Abuse be induced to bestow the same of their Wills upon Strangers'; that widows and creditors also derived benefit from the custom; and furthermore, they added darkly, various dire results would ensue for the city and all concerned if freedom was allowed in this matter. Certainly dire results did ensue from Sir James's will since he died before the dispute was settled and the wretched Sebastian promptly left the City without accounting for his father's property and putting his sister Claire 'out of doors and left her to the world'.[1]

Whilst the idea of profit to the City can hardly ever have been absent when the Court insisted on its rights, it is impossible to read through the records of its activities without gaining the impression that their careful concern for the rights of these orphans was a sign of a genuine interest in their welfare rather than merely an indication of municipal greed. Frequently they write letters reminding guardians of their obligations to their wards. Mr. Benyon, servant to the Bishop of London, had to be

[1] See *Remembrances of the City of London, 1579–1664*. 1878. pp. 312–14.

reminded of his duty 'to give assurance for the portions of his wife's children, being orphans and in the charge of the City' which he had neglected to do and who was thus threatened with legal proceedings if he continued to fail to do so in the light of this reminder.[1] Nor did they hesitate to send similar 'reminders' to those of far higher degree. In 1622, a letter was despatched to Lucy, Countess of Bedford, 'reminding her of their frequent applications on behalf of the orphans of Richard Clarke, late of London, Merchant Taylor, deceased, for the payment of the money due by her Ladyship to them'.[2] Time after time they resisted pressure put on them not least by the Lords of the Privy Council, to dispose of the guardianship of a child to some personal nominee. In sharp contrast to the general usage relating to the Royal Wards at this time, the London Court of Orphans did attempt 'to commit them [the orphans] and their portions to the custody of those who would be mindful of their education'. Indeed, the Court of Orphans' concern for the well-being of the children under its authority does in general seem to have been very different from the Crown's attitude to its wards. But, of course, these municipal authorities were in a way representative of the class from which the deceased parents came, which the Crown and its guardians of the Royal Wards were not. And certainly, City Officers were expected to be a great deal more scrupulous in regard to their dealings with the City orphans than were the officers of the Royal Court with its wards. In 1610, the resignation of Mr. Francis Morgan, Reader of the Middle Temple, from the Judgeship of the Sheriff's Court followed upon the disgrace of his son, who acted as his deputy. The son had been dismissed from office for enticing away and marrying without licence of the Court of Orphans, the orphan grandchild of Sir Thomas Campbell, the Lord Mayor, at whose house the girl lived. (Shortly afterwards due, so it was said, to the younger Morgan's example, an apprentice 'of mean friends and estate' enticed away another of the Lord Mayor's granddaughters!)[3]

But despite differences in the character and quality of the care they respectively took in the children who came into their

[1] ibid., pp. 308-9.
[2] ibid., p. 317.
[3] ibid., p. 292.

charge, both the Courts of Orphans and the Court of Wards shared one essential characteristic; both were concerned with the custody and control of property and it was in essence precisely because the exercise of their powers in this sphere increasingly ran counter to the concepts of individual property rights necessary to the development of a capitalist society that ultimately their authority was successfully challenged.

VI

The Vagrant and Delinquent Child

THE problem of the care and training of poor and destitute children was one which exercised the minds of the legislators and municipal reformers throughout the sixteenth century. In this respect it was one aspect of a most difficult and intractable problem that faced all governments of Western Europe – the necessity to found a system of poor relief to deal with the increase in distress and destitution, and to replace on a systematic basis the inadequacy of ecclesiastical charity and the slackening of private alms giving. 'The evolution of the Elizabethan poor law,' says Sir William Ashley, 'was but the English phase of a general movement for reform, and was probably stimulated by continental examples.'[1] English concern for the education of the children of the poor may well have been stimulated by the views of Vives, the Spanish humanist, whose practical treatise *On the Relief of the Poor* – probably the 'best seller' of its time[2] – was written in 1524 while he was resident at the Court of Henry VIII. It is significant that in his comprehensive plan for a poor law policy Vives laid great stress on the education of the children of the poor as one means of securing their moral improvement. In this treatise (written for the citizens of Bruges) he emphasised that the young children of the poor were 'villainously brought up', their sons wandering about begging, their daughters at an

[1] *English Economic History and Theory*, vol. II, p. 350.
[2] S. and B. Webb, *English Poor Law History*. 1927. pt. I, p. 36.

early age selling themselves cheap into prostitution, 'nor can they be drawn away from this most evil way of life'. Although work was available in industry, they refused to take it, 'for their parents say they bring home more money from begging'; and he advocated that begging should be forbidden and that such children should be placed by the municipality with individual manufacturers for work and training. As for the destitute children, he continued, 'let there be a hospital where abandoned children may be nurtured, to whom appointed women shall act as mothers; these shall nurture them until the sixth year: then let them be moved on to the public school, where they shall receive education and training, together with maintenance ... In selecting teachers of a ... suitable kind let the magistrates spare not expense. They will secure for the city over which they rule a great boon at small cost ... I would say the same about the girls' school in which the first rudiments of letters are taught. If any girl show herself inclined for and capable of learning, she should be allowed to go further with it.' After preliminary training, those boys who were 'quickest at learning' were to be kept on in the school, and the others were to 'move on into workshops according to their individual bents'.[1] Although no English version of Vives' book appears to have been made at the time, it is unlikely that his plans were not discussed with the legislators, Court officials and scholars of Oxford (where he held a Lectureship in Rhetoric), with whom he was then actually associating; and indeed, the later London plans for destitute children, which resulted in the foundation of Christ's Hospital, are largely based upon the principles enunciated here. Moreover, a plan entirely in accordance with Vives' principles and possibly based on earlier advice given to the citizens of Ypres,[2] was put into operation there in 1525 and achieved wide notoriety throughout Christendom. The Ypres scheme – the practical working out of Vives' principles – became a noted model for legislators dealing with poor relief all over Western Europe. An English translation of the Ypres regulations was produced here in 1535 by William Marshall, an ardent reformer employed by Thomas Cromwell, and in the dedication to Anne Boleyn, Marshall suggested that similar rules should be made for the poor and needy in England.[3]

[1] op. cit. printed in F. R. Salter, *Some Early Tracts on Poor Relief*. 1926. pp. 8–9.
[2] ibid., p. 32.
[3] ibid., p. 36.

An examination of subsequent legislation, especially in connection with the care and training of destitute children, leaves little doubt that this publication influenced public opinion in favour of state policy on similar lines.[1]

The new and terrifying problem which faced legislators everywhere was the increase in vagrancy and vagabondage. The beginning of the sixteenth century was a period of economic transition and stress and the bands of 'sturdy beggars' who swarmed on the roads and terrorised both 'towne and contrie' were recruited from many sources. There were the families uprooted by agrarian changes, industrial workers displaced by temporary fluctuations in industry and commerce, discharged soldiers, sailors and retainers, the old and impotent poor, the rogues and harlots, and the incorrigible vagrant and idle, and accompanying these groups, children. 'For this is sure,' wrote Starkey, 'that in no country of Christendom, for number of people, you shall find so many beggars as here in England.'[2] Distress and hunger, despite the many whippings imposed by penal statutes, drove many men to theft and crime and to rear their children in roguery. An anonymous tract of 1546 thus described the process: 'Many thousands of us which here before lived honestly upon our sore labour and travayl, bryngyng up our chyldren in the exercise of honest labour, are now constrained some to begge, some to borrowe, and some to robbe and steale, to get food for us and our poor wives and chyldren. And that wych is most lyke to growe to inconvenience, we are constrained to suffer our chyldren to spend the flour of theyr youth in idleness, bryinging them up other to bear wallettes, other else, if thei be sturdy, to stuffe prisons, and garnysh galow trees.'[3]

It was the persistence of begging, crime and disorder, and the failure of repressive policies to suppress vagrancy, that ultimately led the authorities to accept responsibility for the various groups of destitute.

Sixteenth-century writers commonly classified the poor into

---

[1] Thomas Starkey, in his *Dialogue*, refers to these plans 'lately devised by the wisdom of the citizens of Ypres, a city in Flanders, the which I would wish to be put in use with us, or else some other of the same sort'. Ed. K. M. Burton, 1948, p. 160.
[2] ibid., p. 89.
[3] *A Supplication of the Poore Commons, in Four Supplications 1529–1553*. Ed. Furnivall and Cowper, 1871. p. 79.

three groups, each of which included children. The 'poore by impotency and defect' included 'the poore orphans and others left fatherlesse and motherlesse in the world', and the child who was 'naturally disabled either in wit or member'. The 'poore by casuality' included the poor man 'overcharged with many young children'; and 'the thriftlesse poore' included the children of the idle and dissolute vagrants.[1] For these various groups of children the sixteenth-century reformers tried to devise policies which, they hoped optimistically, would end poverty and teach them the virtue of an industrious and independent way of life.

What, then, were the actual provisions made for the poor child and how were they carried out in practice? In view of the popular fears of vagrants who menaced public safety, it is not surprising that the Tudor State showed its first concern for this class of children.

During the first half of the sixteenth century no clear distinction was made between the unemployed and incorrigible rogues. While the impotent poor might be relieved, vagrants as a class were assumed not to be seeking work but avoiding it. 'As touching the multitude of beggars,' wrote Starkey, 'it argueth no poverty, but rather much idleness, and ill policy; for it is their own cause and negligence that they do beg; there is sufficient enough here in our country of all things to maintain them without begging.'[2] Because of the criminal elements among them, vagrants were feared and detested and treated as enemies of the community, to be driven back to work 'under fear and terror of the whip and the gallows'. It is against this background that the first provision for vagrant children has to be seen.

The first poor law of 1531[3] made no mention of children, but merely licensed begging by the aged and impotent and laid down punishments for sturdy beggars. In 1535, however, and significantly the same year in which William Marshall's translation of the Ypres Ordinances was published, a draft poor law was drawn up (possibly by William Marshall) which made provisions for vagrant children very similar to those which became law in 1536. The preamble to this draft in an enlightened and compassionate way emphasised the misfortune of children

[1] See *An Ease for Overseers of the Poore*, 1601, also Henry Arth[ington], *Provision for the Poore, now in Penurie*. 1597. p. B. 2-3.
[2] Starkey, op. cit., p. 89.
[3] 22 Henry VIII, c. 12.

brought up in vagrancy and pointed out that many adult vagrants have had 'to procure ther livying by open beggyng euen from childehod, so that they nuer knewe any other waie of livyng but onely by beggyng. – And so for lacke of gode ouersight in southe many live in grete mysery in age'.[1] It was therefore the conviction that the vagrant child constituted a danger to society and must be rescued from a life of idleness and from growing up to swell the ranks of yet another generation of adult vagrants and criminals, that led to the provisions of the Act of 1536. By these, the authorities of every parish were authorised to take healthy idle begging children between the ages of 5 and 14 and apprentice them to masters in husbandry or other crafts to be taught, 'by which they may get their livings when they shall come of age'. As far as the 'charitable collections' allowed, the children were to be provided with a suitable outfit of clothing when they entered into service. By this radical measure such children were to be removed from a vicious environment and be provided with maintenance and training to prevent future dependency. And in line with the general attitude to vagrants, children between 12 and 16, who 'without reasonable cause refused service' or afterwards attempted to return to their idle ways, were to be openly whipped 'with rods' at the discretion of the authorities. Lest the soft-hearted should be tempted to spare the rod, parish officers failing to inflict due punishment were to be put in the stocks for two days on a diet of bread and water.[2]

We do not know what efforts, if any, the parish authorities made to execute this Act when it was first passed, though it was used by a number of towns in the second half of the century. In the

[1] British Museum, Royal MS. 18, c. vi, cited by G. R. Elton, An Early Tudor Poor Law. *Economic History Review*, 2nd Series, vol. VI, no. I. August 1953. p. 57.

[2] 27 Henry VIII, c. 25. There is a striking similarity between the provisions of this Act and the Ypres scheme for the training of poor children. 'Thus the boys taken from the bytter and sowre crafte of beggynge ar appoynted to an easyer way and have assygned untoe them a maister to teche theym such crafte and occupatyon as they ar mete to and as their wyttes wil serve them. And lykewise the yonge women leste in idlenesse they shulde lerne sluggerdy . . . hathe one occupatyon as to do servyce to the citizens to dresse the houses to make redy mete and drinke . . . and some are bounden apprentyses to lerne suche thinges as is mete for women to do.' Begging was forbidden, and the 'unruly' were to be 'corrected' with 'rod of justice' (see Salter, op. cit., pp. 53–4). In places, the very phraseology of the English Statute appears to be a paraphrase of Marshall's translation.

changing economic conditions of the time, amid widespread unemployment, suitable homes for children must often have been difficult to find. *A Supplication of the Poore Commons* in 1546 states: we 'can fynd no way to set our chyldren on worke, no, though we prefer them for meat and drynk and poore clothes to cover their bodies'.[1] In such circumstances many masters must have been reluctant to take vagrant children into their households. In the next few years the vagrancy problem grew to alarming proportions; riots and unsettlement throughout the land created a state of panic which resulted in the Act of 1547, the most savage legislation of the century. Recalcitrant vagabonds who refused to work were to be branded and enslaved for two years. A second offence extended slavery to life. Their children 'which brought up in idleness might be so rooted in it that hardly may they be brought after to thrift and labour', as well as any beggar children of between five and fourteen years of age found wandering about on their own, might be taken away from their parents or 'keeper' by 'any manner of person' who promised, in the presence of one of the constables of the parish and 'two honest and discreet neighbours' and a justice of the peace, to bring up the child in some honest labour or occupation, until 20 years of age in the case of a 'woman child' and 24 for a 'man child'. Should the apprentice run away and be recaptured, the master might put the child in chains 'and use him or her as his slave in all points' until it came of age. During such period of enslavement, the child ranked as personal property and could be disposed of 'after such like sort and manner as he may do of any other of his movable goods or chattels'.[2]

This ferocious legislation defeated its own ends and was withdrawn two years later. But in the new Act of 1549, and in similar clauses relating to children of the same age group in subsequent legislation,[3] wandering beggars who carried about with them 'children of tender age . . . brought up in idleness' were liable to forfeit their parental rights. Compulsory apprenticeship continued, but the taint of slavery was removed; instead, runaways were to be punished 'in the stocks or otherwise by discretion'. Moreover, some attempts were made to safeguard the child's

[1] op. cit., p. 81.
[2] I Edward VI, c. 3.
[3] See 3 & 4 Edward VI, c. 16; 2 & 3 Philip & Mary, c. 5; 5 Elizabeth, c. 3.

THE VAGRANT AND DELINQUENT CHILD

interest and protect him from ill-treatment. The bond of apprenticeship was to be formally entered into at Quarter Sessions, and on complaint by 'two honest neighbours' that the master or mistress was 'unreasonable in ordering and bringing up the child', the Justices might discharge him and apprentice him to a new master. The length of service was shortened to 15 or marriage for girls and 18 for boys.

Subsequent legislation modified only slightly – and on the side of stringency – the principles laid down in the 1549 Act as it affected vagrants. The Poor Law Act of 1572,[1] in which the State came to accept the principle of a compulsory poor rate, contained severe measures against idlers, rogues and vagabonds, especially for adolescents, who were for the first time distinguished from younger children. Adolescents over 14 years found begging without licence were to be put in gaol until the next session and, convicted of a 'roguish and vagabond's trade of life', they were to incur the same penalty as adults, unless some honest person were willing to take them into service for a year. A repetition of the offence, however, could not be classed as a felony, as with persons over 18 years. Younger children were to be dealt with by 'whipping and stocking' as in former Acts. In addition, this Act made the first suggestion for providing work for the unemployed. If funds permitted, after the needs of the impotent poor had been met, the justices might place and settle to work the rogues and vagabonds who were either born or had three years' residence in the area.[2] An amending Act in 1576, *An Act for the setting of the poore on worke, and for avoyding ydleness*, showed still more clearly the influence of the work and training schemes in the towns. 'To the Intente Yowthe maybe accustomed and brought up in laboure and worke, and then not lyke to growe to be ydle Roges, and to the Entente also that suche as bee alredye growen up in Ydlenes and so Roges at this present, maye not have any juste Excuse in sayeng that they cannot get any Service or Worke'[3] – the justices were directed to purchase a stock of raw materials at the cost of the rates, and set the poor, young and old, to work, so that they might be maintained by their labour whilst

---

[1] 14 Elizabeth, c. 5.
[2] The length of service of apprenticeship for beggars' children was restored to 24 for boys and 18 for girls.
[3] 18 Elizabeth, c. 3.

in the House of Correction. To this end, a House of Correction was to be established in every county for punishing and employing those who refused to work.

The legislation of 1572-3 was continued until it was replaced by a comprehensive Act for the Relief of the Poor in 1597 which, re-enacted with only slight modification in 1601, remained the basis of poor law administration until 1834. Its importance, so far as children were concerned, was that after half a century of experimentation, their maintenance and training were placed on a systematic basis. The churchwardens and overseers of the poor, with the consent of the justices of the peace, were required to take such measures as were necessary to set to work and apprentice, not merely vagrant and destitute children, but all children whose parents were thought to be unable to keep and maintain them. Such expenses as were required for their apprenticeship were to be paid from the rates.[1] This Act was followed by a series of *Orders* from the Privy Council reminding justices that they were specifically charged with the apprenticeship and training of children.[2] Where parental rights clashed with the security of the State and with the welfare of the child, as in the vagrant and criminal sections of the community, they were to be overridden. And in principle the State accepted the responsibility for securing the proper treatment and training of children by those into whose care the law had entrusted them.

That vagrancy and crime were inextricably mingled both in sixteenth-century legislation and in the public imagination, and very largely in fact too, is obvious from contemporary sources. What is far from clear, however, is just how many children actually took to a life of crime. From the days of Elizabeth onwards, the labour of children was a social ideal explicitly encouraged both by the provisions for parish apprenticeship in the Poor Laws and also by the Statute of Artificers of 1563: an ideal of which the extensive use of child labour in all types of industry was clear evidence. Nevertheless, even where children were employed for long hours when trade flourished, frequent trade depression, regular seasonal unemployment and, in the

---

[1] 39 Elizabeth, c. 3. The terms of apprenticeship were up to 24 for a boy and 18 for a girl but the Act of 1601 (43 Elizabeth, c. 2) specifically stated that marriage ended a girl's apprenticeship, even if she were under 18 yrs. of age.

[2] J. C. Cox, *Three Centuries of Derbyshire Annals*. 1890. vol. I, pp. 4-6.

towns, lack of employment for children, together with the absence of schools for the poorer classes, must have resulted in a good deal of lawlessness and mischief.

The limitations of this type of speculation are, however, very obvious and not the least among them the implicit sanction for the contemporary view that delinquency was largely, if not exclusively, a characteristic of the poorer classes. In fact, we know very little about the social structure of sixteenth- and seventeenth-century juvenile delinquency apart from the obvious bias in the administration of justice against the poor, the latter frequently being punished where the rich escaped. On the other hand, there is some evidence to show that the claims that the bands of professional beggars which swarmed the countryside were peripatetic training grounds for what, even in our own more permissive society, would be recognised as delinquent behaviour, were not all unfounded. The studies of Thomas Harman[1] and Thomas Dekker,[2] those Mayhews of the Elizabethan underworld, both agreed that children figured prominently among its inhabitants. The 'free companies of beggars', who carried out many 'detestable crimes' under pretence and colour of begging, were accompanied by 'great flockes of Chyldren', taught 'evil tatches' by the 'fellowship of lewd persons'. Dekker, not unnaturally, argued that irresponsibility bred irresponsibility:

'The *Tame Rogue* begets a *Wilde Rogue*; and this is a spirit that cares not into what company of what Divels hee falles: In his swaddling clothes he is marked to be a villaine, and in his breeding is instructed to be so. The mother of him (who was delivered of her burden under a hedge) ... will rather endure to see his braynes beaten out than to have him taken from her, to be put to an honest course of life ...'[3]

Harman, a Kent magistrate who carried out a sociological survey of the vagabonds in his county, gave a vivid picture of some of the young delinquent types. There were first the 'dells', young girls who went abroad young, 'either through the death of their parents and nobody to look after them or else by some sharp mistress that they serve do run away out of service', and take to a life of prostitution and crime. The 'wild dells' were the

---

[1] *A caveat or Warning for Common Cursitors, vulgarly called Vagabonds.* 1566.
[2] *The Belman of London.* 1608.
[3] ibid., p. D.

children of harlots, and, 'being traded up by their monstrous mothers, must of necessity be evil, or worse, than their parents'. The 'Kinchin Coes' and the 'Kinchin Morts' were little boys and girls carried at their mothers' backs who, reared from infancy in crime, were used 'to creep in at windows or cellar doors'. They were brought up 'savagely, till they grow to be ripe, and soon ripe, soon rotten', he concludes.[1] If beggars had no children of their own, Dekker claimed, 'they wil steale from others, and by some means disfigure them, that by their parents they may never be knowne'.[2]

These were the children who grew up 'to stuff prisons and garnish gallow trees', and it is hardly surprising that, when England was swarming with such bands, the authorities should have thought that the only realistic solution to the problem was to remove the children from their parents, whether they wished it or not, in the hope of rearing them in a more settled way of life. This was in fact the same solution as that to which the authorities returned at the end of the nineteenth century. The Poor Law Act of 1899 allowed the transference of parental rights to the Guardians, where 'vicious habits or mode of life' of the parents were likely to reflect adversely on the welfare of the child, and many children of habitual vagrants were removed from their parents under this Act in the early years of the twentieth century.[3] Nevertheless, the harsh treatment meted out to young vagrants under the Tudor poor laws is very difficult for the modern reader to comprehend. It must be remembered, however, that discipline was hard for all classes of Tudor children; the rod was not spared either at home or at school. In the circumstances, it is unlikely that many young vagrants, if apprehended, escaped a whipping. An item in the Nottingham Records, for instance, refers to fourpence being paid out 'for whipping of a false boye which was sett uppon the pillorie'.[4] Almost in anticipation of the Act of Settlement of 1662, definite instructions as to the treatment of children found wandering with their parents are contained in some *Resolutions* issued for the use of justices of the peace by the Lord Chief Justice, Sir John Popham, about the turn

[1] Harman, op. cit., pp. 107–8.
[2] Dekker, op. cit., p. D. 3.
[3] 62 & 63 Victoria, c. 37. The Act also provided penalties 'for either assisting or inducing the child to escape from the control of the guardians'.
[4] *Records of the Borough of Nottingham*, vol. IV, 1889. p. 213.

THE EPISTLE

ment of a common wealth is muche like to the Tutorship of a Tutor who ſuch people, or thoſe governors and Tutor is to doe, ſuch and all maner of things which may tend & be for the beſt behoof and pfit of the pupil: & for that cauſe is he called a tutor, quaſi tu- Inſtituris tor, that is to ſay, a carefull defendor and a diligent preſeruer, tutelu & bothe for the good education of their perſonages and of their ſortes. ſo euer to them apperteineth, ſo ought the magiſtrate who beeing the generall Tutor is the eye of the whole Citie, and therfore muſt beholde and ſee euery particuler mans caſe, he is the care and muche of the whole body, and therfore it is to bear all and to ſpeake for all, he is the head of the whole common wealth: and therfore muſt vnderſtand and direct every man in his eſtate and calling. Sic enim temp. tuer. debet, vt omni-bus contulat.

Many good orders I confeſſe haue been deviſed by the pru-dent Magiſtrates and gouernours of this Citie for the good gouernement both of the elder ſorte and of ſuch young Orphans, as vnto whome any wealth is left, and who are to inioy the benefit of their parents travels: but ſuche Orphans, who having nothing left vnto them, & beeing deſtitute of all relief and help: as left to their extreme diſpoſition, theſe as I ſaid, I ſay again, ſo ſwarme in cluſters in euery corner and quarter of your Citie, and for viciouſneſſe of good education and nurturing, dai-grow to be thornes and nettles, and who as the Cattr-pillers, Frogs, graſhoppers and lice of Egypt, ſhalbe the plagues Exod.7.8. of this your common wealth, and if remedy be not provided: ſhall vtterly devoure and deſtroy the ſame. And for theſe there is no care, no regard, no account made, but you beeing the fa-thers of this common wealth: it is your parte, and bounden du-tie to provide alſo for ſuch, not onely in reſpect of the ſafetie and preſeruation

---

ORDERS
enacted for Orphans and for their poſſitions within THE CITIE OF EX-ceſter, with ſundry other inſtructions incident to the ſame. Collected and ſet foorth by Iohn Vowell alias Hooker gen-tleman and Chaum-berlaine of the ſame Citie.

Pſalme. 82.
¶ Doo right to the poore and father-leſſe, and ſaue them from the hand of the wicked.

IMPRINTED at LONDON by Iohn Allde.
1575

11 (a) (*left*) The Title-page of Vowell's *Book of Orders*
11 (b) (*right*) An extract from Vowell's *Book of Orders* in which he warns of the dire con-sequences of neglecting the welfare of the orphans of the poor

12 Title-page of *The Poore Orphans Court, or Orphans Cry*, 1636

of the century: 'The wief must goe with the husband to the parishe where he was borne, and not to be divided from one another, the children that are above 7 yeres of age must, after they are whipped, be sent to the parishes where they were severally borne. But those children under the age of 7 yeres, because they are not within the degree of vagabondes, must goe with their parents, not where they were borne or last abidinge.'[1] The principle of settlement stemmed from the reluctance of parishes to accept responsibility for the support of any save those born within the boundaries of the parish and the provision in Popham's *Resolutions* for the removal back to their parish of birth of all but the youngest children of vagrants only underlines how important an issue this was long before it gained the sanction of statute.

Shocking as this disregard of family ties seems to us now, the paternal governments of the Tudors, used to ordering about almost every section of the community, had no compunction in sending children of tender years separately to places where they were born, there to be provided for by the parish authorities, or to remove children from a settled family environment and place them with strangers for apprenticeship. The Tudor attitude on this question can only be understood in the light of contemporary family patterns. In all sections of society, as we have already seen, the common practice was for children to leave the family environment early in life. In this respect, therefore, poor children who came under the aegis of these Acts were originally not treated very differently from children in other sections of the community, although the pattern established by statute in the sixteenth century involved untold misery for the children of the poor in later centuries, by which time, in other classes, separation of parents and children had been largely abandoned.

Of course, the bands of beggars were not the only training grounds for juvenile delinquency. Fagin had his sixteenth-century counterpart in one Wotton, 'a gentilman borne, and sometyme a marchauntt man of good credyte', who, falling on bad times, kept an alehouse and later 'procured all the Cuttpurses abowt this Cittie (London) to repaire to his said Howse. There

---

[1] *Lothian MSS (Hobart Papers) Hist. MSS. Com.*, 62, 1905, p. 76. See also, William Lambard, *Eirenarcha*. 1602 edn., pp. 192-3.

was a schole howse sett upp to learne younge boyes to cutt purses. There was hung up tow devises, the one was a pockett, the other was a purse. The pocket had in yt certen cownters and was hunge abowte with hawkes bells, and over the toppe did hange a little sacring bell; and he that could take a cownter without any noyse was allowed to be *a publique Foyster:* and he that could take a peece of sylver owt of the purse without the noyse of any bells, he was adjudged *a Judiciall Nypper* . . .'[1] The punishment for theft demanded by Tudor criminal law was in many cases death, and for as long as life was held cheap, delinquency deemed wilful rather than coincidental and young and old held to be equally responsible for their actions, children over seven years of age were not exempted from offering their pathetic tribute to public order from the arm of the public gallows. The petty offender, also regardless of age, was committed to the local House of Correction or 'Bridewell'.

As we shall see, the Bridewells ultimately came to be the local workhouses, but they were originally conceived as being something in addition to this – a type of prison to which sturdy beggars might be sent for corrective 'treatment' in the form of whipping and forced labour. In the house of Bridewell, juveniles and adults were herded together, women and girls always being kept separate from men and boys, but young and old lodged and worked together and given the same treatment. The Orders and Rules for the treatment of offenders, drawn up by the justices of the County of Suffolk, who had been convened for the purpose at Bury St. Edmunds in 1589, give us some idea of what this treatment was like:

'It is ordered and agreed uppon,' say the justices, 'that every stronge or sturdie roag shall have xij stripes upon his beare skynne with the said whipp provided for the said house, and every yong roag or idle loyterer vj stripes with the said whipp. And that every one of them withowte fayle at their fyrst comminge into the said house shall have putt upon hym, her, or them, some clogge, cheine collers of iron, ringle or manacle, such as the keper of the said house shall thinke meete so as he maie answer for everyone as well for his forthcomminge, as also that they

[1] Fleetwood to Burghley, 7 July 1585, Landsdown MSS. no. 44, Part 38, printed in H. Ellis, Original Letters. 1st Series, vol. II, pp. 295–303, quoted by Tawney and Power, *Tudor Economic Documents*, vol. II, pp. 337–8.

shall be quiette and doe noe hurte for the tyme they shall contynue in the said house.'¹

The importance that the justices attached to the deterrent element of committal to the House of Correction is immediately obvious from this account, the more so since it was this, rather than equally detailed directions as to the way in which the inmates of the House should be employed, to which they addressed themselves. On the other hand, at least until the end of the sixteenth century, the Houses were cleanly kept and strictly managed under the supervision of the local magistrates. The food allowance laid down by the Suffolk magistrates in fact compares very favourably with later prison diet sheets:

'It is ordered that every person committed to the said House shall have for theire diets . . . at every dynner and supper on the fleshe daies, bread made of rye, viij ounces troye waight, with a pynte of porredge, a quarter of a pound of fleshe, and a pinte of beare . . . And on every fyshe daie, at dynner and supper the like quantities made eyther of milk or pease or such lyke, and the thurd part of a pound of chese, or good heringe or twoe white or redd accordinge as the keper of the house shall thinke meete . . .'²

Moreover, although deterrence was the immediate aim of the committal of vagrants, rehabilitation was the long-term objective of the Bridewell system. In a society in which child labour was the ideal, the forced labour system of the Bridewell was the natural panacea since it was believed that it must inculcate industrious habits in those on whom it was imposed: 'It was too evident to all men that beggary and thievery did abound,' wrote the citizens of London in 1552 to the Privy Council concerning their suit to the King for the use of Bridewell Palace, in London, which was to be converted into the first of these Houses of Correction and thus to give its name to the many later institutions established to serve the same purpose. After due examination of the problem, they claimed, 'we evidently perceived that the cause . . . was idleness: and the mean and the remedy to cure the same must be by its contrary, which is labour . . .'³

No case-histories remain to tell us how successful the Bride-

[1] Harleian MSS. no. 364, B. M., printed in F. M. Eden, *The State of the Poor*. 1797. vol. III. App., pp. CXLII, CXLIII.
[2] ibid., p. CXLIII. Also quoted by W. D. Morrison, *Juvenile Offenders*. 1896. pp. 229–30.
[3] Quoted Tawney and Power, op. cit., p. 307.

wells were in individual cases, but there is ample evidence from the following centuries that they failed to stamp out juvenile delinquency. In the towns, and in London in particular, the gangs of children roaming the streets were a recurring theme for writers on social subjects and anxious for public safety. Among the more remarkable of the many pamphlets devoted to this particular theme was that written by T. Firmin in 1678, *Some Proposals for the Employment of the Poor:* 'Let any man that hath occasion either to walk through the outparts of the city (where mostly our poor people inhabit), tell but what he hath seen of the rudeness of young children, who for want of better education and employment, shall sometimes be found by whole companies at play, where they shall wrangle and cheat one another, and upon the least provocation swear and fight for a farthing; or else they shall be found whipping of horses, by reason of which they sometimes cast their riders, to the hazard or loss of their lives or limbs; or else they shall be throwing of dirt or stones into the coaches, or at the glasses, in so much that I have been found a 100 times greatly troubled to see the rudeness and misbehaviour of the poorest sort of children (especially of late years), they having been generally too much neglected, that they have neither been taught their duties either towards God or man . . .' It is very noticeable, however, that for Firmin in the seventeenth century, in contrast to Vives with his pleas for schooling in the sixteenth, the solution to the problem appeared to be some sort of industrial training, not better education facilities for the poor: 'Why, I pray, must a poor boy that is designed for a mason, bricklayer, shoemaker or the like honest and necessary trade, be taught to write as if he were designed to be a merchant? Is it not enough that such children are taught to read the Bible, and so much of arithmetic and writing as may fit them for such trades and employment as they are intended to be put into?'[1] Idleness, of course, was then, as it had always been the most publicised of the causes of delinquency. But the absence of any effective police system made it comparatively easy for gangs of mischievous and semi-delinquent juveniles to deteriorate into lawlessness and graduate into crime. Children under apprenticeship indentures, although no more law-abiding, continued to be disciplined by their masters or mistresses who were long accustomed to deal

[1] op. cit., p. 15–16.

summarily themselves with delinquents and did not hesitate to mete out harsh punishment for any misdemeanour they detected among their employees. But for the unemployed poor, the lack of a police force was only exacerbated by the maladministration of justice to which Defoe refers in *The Poor Man's Plea* (1698), in the course of a general condemnation of 'the Passive Magistrate'.[1] In the event, therefore, since the ineffective administration of local justice combined with only a very limited understanding of the fundamental causes of juvenile crime and an even more restricted understanding of how to deal with it, it is scarcely surprising that there should have been at the end of the seventeenth and beginning of the eighteenth centuries a considerable problem of the vagrant and juvenile delinquent, many of whom escaped being even brought before the magistrate.

Confronted by the obvious failure of traditional policies, two attempts were now made, one in 1703 and one in 1717, to get rid of vagrant, begging and thieving boys from the streets by literally shipping them out of the country. This rather drastic solution to the problem of juvenile delinquency had in fact been adopted on a far more limited scale a hundred years before (and notably in London) by the astute manipulation of the apprenticeship clauses of the poor laws. In 1609, the Privy Council had informed the Mayor of London that 'the ills and plagues' of the city were chiefly due to the numbers of poor within its walls and suggested that the Corporation, together with the chartered Companies, should raise a fund to ship many of them to Virginia, one of the many colonies well known to be in need of labour. A considerable sum of money was in fact raised for the purpose, but nothing more seems to have been done at this stage until, about 1617, the Lord Mayor authorised a charitable collection for the purpose of sending a hundred poor children to the colony. The City was to grant five pounds apiece for equipment and passage money, while the children were to be apprenticed until they were twenty-one years of age and afterwards to be granted fifty acres of land in the plantations, to be held in fee simple at a rent of one shilling a year. Amounts subscribed appear to have varied a good deal in size, one parish is recorded as only subscribing twelve and threepence 'towards the transportation of a hundred children

---

[1] Printed in *The Genuine Works of Mr. Daniel Defoe . . . containing 39 Scarce and Valuable Tracts upon many Curious and uncommon subjects*, pp. 295–6.

to Virginia by the Lord Mayor's appointment', but the necessary sum of five hundred pounds was eventually collected and the children, who had meanwhile been lodged in Bridewell to await 'despatch', left for Virginia in the spring of 1619. How far this exercise was looked upon as a solution to the delinquency problem may be seen from a letter dated January 1618 from James I to Sir John Smith, who became Governor of Virginia the following year:

'Whereas our Court hath been troubled with divers idle young people whoe although they have been twise punished still continewe to followe the same haoeing noe ymploymente. Wee haveinge noeother course to cleere our court from them have thought fitt to send them unto you, desireing you att the next oportunitie to send them away to Virginia and to take such order that they may bee sett to worke there, wherein you shall onlie doe us good service, but also doe a deed of charitie by ymploying them whoe otherwise will never be reclaimed from the idle life of vagabonds . . .'

In November 1619, the Company wrote to the Lord Mayor asking for another hundred children, the City to pay five hundred pounds as before. These children, however, at the expiration of their apprenticeship, were to be tenants on the public land, with a house and a stock of cattle. The Common Council of London met and decided to send the children asked for, levying the taxpayers to do so. But as to the terms on which the children were to be established in Virginia, they proceeded to haggle with the Company, and it was finally agreed between them that, after a seven years' apprenticeship, each child was to be given twenty-five acres of land, to be held at an annual rent of sixpence a year – a much better bargain for the children and an interesting indication of the City's genuine interest in the ultimate fate of the children of whom it wished to rid itself. A second group of children was sent out in 1620; but not altogether without some difficulty, since not all of them were willing to be rescued from a life of 'mysery and ruyne' by transportation oversea. Unwilling that the City should be frustrated in 'so good a worke' the Privy Council had had to authorise 'such as shall have the charge of this service to imprison, punish, and dispose any of those children, upon any disorder by them committed, as cause shall require, and so to shipp them out for Virginia with as much expedition as may stand with convenience . . .' Fortified by this warrant, the City continued with its shipments, making more collections of money as they were needed.

In 1627 it was claimed that 1,400 or 1,500 children had been 'gathered up' that year 'from divers places' and sent out to Virginia, and although these figures may not be entirely accurate there is evidence enough to show that during this period several hundred young people were taken to the colony and their passage paid by the charitable contributions of more fortunate Englishmen. Most of the children sent to New England after 1622 were sent out by private donations. Anthony Abdy, a citizen and Alderman of London, made a will in 1640 in which £120 was left 'to be disposed and bestowed by my Executors upon twenty poore Boyes and Girles to be taken up out of the streets of London as vagrants for the Cloathing and transporting of them to Virginia New England or any other of the Western Plantations, there to be placed'. Abdy's two sons also made identical bequests in their own wills.

Other large towns, notably Bristol and Liverpool (who shipped 'dyvers yong Children and Beggars wch are much p'judiciall to ye Towne . . . Wandring and begging, contrarie to Lawe', to work in the plantations of Barbados) were still transporting groups of children to work on the plantations in the Colonies in the middle of the century, but the last wholesale shipment from London seems to have been in 1643, when the House of Commons authorised a collection to be made on two Sundays to finance the emigration of poor children from the City. Although £832 was collected, owing to misuse of the money by the agents, only a small number of children – somewhere around twenty – were actually sent out. Perhaps it was this disillusioning experience which discouraged any further activities in this sphere by the City.

These local, seventeenth-century attempts to transport vagrant and potentially delinquent children overseas were not, of course, technically exercises in penal transportation. But it is clear that some of them were in fact forced to go against their will, and one can but sympathise with Abbot Smith's comment in *Colonists in Bondage:* 'It is to be feared that nearly all of them were persons on whom charity descended as a heavy penalty rather than a gentle mercy.'

THE VAGRANT AND DELINQUENT CHILD

The first of the eighteenth-century statutes whose aim was to rid the country of the same troublesome type of child sanctioned a policy of rather a different character to achieve exactly the same end. In practice, the Act of 1703 was a new method for the impressment of men into naval service. Using the powers vested in them by the *Act for the increase of seamen and better encouragement of navigation and security of the coal trade,* magistrates or local overseers of the poor might 'bind or put out any boy or boys, who is, are or shall be of the age of 10 years, or upwards, or who is, are or shall be chargeable, or whose parents, are or shall become chargeable to the respective parish or parishes wherein they inhabit, or who shall beg for alms, to be apprentices to the sea service, to any of Her Majesty's subjects, being masters or owners of any ship or vessel used in sea service . . . for so long time, and until, such boys shall respectively attain or come to the age of one and twenty years . . .' provided always that no apprentice was to be compelled to enter sea service until he was fully eighteen years old. Clause XVI of the Act further provided that: 'forasmuch as divers dissolute and idle persons, rogues, vagabonds and sturdy beggars, notwithstanding the many good and wholesome laws to the contrary, do continue to wander up and down, pilfering and begging through all parts of this kingdom, to the great disturbance of the peace and tranquillity of the realm; for the more effectually suppressing such disorderly persons, and to the end that they may be made serviceable and beneficial to their country; be it further enacted . . . that all lewd and disorderly men servants, and every such person or persons, both men and boys, that are deemed and adjudged rogues, vagabonds, and sturdy beggars (not being felons) . . . shall be and are hereby directed to be taken up, sent conducted and conveyed into Her Majesty's service at sea . . .'[1] Masters of ships were obliged to take these apprentices, one for the first 30 to 50 members of their crew, one for the next 50 and one more for every 100 men after that, on a penalty of £10 for refusal. This was slightly modified two years later by an Act of Parliament under which no master was to be obliged to take a boy of under 13 years 'or who shall not appear to be fitly qualified both as to health and strength of body for that service, . . .'[2] From later

[1] 2 & 3 Anne, c. 6.
[2] 4 & 5 Anne, c. 6.

evidence, it seems that this Act, passed in time of war, when men for the navy and the colliers were urgently needed, was in fact most frequently used during the constant wars of the eighteenth century and throughout the Napoleonic wars, when the press-gangs were active to impress men other than vagrants, and tended to lapse in times of peace. Sir Richard Binns, in 1828, in evidence before the Select Committee on the Police of the Metropolis, stated that masters of ships would not accept men and boys taken up under the Act. Further statements to the same Committee indicated that the demand for such recruits had ceased with the recent war.

The alternative method of exporting juvenile delinquents provided by the Act of 1717 went – quite literally – a good deal further since it permitted the penal transportation (provided they consented) of young people of between fifteen and eighteen years of age to the plantations of North America for periods of up to eight years.[1]

Alas! Neither individually nor in concert did these attempts to shovel out some of the human debris of the streets and alleyways into merchant ships and distant colonies seem to prove any more salutary a solution to the problem to which they had been addressed than the more traditional methods. In 1732, the justices of the parishes of Westminster, Middlesex and Southwark petitioned the House of Commons, complaining of the mischief caused by vagrant children 'who infest the Streets unapprehended . . . and instead of being employed in apprenticeships or services, according to the law, habituate themselves to an idle and profligate course of life and become dangerous as well as unprofitable to the Publick . . .'[2] Although it was decided to have a Committee of the whole House to consider this petition, and to decide what steps should be taken, none seems to have actually been appointed – perhaps because there were none with new ideas on the subject to offer.

Outside Parliament, however, there had been for some years the lurking suspicion that here, as elsewhere, the real solution lay more with prevention than rehabilitation. Such was the tenor of R. Nelson's *Address to Persons of Quality and Estate*, in 1715. It was also the theme of a number of articles and letters to the

[1] 4 Geo. I, c. 11.
[2] *Journals of the House of Commons*, vol. XXI, 1732, p. 931.

influential *Gentleman's Magazine* in the 1730s and notably one from Clemens Dunbar, who argued that, 'If Hospitals were erected for the Education of the Poor, and so constituted as to receive the Children of all who are unable to learn themselves any trade, and if Parents who are able were obliged by law . . . to add some Handicrafts to their other education, we should soon see that this Method would more effectually reform and prevent crimes of all kinds than all the Sanguinary Laws that can be devised, tho' executed with the utmost Rigour . . .'[1] Pertinent though these observations were, they dealt only indirectly with the practical problem of the child who had been corrupted by vicious and irresponsible parents and who so often became the magistrates' concern. In *An Account of the Origin and Effects of a Police*, Sir John Fielding, the Bow Street magistrate and one of the first of a long line of reforming justices to take seriously the problem of the delinquent child and to think about it in preventive terms, drew very particular attention to this cause of delinquency when he analysed 'the vast shoals of Shop-lifters, Pilferers, and Pickpockets' who infested the London streets in the mid-eighteenth century: 'These consisted chiefly of boys from 12 to 15 years of Age, either the Children of Thieves or the deserted Offspring of idle and profligate Parents; many of whom, especially Mothers, shamefully subsisted from their Robberies. And what was very remarkable, four infant Thieves the oldest of which was but 5 yrs of Age, . . . which appeared to be Children of different Persons, collected together by one Woman to beg and steal to furnish that Beast with Gin . . .'[2] Reluctant to commit such offenders who appeared before him to prison, because of the harmful and vicious effect of mixing with hardened criminals, and anxious to protect young people from the severities of the criminal law under which children were still commonly hanged, as John Peverly was hanged in 1731 at the age of 13 for stealing 48 guineas;[3] or transported overseas like Thomas Armson, 'a Boy' for stealing from John Ward eleven pounds.[4] Fielding was concerned to think of some way of preventing delinquency among the young. 'There are at this time in London', he wrote in 1754, 'hundreds of this kind of boy who

[1] op. cit., vol. VIII, January 1738, pp. 14–15.
[2] op. cit., 1758. pp. 19–20.
[3] *Gentleman's Magazine*, Vol. I, May 1731, p. 216.
[4] ibid., vol. IV, September 1734, p. 510.

might be made useful to society if they were collected together before they commenced thieves and placed either in men-of-war or in the Merchant's Service.'[1] In short Fielding was convinced that a complete change of environment would prevent at least some children from deteriorating into a life of crime. Little more than a year later, in January 1756, Fielding was to receive a letter from an old acquaintance, Lord Harry Paulet, which was to prompt him to try his theory in practice. Paulet was Commander of the *Barfleur*, a vessel of the Home Fleet. Knowing something of Fielding's ideas of sending boys to sea, he wrote to ask him for 30 boys, to be fitted out at Fielding's expense, who might be used as servants to the officers of his ship. According to his own account, Fielding 'now began to think that this would be an excellent Provision for the numberless miserable, deserted, ragged and iniquitous pilfering Boys that at this Time shamefully infested the Streets of London'. The great difficulty was to get the boys clothed 'and cured of the various Distempers which are the constant Consequences of Poverty and Nastiness'.[2] To raise the necessary money, Fielding advertised in the press for funds and within six months over six hundred pounds had been subscribed for clothing such boys with the result that, with the help of Saunders Welch (another magistrate interested in juvenile delinquency) and with the co-operation of the Admiralty, Fielding was able to equip not merely the thirty boys for the *Barfleur* but nearly four hundred others for other ships of the fleet. By July 1756, the money had all been spent, but not Fielding's enthusiasm for his project. He accordingly applied for assistance to the Marine Society, recently founded that same July, by Jonas Hanway and a group of fellow city merchants, bankers and shipowners. Originally, the promoters of the Society had decided at the outbreak of the Seven Years' War, the same summer, to concentrate on clothing men for the navy. 'The part relating to the boys had been at the first proposal declined on the principle that it was already in hand [through Fielding's efforts], though it was alleged that a design of such consequence could not be executed with propriety . . . unless it was adopted by a society, acting under a regular and permanent economy . . .'[3] wrote

[1] R. Leslie-Melville, *The Life and Work of Sir John Fielding*, vol. III, 1934, p. 113.
[2] *An Account of the Origin and Effects of a Police*. 1758. p. 21.
[3] *The Origin, Progress, and Present State of the Marine Society*. 1770. p. 5.

Hanway some years later. Fielding's application to the Society for its support, only a few days after its formal inauguration, however, caused them to change their minds. He was invited to become a member of their Society, which for a time he did, and the Society reinstated boys in their own plans to such effect that at the end of the war in 1763, the Society became an organisation interested exclusively in the welfare of boys. By the beginning of 1757, the Society, and not Fielding, was completely in charge of the recruiting, clothing and despatch of the boys, but that it was he who was the originator and chief sponsor of the policy of the Society as it actually developed is beyond doubt.

Subscriptions to the Society flowed in; from royalty, from the citizens of London, the leading provincial towns, the merchants and the City Companies. A great deal of this very substantial support was prompted by a desire to help English naval strength during the current war rather than from a humanitarian interest in delinquency among juveniles. Indeed, Hanway canvassed public support precisely on the ground that the Society's work was a contribution to the war effort and a means of maintaining the navy's strength, only averting incidentally to the Society's redemptive work with the actually or potentially criminal youth of the country. It must have been an added satisfaction to donors to know that their investment in Britannia's maritime strength was inextricably linked with a long-term spiritual bonus for themselves: 'The *choicest* blessings are annexed to *the saving of a soul from death*; but to rescue *numbers* of these young persons from the *jaws of perdition*; to breed them up to *social* and *religious* duties to prevent their being disturbers of the quiet enjoyment of their fellow subjects; to present them a fair prospect of *everlasting happiness:* and at length to teach those who would have had otherwise totally lost to *God* and their *country*, an occupation on which *commerce* and *naval* strength depend: are *objects* which constitute the very essence of the *sublime charity* of a christian, and include the truest and most exalted *patriotism* . . .'[1]

Between 1756 and 1862, at a total cost of some £23,000, the Society fitted out and sent to sea more than 10,000 children:

[1] *An Account of the Marine Society, recommending the Piety and Policy of the Institution, and pointing out the Advantages accruing to the Nation.* 1759. p. 12.

THE VAGRANT AND DELINQUENT CHILD

5,451 adolescents and 4,787 boys both destitute and delinquent. It is evident that some – we have no idea how many – came into the Society's hands as a consequence of the local operation of the 1703 Act to which we have already referred. 'There is yet another order of their fellow subjects which calls forth and exercises the humanity of the Marine Society,' wrote Hanway. 'Many objects of real compassion offer, in the cases of petty delinquency, who are sent on board the *Tenders* by the *Civil magistrates*, many of these are detained as very proper persons to serve the KING ...'[1]

Not all those who had the authority to apprentice vagrants and delinquents to sea service appear to have understood the limits of their authority and made sure of the consent both of the child and his parents and master (if he had any) before they thankfully passed them over to the Society. Hence the Society had to publish the following announcement in 1759:

'Whereas several *boys* have been sent up to this Society by the *church-wardens* and *overseers* of parishes, from distant counties as well as the neighbourhood of *London*. And whereas some of the said boys, when they have been presented to the *committee* of the said Society have persisted in declaring that they were sent against their will, and without their consent; the SOCIETY have thought proper to return such boys to their respective places of settlement.'[2] Thus Bury St. Edmunds received back five boys who declined to go to sea, and with them, a request for £2 10s. – the cost of the children's temporary maintenance by the Society and of their transport back home.

In addition to their being willing, the boys had to be of at least thirteen years of age and for admission to the Royal Navy, where they were either employed as officers' servants or as warrant officers' apprentices, they had to be at least 4ft. 3 inches in height. Shorter boys could be sent to the merchant ships but some, too stunted by their miserable diet, were considered too small even for this and had to be turned away. Once accepted, however, the boys were lodged in the Society's boarding house in Grub Street until they were assigned to their ship and were fed and cared for there on a scale which must have seemed unbelievably generous to many of the boys who had come 'infected with distempers which are the frequent attendant of excessive

[1] ibid., p. 15.
[2] ibid., p. 74.

poverty... polluted with filth, and covered with rags, the very stink of which is pestilential...' Even by twentieth-century standards, the instructions to the 'Proveditor' of the boys in the house make heartening reading:

'You are desired to treat these boys well, particularly in the following instances. The rooms which they occupy must be kept clean; and you will also see that they use such beddings and clothing as the Society will furnish you with...

'These boys must be always supplied with three meals a day, distinguishing those who are under a Regimen, to give to such only spoon meats, as the Apothecary may require. But in general you are to supply good beef and mutton, one day hot, the other cold, with good bread and small beer, for which we agree to pay you fourpence each boy for a dinner. For breakfast, you are to allow good milk porridge and bread one day and beef-broth and bread the next; for which we allow *two-pence*. At supper, bread and butter with beer one night, and bread, cheese and beer the next night...'[1]

The apothecary, who is referred to in these instructions was a Mr. Haskey, 'a person of skill and humanity'. This regimen and the kit which they took with them to sea – which included cap, jacket, 'half-thick waistcoat and half-thick breeches', shirts, hose, shoes, buckles, buttons and comb, and needle and thread to keep all in repair, – must have transformed the appearance of many of these miniature mariners. Indeed, many a London citizen must 'have received sensible pleasure at seeing forty or fifty children neatly dressed, marching in order, with colours flying, and drums and fifes playing' as yet another group of boys set off to their ships. A pleasure heightened by thoughts of 'their laudable destination, and the miserable lot from which they were probably redeemed'. But whether the care they received on the ships to which they were assigned always contributed to a comparable change in character for which Fielding so hoped, some begged to question. A letter to the *Grand Magazine* for May 1760, alleged that the results of sending boys to sea as officers' servants in the Royal Navy were deplorable: '... they are received by the name of *Scape Gallowses* [and] are distributed among the officers as their servants: after which no farther atten-

[1] J. Hanway, *Three Letters on the Subject of the Marine Society*. 1758, third letter, p. 37.

tion is paid to them. There, the first qualifications they acquire are *blasphemy, chewing tobacco* and *gaming*; from whence they proceed to *drinking* and *talking bawdy*. . . . if they ever happen to be called upon to lend a hand, their master's business is a constant pretence for stealing out of the way. They herd . . . in the hold, the round tops or the booms, with their other boys, where they improve each other in a peculiar species of vulgar wit and insolent *jaw*, at which they are so ready that no man in the ship is a match for them at discourse, . . .'[1] In practice, as one might expect, the care of the boys seems to have varied from ship to ship, the ship's commander and the character of the officer to whom the boys were assigned. With a good commander, the boys were well looked after and carefully treated: several ships at Spithead and the Nore established regular schools for the boys on board.[2] But even on the best ship, of course, the boys were cut off from family and friends and, inevitably among the many who could not write, gradually lost touch with them as the months went by. The Society itself appears to have done virtually nothing to maintain the family ties of boys whom it had sent to sea. Maybe it was thought that the children were the better for the breaking of ties with parents, many of whom cannot have been a desirable influence on their lives. Nevertheless, the lack of concern of the Society on this point makes rather startling reading for us today. As late as 1818, the Secretary of the Society was asked: 'When you part with a boy, do you make any communication to the parish or to his parents what has become of the child?' – 'The boys generally write to their parents, to tell them where they are going themselves.' 'Is that a duty required of them?' – 'I leave it optional to them' 'If they omit to do it, do you feel it your duty to do it?' – 'No.'

Time was also to affect the interests of the Marine Society. Inactive between 1763 and 1769 because of a lawsuit, by 1770, partly because other societies had been formed to rehabilitate the wayward and partly because they had proved difficult for the Society itself to place, it had become noticeably less interested in helping the vagrant-delinquent boy and more ready to assist the honest poor in distress – 'boys occasionally employed on errands or in markets, brick-kilns, glass-houses, or by hackney

---

[1] Printed in J. Hanway, *An Account of the Marine Society*. 1759. pp. 148–9.
[2] ibid., p. 152.

coachmen, draw boys and such like . . . [who are] often unemployed and without livelihood . . .'¹

Not surprisingly in these circumstances, Fielding started a new scheme of his own, this time for clothing and sending boys to sea in the merchant navy and confining his activities to those parts of London with which he was concerned as a magistrate. Again he appealed for money to make his scheme practicable and, the funds collected, between February 1769 and April 1770 he had managed to apprentice 234 boys. Equally not surprising was the agitated reaction of the Marine Society who feared that Fielding's rather sanguine announcement of his new scheme would deflect public support for their own work. (As Fielding had chosen to use one of their own appeal gambits in claiming that his scheme was 'a national object, to raise a nursery for a sufficient number of seamen, to answer the demands of Commerce and the exigencies of the Navy' one has a certain sympathy for them!) Even so, there seems to have been little actual ill will involved and, after the Marine Society was incorporated in 1772, Fielding actually wrote to the Governors hoping that they would 'assist the police of this metropolis, by taking under their care and protection such friendless, deserted and criminal boys, as may be brought before the magistrates or the courts'² – in this last, as evidence to a Select Committee in 1828 was to show, he was to be disappointed.³ By 1828, the Society had an annual turnover of some 424 boys and actually rejected between two and three thousand each year. But although it was said that no particular enquiries were made as to character, certainly none known to have a criminal record was accepted.

It would be misleading and a gross injustice to both Fielding himself and to the groups of philanthropists who had been associated with the Marine Society, to give the impression that, all these years, their only concern had been for the welfare of boys. Only four years after his letter to the *Public Advertiser* on the care and protection of boys, Fielding was canvassing public support for *A Plan for Preserving Deserted Girls*. Both John Fielding and his brother Henry had been active in the campaign which had led to an Act of 1752⁴ which had attempted to make

¹ *The Origin . . . of the Marine Society*, pp. 23–4.
² Leslie-Melville, op. cit., p. 121.
³ *Report from the Select Committee on the Police of the Metropolis*, 1828, p. 118.
⁴ 25 Geo. 11, c. 36.

13 Thomas Coram 1668–1751

14 *The Industrious 'Prentice.* William Hogarth

both more efficient and expeditious the prosecution of bawdy-house keepers. But neither they, nor those who had been writing to the influential journals of the day, such as the *Rambler* and the *Gentleman's Magazine*, were under any illusion that the problem of prostitution would be solved by attempts to close the doors of these Augean stables.[1] Prostitution and in especial juvenile prostitution was a state into which many were driven by a morally corrupt society, in which to sell her body was commonly a girl's chief resource. Writing of the many children who appeared before his court during the twelve months of 1755 and 1756, Fielding comments '... these deserted Boys were Thieves from Necessity, their Sisters are Whores from the same cause; and having the same education with their wretched Brothers, join the Thief to the Prostitute.... The lives of their Fathers being often shortened by their Intemperance, a Mother is left with many helpless Children, to be supplied by her Industry: whose Resource for Maintenance is either the Wash Tub, Green Stall or Barrow. What must become of the Daughters of Such Women, where Poverty and Illiterateness conspire to expose them to every Temptation? And they often become Prostitutes from Necessity before their Passions can have any share in their Guilt...' It was girls such as these – some even sold into prostitution by their mothers – that fell into the clutches of the brothel keepers and were found by the Constables in their searches of houses suspected of being run for immoral purposes. 'On a search night, when the Constables have taken up near forty Prostitutes,' wrote Fielding, 'it has appeared on their examination, that the major Part of them have been of this kind, under the age of eighteen, many not more than twelve, and these, though young, half eaten up with the foul Distemper.'[2] For these girls, as for their brothers, Fielding believed in a policy of prevention whilst at the same time trying to rehabilitate such girls as had already become prostitutes. Thus his original plan for a *Preservatory and Reformatory*, which was to take the form of a 'public laundry', allowed for the admission of 'Daughters of the Industrious Poor' aged between 7 and 15 years and as yet 'uncorrupted'; and 'Prostitutes anxious to be reformed' who were to be taken in up to the age of 23 (and by implication, to

[1] See the *Rambler*, no. 107, 26 March 1751, and the *Gentleman's Magazine*, April 1751.
[2] *An Account of the Origin and Effects of a Police.* 1758. pp. 43–5.

be lodged separately). In addition, and this is an interesting comment on parish apprenticeship in the eighteenth century, there were to be admitted 'Poor Girls put out by the Parish Officers from the Workhouses, as they are generally placed in the worst of Families and seldom escape Destruction.'[1]

In principle, the Preservatory and Reformatory was to be a domestic science training centre for whose products places would be found in reliable households. And this, basically, was the principle adopted for the Female Orphan Asylum, opened in Lambeth in 1758 as a result of the publication of Fielding's *Plan*. Financed by public subscription; the proceeds of theatrical performances – probably due to Fielding's connections with the theatre and his personal friendship with Garrick; and by half Fielding's share of 'the fees levied from careless carmen, bakers who gave short weight and other nuisances' to which he was entitled as a Bow Street magistrate, the Asylum was open to girls of between 9 and 12 years of age, who were orphans and had been resident for six months 'within the Bills of Mortality' but whose settlements could not be found. It was especially designed to preserve friendless and deserted girls from those dangers and misfortunes to which their distressed situation exposed them. The girls were to be apprenticed for seven years to the Matron of the Asylum who was generally responsible for their training and, at the end of this period, the girls were expected to produce for the Committee's inspection 'a shirt cut out, washed and ironed by their own hands'. The girls were also to be able to cut out and make their own linen, to understand plain cookery and to clean kitchen and other household furniture. No less important, they were to be able to read a chapter of the Bible, write a legible hand – to which end a writing master visited the Asylum twice a week – and cast up a sum in addition. Not until they had acquired these many skills, at the age of fifteen or sometimes earlier 'if the objects were by then properly qualified', were they placed as servants in respectable households, the character of whose master and mistress had been first carefully scrutinised by the Asylum's Guardians. If for some reason a girl was incapable of domestic service, possibly through some infirmity, she was to be put out to some trade the premium for entry to which had to be not more than £10.

[1] ibid., p. 50.

During the period 1758 to 1768, the Asylum admitted 282 girls of whom, by 1769, it had placed 125; 146 remaining in the Asylum and 11 having died. None of these, of course, was a penitent prostitute: the Lambeth Asylum was in fact the materialisation of only the *Preventory* part of Fielding's *Plan*. Others, among them several of that same group of London merchants who had sponsored the Marine Society – Hanway himself, Charles Dingley, a timber merchant, Robert Nettleton, a Governor of the Russian Company, John Thornton, a Director and Governor of the Bank of England, and Robert Dingley, brother of Charles Dingley, a business partner of Hanway and prime mover in the founding of a second institution – sponsored the Magdalen Hospital, which was intended as 'Public Place of Reception for Penitent Prostitutes'.

Although the Hospital effectively represented the fulfilment of the second part of Fielding's *Plan*, he himself was not directly concerned with its foundation although some of the inspiration for the idea was probably due to him. And although he and Welch, who had assisted him in his efforts to found the Asylum, were both made governors of the Hospital, he made no attempt to fuse the two schemes, maintaining the same independent though amicable relationship with the group on this particular project as he was, after a very few years, to do with their Marine Society for the welfare of boys.

The Hospital was opened on 10 August 1758, in a house in Prescot Street, Goodmans Fields with a total of eight inmates. Admission was by petition and, unless she herself was willing to pay £10 a year towards her keep, a girl normally had to agree on admission to stay three years. Once accepted, none was allowed to go out of the Hospital save with the special permission in writing of either the Chairman or the Treasurer and of two members of the Hospital's Committee. Each was given a uniform of light grey, a discretion in dress to which, if they wished, they might add the discretion of a feigned name. After a trial period in what was known as 'the Admission Ward' – to see whether the girls could settle down in the Hospital's sobering atmosphere – the penitents were each assigned to a particular Ward 'according to the Education or Behaviour of the Person Admitted'. The lower Wards 'shall consist of Inferior Persons and those who may be degraded for Misbehaviour'. But despite appearances to

THE VAGRANT AND DELINQUENT CHILD

the contrary, it was not the intention of the founders of the Hospital that it should in any way be viewed as a punitive establishment. 'In their Work, as in every other Circumstance, the utmost Care and Delicacy, Humanity and Tenderness will be observed, that this Establishment may not be thought a House of Correction or even of hard Labour, but a safe Retreat from their distressful Circumstances'.[1]

Of course, the girls were expected to contribute to their keep and they were thus employed not only in making their own clothing, but in knitting stockings, spinning, making artificial flowers and toys, glove making and carpet making. As an incentive to acquiring habits of industry and diligence some portion of the profit from the sale of their handiwork was credited to them. After three years in the Hospital, or upon an earlier application from a parent or friend (or from 'any Housekeeper of sufficient Credit') – 'if such friends declare they will forgive her past Offences and will provide for her; or if such Housekeeper will receive such woman as a Servant' – the Governors would discharge the girls, returning their own clothes to them and any earnings they had credited to them together with a certificate of good conduct. At their discretion, the Governors might also give a bounty to assist girls 'who marry in a Manner satisfactory to the Committee' or who needed it to 'set up trades in whatever Way they shall have gained a Proficiency'.

Between 1758 and January 1793, the Hospital had admitted 2,851 girls of whom 1,874 had been reconciled to friends or placed in service; 358 had been discharged at their own request; and 402 had had to be discharged for improper behaviour. Since most of them were under 20 at the time of their discharge, it seems as though the Hospital largely admitted young girls of the age of sixteen or seventeen. George Dyer, interested to find out what happened to the girls after their discharge, analysed the records of the 246 who left the Hospital between May 1786 and May 1790. He found 157 of them to be with friends or in service and behaving well; 74 in similar circumstances but whose behaviour was by no means satisfactory; 4 insane and in confinement; 1 dead; and 10 of whom nothing was known. On

---

[1] *The Plan of the Magdalen House for the Reception of Penitent Prostitutes. By Order of the Governors.* 1758. p. 18.

this reckoning, two out of every three girls discharged had made good.[1]

Whilst it is impossible not to be impressed by the several efforts to prevent delinquency and reclaim the delinquent with which Fielding was associated and also by the several other similar schemes which others were pioneering both in London and elsewhere, it was clear even at the time that private charity was an insufficient basis of financial support for such efforts and which must necessarily limit their effectiveness. J. Massie, a well-known eighteenth-century writer on trade and finance, argued that a rate should be levied on 'all the opulent and the substantial Inhabitants' in the Metropolitan area 'for, equitably speaking, the exposed or deserted Women and Girls, as well as the common Prostitutes whom it is intended to Relieve and Reclaim' (by the Magdalen Hospital scheme) 'are Part of the poor of *London, Westminster* and *Southwark,* considered collectively as one great City without regarding the legal Subdivisions of them into Parishes'.[2] It may well have been that Massie's idea was prompted by his reading of early tracts on social and economic questions; certainly his proposal for a municipal rate in aid of local welfare has a very sixteenth-century ring to it. On the other hand, his obvious scepticism of the usefulness of the Parish as the unit of administration for social policy, shared by few others of his day, anticipated one of the fundamental reforms of the Poor Law Act of 1834 passed nearly a hundred years later.

Taken together, the ideas of Fielding and Massie contain a great deal that is familiar in modern policies for the juvenile delinquent. In the eighteenth century, such ideas were too unusual to command general public sympathy and approval. Familiar with the sight of young prostitutes walking the streets and more anxious for the protection of persons and property than for the welfare and reclamation of the semi-delinquent children who roamed the towns, official social policy toward the vagrant and delinquent continued very much on the lines laid down by previous generations and shows little awareness of the considerations which prompted both men to re-examine the basis of social

[1] George Dyer, *A Dissertation on the Theory and Practice of Benevolence.* 1795. pp. 44-5.
[2] J. Massie, *A Plan for the Establishment of Charity Houses for Exposed and Deserted Women and Girls and for Penitent Prostitutes* ... *etc. etc.* (the full title runs to some twenty-eight lines!), 1758. pp. 15-18.

action in this particular field. Even the language of eighteenth-century legislation underlines how true this was. *An Act for reducing the Laws relating to Rogues, Vagabonds, Sturdy Beggars and Vagrants into One Act of Parliament and for the more effectual punishing such Rogues, Vagabonds, sturdy Beggars and Vagrants and sending them whither they ought to be sent* (1713) was mainly concerned, as one might suppose, with continuing and 'improving' the old laws relating to rogues and vagabonds. The treatment recommended – that rogues and vagabonds were to be sent back to their place of settlement and 'whipped till their body be Bloody' if the local justice saw fit – stands in sharp contrast to the ideas of Fielding. Clause XVIII, however, was slightly less severe and from its nature and the fact that it suggests the apprenticeship of rogues and vagabonds, may have been framed with an eye to the young. It enacts that the justice 'instead of punishing or passing him, her or them away in the manner before directed . . . [may] . . . Commit the Person or Persons so apprehended to the Custody and Power of him or them who procured such Apprehension, or in the case of his or their Refusal, to the Custody and Power of any other Person or Persons Body Politick or Corporate willing to receive him, her or them as his or their Apprentice or Servant for the space of Seven Years next ensuing and no longer . . .' It is rather alarming, however, to discover that 'The Master shall and may detain, keep, imploy and set to work either within the Realm of Great Britain or in any of her Majesty's Plantations or any British Factory or Factories beyond the Seas', provided that rogues and vagabonds were not to be sent 'beyond the Seas' until the Master had entered into a recognisance that the rogue would be employed in a Factory or Plantation in British hands and would be discharged after seven years and 'not sold into slavery or disposed of to any Alien'.[1] From this to the Transportation Act of 1717 was but a step and, for those apprenticed overseas under this Act, the implications must have been indistinguishable.

What clearly puzzled administrators as much as it concerned men like Fielding, was how best to train the vagrant child in diligence and self-reliance. The difference between them, however, was that the law only proposed to treat with the problem

[1] 13 Anne, c. 26.

of such children who for one reason or another had come within its purview as transgressors. Hence the new Vagrancy Act of 1744, which raised to fourteen the age at which children might be separated from their parents under the requirements of the laws relating to the committal of vagrants to the Houses of Correction, makes constant reference to the fact that children of such parents were brought up in a dissolute course of life destructive to such children and prejudicial to the kingdom 'in which a race of disorderly persons will grow up if such children are suffered to remain with such offenders'.[1] Just as there was nothing new about the problem which so much concerned them there was certainly nothing novel about the solution which was recommended. Any child over the age of seven might, by order of the justices in Quarter Sessions, be placed out as servant or apprentice to any person willing to take it 'until the child shall arrive at the age of 21 or for such time as the Justices may see meet'.

Already we have seen in Fielding's work a hint that by the eighteenth century parish apprenticeship did not always provide that careful, supervised training of the child that had been hoped for by Tudor legislators. To this we shall have to return in much more detail later. At this point it is very important to notice that, in law at least, over a period of all but two hundred years, the State's attitude to the vagrant and semi-delinquent child remained virtually unchanged despite the many differences in social framework which had emerged. Whatever else may be said of the increasing irrelevance of Tudor social policy to later generations, two of the major factors inhibiting any fundamental changes in it were the continuing inability to distinguish between vagrancy and delinquency and the traditional conviction that a juvenile delinquent was merely a miniature criminal.

If it was Fielding who introduced the idea of prevention in the treatment of the vagrant and delinquent child it was John Howard whose contribution it was to point to the necessity of classification of delinquents and thus to the necessity of providing quite separately for them. In his famous *State of the Prisons of England and Wales* published in 1777, four years after he began his personal investigation of them, there are two interesting references to the hard and unadvantageous lot of the young

[1] 17 Geo. II, c. 2. 5. s. 24.

criminal detained in them. But the main importance of his book was that it drew attention to the state of contemporary gaols generally. His particular interest in them was the health of the inmates and his evidence that many prisons were little plague spots, discharging from time to time men who spread disease over the country, thoroughly aroused the self-interest of the country over and above any charitable emotions that individuals might feel. A series of intensive investigations into the gaols followed which, apart from problems of health and sanitation included also – at first incidentally and then primarily – general questions of administration and discipline. The reform of classification became quickly and obviously desirable, the problem of juvenile delinquency *per se* sprang to light and interest in this particular issue was reinforced by the apparently huge increase of crime at the beginning of the nineteenth century. This was in any case probably considerable in actual fact owing to the development of urbanisation and the great growth of population, but seemed immense to contemporaries as a result of the great increase in committals following on Peel's institution of the first regular police force and also to various changes in the law which encouraged prosecutions.

Just how important the need for the reclassification of prisoners was at the end of the eighteenth century can be seen in the *Report from the Committee who were appointed to consider the Several Returns which have been made to the Order of this House . . .* (of 16 December 1778) . . . *that there be laid before this House an Account of Persons convicted of Felonies or Misdemeanors.* The evidence showed that not only were little boys in prison but that a number were in the hulks, intended for the most degenerate criminals. The Committee recommended that power should be given to two justices to release any youth under 15 brought before them charged with a misdemeanour or petty larceny, with the approbation of the prosecutor, on condition that the youth consented to serve in the land forces of the Crown, in the East or West Indies, or in the navy, for at least three years. But although many of the Committee's recommendations were adopted, their suggestions regarding young persons were not even put in the Bill which was shortly presented to Parliament. Nevertheless, here at last were the beginnings of some flickering and official recognition of the peculiar and especial needs of at least one category of children with which the State had – perforce – to deal. More than another half century was to pass before these needs were sufficiently recognised to produce some policy of reform.

VII

'The Succourless Poor Child'

1. *Tudor Policies for the Deprived Child*

Up to the middle of the sixteenth century, the State's concern was primarily with the vagrant child, but in the next few decades important steps were taken by the larger towns to organise a comprehensive system of relief for all classes of the poor, which bear strong resemblances to the proposals made by Vives and the experiments described in Marshall's book. Thus the municipal authorities attempted to make an accurate census of the various categories of the poor which revealed for the first time the seriousness and magnitude of the problem of the 'succourless poor child' and stimulated plans for its solution. In London, John Howes tells us, the survey made throughout the wards of the City in the early 1550s, showed a total of 2,160 persons in need of relief, of which 300 were 'fatherless children' and 350 'poore men overburdened with theire children'.[1] In Norwich, a few years later, the census revealed some 2,000 people in need of relief out of a population of around 15,000; and of these nearly 1,000 were children, although a surprising number of them were shown to be at school.[2] In Exeter, the City Chamberlain writes: 'It is lamentable to see what troupes and clusters of children, boyes and elder persons, lye loitering and floistering in every corner of the Citie, but more lamentable is that no care, no order

---

[1] John Howes' M S., ed. W. Lempriere, 1904. p. 21.
[2] *The Records of the City of Norwich*, ed. W. Hudson & J. C. Tingey, 1910. vol. II, p. ciii.

nor redresse is had therof, which if it be not looked unto in time, it will rebound to the peril of the publique state of your Citie.' He goes on to contrast the care and protection given by the city governors to the orphans with property, with 'such orphanes, who having nothing left unto them, and being destitute of all relief and help, are left to their own dispositions, these ... swarme in clusters in every corner and quarter of your Citie, and for want of good education and nurturing, also growe to be thornes and thistles: and who as the Caterpillars, Frogs, Grasshoppers and Lice of Egipt, shalbe the plagues of this your common welth, and if remedy be not provided: shall utterly devoure and destroy the same ... it is your parte and bounded dutie to provide also the education, instruction, and what soever is necessary for such ... let them be provided for, that by your meanes and under your government they being taught and instructed in some honest art and discipline, they may become to be profitable members to the common welth ...' To this end he advocates the erection of a hospital and the founding of a free grammar school for the 'poor destituted and helpless children'.[1]

During the second half of the century many of the large towns, led by London, developed schemes for coping with the problem of their own destitute children – schemes in which compassion and benevolence often contrasted strangely with the harshness evinced towards vagrant children. Alarmed by the great and increasing number of people begging in the streets 'and wandring in the fields so ydellye, being readie to attempt any myschiefe upon any lighte occasion', the City was inspired to obtain from Henry VIII and Edward VI possession of the Hospitals which had been attached to the various London monasteries, in order to provide for the various groups of the destitute. As a result of the efforts of successive Lord Mayors and in particular, of Nicholas Ridley, Bishop of London at the time of Edward VI, agreements were finally made between the City and the Crown whereby four foundations, the so-called 'Royal Hospitals', passed into the control of the City; St. Bartholomew's and St. Thomas's for the sick and aged poor, the house of the Grey Friars (Christ's Hospital) for the children, and Bridewell, as we have seen, for the vagrant and thriftless poor. According to the final agreement concluded in 1552 with Edward VI, the Hospitals

[1] John Vowell, alias Hooker, *Orders enacted for Orphans* ..., pp. 9–11.

were to be run as a group under the direction of a Committee of thirty, six of whom were aldermen, the rest being citizens nominated by the City. It was this Committee which made the census of the London poor to which Howes refers and it was this Committee which set about raising the necessary funds to maintain their Hospitals.

The importance attached in these schemes to the question of children is clearly shown in a letter from the citizens of London to the Privy Council in 1552. 'Among the whole rout of needy and miserable persons, we espied three sundry sorts which were diversly to be provided for; . . . And first, we thought to begin with the poor child, that he might be harboured, clothed, fed, taught, and virtuously trained up.'[1] The motive behind this primary concern was a dual one: compassion undoubtedly played an important part, but there was also the widespread conviction that the cause of the poverty and misery everywhere was the 'ill and idle bringing up of youth'. With equal simplicity it was believed that destitution could be cured, there and then, by adequate education and training. To this end, Starkey's *Dialogue* advocated the compulsory education of all children above seven years of age, 'either to letters or to a craft, according as their nature requireth'.[2] The London citizens acknowledged these motives in their aim for Christ's Hospital, that 'neither the child in his infansie shall wante the vertuous education and bringing up, neither when the same shall growe into full age shall lack matter wheron the same maye vertuously occupe him sealf in good occupacion or science profitable to the common weale'.[3]

London's plan for the children was in many ways excellent, conceived in terms of broad humanity that does credit to the benevolence of the administrators. Christ's Hospital was designed 'to take oute of the streates all the fatherless children, and other poor mens children, that were not able to kepe them',[4] while Bridewell was to relieve and provide technical training for the older child 'unapt for learning'. These two institutions would

---

[1] Thomas Bowen, Extracts from the Records and Court Books of Bridewell Hospital. 1798. Appendix, p. 3. (Cited by Tawney and Power, *Tudor Economic Documents*, vol. II, p. 307.)

[2] Starkey, op.cit., p. 142.

[3] *Memoranda, References and Documents relating to the Royal Hospitals of the City of London*, ed. J. F. Firth. 1836. Appendix, p. 57.

[4] Howes, op. cit., p. 11.

'THE SUCCOURLESS POOR CHILD'

thus, it was optimistically believed at the outset, solve the problem of the 'innocent and fatherless' who were, in Holinshed's words, 'the seede and breeder of beggerie'.

A vigorous campaign for funds for these and the other two Hospitals was conducted by the City's Committee of aldermen and citizens. First, they each contributed ten or twenty pounds apiece and the total they collected, together with 'two sheriff's fines' was £748. Having given so practical an example themselves, they then embarked on a public campaign for raising the rest of the necessary funds by methods which have a startlingly eighteenth-century character. The inhabitants of the City were summoned to St. Paul's to be harangued from the pulpit by Sir Richard Dobbs, the Lord Mayor. The Committee themselves approached 'preachers, mynisteres, churche wardeines and sydemen' and exhorted them to obtain a weekly 'pencion' from their parishioners. To make sure that the urgent need for subscriptions to the Hospitals was adequately conveyed, they had printed and circulated 'a very fyne wittie & learned oracon', giving a copy to every preacher and minister 'the better to instruct and persuade the people in every paryshe to give liberallye'. In addition, each housholder was given a slip to fill in, on which he was to state the amount he was prepared to subscribe regularly to the support of the Hospitals.[1] In the immediate event at least, their campaign bore more than adequate fruit, 'for men gave franckly, the worcke was so generally well lyked'.[2] On 22 July 1552, preparations were made to re-open the old Hospital of the Grey Friars to accommodate 500 poor orphans of the City; and some time between September and November of the same year, three hundred and eighty children were received into the new Christ's Hospital. On Christmas Day 'in the afternoone, while the Lord Mayor and Aldermen rode to Powles [St. Paul's], . . . the children of Christ's Hospital stood, from Saint Lawrence lane end in Cheape, towards Powles, all in one livery of russet cotton . . .'. The following Easter, the colour of these uniforms was changed to 'blew', which it has remained ever since.[3]

No ideas of 'less eligibility' hampered the administrators in

[1] E. H. Pearce, *Annals of Christ's Hospital.* 1908. pp. 20–1.
[2] Howes, op., cit., p. 25.
[3] John Stowe, *A Survey of London*, edit. C. L. Kingsford. 1908. vol. I, p. 319.

'THE SUCCOURLESS POOR CHILD'

the equipping and staffing of the Hospital; these were luxurious indeed in comparison with what was thought necessary for poor children in the nineteenth century. Howes gives a brief list of the bedding considered necessary before children could be admitted. A Mr. Callthroppe, one of the thirty members of the Committee working on the Hospitals scheme, took upon himself to provide '500 featherbeds & 500 padds of Strawe to laie under the featherbedds & as manye blancketts & a thousande paire of shetes to be allowed for the same when he had furnyshed as many as shoulde come to a thousand marcks'. (A provision all the more remarkable at a time when the majority of citizens and rich men's sons at their public schools were still sleeping on pallets of straw.) The officially recorded cost of all this was some £3,000: in fact it actually cost a great deal more but 'god so wroughte in the herte of a number of good men . . . [that they] disbursed greete somes of moneye . . . wch never came to any publique accoumpte so that god's secreate broughte greate things to passe in the advancemente of this foundacon.'[1] The detailed accounts of the food and provisions bought in for the children; beer and bread, milk, mutton and beef, whiting, herring and plaice, also testify to a greater generosity towards the poor child than was to be tolerated by later generations. Not only was the food to be adequate to the appetites of the 'Blue Boys', it was to be of good quality: 'Wm Hawer bucher is agreed withall to serve this House with beefe, mutton and veale for one whole year to Shrowetide 1593, and the same to holsom and good, the bones to be taken out of the beef and he to have xi^d p. ston for witness whereof he hath put his mark'.[2] So unused were some of the poor orphans to such a diet that some, 'being taken from the dunghill when they came to swete and cleane keping & to a pure dyett, dyed downe righte . . .'[3]

Twenty-five sisters were appointed to look after the children 'the same holesomly, cleanely, and sweetly nourishe and bringe up'; and these were supervised by a matron – 'an office of great charge and credite' for she had 'the governance and oversight' of all the children. Detailed instructions were issued to all officials concerned to ensure efficient administration.[4] Education was to be

[1] Howes, op. cit., p. 42.
[2] Pearce, op. cit., p. 175.
[3] Howes, op. cit., p. 39
[4] *Memoranda* (op. cit), Appendix, pp. 91 et seq.

'THE SUCCOURLESS POOR CHILD'

by aptitude and ability – a remarkable anticipation of the Act of 1944 – and the number of teachers was generous for the time, as Vives had advised. These included a grammar school master, an usher, writing teacher, a schoolmaster 'for the Petties A.B.C.', and a master to teach music, as well as teachers of various crafts to prepare the children for apprenticeship.[1] When the children arrived at a suitable age, and, in the case of boys, could read and write and cast accounts, the greatest care was to be taken in choosing suitable masters for them 'chieflie, that they be honest persons, and such as be well able to kepe them, and to bring them up in such facultie, service or occupation, as they may hereafter be good members in the commonwelth'.[2] Boys who were found 'very apt to learning' were to be 'reserved and kept in the grammar-schole, in the hope of preferment to the Universitie; where they may be vertuously educated, & in time become learned and good members in the commonweale'.[3] Thus the educational ladder to the highest offices in Church and State was to be accessible to the poor child, and, in the early days, to the unwanted foundlings, such as 'the younge Tenter infant' left on St. Pancras Church steps, who were in the early days admitted to the Hospital.

The original intention had been that Christ's Hospital should receive not only the orphans, but all the destitute children of London; however, within a few years the number of foundlings left at the gates or elsewhere in the streets proved too great for the resources of the Hospital.[4] Presumably many of them were illegitimate children, since the Governors' Order of 1557 maintained that putative fathers should be compelled to support them (a suggestion which took effect in the Act of 1576) 'to avoide the laying of such children in the streets, whereby this hospitall upon such extremities should otherwise be charged thereby'. Consequently the rule was made that henceforth only children born in wedlock were to be admitted, except 'in cases of extremity, where losse of life and perishing would presently followe, if they be not received into this said hospitall'.[5]

A later rule further restricted admission to the children of

[1] Howes, op. cit., pp. 35–6.
[2] *Memoranda*, p. 90.
[3] ibid.
[4] Pearce, op. cit., pp. 35–8.
[5] *Memoranda*, appendix, pp. 89–90.

'THE SUCCOURLESS POOR CHILD'

citizens and freemen in view of the overwhelming number of country children seeking admission. In 1556, the Governors of the Hospital laid down the numbers of children who might be admitted to the Hospital: 'Of Sucklings to be comitted to nurse not above CL^{ii} [150] and of children to be admitted to lodginge and learninge not above CCL^{ii} [250].'[1] Of the 380 children who had been admitted in the autumn of 1552, a hundred were infants who were sent into the country to be nursed at the Hospital's expense and elaborate instructions were issued for their supervision and welfare. Twenty-five years after its foundation, John Howes tells us that 540 poor children were maintained at Christ's; of these, 150 were 'yerely preferred to sundrie services and the universities' and, in addition, allowances were paid weekly to poor men overburdened with children. Yet despite this admirable achievement, the City was still overcharged with poor children; boys and girls who wandered up and down the streets, loitered around St. Paul's, and slept under hedges and stalls at night. Some of these were 'honest men's children out of the Countrie', brought in as cheap labour by artificers when work was plentiful and turned adrift in time of depression. Country carriers ran a regular traffic in such children. Others came in with the streams of vagrants who flocked to London, either seeking work, or 'hearinge of the greate lyberallitie of London cometh hither to seke reliefe'.[2] 'London cannot releve Englande', reiterates Howes, and already it was clear that London's grandiose aims of solving the problem of child destitution could not be achieved on a municipal basis.

The new London institution of Bridewell, so far as the children were concerned, was closely connected with Christ's Hospital, and in the eyes of the city authorities was an ancillary training institution. Bridewell had two distinct functions to perform. As a House of Occupation, it was to provide work for the unemployed, and coercion and punishment with a chance of training and

[1] Pearce, op. cit., p. 37.
[2] John Howes, *Second Famyliar and Frendly Discourse*. 1587. Cited in Tawney and Power, op. cit., vol. III, pp. 425, 431, and 438.

An Order of the Common Council of the City of London, 1579, ordered any Carrier bringing children to London and leaving them unprovided for, to be punished by imprisonment 'as sharply as the law will permit', and then to convey the children back where they belonged. Any innkeeper wittingly receiving such a child was either to be responsible for keeping it or for conveying it back. (See *Charity Commissioners' Reports*, vol. 32, pt. VI, 1840, pp. 395 and 403.)

'THE SUCCOURLESS POOR CHILD'

reform for the 'sturdy vagabond'. On the children's side, it was to act as a school for technical training 'to train up the beggar's child in virtuous exercise, that of him should spring no more beggars'.[1] As the foundation documents show, the first concern of the City authorities was to reclaim, by training, the child reared in a vagrant and semi-criminal way of life who, 'grown to years, and found unapt to learning, neither any honest person desireth or would have his service'.[2] This original purpose continued throughout the century. It was one of the duties of the Beadle of Christ's Hospital to round up every Sunday all begging and vagrant children in the streets round St. Paul's and take them to Bridewell,[3] and the records make frequent mention of destitute children who slept in the streets being taken up and relieved there.[4] But other categories of children were also sent to Bridewell for training during the sixteenth century. Sometimes the sons of poor freemen were received, while at the end of the century many of the London parish apprentices were placed there. Some of Christ's Hospital children also learned their crafts there, while being fed and lodged in the Hospital.[5]

The entries of the first Court Book, 1552–92, show that children were sent, four or five at a time, to learn a trade in Bridewell, returning to Christ's for their meals. In other cases, an arrangement was made for 'Blue children' actually to live in Bridewell, paying twelve shillings for a period of eight weeks and then remaining free of charge. Bridewell could also be used as a place of punishment for Christ's Hospital children if they were 'lewd and idle'.

London's example in devising new methods of dealing with child destitution was followed by a number of provincial towns during the second half of the sixteenth century. Some of the larger towns, such as Bristol, Exeter, Plymouth and Norwich, founded orphanages on the model of Christ's Hospital, though much smaller in scope, while Christ's Hospital at Ipswich, the Hospital at Reading, St. John's Hospital at Nottingham, and St. Thomas's at York, among others, had training schools

[1] Ordinances and Rules, drawn out for the good government of the House of Bridewell. 1557. Printed in T. Bowen, op. cit., appendix, p. 9.
[2] ibid., pp. 3–4.
[3] *Memoranda*, appendix, p. 107.
[4] Bowen, op. cit., pp. 19, 27, 28, and appendix, p. 9.
[5] ibid., p. 25.

similar to those of Bridewell, in which many poor children of these towns were trained to various crafts. Ipswich first attempted to suppress begging by children in 1557 by a curiously illogical order: 'Noe children of this town shall be p'mitted to begg, and suche as shall be admitted thereto shall have badges'.[1] But later, in 1569, when the citizens established Christ's Hospital on the site of the Black Friars, a training school was provided for poor orphans; a house of correction for the unemployed, and a hospital for the sick and aged. By orders made in 1598, on payment of a shilling, parents could send their children, and masters their apprentices, 'to be corrected by the Town',[2] – an early example of municipal authority being called in to deal with 'the child beyond control'. The Reading Hospital housed twenty-one children and fourteen old persons in 1578, and the cost was defrayed by voluntary contributions, by compulsory collections in the parishes, and by the work of the inmates.[3] York, like many other towns, carried out a census of the poor; after which the unemployed including the older children were set to work, the poor boys being lodged and trained in St. Thomas's Hospital.[4] The City authorities further ordered that 'Laborers wyves and children may be barred from going abegging, and that their husbandes who get sufficient to maintaine them withall may be restrained from the ale-howse, where they drinke all that should maintaine ther poor wyves and children at home'.[5] Unfortunately, no indication is given of just how this rule was to be put into effect! York also provided for the children of prisoners,[6] and the civic records confirm that the municipal authorities there, as in London, approached the problem of the poor child in a genuinely humanitarian spirit. The children of the Hospital were not only to be clothed but to have 'Money to be pute in their purses'. Turves, 'at 2s. 4d. a thousand', as well as six horse loads of coal at 6d. the load were to be delivered at the Hospital. Special provision was made for childish ailments. Thus four and sixpence was to be paid 'to Johnstone's

[1] Nathaniell Bacon, *The Annals of Ipswich*. 1884 edn., p. 247.
[2] *An Account of the Gifts and Legacies . . . in the Town of Ipswich*. 1819. p. 63.
[3] C. Coates, *The History and Antiquities of Reading*. 1802. pp. 307-8.
[4] M. Sellers, The City of York in the Sixteenth Century, in the *English Historical Review*, vol. IX, 1894. pp. 286-7.
[5] *York Civic Records*, edit. Angelo Raine, vol. VIII, 1953. York. p. 159.
[6] ibid., vol. VII, 1950. p. 163.

'THE SUCCOURLESS POOR CHILD'

wife in Skeldergate for healing 2 boys heads at St. Thomas's house which were scalled and stuff for them' whilst eight shillings had to be paid to Robert Blake 'for curing a young Spanyghte & for stuff that went to it'.[1]

Norwich, the leading manufacturing town of England at that time, became famous for the methods it adopted in dealing with the poor, especially its training scheme for the young. Reference has already been made to the census taken there in 1570, which showed some two thousand of its small population in need of relief, of whom slightly less than a half were children. In the following year, Orders for the Poor were issued, forbidding indiscriminate charity which had encouraged begging, and in particular had made children 'so brought up . . . altogether unapt ever to serve or do good in the Commonwealth'. Henceforth, anyone relieving beggars at the door was to be fined 4d. for each offence, anyone begging, young or old, was to receive six stripes. A compulsory rate was established to maintain a few poor children in the Hospital of St. Giles, where they were to be taught their 'letters and other exercises', and to provide work for older children and women who needed help. In each ward of the City, 'select women' were appointed, each of whom was to take up to twelve poor women and children into her house, and to supervise their work in the cloth industry. Every 'select woman' that did her job properly was to get twenty shillings a year. Any woman chosen by the committee who refused to do the job, was liable to a minimum period of imprisonment of twenty days. The children of the poorest, 'whose parents are not able to pay for theyr learninge', were to be taught their letters, as well as to work, and elaborate rules were drawn up as a guide to the 'select women' in their functions. No children were to be allowed to be idle; all of a suitable age were to be set to work, or to be apprenticed.

If a child refused to work, the 'select women' had a carefully regulated system of punishments which they might inflict. At first, idlers were to be given six stripes with a rod. Failing a rod, they were to have six to ten stripes from a rope's end or 'a holie wande or hesell or somme other reasonable stick'. If still recalcitrant, the 'select woman' had to send for the deacon of the poor for her ward and, in his presence, she was to give the culprit

[1] M. Sellers, op. cit., p. 287.

'THE SUCCOURLESS POOR CHILD'

double the above number of beatings. Any who yet remained incorrigibly idle and 'would neither be rewled by their frindes nor by the select women' were to be sent to the City Bridewell, the Normans, 'ther to receive punisshment and coller of yron'. These various measures for the employment of destitute children appear to have been remarkably successful for some years, coinciding as they did with the expansion of the cloth industry. A later entry in the City records speaks of nine hundred children, 'which dailie was ydle and did nothinge butt begge, the same now kepte in worke', whereby the city gained 'great commendacion'. So much so, that 'the Lorde of Cannturburies grace [Matthew Parker – a native of Norwich] bearinge good wylle to ye citie as it seamed, sent unto the Maiour to understande of the orders and the profytt that the citie reaped therbye, wherupon in hope that some further benefyt (from hym) was hoped to redounde to the citie, was a book made & sent to him, the contentes . . .'[1]

At this time, it is clear that neither in London nor in the provinces was there any notion of the 'workhouse test' for poor relief that was to be so much a feature of the 'reformed' poor law of the nineteenth century. Just as outdoor relief was allowed in London, so also for example, in Norwich, weekly allowances were made to the poor in the city at the discretion of the deacons of the poor. Other types of outdoor relief were also provided, notably for the care of sick children. The city's records note that some time in 1580, 'Robert Thacker [presumably an official of the corporation] is commaunded to buye a rack [neck] of mutton for George Cannold, a pore lame boye wch it putt to William Fever, Surgeon, to be cured. And it is agreed that every Saterdaie and Wednesdaie for a moneth next to coom shalbe bought for the dyett of the said George a rack of mutton or vealle wch shalbe be payed for owt of the hamper'. (The hamper was the Mayor's fund.)[2]

The work accomplished in London and the more progressive towns, Norwich, Ipswich, York and the rest, in rescuing destitute children from the streets, and giving as many poor children

[1] *The Records of . . . Norwich*, vol. II, pp. 344–7, 352–6.
For somewhat similar schemes for putting poor children to technical training and work, though on a smaller scale, see John Latimer, *Sixteenth Century Bristol*, 1908, p. 96: *Records of the Borough of Leicester*, vol. III, p. 327; Leonard, op. cit., p. 42.
[2] *The Records of . . . Norwich*, vol. II, pp. 190–1.

'THE SUCCOURLESS POOR CHILD'

as possible the sort of education and technical training then thought desirable, was a remarkable achievement for these small Elizabethan communities, with their limited resources, and a tribute to their imagination and administrative ability. There was nothing comparable again to this first Elizabethan concern for the poor child until the mid-nineteenth century, when once more philanthropists were moved by the sight of hordes of neglected and homeless children in the streets of the growing industrial towns, and founded a spate of ragged schools, reformatories and children's homes for the 'street Arabs' of their day. But under Elizabeth, the provincial towns ultimately failed, as indeed London had failed, to solve the problem, partly through lack of financial resources (as early as 1561, the Lord Mayor of London was complaining of the difficulties in continuing the City's great work for the poor and especially for poor children because of the reluctance of many to continue their weekly contribution of alms) and partly because the relief schemes themselves acted as a magnet for the poor of the surrounding areas. The town records of the time are full of complaints of the disorder caused by rural immigrants. Strenuous efforts were made by town after town to prevent their settlement, especially of those who concealed themselves in the slums and afterwards proceeded surreptitiously to bring in their children.[1] Undoubtedly some vagrants were evicted by the vigilance of the beadles and citizens, but many more seem successfully to have evaded it. In such circumstances, the idealistic aims of the towns to solve independently the problems of child destitution were bound to fail. It could only be dealt with, like the whole of the problem of poverty, on a national scale. As this was gradually recognised, in the second half of the century, some of the more successful orders and experiments tried out in the towns were incorporated in parliamentary legislation applying to the whole country.

Thus the State came to accept the principle of a compulsory poor rate, following the example of London, Ipswich and Norwich. And it is interesting to note that the State supported the work of Christ's Hospital in directing that all the poor rates collected in the City of London should be paid to the Governors of the Hospital to be used according to their 'wisdoms and dis-

[1] R. H. Tawney, *The Agrarian Revolution of the Sixteenth Century.* 1912. pp. 275-6.

'THE SUCCOURLESS POOR CHILD'

cretions'.[1] The Act of 1572 ordered a Census of the aged and impotent poor to be made in all places, on the lines previously carried out by London and the progressive towns – the ascertainment of their needs, and arrangements for their maintenance from the rates.

As we have already seen, both the 1572 and the amending Act of 1576 were principally directed towards the problem of the vagrant child and 'the young rogue'. The 1576 Act was also important for the first regulations regarding the maintenance of illegitimate children whose treatment under this and other legislation will be dealt with separately. These two Acts continued in force until they were replaced by the comprehensive Act for the Relief of the Poor of 1597 which, re-enacted with only slight modification in 1601, remained the basis of poor law administration until 1834. Its importance, so far as children were concerned, was that after half a century of experimentation, their maintenance and training were put on a systematic basis. The churchwardens and overseers of the poor, with the consent of two justices of the peace, were required to take such measures as were necessary to set to work and apprentice, not merely vagrant children, but all children whose parents were thought to be unable to keep and maintain them. Such expenses as were required for their apprenticeship were to be paid for out of the rates. This Act was followed by a series of *Orders* from the Privy Council, reminding justices that they were specifically charged with the apprenticeship and training of children.[2] Thus by the end of the sixteenth century, certain principles had been established as to the obligations which the State should accept on behalf of the poor child – principles which bear a close resemblance to some of those of the twentieth century. It was to be responsible, through the intermediary of the parish or of the municipality, for the maintenance of orphans and destitute children during their early years and, if coercion of parents failed, for base-born children too. The poor man 'overcharged with many young children' was to receive a supplement to his wages, so that in infancy they might be properly nourished. All children whose parents could not provide adequate training for

[1] 2 & 3 Philip and Mary, c. 5, clause XII, which was repeated in 5 Elizabeth, c. 3, clause XIV and 14 Elizabeth, c. 5, clause XXIX.
[2] J. C. Cox, *Three Centuries of Derbyshire Annals*. 1890. vol. I, pp. 4–6.

'THE SUCCOURLESS POOR CHILD'

them were, at a suitable age, to be given an industrial training or be apprenticed until 24 – or 21 in the case of girls – so that they would be properly equipped to maintain themselves in later life. And, as we have already seen, the children of vagrant and demoralised parents were to be removed to other environments to secure their welfare. Finally, the State accepted in principle the responsibility of securing the proper treatment and training of children thus brought into community care.

The translation of principle into practice was no easy matter in a society lacking the administrative paraphernalia of the twentieth century Welfare State. Here, the efficiency of local administration of the Acts was necessarily influenced both by the willingness and the ability of local justices, churchwardens and overseers to perform the tasks allocated to them by law. Today, we take it very much for granted that the day-to-day administration of the social services should be in the hands of permanent civil servants and professionally trained social workers: Tudor social legislation had to be operated by amateurs. There is, as we have tried to show, a good deal of evidence that in London and some provincial towns many of these amateurs engaged in sixteenth century voluntary welfare schemes were both gifted and enterprising. The statutory schemes put on foot by Tudor legislators, however, required on a national scale the exercise of judgement and skills which, up till then, had only been demonstrated to exist on a local, much smaller and often *ad hoc* basis. The administrative hazards of transforming a local and voluntary social service into a compulsory system of national relief, were as evident in the sixteenth as in the twentieth century. Hence numbers of tracts were published on the interpretation of the statutes and the correct means whereby the laws could properly be executed. The *Ease for Overseers*, 1601, was one of the earliest of these and is designed as a *vade mecum* for the parish officers. The author outlines the meaning of the word 'overseer'; the sort of man he should and should not be; and the manner in which he should discharge his duties. He goes in detail into the various sorts of poor to be helped, given work or punished as the case may be, and concludes his little volume with a chapter headed 'A Prospect for rich men to induce them to give to the poore', (like many of his contemporaries, he deprecated the lack of funds which made compulsory poor laws necessary, almost as much as he deplored the slothfulness which made so many a charge on parish relief and private charity alike) and another one on 'A Patterne for poore men, to provoke them to labour'. His association of poverty with idleness in some cases did not, however, lead him, as over the years it was increasingly to lead others, to a harsh insensitivity to the poor themselves; 'those whom God hath punished with povertie, let no man seeke to oppresse with crueltie...'. On the contrary, the overseer is defined as a man whose office is to have charge over the poor 'as the shepheard over his sheep'. A man who, when chosen, should 'consider God, that they oversee others as he over seeth all'. An overseer should thus show malice to none in his power, but consider 'the rule of charity to doe as they would be done to...'. In respect of setting the poor to work, therefore, the overseers 'must tender the poore and lay no more upon them, than they are able to beare, as we intreat God to lay no more on us than he will make us able to bare: ...'

The same humanitarian spirit emerges when the anonymous author outlines the responsibilities of his readers to children in their charge. He draws their attention to the fact that under the heading of 'impotent poor' mentioned in the statutes, all infants without parents or proper support as well as the aged, sick and disabled poor are to be included. Children he points out, are to be relieved either 'by infancie' or 'by familie'. 'By infancie, when poor orphans and other be left fatherlesse and motherlesse to the world, and by reason of their tender yeares, cannot worke, or be unable to live of their worke, it is fitte they should have reliefe: for if the bird will cherish her young till they be able to flie, wee are bound by nature to nourish these till they be able to shift.' The man overcharged with young children is also a worthy object of relief 'for if a man in pittie will ease his beast which is oppressed with burthen, he must in nature relieve his neighbour which is oppressed with charge'.[1]

It was for the first of these two categories of children, the poor, succourless child, that the need for extensive provision was most keenly felt in the sixteenth century. In contrast to the demoralised parents whose children were removed to a new environment, the poor but honest widow was usually given a weekly allowance to enable her to provide for her children her-

[1] *An Ease for Overseers of the Poore*, 1601. See particularly pp. 7–10.

'THE SUCCOURLESS POOR CHILD'

self during their infancy. As for orphans and destitute children, the authorities practised both methods in use today; institutional care and boarding out. Provision for 'further education' of orphans had been one of the most popular medieval charities, and voluntary effort for the provision of orphanages continued side by side with the new statutory requirements. Reference has already been made to the orphanages established on the model of Christ's Hospital in such towns as Bristol, Exeter, Plymouth and Norwich, and to the training school for poor orphans at Ipswich, Reading, Nottingham and York; and after the Act of 1597, public provision for orphans was especially emphasised. In 1599, for example, the small town of Beverley was maintaining and educating eighty orphans under the Act.[1] But institutional provision was inadequate for the large numbers of orphans and destitute children of the times, and both in town and country, fatherless and abandoned children as well as illegitimate children, were boarded out with foster-parents. The numerous entries in local records, itemising payments to foster-parents for keeping 'a fatherless chylde' or 'a childe that was founde in this towne', indicate the activity of the local authorities in boarding out such children.

The *Ease for Overseers* recommended the payment of a weekly allowance of 1s. for each child boarded out, and gave an example:[2]

'Thomas Figge
keepeth
Ro. Segge ⎫
Th. Rere   ⎬ orphans   Weekly   IIIs.'
Hen. Tod ⎭   allowance

This allowance, taking into account the higher value of money in the sixteenth century as compared to the nineteenth century, was far more generous than the 4s. maximum weekly allowance permitted by the Boarding-out Order of 1870. In practice, the actual size of the allowance in the sixteenth century varied a good deal from place to place. Whilst in Nottingham 'a poore woman that keepes a childe that was founde in the towne' was to have 16s. paid to her quarterly,[3] the justices of Chester Quarter Ses-

---
[1] G. Oliver, *History and Antiquities of Beverley*. 1829. p. 192.
[2] op. cit., p. 4.
[3] *Records of the Borough of Nottingham*, vol. IV., p. 231.

sions ordered 'the gents, churchwardens and parishioners of Wybumbrie to make a yearlie collection and allowance' of 20s. to Roger Harding 'toward the educacon and bringing up of Samuel Eaton', an orphan, this allowance was also to be paid not weekly but quarterly.[1] Where parishes neglected their statutory duties, apparently in the hope that relatives or private charity would provide for the children as in the past, some of the local justices did not hesitate to fine them. Thus, in 1598, the parish of Silkston, which had refused to pay 6d. a week to John Mitchell towards the education of two orphans, Mary and Elizabeth Mitchell, the children of the lately deceased Thomas Mitchell, was fined £3. 6s. 1d. in default, and the justices directed that the churchwardens and overseers were to make proper provision for the children's education 'according to the last Statute [1597] in that case made and provided'.[2] In certain very special circumstances the county, and not the parish, was ordered to provide the necessary money for the boarding out of a child, as for example, where a child's parent was in prison, or had been executed.

One of the ideas of the Tudor paternal State, which anticipated in part the later development of the Welfare State, was the belief that some additional assistance, in the form of family allowances, was essential for the over-large poor family. This idea probably took root with the publication of Marshall's book describing the Ypres experiment where such allowances were paid. The poor law drafted the same year (1535) actually made provision for such payments but this and other radical suggestions were dropped in the modified version which became law in 1536, and the implementation of the idea had to wait until the end of the century. The Act of 1597 did not specifically mention such allowances, but the *Ease for Overseers*, as we have seen, includes them along with various other payments to the impotent. There is certainly evidence that such allowances were being paid to fathers of large families in Bedfordshire and elsewhere after the Act of 1597.[3] The justices of the North Riding of Yorkshire ordered in 1618, for example, 'that whereas Geo. Ward is

---

[1] *Cheshire Quarter Sessions Records*, ed. J. H. E. Bennett & J. C. Dewhurst, vol. I, 1940, p. 51.
[2] *West Riding Sessions Rolls, 1597–98, 1602*, ed. John Lister, 1888, p. 6.
[3] See F. C. Emmison, Poor Relief Accounts of Two Rural Parishes in Bedfordshire. *Economic History Review*, Jan. 1931, vol. III, no. 1, p. 106.

'THE SUCCOURLESS POOR CHILD'

greatlie surcharged with children, and beinge verie poore, doth want an habitation, the parish of Burneston shall weeklie give 12d. to the said Ward . . . untill they shall provide a house for him to live in, and that then the said parishioners shall pay him 6d. weekelie'.[1] The practice of giving such allowances continued through the seventeenth and eighteenth centuries and until the abuse of the Speenhamland system ended any supplementation from the poor rates by the Poor Law Act of 1834.

Whilst it is comparatively easy to point to particular examples of the Elizabethan statutes being applied both in the letter and in the spirit advocated in the *Ease for Overseers*, their effectiveness over the whole country depended on the extent to which the Privy Council interested itself in their local implementation by the local justices of the peace, in whose hands lay day-to-day supervision. In 1597, a letter advising the good execution of the new poor laws was sent to all justices in England and Wales. But between 1597 and 1629, this kind of action was exceptional. The Council interfered in particular cases, and in times of scarcity commanded general measures of relief, but before 1629, it did not steadily enforce the administration of general measures with regard to the relief of the poor in ordinary times. According to Leonard, in *The Early History of English Poor Relief*, the Orders in Council of 1597 which followed upon the statutes of that year were effective in securing the local relief to the poor, but between 1605 and 1629 when the Privy Council did not make continuous efforts on behalf of the deserving poor, the law appears to have been badly administered: 'rogues soon swarmed again', wrote Lord Coke in 1624. Numbers of pamphlets appeared deploring the increase of beggary and rogues and lamenting the failure of the parishes to collect and administer a poor rate and a stock of materials on which to set the poor to work. A Mr. Williamson, writing in 1624 to Sir Julius Caesar, the Master of the Rolls, asserted that the failure of the overseers to apprentice children was the fundamental cause of this upsurge in vagrancy. The seventeenth century vagrant, he tells Sir Julius, was very seldom a man who knew a trade and the existence of untrained men was due to the faulty administration of the poor laws. 'These intolerable offences haue originally growen from the

[1] *North Riding Quarter Sessions Records*, vol. II, 1884, ed. J. C. Atkinson, p. 177.

'THE SUCCOURLESS POOR CHILD'

Ou[er]seers of the poore who heretofore and att this day haue and doe so ou[er]see as though they did not see at all.'[1] Between 1629 and 1644, however, the Privy Council made renewed and continued efforts to enforce the laws. With regard to apprenticing, they made special efforts at enforcement and from all over the country there is evidence that it was enforced, though not always with favourable results.

The distraction of the attention of the Privy Council to more urgent political matters prior to the outbreak of the Civil War and the diversion of the zeal of the justices to raising troops and meeting demands for money made both by King and Parliament, inevitably resulted in some dislocation of poor law administration. Nevertheless, the impotent were still relieved and children still apprenticed, though perhaps less efficiently than before.

The dislocation of poor law administration was paralleled by the disorganisation of the semi-voluntary charities. The four royal Hospitals were the most conspicuous instances of charities which were under public management, although partly supported by private contributions. From the Hospitals came numerous complaints of partial breakdown owing to the Civil Wars and the figures given by the Governors speak for themselves. In 1641, there were over 900 children in Christ's Hospital; in 1647, there were only 682. At St. Bartholomew's and Bridewell, the numbers had also substantially decreased. The Governors of Christ's believed that the reasons for this were to be found 'in respect of the troubles of the times, the meanes of the said Hospital hath very much failed for want of Charitable Benevolence which formerly have beene given, and are now ceased; and very few legacies are now given to the hospitals, the rent and revenues thereunto belonging being all very ill paid by the tenants who are not able to hold their leases . . . by reason of their quartering and billeting of soldiers and the taking away of their corne and cattell from them'. A few years later, the billeting had apparently ceased, but the tenants then suffered 'by reason of the severall charges and taxes laid upon them'. Even in 1653, the Governors report that their revenues 'hath divers wayes fallen very short of means formerly received, viz. heretofore many have given monies privately, others very bountifull at their deaths. And in several parishes in London have sent in

[1] Leonard, op. cit., p. 242–4.

'THE SUCCOURLESS POOR CHILD'

large contributions and now but one that sends in anything at all'.[1] The Civil Wars had reduced many of the rich to poverty, and probably most institutions which had been maintained by their contributions, either in whole or in part, suffered in the same way as the London Hospitals. This was certainly the case with the Hospital at Dorchester, for example, which had been founded in 1617 and was actually forced to close between 1643 and 1646 owing to the disruption of its finances during the Wars.[2]

From London also came complaints of increasing numbers of vagrants roaming the streets, begging during the day and pilfering at night 'to the scandall of the governments of this City'. As soon as the Commonwealth was fairly established, many efforts had been made to relieve the poor of London. As early as 1647,[3] a new body was established, the Corporation of the Poor, which was empowered to erect workhouses and houses of correction. The store houses situated in the Minories and the Wardrobe-house were granted to them, and here orphans were maintained and poor families employed and relieved by the Corporation by spinning and weaving.

The President and Corporation of the Poor were soon hindered in their work by want of funds, and were not at all successful in maintaining order in the London streets. In spite of the new orphanage at the Wardrobe, few children were educated there, probably because no money could be got. (According to a Report for 1655, only 100 orphans and deserted children were in the house.) The hymn sung by the children implores Parliament to do something to relieve the matter:[4]

> Grave Senators that sit on high
> Let not poor English children die
> And droop on Dunghills with lamenting notes;
> An Act for Poor's Relief they say
> Is coming forth; why's this delay?
> O let not Dutch Danes Devils stop those
> Votes . . . .

---
[1] ibid., p. 269.
[2] *The Municipal Records of the Borough of Dorchester, Dorset*, ed. Chas. Herbert Mayo. Exeter, 1908. p. 517.
[3] See *Acts and Ordinances of the Interregnum, 1642–60*, ed. C. H. Frith & R. S. Rait, 1911. vol. I, pp. 1042–5.
[4] *Poor Outcast Childrens Song and Cry.* 1653.

'THE SUCCOURLESS POOR CHILD'

Neither in London nor the provinces did Parliament prove equal to the task of ensuring that effective administration of the poor laws which the Royalist Privy Council had worked so strenuously to achieve.

Not only did Parliament fail to provide any alternative means of co-ordinating central and local authority. In addition, the development of Puritanism, with its special emphasis on work and thrift, and the corollary that poverty itself was disgraceful, led to an increasingly negative attitude towards the poor themselves. The new mental climate, together with the falling off of charitable funds due to general impoverishment after the Civil Wars, combined in the mid-seventeenth century to produce an increasingly harsh and repressive policy with regard to the poor, in strong contrast to aspects of earlier benevolence. The poor, it was now argued, even the children, should be made to keep themselves. Hence there gradually developed the new movement for the establishment of children's workhouses which in their turn strengthened and officially sanctioned a tradition of child labour which was all too readily accepted and exploited by the factory- and mine-owners of later generations.

2. *The Children's Workhouse Movement*

The London Corporation of the Poor was itself an illustration of the new attitude. In practice, its main function was the suppression of vagrancy in the City. This was made very clear in the Act of 1647 under which it had been set up and underlined by the subsequent *Act for the Relief & Imployment of the Poor, & the Punishment of Vagrants, and other disorderly Persons Within the City of London*. Not only did this further Act authorise the Corporation to set vagrants to work, to whip and stock them and send them back to their place of birth or their last abode, it was also considerably more severe towards non-vagrant children than the legislation of 1597 and 1601. 'And also That it shall be lawful ... to apprehend, or cause to be apprehended and kept at work, All such poor Children able to work and inhabiting within the said City and Liberties who are chargeable to any Parish, or have not sufficient to maintain themselves, and in case of their refusal to work, That it shall and may be lawful ... to punish,

'THE SUCCOURLESS POOR CHILD'

or cause to be punished as Vagrants, such persons so refusing to work...'[1]

As significant as the unprecedented authority this Act granted to the Corporation over the non-vagrant poor child is the emphasis placed by contemporaries on the virtues of the institutional provision made by the London Corporation for poor children. Samuel Hartlib, in a pamphlet which seems to have been issued in conjunction with the inauguration of the Corporation's workhouses in 1649, declared that 'of all parts and peece of Reformation, this of the Work-houses to train up children in godly education, will be one of the great masterpeeces'.[2]

Of course, there was nothing new in the idea of collecting children together under one roof to give them some sort of industrial training. This had always been provided for both in Elizabethan and Jacobean legislation and had been the object of the original Bridewell scheme as well as many others. Moreover, as Leonard shows,[3] by the 1630s, municipal and parochial workhouses where the able-bodied were sent that they might be trained and employed at the same time were fairly numerous before the Civil Wars. What was new, was the conviction, which many of Hartlib's contemporaries had come to share, that this sort of provision was not merely a possible solution but the panacea for the problems of the poor child.

Some of the reasoning which lay behind this conviction was set out in a pamphlet by Sir Matthew Hale (lately a Lord Chief Justice of the King's Bench) in his much discussed *Discourse Touching Provision for the Poor* (1659). Hale claimed that 'no provision is now made in England to give the poor honest employment' – by which he meant setting the poor to work on a stock of materials provided by the parish – 'thus they do unavoidably bring up their Children either in a Trade of Begging or Stealing; or such other Idle course, which again they propagate over to their Children, which fills the Gaols with Malefactors, and fills the Kingdom with idle and unprofitable Persons ... that daily increase to the desolation of time ...'[4] There is a lot

[1] Firth & Raith, op. cit., vol. II, p. 106.
[2] S. H. (Samuel Hartlib), *London Charitie, stilling the Poore Orphans Cry.* 1649. p. 5.
[3] Leonard, op. cit., p. 260.
[4] Hale, op. cit., 1683 edn, pp. 79–80.

'THE SUCCOURLESS POOR CHILD'

in Hale's pamphlet that reminds one of many similar effusions on the causes and consequences of child destitution which had been circulated during the previous hundred years. Perhaps it even struck some of his contemporaries as rather old-fashioned. Certainly there was an additional argument in favour of workhouses which was constantly reiterated in later seventeenth century pamphlets, which seems to have told more heavily with a generation as inclined to weigh the economics as the ethics of poverty: the argument, quite simply, that the workhouse was a place where the poor could be compelled to work, and by their work, both support themselves and relieve the rates. But in his view that the individual parish was no longer a satisfactory unit for the administration of the poor law, Hale was a good deal more foresighted than legislators of his day who, by the Act of Settlement of 1662 – the first Act relating to the poor after the Restoration – had statutorily reaffirmed the traditional assumption of the individual parish's exclusive responsibility for its own poor and granted the overseers the legal right 'to remove and convey to such parish where they were lastly settled either as a native Household Sojourner or Apprentice or Servant for the space of forty days at the least' any newcomer whom they suspected as likely to become a charge on the local rate 'unlesse he or she give sufficient security for the discharge of the said Parish'. As Leonard remarks, the Settlement Act was a curious example of the adoption by statute of a custom that had long existed and been enforced, as we have already seen in the case of vagrants, to the extent of cutting family ties. This was only one of the ways in which the principle of settlement was asserted. In St. Alban's, at Norwich, where settlement regulations were very extensive, sureties against chargeability on the rates were being demanded three-quarters of a century before the Act of Settlement. John Palmer, for example, was admitted a freeman on Thomas Browne's undertaking that Palmer's children should not become chargeable to the borough.[1] These customs had been enforced without statutory authority, while the town government continued to possess semi-independent powers, but it could not be enforced without statutory authority at later times.

It also stereotyped a unit of administration which, before 1662, had already proved itself totally unfitted to perform one of

[1] Leonard, op. cit., p. 260.

'THE SUCCOURLESS POOR CHILD'

the principal tasks laid upon it by the Poor Laws of 1597 and 1601, that of getting the poor to work on a stock of materials provided by the parish.

During the Interregnum, the creation of the London Corporation of the Poor had been the only recognition by Parliament that some larger unit of administration was necessary if Poor Law administration was to be made effective; and only for London (the City of London, Westminster, and the parts of Middlesex and Surrey within the Bills of Mortality) did the Restoration Parliament acknowledge the same administrative necessity by providing for Corporations of the Poor, consisting of a President (the Lord Mayor in the case of the City), a Deputy President and a number of aldermen who were empowered to set up workhouses within their respective areas in which the poor might be employed.[1] For the time being, the only workhouse built under the Act, at a cost of £5,000, was at Clerkenwell in Middlesex, on which work began in 1663. It was the intention of the Middlesex Corporation to accommodate 600 able-bodied and 100 impotent poor in this House. For reasons which are far from clear, however, the activities of the Corporation came to an end in 1672. Possibly their original plan had proved too expensive to run. But in 1685, the justices of the Middlesex Quarter Sessions, 'having observed great inconveniences from the loose way of breeding up parish children, whereby few of them come to good',[2] acquired a large part of the Corporation's workhouse at Clerkenwell to be set apart 'for the Reception and Breeding up of poor Fatherless and Motherless children, left to the Parish care, and for the Instructing them in Religion and Virtue, & making them Capable of getting an honest Livelihood by their Labour'.[3]

The objectives of the scheme are exactly reflected in the staff engaged to run the 'Nursery' or 'College of Infants', which was to be placed under the authority of one of the Middlesex justices, as non-resident Governor. Beneath the Governor, there was a resident Minister, whose job it was to read prayers twice daily, to catechise the children weekly, preach occasionally and super-

[1] E. G. Dowdell, *A Hundred Years of Quarter Sessions*. 1932. pp. 45–7.
[2] ibid., p. 59.
[3] *An Account of the General Nursery, or Colledge of Infants, set up by the Justices of the Peace of the County of Middlesex, With the Constitutions and Ends thereof.* 1686. p. 1.

vise the work of the rest of the very considerable staff of the Nursery. This included a physician, apothecary and surgeon, visiting weekly; a writing master, who was to teach all the children to write; a schoolmaster who was to teach the boys to read and say their prayers and catechism; a schoolmistress; 'and several other persons of several trades, to teach the children several sorts of works, & bring them up therein' – a seamstress to instruct the girls is specially mentioned; a porter, to supervise the children at play; a matron or housekeeper; a cook and laundress; as well as 'an old Nurse, to take care of all sick and weak children; the Nurse hath her Assistants if required'; together with domestic servants to do household work. Both the size of the staff and the character of the Governor appointed to the Nursery, Sir Thomas Rowe, point to its being a charitable experiment based on humanitarian principles rather than a rate-reducing exercise based on narrow economic considerations.

It had been Rowe, together with some friends, who had in fact been responsible for taking a lease on part of the workhouse, and for fitting it out 'at a great charge' as an act of private charity on the ground that, although private charity was active in the education and upbringing of 'youth', no systematic attempt was being made to deal with the problem of the 'poor infants' . . . 'For want whereof, many great Evils and Inconveniences are daily found, by the wilful & careless causing or suffering more Infants to perish, or to suck in the wicked & debauched Principles to their Ruin, as 'tis to be feared often their Souls as well as Bodies'. Started as a charity, the College of Infants it was hoped, would attract further benefactions 'whereby the Charge of the Maintenance and Education of the Poor may at least be eas'd, if not wholly taken off'. For a donation of £50, a benefactor could nominate a poor child to be educated in the College, bound apprentice and given £10 at the end of his term to help him set up on his own. For a £200 donation, a child could be educated, 'bound to a very good trade' and given £100 at the end of his training. 'Poor orphans' might be entered at the College by a parish for a payment of 20s. on entrance (to provide new clothes and bedding) and a weekly payment of 3s. for the child's food, drink and maintenance. The details of the cost of entering children in the College shows only too clearly the confusion of thinking among the College's sponsors as to the

'THE SUCCOURLESS POOR CHILD'

categories of children for whom the institution was primarily intended. This also manifests itself in the claims made concerning the type of persons likely to benefit from the College's work. 'Fatherless and Motherless' children are first mentioned, but it was also asserted that the College would be an advantage 'to the Poor: the Trouble & Charge of Breeding up such Infants, taking them much off from earning their Livelihood: . . . & all such whose Employments require, or cause their Absence from their Dwellings, or seafaring Men, users of Fairs & Mkts; and to all such as would not otherwise keep Houses, unless it were for the looking after, & Breeding up of their Children'. It was also believed that the College would 'prevent the great Trouble and charge to all persons by Children left & laid in the several Parishes . . . And by their Education, we may be assured there will be better Subjects better Masters and better Apprentices & servants for all persons that shall need them'. Obviously, the College was in fact to be something more than a residential school for parish orphans, and certainly there is no evidence that they were only thinking of parish orphans when, in February 1686, the Middlesex justices ordered the churchwardens and overseers of the poor of parishes which lay within the London Bills of Mortality to send in to the College by March 18 a specified quota – usually 5 – of parish children. In April, the Westminster justices at their own Quarter Sessions, made similar orders for children to be taken to the College and in July, well pleased with their new institution, the Middlesex justices decided to advise justices outside the Bills of Mortality that they should recommend their parish officers to send at least two children to the College from their respective parishes. Several parishes not only took up this advice but published a joint address, thanking the justices for their excellent scheme which, they said, was 'a very great Advantage to the Poor Children, they being provided for & Educated much beyond the Imagination of any Persons that do not go to see them, & to the great Satisfaction of all that do'. When an inspection was made of the College in August by the Middlesex Grand Jury, they reported: 'We find that all the Children there are well Lodged, well Cloathed, kept Neat and Clean, taught to Read and Write, & well instructed in the Religion of the Church of England, as it is now Established by Law.' The following June [1687], it was

'THE SUCCOURLESS POOR CHILD'

claimed that the College was 'one of the best & most charitable works that has for these many years been set on foot'.

No charitable work has ever been attempted, however, that did not have its opponents, and the parish of St. Clement Dane 'did absolutely refuse to obey the order of the Quarter sessions' to send in their quota of 5 children on the ground that they could save 2s. 6d. a week by educating the children themselves. Since the justices had no coercive power to make them do so – the greatest drawback to their scheme and the one which was ultimately to undermine it altogether – it was only possible for them to order an enquiry into the state of the infant parish poor of the recalcitrant parish. The investigation which was promptly ordered revealed, among several other peculiarities of the administration of the finances of the parish, that it was quite clear that the accounts showed payments being made for children who had, over the past seven years, either been lost, died or had never existed at all.

Much later, Jonas Hanway, writing in 1766, remarked that the inability of the justices to order children to be brought in to their institution inevitably undermined the vitality and viability of the College as a means of providing for the infant poor within the Bills of Mortality.[1] St. Clement Dane was able to contract out of the scheme only a short time after its inception: by 1690, other parishes which had earlier co-operated with the justices were far less regular in sending in their quotas of children. Rowe himself died about 1690, and a year later the College was transferred to Hornsey, after which records of its activities cease.

The College of Infants had been an attempt to harness on a voluntary basis private charity to public responsibility at a time when expressions of both were becoming markedly less liberal and less humanitarian. At most it had only housed sixty children and had never become large enough to constitute an adequate solution to the problems of even one of the several categories of children to whose needs it was supposedly addressed. The potential value of being able to draw children from an area larger than

[1] Jonas Hanway, in *Letters on the Importance of the Rising Generation of the Laboring part of our fellow subjects* (published in 1767), argues that the lack of authority of the justices to coerce the parish authorities to place children in the College was one of the principal reasons for its collapse. See vol. I, Letter XV, p. 51.

'THE SUCCOURLESS POOR CHILD'

that of the individual parish thus never found practical expression in an institution whose limited size effectively prevented potential economies of scale.

Elsewhere in London, however, another attempt was being made to cope with the large numbers of children chargeable on the poor rate. In this case, the scheme had behind it all the authority of statutory sanction. As we have already seen, the work of the original London Corporation of the Poor of 1647 had been largely abortive. In April 1698, on the application of some wealthy citizens, the Common Council of London elected, as they believed themselves empowered to do under the terms of the Act of Settlement, a new Corporation of the Poor, composed of the aldermen and fifty-two 'leading citizens', who were deputed to establish a workhouse for the poor, towards which some of the Aldermen made loans until the Common Council voted the necessary subsidy. The Council had originally intended the workhouse to be a kind of work centre, to which up to a thousand able-bodied poor between the ages of 7 and 50 could go to be trained to spin, and made employable in the woollen industry. The training was to last six weeks, during which they were to be kept warm and fed on broth and boiled meat. When trained, they were to be found employment in their own homes by their local parish officers. Not very surprisingly in view of the contemporary inefficiency of parochial poor law administration, this scheme broke down because the parish officers failed to find the trainees work when they came back from the centre, but continued to pay them relief 'so that all the charges and pains of the Corporation was at were rendered ineffectual'.[1] In August 1699, therefore, the Corporation took a number of houses in Half-Moon Alley, Bishopsgate, 'at a considerable yearly rent', which they proceeded to fit out and furnish at no small cost as a residential workhouse.

The Corporation directed its immediate attention to providing for the poor child as 'the original cause' of the adult poor, ordering vagrant children found in the City without settlement to be brought in to the workhouse as well as 'all such Poor Parish Children that belonged to the several Parishes of the City, that were above Seven Years old (who were heretofore

[1] *A Short Account of the Work-House belonging to the President and Governors for the Poor, in Bishopsgate street, London.* 1702. p. 2.

'THE SUCCOURLESS POOR CHILD'

generally bred very idle, little Care being taken to Educate & Imploy them)'.[1] The children were to be taught reading, writing and arithmetic and employed in spinning wool and flax; knitting stockings, as well as making their own clothes and shoes 'to insure their fitness to honest Labour and Industry'.

The Bishopsgate Workhouse, like the College of Infants, had a considerable staff: a secretary (who was in fact the master), a steward, a schoolmaster 'who is a minister', a writing master, three matrons, a schoolmistress, thirteen nurses – one to every 30 children, 15 teachers of various trades, a messenger, porter, 2 cooks and 2 under cooks. Four physicians and a surgeon also attended the House, a provision made all the more desirable since many of the vagrant children arrived 'almost naked & in the last degree miserable, eaten up with vermin, & in such nasty Rags, that one could not distinguish by their Clothes what Sex they were of'.[2]

On entry, each child was given a kind of uniform to wear which, like the food provided for them to eat, was probably of a far better quality than they could ever have expected outside the workhouse. On Sundays, for example, a breakfast was provided of three ounces of bread 'and beer sufficient, not exceeding a pint to each, of 7s. 6d per barrel'; a dinner of four ounces of bread, eight ounces of beef, again with 'beer sufficient'; and a supper of four ounces of bread, one and a half ounces of cheese, or one ounce of butter 'and beer sufficient'. Saturday was perhaps their least satisfying day, with milk pottage for breakfast, and bread and cheese for supper and only 'a plain flower suet Dumpling' for dinner. But on the whole their food was good, with dinners varying between 'Pease-pudding', 'Plumb-pudding-pye', 'Butter'd Parsnips and Carrots' and beef.

At night, the children slept in wards, two to a bed, which were 'boarded and set one above another, a Row on each side of the Ward, a Flock Bed, a pair of sheets, 2 Blankets and a Rugg to each'.[3] Their life by day is described in such unusual detail by Edward Hatton, that it is worth recording here in detail:[4]

[1] *A True Report of the Poor, Maintained and Imployed in the Work-House, Easter,* 1703.
[2] *A Short Account* . . ., p. 65.
[3] *A Short State and Representation of the Proceedings of the President and Governors for the Poor of the City of London.* 1702. p. 2.
[4] Printed in full in Ashton, *Social Life in the Reign of Queen Anne.* 1882. p. 436.

'THE SUCCOURLESS POOR CHILD'

'The Bell rings at 6 a Clock in the Morning to call up the Children and half an Hour after, the Bell is rung for Prayers and Breakfast; at 7 the children are set to work; 20 under a Mistress to spin Wool and Flax, to Knit Stockings, to wind Silk, to make and Sew their Linen, Cloaths, Shooes, & etc. All the Children are called down for an Hour every Day to Read, and an Hour every Day to Write (viz) 20 at a time.

'At 12 a Clock they go to Dinner, and have a little time to play till One, then they are set to work again till 6 a clock: They are rung to Prayers, to their Supper, and are allowed to play till Bed time.

'Every Nurse combs her Children with a small tooth-comb three times a Week; mends the Children's Cloaths; makes their beds, washes their hands: and sees that the children go neat and clean, and that they wash and comb themselves every day.

'Some Children earn ½d some 1d & some 4d a day.

'The Children are taught their Catechism and often Catechised by the Minister, especially every Sunday.' (When they were taken twice to Great St. Helen's Church.)

As in ordinary schools, so in Bishopsgate, even the most carefully organised of timetables did not entirely dispose of problems of discipline. It is refreshing however to notice that, in contrast to contemporary school discipline, the punishments meted out in this workhouse do not reflect an unqualified belief in the merits of physical violence. True, Sarah Fry and Mary Story were ordered to be 'publickly whipt' for stealing from their nurse, but the Governors were not prepared to sanction whipping indiscriminately and were certainly not disposed to allow the teachers to take the administration of physical punishment into their own hands. Hence three teachers were actually dismissed 'for misusing the Boxmakers Apprentice by whipping him with Rods', and the Governors required that 'Mr Iles do provide others in their Room'. On another occasion, they record 'That Wee have Ordered the Children for their faults to be Tyed to a Rope at ye Lower End of ye Dineing Room without any Supper or time to play every Evening instead of Whippeing',[1] an alternative punishment which may not entirely commend itself to the twentieth-century mind but which was a good deal more

[1] *Corporation of London Records, 1702-5.* (MS), fol. 219v, June 1705.

'THE SUCCOURLESS POOR CHILD'

enlightened than the beatings so often referred to in records of seventeenth-century schools.

There was, in fact, a great deal about this early example of municipal workhouse management which appears far more careful and enlightened than was the case with later establishments both in London and elsewhere. Great care was taken, for example, that the children should be housed separately from the adult 'Beggars, Vagrants, and other Lewd, Idle and Disorderly Persons' who were admitted to Bishopsgate after November, 1700; and special attention was paid to the needs of the sick and handicapped. Among the records of the workhouse is one, dated July 1703: 'That there being Severall Lame Children in the House wee [presumably the master] have ordered them at present to be employed in knitting but do think ye air might do them Good if they were sent five or six mile out of Town for some time & wee desire this Court [of the President and Governors of the Poor of London] would please to Give directions Therin if the Doctors think it advisable'. In response to this request, the Court did order 'that Lame Children be sent to the Sick House in Bunhill fields [which had been lent the Corporation free by its Deputy President] for the Benefit of the Air and that they be there employed in Knitting'.[1]

One may well ask how an enterprise such as this was financed and to what extent it was self-supporting. It was considerably bigger than the College of Infants, taking about 200 children from the parishes and anything between 150 and 200 vagrant children, and its overheads and running expenses were thus very much heavier. The rent of the original four houses in Half-Moon Alley amounted to £41 a year to which was soon added another £59 a year for the rent of additional accommodation when the work of the Corporation really got under way. The salaries of the staff totalled another £290 a year. And to these sums must be added the cost of supplies and the cost of the children's uniform, estimated at a pound a head, and the host of incidental expenses a large residential establishment necessarily incurs. Like the College of Infants, the Bishopsgate workhouse hoped for private benefactions, and from October 1701, operated a similar scheme for encouraging them by allowing benefactors certain privileges. Every benefactor that contri-

[1] ibid., fol. 36, July 1703.

'THE SUCCOURLESS POOR CHILD'

buted £25 (later raised to £50) was allowed to recommend a child for acceptance. This particular arrangement soon proved an unexpected embarrassment to the Corporation, not only in that too many children were commended in this way but because some of the children, though certainly not within the category of 'vagrant', had no settlement in the City of London. In 1708, therefore, a Committee of the Common Council which had been appointed to look into the matter, advised that only persons giving more than £50 should have the right to present children and that, in such cases, the child had to be known to have its settlement in London. Only in very special circumstances might even a London child be presented for a smaller benefaction although, loth to alienate the charitably disposed and 'that the Charity might not be too strictly confined', it was further ordered that any benefactor giving £70 'might put in a Child from what Place he thought fit', provided its settlement were known.[1] According to the records of the Corporation of the Poor for 1712, the only year for which we have an analysis of the number of benefactors and the size of the benefactions, the usual amount contributed to the workhouse by the 76 benefactors of that year was between £50 and £100, but some gave as little as £2 or as much as £826; benefactions of £200 were quite frequently recorded. Unlike the College of Infants, however, since the workhouse was founded by statutory authority, the Corporation had additional means of raising money. According to the provisions of the 1662 Act, the Common Council of London were empowered to levy a rate on the citizens from time to time as was necessary and 'not exceeding one Year's rate for the Relief of the Poor', towards the maintenance of the Corporation's workhouse, although in practice, they do not seem to have raised more than the equivalent of a half-year's rate. In addition, until 1710, when the charge was discontinued, the parishes were charged a shilling a week for each child they sent to the House.

The history of their attempts to harness municipal to voluntary effort can scarcely be said to have been harmonious. Where the Corporation's right to levy a tax for a workhouse for any other than vagrants was not directly disputed – to which the crisp retort was that 'If the Poor are not taken into one side of the House when they are Young, its great odds but they will

[1] *An Account of Several Workhouses . . .* 1725. p. 2.

deserve to be sent to the other when they are grown up'[1] – the complaint was made that, by refusing to take children into the House under seven years of age, the parish was left to provide for the infant poor who, unlike their elder brothers and sisters, could contribute nothing by their own labours to their maintenance and were thus a heavier burden on the parish . . . 'so that this Corporation seems calculated for the Benefit of the Corporation and the Agents only'.[2] To this there were two replies. First, that the Corporation's activities saved the parishes at least £800 a year, and second, by way not merely of refuting but returning in good measure the insult to their integrity '. . . the Corporation do imploy a great part of their time in serving the Publick, without a penny benefit to themselves; but on the contrary, they spend their own Mony, and did advance a considerable sum for carrying on that Work before any Mony could be raised by the Common Council for that end. Whereas in one or two of the Parishes in Farringdon without, it has been customary to spend twenty pounds at a Scavenger's and three or four and twenty pounds at a Perambulation dinner; which Mony is generally rais'd by overrating the inhabitants . . .'[3] Another objection against the Corporation was that the children could be maintained more cheaply in the parishes than in the workhouse. The reply to this allegation in an anonymous pamphlet written in 1713 to uphold the London Corporation of the Poor and their work at Bishopsgate is an interesting contemporary reflection on the standard of parochial care of poor children in London at this period.[4] First, the author asserts that, since the Corporation's opponents constantly underestimate the cost of parochial care of children, by neglecting to include such items as churchwarden's visitations, medicines, clothing, etc., the comparisons made of relative costs are meaningless. But, he continues, '. . . will those who Object, say what they so allow the poor children is sufficient, or does

[1] *An Account of the Corporation of the Poor of London; Shewing the Nature, Usefulness and Management of the Workhouse in Bishopsgate Street, And that the Relieving, Educating and Setting Poor Children to Work therein, is one Principal Design of its Institution: And of Great Advantage to the Publick.* 1713. p. 14.

[2] *REASONS Humbly offered to this Honourable House, why a Bill pretended to give further Powers to the Corporation for setting the Poor of the City of London and Liberties thereof to Work, should not pass into a Law.* 1700.

[3] *Observations upon a Paper intitled, Reasons humbly offered to This House why a Bill . . .*, (n.d.).

[4] See note 1, above

indeed wholly Support and keep them? No, it is manifestly otherwise, and in fact, such Children are often sent a Begging, and found Pilfering to supply their Necessities, and what is likely to be the End of many of them, one cannot but dread to think of'. Moreover, the author contends that the ordinary kind of upbringing of pauper children in their own parishes neither teaches them to read nor does it bring them up in the fear of God and the doctrine of the Church of England. Certainly, he argues, the parish fails to train them up in habits of industry before placing them out as apprentices. 'No such matter; they are commonly, when put out, rude, and untractable, and therefore few will take them, who want not the Money usually given with them.'[1]

One question relating to workhouse finances which all these allegations and counter-allegations raise directly or indirectly is the extent to which the children's own labour contributed to their support. As we have seen, the Corporation's detractors were wont to imply that the value of the children's work was a substantial advantage to the operation of the workhouse. In fact, this was quite certainly not the case. A Report on the Workhouse, dated 26 March 1705, analyses the numbers of children in the House at that time, some three hundred and twenty six in all, and comments: 'Which being Many in Number, the Profit gain'd by their Work Little, and the Income for their Maintenance very short of the Charge, it is hop'd many Worthy and Good Christians will liberally assist towards so Useful and Beneficial a Charity, which tends so much to the Reformation of the Vicious Youth, and the Incouragement of Honest Labour and Industry . . .' Charitable enterprises are, of course, prone to underestimate their private sources of support the better to move the public to benefaction, but the accounts of the President and Governors of the London Corporation of the Poor for this and other years do endorse the grounds for this particular appeal. In 1715, for example, the earnings of the children were estimated as follows:

	£	s.	d.
By spinning wool and winding silk	408	7	4
By making their own shoes	59	11	6
By making their clothes	31	2	11

[1] ibid., pp. 16–19.

The next year, when there were 317 children in the House, their earnings were much about the same:

	£	s.	d.
By spinning wool	316	12	2½
By flax spinning	3	18	3¼
Stocking knitting	17	0	0
Linen sewing	18	18	11
Making own clothes	44	15	2
Making own shoes	47	17	0
	449	1	6¾

On these figures the children each earned roughly thirty shillings a year. Since the cost of maintaining a child at Bishopsgate was estimated at about £8 a year, the necessity for outside financial support, voluntary or municipal is all too obvious. Equally obvious was the reluctance of London parishes to support such a scheme as the Corporation of the Poor had started at Bishopsgate, and time and again the advice of lawyers was sought as to whether, in fact, the Act of Settlement really gave the Corporation power to levy a rate to maintain a workhouse for non-vagrant children. Yet when, in 1700, a Bill before Parliament for *Relieving and Employing the Poor of this Kingdom* gave detractors of the London Corporation one of their earliest opportunities to ventilate their criticism publicly, others seized the occasion to advocate, equally publicly, the great virtues of municipally organised workhouses for the non-vagrant child and to illustrate their argument from practical experience. The experience to which reference was made, however, was not to that of the Bishopsgate Workhouse but to one run by the recently constituted Corporation of the Poor of Bristol. In the light of the constant friction between the Corporation of the Poor and the parishes in London, it would, indeed, have been tactically unwise to use its Workhouse as a model for all to copy. But it was not on the grounds of administrative harmony that the Bristol Workhouse was being commended to the nation so much as its apparent economic success.

The notion of a Workhouse as a place where the poor might be either taught or compelled to labour to support themselves and relieve the poor rates had been specifically canvassed for some years past. Only a few years after the appearance of Hale's

'THE SUCCOURLESS POOR CHILD'

pamphlet, Thomas Firmin, the London philanthropist, published two pamphlets, both of them vigorously advocating the provision of workhouses for children on precisely these grounds.[1] 'If any parish that abound with poor would set up a school in the nature of a workhouse, to teach poor children to work who wander up and down the parish and parts adjacent, & between begging and stealing get a living . . . it would in a short time be found v. advantageous, not only for the poor children, who by this means whilst young should be inured to labour & taught to get their own living, but also to their parents, who should hereby both be freed from any charge of keeping them & also in time be helped by their labour, as in other places. . . and further, the parish would by this means be freed from such charge that now they are at, either to keep these children or to allow their parents something towards it, nothing being thought a greater argument for a large pension than that a man or woman hath six or seven children . . .'[2]

In 1677 Firmin had actually set up a workhouse, in the shape of a linen manufactory, in Aldersgate, admitting children between three and ten years of age. He had thus the advantage of being able to reinforce theory with examples from experience, in the light of which he claimed that 'as to young children, there is nothing they can more easily learn than to spin linen, their fingers though never so little being big enough to pull the flax and make a fine thread'.[3] At the time of writing, Firmin had 'some children not above seven or eight years old, who are able to earn twopence a day' or a little over one shilling a week. The children remained in his school until they had learned to spin, when they took work home, so as to make room for others to be taught. Here, they laboured on until they were old enough to be apprenticed or put to service 'and no longer'. 'I have taken special care', Firmin writes, 'that no person that is fit to go to service, or to prentice, shall have any of my work.'[4] Although at Aldersgate, two hours a day were set aside for the children to

---

[1] Thomas Firmin, *Some Proposals for the Employing of the Poor, especially in and about the City of London.* 1678.
Also, *Some Proposals for the Employment of the Poor and for the Prevention of Idleness and the Consequence thereof, Begging.* 1681.
[2] Firmin, op. cit., 1678. p. 2.
[3] ibid., p. 4.
[4] Firmin, op. cit., 1681, p. 19.

be taught to read, and to learn the Catechism, Firmin had little patience with those who had a larger view of the education of the poor: 'nothing can be more advisable (in my poor judgement) than that all these children, except for some few who may be designed for more liberal employment, should together with their learning to read [no hint of writing here!] be taught to work as it is in Holland and other places and not all their time from 7 to 15 years spent in play or poring upon a book; for by this means they get such a habit of idleness, that many times they will never take to any labour at all; or if they be forced unto it, it is with great reluctancy; whereas, if whilst young they were taught to work, they would fall in love with it, and when old would not depart from it'.[1]

Firmin thus urged private benefactors and individual parishes to set up their own spinning schools ('or knitting, lace-making ... or any other work which the children shall be most fit for') as a sure means of relieving the rates; of providing semi-skilled labour for the textile trades at a cheap price; as a means of 'inuring the poor child to labour'; and a way of removing the children from the life of the streets.

In fact, attempts had already been made by some parishes to set up such a scheme as Firmin was advocating. In 1653 and again in 1679, Bristol had tried to establish manufactures for the employment of the poor, including poor children, in which the commercial management had been handed out to a local contractor. Neither of these attempts had proved successful. But in 1695, John Cary, a Bristol merchant, revived the idea in *An Essay on the State of England, In Relation to its Trade, its Poor, and its Taxes, For carrying on the Present War against France.* Cary, however, introduced his own notions of how a workhouse scheme should operate in so far as he believed that 'Imployment must be provided in them for all sorts of People, who must also be compelled to go thither when sent & the work houses to receive them'. Entry to the workhouse was thus the condition of receiving relief in Cary's scheme.

Since children were to be accepted in the workhouse only until the appropriate age for apprenticeship, Cary also recommended that the local justices should be given powers to assign workhouse boys to 'Artificers, Husbandmen, Manufacturers, and Mariners

[1] Firmin, op. cit., 1678, p. 5.

when of fit age for service and that the Employers should be bound to receive them'.

The general effect of the scheme, it was claimed, would be that the cost would be substantially reduced, since the children would by their own work maintain themselves, and the aged and impotent, who were also to be in the House, would care for the young children for nothing. Further, such a scheme, if adopted, would 'prevent Children from being murthered and starved by the neglect of the Parish Officers and Poverty of their Parents, which is now a great loss to the nation . . . and a great number of Manufacturers will be bred up, which are the riches of this City'.

In 1696, a private Act of Parliament was obtained to allow the eighteen parishes of Bristol to incorporate themselves 'for erecting of Hospitals & Workhouses within the City of Bristol, for the better employing of the Poor thereof'. The Corporation of the Poor, consisting of the Lord Mayor, the aldermen and 48 guardians elected by the ratepaying citizens, were not merely given powers to erect workhouses but to compel the poor to enter them as a condition of receiving relief. From the workhouse, children were to be bound apprentice at 16 (instead of the more general age of 14) for a period of seven years.

Immediately after the Act was passed, the Corporation turned its energies to establishing, at a cost of £500, a workhouse to accommodate 100 girls of from six to sixteen years of age. A Master was appointed to be in charge of the work and to act as accountant. A Mistress was to be in charge of the household. And in addition, there were to be a 'Tutress' to teach spinning and a schoolmistress to teach them to read – though not to write. On reception, the girls were given a bath and clean clothing 'which, together with wholesome Dyet at set hours, and good Beds to lye on [some sleeping two and some four to a bed] so incouraged the children that they willingly betook themselves to their work'. The main difficulty with which the Committee had to deal apparently, was not the recalcitrance of the children but the resentment of their parents at being deprived of such money as their daughters might have contributed to the family income had they remained at home. '. . . We appointed them [the girls] set hours for working, eating and playing; and gave them leave to walk on the Hills with their Tutress, when their work was over, and the weather fair; by which means we won them into Civility & a love of their labour. But we had a great deal of trouble with their Parents, & those who formerly kept them, who having lost the sweetness of their Pay, did all they could to set both the Children and others against us ...' The girls worked ten and a half hours in summer and an hour less in winter. After initial difficulties in discovering the right kind of yarn to be spun for the greatest reward, the value of the girl's labour amounted to nearly £6 a week 'and would have been more, but that our biggest Girls we either settle forth, or put in the Kitchen: and those we receive being generally small, are able to do little for some time'.[1]

As a result of these encouraging beginnings, the Corporation decided to start another workhouse for remaining categories of the poor: the aged and impotent, boys and very young children. This House they named 'the Mint'. In the early days of the Mint, it seems that not only did the Corporation of the Poor bring into the House all children of families receiving relief, but also kept in the House, under the care of nurses, the very youngest children. Within a few years, however, the custom changed and the very young were either put out to nurse or allowed to remain in the care of their own parents who were given an allowance to bring them up. The boys were kept quite apart from the old people and given a special uniform of blue coat 'with tin buttons', a blue waistcoat 'with Clasps', white breeches, blue stockings and blue cap. From October to March, they rose at six o'clock 'that their faces and hands be washed & their heads combed & that they go to work at seven'. Between seven and nine, they worked, breaking off at nine for prayers, breakfast and play. From ten until noon, they worked again, then had an hour for dinner and more play, after which they worked solidly from one until seven o'clock. From seven until nine in the evening was allocated to prayers, supper and play and at nine they went to bed. In summer, the children rose at five and an extra hour of work was inserted at the end of the morning. If this seems a rather grim daily round for the young, it was certainly no worse than children of a later generation were to sustain in the factories and in fact compared very favourably in its regular provision for play with many contemporary schools.

[1] John Cary, *An Account of the Proceedings of the Corporation of Bristol in Execution of the Act of Parliament for the better Employing and Maintaining of the Poor of that City.* 1700. p. 15.

'THE SUCCOURLESS POOR CHILD'

Children who misbehaved themselves or ran away were severely disciplined. John Webly, for example, who had been found guilty 'of great misdemeanours refuseing to follow his work & breaking out of the house severall times and very Ill language to the Officers and tutores' was ordered to be stripped to the waist and given 'nine strips with a birching rodd at the Whipping post by the Beadle' and afterwards to be kept in the workhouse 'place of Confinement' till the Committee ordered his release.[1]

If the discipline was severe, the food provided for the children was no small compensation. Monday's meal consisted of:

Breakfast: Broth thickened with oatmeal & six ounces of Bread.
Dinner: 1 pt of Green Beans. 1 oz Bacon, 2 horns of beer.
Supper: 1½ pts Milk porridge to be ½ milk.

Thursday's menu comprised:

Breakfast: 1¼ pts milk porridge
Dinner: ¼ lb beef, 4 ozs bread, 2 horns of beer, Garden stuff 3d for 20
Supper: Bread 1½ oz. and cheese and a horn of beer.[2]

As a result of their labours, the boys were said to bring in to the House over £6 a week at the same time as they were being educated in habits of industry.

Entranced by the success of the Bristol scheme, Cary urged the adoption of similar schemes throughout the kingdom: 'we are freed from Beggars, our old people are comfortably provided for; our Boys and Girls are educated to Sobriety, and brought up to delight in Labour; our young Children are well lookt after and not spoiled by the neglect of ill Nurses'. Cary's success fired the public imagination. Within two years of its inauguration, Tiverton, Exeter, Hereford, Colchester, Kingston and Shaftesbury all obtained private Acts to allow the incorporation of individual parishes to start similar schemes of workhouse provision themselves. Before the end of the next reign, King's Lynn, Sudbury, Plymouth, Gloucester, Worcester, and Norwich had followed suit.

---

[1] *Bristol Corporation for the Poor, selected records 1696–1834*, ed. A. Ruth Fry, 1935. p. 76.
[2] ibid., pp. 68–9.

'THE SUCCOURLESS POOR CHILD'

Parallel with the development of the large workhouses maintained by a group of incorporated parishes was the steady growth in the number of small workhouses built by individual parishes by the consent of the local Quarter Sessions. Such a one was built at Stroud in 1721, with the intention of housing within it the parish orphans, the aged, sick and impotent as well as poor widows and their children. Opened in the summer of 1722, the House took in about fifteen children who, until old enough to be apprenticed or put to service 'are employ'd in Spinning Jersey by a Person of the Parish, who twists and dies it, and then sells it for Stockings; and some can earn 2d. a day in Winter, and 3d. in the Summer. The Officers receive their Money, and provide everything they want. These Children us'd to be kept in Poor Families at 2s. per week, and bred up in the grossest Idleness and Vice! But now they are inur'd to Labour, and help to maintain themselves, earning at least their Diet. And by this Method, a great deal is sav'd to the Parish, and the Children themselves virtuously and christianly brought up and made fit for good Services . . .'[1]

The passing of the 1722 Poor Relief Act, whereby general permission was granted to the churchwardens and overseers of the poor in any parish, with the consent of the majority of the parishioners, to 'purchase or hire any house or houses in the same parish . . . for the lodging, keeping, maintaining and employing any or all such poor in their respective parishes . . . as shall desire to receive relief . . . from the same parish', was thus a mark of the importance of the workhouse movement throughout the country rather than a sign of its inauguration. After the Act, there was certainly a great increase in the number of workhouses, but the more important continued to be built under special Acts. The 1722 Act made special provision for two or more parishes to join together to build a common workhouse, and for such a union, the consent of the justices alone was necessary. But in the majority of cases, parishes do not seem to have availed themselves of this offer, the greater number of workhouses built under this Act being the property of separate parishes.

According to one account, the number of workhouses existing in the various counties of England in 1725 was about 129.[2]

---
[1] *An Account of Several Workhouses . . .*, 1725, p. 37.
[2] ibid., pp. 110–13.

'THE SUCCOURLESS POOR CHILD'

Some of them had been established primarily with a view to protecting the ratepayers, but this was not always either the only or the main reason. Some parishes were keener on keeping the poor in health and from worklessness, than on merely saving money. 'Give me leave to warn you', wrote one man from St. Albans, 'not to promise your selves too much from the produce of the Labour of the People [in the workhouse] . . . It must be considered, the Men and Women are generally old and helpless, and the children perfectly new and inexperienced in everything; so that if you keep them employed tho' the Produce be no more than what will pay for the Articles of Firing and Candles, . . . it is something not be be despised: And what is still of greater Consequence is, that by keeping them employed you keep them in Health and from Idleness, the Parent of most Disorders in Society . . .'[1]

An outstanding example of a parish workhouse which reflected this humanitarian concept of workhouse provision for the young was the Stroud workhouse to which we referred earlier. Founded largely on the basis of *Proposals* made to the parishioners by Caleb Parfect, the Minister of Stroud, the detailed Orders issued in November 1722, regarding the treatment of children in this particular workhouse are a revealing indication of local attitude to the poor child:[2]

'VII. That the Children spin Jersey and be moderately task'd; and if they are idle or do not their Tasks, or make great Waste, that they go sometimes without their Meals, and sometimes have corporal Punishment, at the discretion of the Master and Mistress

'XI. That each Child have every Day two hours to learn to read etc. at the Discretion of the Master and Mistress

'XV. That neither Children nor others, go abroad on Sundays, but continue together in the House, and read some portion of Holy Scripture, or a Chapter out of the *Whole Duty of Man*

'XIX. That all the Children appear then (on Sunday evening) before the Governors, to show the Condition of their Cloaths, and to be examined in the Progress they make in their Learning;

---

[1] ibid., p. 68.
[2] Caleb Parfect, *Proposals Made in the Year 1720, to the Parishioners of Stroud, near Rochester in Kent, for Building a Workhouse there* . . ., 1725. pp. 12–14.

that the Master and the Scholars may have their due Commendations, and the Benefactors all the Comfort they propose to themselves, by encouraging this Design.' A rule which makes it clear that this, like almost all the workhouses of this period, private benefactions as well as local poor-rates contributed to the support of the House.

The emphasis on the formal education of the children in the Stroud workhouse was one of its more remarkable features and was facilitated by the provision of a charity school which was attached to the workhouse. Elsewhere in Essex and Kent, Parfect noted in a brief survey of some of the other parish workhouses, that educational provisions for the workhouse children were rather poor.[1] Similarly, the food provided in the Stroud workhouse seems to have been of an exceptionally high standard; meat being provided for dinner every day of the week except Saturday.

Parfect was making a comparison between the conditions existing in the 1720s in various small parish workhouses in country districts. It is salutary to contrast the Stroud workhouse with one of the much larger ones supported by unions of parishes in urban areas such as the House at St. Giles, London, which belonged to the united parishes of St. Giles in the Fields and St. George's, Bloomsbury. The 'Family' of this House consisted of between 200 and 300 persons – old, lame, sick, lunatics, idiots, lying-in women, and young children – for whom 156 beds were provided, distributed through the workhouse's several wards. On the whole, it seems that the children were separated from the adults in a special 'Children's ward'; certainly there was a quite specific regulation requiring that children between the ages of three and five years should be kept to themselves in a special 'school'. Above the age of five, the children were set to spinning, knitting 'or such other Work as shall be thought most proper for the Benefit of the Parish' until they were of an age to be placed out as apprentices or put to service. In addition, the children between five and nine years of age were to have two half-hourly periods a day being taught to read; whilst those above nine years of age were to spend a similar amount of time learning to write and to cast accounts. It is noticeable that where the children were old enough to work, the time allocated for schooling was not

[1] ibid., pp. 22–4.

allowed to reduce working time: they were simply made to get up earlier in the morning![1]

The character of individual workhouses varied a good deal, and was inevitably influenced both by the motives which had prompted their establishment and by the size of the actual house. Prominent among the motives for the establishment of the St. Giles House was the desire to cut down the cost of the local poor rate. One citizen quoted the use of the workhouse to such an effect in Tring, Hertfordshire, where in four years the introduction of the workhouse as the principal means of obtaining assistance had reduced the rate from 3s. 6d. to 1s. 4d. in the pound. Additional advantages were also hoped for at St. Giles: 'all the poor children now kept at Parish Nurses, instead of being starved or misused by them, as is so much complained of, will be duly taken care of and be bred up to Labour and Industry, Virtue and Religion',[2] the 'Lazy-grown Poor' would be compelled to work, and the aged and infirm supported. Profit to the parish from the labour of the poor was also expected, but above all, the introduction of the workhouse into the united parishes was confidently expected to scare away the feckless and idle poor. Established from these very mixed motives, it is interesting to see which eventually dominated and what sort of régime it led to. The instruction to the Governor of the House gives an immediate clue: 'he is to maintain the poor [in the House] as cheap as may consist with reason'. Hence the monotony of the diet, in which some form of porridge appears seven times a week, bread and cheese every evening, and meat on Sundays, Tuesdays and Thursdays only for lunch. Hence also the very strict regulations regarding admission to the house: 'That no Person be admitted or received into the Workhouse, but by order of the Vestry . . . (or the Justices) . . . And if any Person offer themselves, or are sent by any others, they are not to be taken in, unless so ill, as they must probably perish if refused, or Women ready to fall into labour . . .'[3] The importance attached to keeping the local rate at a minimum by scaring people from asking for assistance which obliged entry into the House, undoubtedly resulted in

[1] See *Rules and Orders to be observed by the Officers and Servants in St. Giles Workhouse, and by the Poor therein*. (n.d., ? 1726.) pp. 7–11.
[2] *The Case of the Parish of St. Giles's in the Fields, as to their Poor, And a Workhouse designed to be built for employing them.* (n.d.) p. 3.
[3] *Rules and Orders . . .*, pp. 13,. 25 et seq.

'THE SUCCOURLESS POOR CHILD'

the internal discipline of the House being far more rigorous than was strictly necessary merely to maintain order in an admittedly large, residential institution. Inmates were not allowed out of the House without leave of the Governor: 'And if any desire to see or speak with any of the Poor, though their nearest Relation, the Door-keeper is not to call them without leave'; if any visitor were suspected of bringing in extra clothes, food or drink for one of the inmates, they were to be stopped and searched if necessary. Anyone causing trouble in the workhouse, risked being sent to 'the Dark-Room', or deprived of their meals, or stood on a stool in the corner of the work-room or expelled from the House and thus deprived of relief. Such was the character of at least one of the institutions in which young children were expected to learn the joy of work and the ways of Christian virtue. Small wonder that strange tales of sudden death, starvation and of children's corpses being smuggled out of the House at dead of night for the fell purposes of the 'Anatomists' began to circulate both by word of mouth and in crudely printed handbills![1]

The glowing account of the Stroud workhouse by the man who had largely been responsible for its establishment and the horrific rumours of the St. Giles workhouse, which lost nothing in the telling, represent two extremes of popular opinion about the practical operation of workhouse schemes and both undoubtedly contained their own modicum of truth. As regards children, if their diet was limited and monotonous it was probably no more so than that of children of the same class being fed in their own homes, and at least they were regularly fed: if the hours the children worked seem to us now inordinately long, there is no evidence to show that they compared unfavourably with hours of work which prevailed generally at that time and were almost certainly better for being organised within known limits. If the care of the children in some houses was organised on far less humanitarian lines than in others, it would still be difficult to argue that, left to the care of their own parents, or abandoned in the streets, or handed over to the doubtful care of parish nurses, their welfare would have been better catered for.

Nevertheless, the question still remains as to whether the high hopes of the workhouse advocates were fulfilled by the

[1] *The Workhouse Cruelty, Workhouses turn'd gaols, and gaolers executioners.* (n.d.), p. 1.

'THE SUCCOURLESS POOR CHILD'

establishment of these institutions on either a union or a parochial basis. Since these houses were the result of local enterprise, the quality and character of individual workhouses necessarily varied from place to place. It is interesting, however, to examine the experience of the Bristol workhouse, for which so much had been claimed at the turn of the century. As regards children, the original idea had been to train them to some profitable, and therefore skilled, occupation even though their inexperience might make this unprofitable to the workhouse. But very soon the desire for the ultimate benefit of the children was outweighed by the demand for immediate profit to the Corporation, who seem to have been unprepared for either the cost or the consequences of such a scheme as was originally envisaged. 'For as soon as any (of the children) came to do any thing tolerably well, that they might have been assisting the younger and less practised, they went off to Sea or were Apprenticed in the City; by which Means the Publick were so far benefitted, though the Corporation bore the Loss of the Charge of Teaching them, and of all the Tools with which they were to work, and of the materials for it. For they made nothing perfect, or Merchantable from their Work, but only spoiled the Materials. So that instead of lessening the Charge of Maintaining the Poor, they increased it . . .'[1], which aroused a good deal of local opposition. In 1701, therefore, there were already signs of the boys of the Mint being put to unskilled, but more immediately profitable employments, such as pin-making, instead of being taught weaving; and in 1711, one anonymous pamphlet alleged that all attempts to teach the boys a skilled trade had been laid aside 'and for some considerable Time there has been no Employment but Picking a little Oakum, which is scandalous Labour for Children, and which they only rob the Aged Poor of, in St. James and other out-Parishes: Nor can any Work be thought of hitherto for them by which we should not be the Loosers'.[2] This attack on the workhouse scheme, which at first sight may appear to be merely the exasperated reaction of a local ratepayer, gains support from the history of the Mint in the years immediately following, for in 1714 the Corporation had not

[1] *An Account of Several Workhouses . . .*, 2nd edn. 1732. p. 132.
[2] *Some Considerations Offer'd to the Citizens of Bristol, Relating to the Corporation for the Poor in the said City.* 1711. p. 2.

only spent its annual income, exhausted all their benefactions and borrowed several thousand pounds from the City of Bristol, it had to seek parliamentary sanction to levy a tax of £3,500 a year on the citizens to make their losses good. After this financial disaster, the Corporation only very intermittently attempted to put the children to skilled labour, in fact there appear to have been periods when they were not put to any work at all. At one juncture, in 1730, a local dealer in malt and corn undertook to give between 50 and 60 of the boys employment in weaving and making up sacks for his corn. He himself employed a masterworkman to teach them and the work was done not in the workhouse but in the merchant's shed by the river. The arrangement was that the merchant should have all the benefit of the boys' labour, apart from giving them each a small gratuity; the sole advantage to the Corporation being that it gave the boys something with which to occupy their time instead of leading 'an idle and profligate life' in the House.

This in itself is a revealing side-light on the virtues of the Mint as a place where children were trained up in not merely industrious but virtuous habits. The anonymous pamphlet from which we have already quoted,[1] contains some astringent remarks on the quality of the education, apart from industrial training, of the Mint's younger inhabitants. According to its author there were, in 1711, 55 children at that time being taught in the House, 'which should make them sought after by tradesmen and artificers as apprentices, but 'tis quite the Reverse; very rarely any honest industrious Man desiring any of the Family. Indeed a great many have been placed out to poor Weavers, or other poor Tradesmen',[2] who only took them for a premium. Some went to sea, but this, he argues, was only possible because the law obliged masters of ships to accept such children. From the actual records of the Mint, it is quite clear that the education given to the children was constantly of a low standard, economy outweighing efficiency in the selection of the teachers. An entry in the records of 1753 implies that, for a time at least, economy had overridden one of Cary's most advertised plans for the workhouse – that the children should be instructed in the principles of religion: 'A MOTION having been made and agreed on That Prayers and the Common Service may be of great Use to assist

[1] ibid., p. 59. [2] ibid., p. 5.

'THE SUCCOURLESS POOR CHILD'

the Minds of our Family, who are too much prone to a loose and profligate Behaviour, and that Care be likewise taken in the proper Educating and instructing the Children. RESOLVED That 'tis the Opinion of the Court, That a Regulation be attempted at as easy an Expence as possible, under the Conduct of the Governor, Deputy Governor and Committee, who are requested to put the same into Execution'.[1]

In effect, what the Bristol workhouse records amply demonstrate is the wisdom of the man from St. Albans who cautioned against hoping that the establishment of a workhouse would not merely be a protection but a profit to the local ratepayers in that the value of the children's labour would be sufficient for their support. Despite the euphoric descriptions of the Bristol scheme, it had never been self-supporting and continually relied, as did many other workhouses, on the generosity of benefactors. When the real cost of putting Cary's original scheme into effect was fully appreciated, the immediate reaction of those responsible for the running of the House as well as those who had hoped for substantial economies from its establishment, was to reduce the quality of the training and services it provided.

Since workhouse conditions varied so widely, both as between town and country and within either category, it would be foolish to attempt to generalise from the experience of this one workhouse, yet it is perfectly clear that the criticisms we have seen levelled against the Bristol workhouse could be, and indeed were throughout the eighteenth century, levelled against many more. In 1776, a 'Kentishman' observed of the Canterbury workhouse that the children there 'were not so industrious as those bred outside, not so suitable for servants . . . They are totally ignorant of every domestic business . . .'[2] In the previous year, R. Potter, in *Observations on the Poor Laws, on the Present State of the Poor, and on Houses of Industry*, refers to parish workhouses as 'those filthy nurseries of shameless and abandoned vice'. He describes the children reared in them as 'for want of necessary food and covering . . . emaciated, dispirited, and unfit for any work; for want of instruction . . . ignorant of all goodness; and the evil practices, in which they are early initiated, harden them

---

[1] *Bristol Corporation for the Poor, selected records . . .*, p. 104.
[2] *Thoughts on the Present State of the Poor, and the Intended Bill for their better Relief and Employment.* 1776. p. 43.

'THE SUCCOURLESS POOR CHILD'

to vice' with the result that the local farmers are unwilling to take children from the parish poor houses.[1] Elsewhere, Edmund Gillingwater, a workhouse reformer and an overseer of the poor at Harleston, Norfolk, speaks of 'the great neglect of educating the children' in the workhouses, and argues that 'the result of this neglect will be that children of exceptional natural intelligence will become exceptionally vicious since there is no other outlet for their talents'.[2]

In all probability, since the merits of educating the working classes was a matter much disputed at this time even by some social reformers themselves, the neglect of the education of children in the workhouses was to be expected where there was no local enthusiast like Caleb Parfect. How far idleness as well as ignorance was permitted in the workhouses seems a much more debatable matter. When the House of Commons appointed a Committee to enquire into this and other matters relating to workhouse management in the early 1770s, quite a number of parishes neglected to enter on the schedules they were required to return to the Committee any details of children's employment. This was particularly the case with the schedules relating to the London Parishes and Bills of Mortality. In some cases, this neglect was no doubt due to the fact that the rewards for such work were so small, and benefited the parish so little, that it was not thought of sufficient importance to refer to it other than that 'the masters take the earnings'. In other cases 'no employment' is entered regarding the children in the house, as in the case of St. Anne's, Aldersgate, which explained that 'the poor are aged and infants and therefore not employed in anything'. Most workhouses, however, did record their children as being employed, mostly on unskilled tasks such as spinning, knitting, sewing, pin-making and occasionally oakum picking. In some cases, where the children were hired out to a contractor (a growing practice because of the inability of the workhouse governors to make their institutions profitable), no indication of how they were employed is given.[3]

[1] R. Potter, op. cit., pp. 47–8.
[2] *An Essay on Parish Work-houses: Containing Observations on the Present State of English Workhouses: with some Regulations proposed for their Improvement.* 1786. pp. 5–6.
[3] See *First and Second reports from the Committee appointed to enquire how far the orders of the last Session, respecting the poor, have been complied with.* P.P. 1776. vol. IX, pp. 273, 275 and 277.

'THE SUCCOURLESS POOR CHILD'

These eighteenth-century accounts of the children's workhouse movement bear eloquent testimony to the deterioration in social attitudes towards the children of the poor since the sixteenth century. Elizabethan reformers had set out in a burst of generosity and idealism to end poverty by education and training. Great emphasis was laid on the raising up of children to become responsible citizens of the commonwealth. When these early hopes failed, the mid-seventeenth century produced the children's workhouses, where the emphasis was to be on work, with only a modicum of education. Here too, the original ideal of giving children some kind of skill was soon abandoned in favour of the principle of using the labour of the children of the poor in any kind of unskilled work to reduce the poor rates. And when this could not be achieved because their earnings were so small, children were left untrained and in idleness in the interests of 'economy'. From the end of the seventeeth century onwards economy in relation to the children of the poor became the dominant idea in the minds of most administrators, and persisted until the early nineteenth century, when it was seen at its worst in connection with the principle of 'less eligibility'.

3. *Workhouse Innocents*

Although economy, training and education had been the principal arguments in favour of the establishment of workhouses for children, it had also been believed that, by giving shelter, regular food and some medical attention, the workhouse child would also benefit in health. This was either argued by reference to the general condition of poor children outside the house or, alternatively, by reference to poor children put out by the parish to nurse. The possiblity of a parish boarding out children with a nurse had first been mentioned in the Poor Law Act of 1536, and had been provided for in the subsequent legislation of Elizabeth's reign. It had been practised in the second half of the sixteenth century and throughout the seventeenth and continued to be used as a means of relief for orphans and illegitimate children who became a charge on the parish in the eighteenth century, even where, as in Bristol, there was a local workhouse – although here, as in some other instances, the children were often brought into the workhouse when they were three or four.

'THE SUCCOURLESS POOR CHILD'

Despite the generous terms envisaged in the *Ease for Overseers* and despite the fact that there is evidence to show that some justices undoubtedly tried to force the parishes to administer the law in the light of Elizabethan idealism, the boarding-out system had never been very satisfactory from a number of points of view. Time and again there had been complaints from foster-parents that the money allowed them for the care of the children in their charge had not been regularly paid to them. Thus, in 1611, Anne Leiftwicke petitioned the justices of the Cheshire Quarter Sessions complaining that, although the local minister, churchwardens and collectors of the poor of Nantwich had agreed to allow her 2s. a week for each of three pauper orphans they boarded with her, the allowance had not been paid in full, since the parish authorities could not get the money from the local inhabitants. In the circumstances, she asked the justices either to see that she was paid according to the terms of the original bargain 'or else that the children may be taken from her, she herself being a poor woman and having three children of her own'.[1] In other cases, even where the payment to the foster-parents was at least regular, it was said to be inadequate, leading to the malnutrition and death of numbers of children throughout the country. The breakdown of the effective supervision of the poor law administration in the second half of the seventeenth century was to influence the boarding-out system as it did all other aspects of poor relief, as the irregularity of payments to the foster-parents shows. Hence, in the eighteenth century, at a time when English society was experiencing a rapid increase of population for whom provision had to be made, the hazards of hand-rearing were exacerbated by the growth of a large class of unskilled nurses who made a livelihood by receiving such children and who frequently sacrificed the welfare of their charges for their own financial gain.

Writing in 1768, Fielding deplored the small sums given by parish officers to the nurses, especially the nurses of very young children under two years of age which 'occasions the Loss of an amazing Number of his Majesty's Subjects yearly',[2] and suggested that a fixed weekly allowance of 2s. 6d. instead of the

[1] *Cheshire Quarter Sessions Records*, ed. Bennett and Dewhurst. vol. I. 1940. pp. 71-2.
[2] John Fielding, *Extracts from such of the penal laws as particularly relate the the peace and order of the Metropolis, etc.* 1768 edn. p. 415.

'THE SUCCOURLESS POOR CHILD'

1s. 6d. then generally allowed should be required by statute. Fielding's plan, had it been adopted, would have had the additional advantage of placing a premium on the nurse's keeping the children in her care alive, instead of giving a bonus on their early death as was all too often the case in those parishes where, instead of a weekly or quarterly payment, a lump sum was given to the nurses to discharge the parish of any further liability for the children – a sum often quickly spent or misused. Basically, a great many of the scandals of the boarding-out system, which were increasingly advertised during the eighteenth century, arose because the parishes had neither the duty nor in many cases the inclination to scrutinise the characters of the nurses or the quality of the provision the nurses made for the children entrusted by the parish to their care. When one remembers how inadequate was the contemporary understanding of infant and child management, it is obvious that some of the hazards to infant life which the boarding-out system entailed, were inescapable and not necessarily confined to poor children put out to nurse. On the other hand, at a time when a high death-rate among infants caused no surprise, it is equally clear that the poverty of the parish nurses was in many cases an incentive to culpable neglect.

We have seen that, when the idea of a union workhouse for the parishes of St. Giles and St. George's, Bloomsbury was being canvassed, the advantage of an alternative to boarding out children with nurses was one of the specific arguments presented in favour of the workhouse. It was not, as it happens, an argument which would have found much favour in the eyes of a later workhouse reformer, Jonas Hanway, whose investigation of the infant mortality of London workhouses between 1757 and 1763 led him to call this very workhouse 'the greatest sink of mortality in these kingdoms'[1] and to aver: 'Parish Officers may amuse themselves till Dooms-day, but to attempt to nourish an Infant in a Workhouse, where a Number of Adults are congregated, or where a Number of Nurses are assembled in one Room, and consequently the Air becomes putrid, be these nurses ever such proper Persons, I will pronounce, from the most intimate

---

[1] Jonas Hanway, *Serious Considerations on the Salutary Design of the Act of Parliament for a regular, uniform Register of the Parish-Poor in all the Parishes within the Bills of Mortality.* 1762. p. 10.

'THE SUCCOURLESS POOR CHILD'

Knowledge of the Subject, is but a small remove from Slaughter, for the Child must die . . .'

At St. Giles, of 122 children aged under three years admitted to the house during 1765, 40 per cent. (53) had died after about one month and a further 40 per cent. (54) had been discharged to their mothers at the end of a similar period. In the workhouse of St. George's, Middlesex, where nineteen children under three years of age had been admitted that same year, twelve had died within fifty days, four within nine months and three had been taken out of the House. 'There is *no wonder* in this', wrote Hanway, 'when it is considered, that these children were put into the hands of indigent, filthy or decrepit women, three or four to one woman, and sometimes sleeping with them. The allowance to these women being scanty, they are tempted to take part of the bread and milk intended for the poor infants. The child cries for *food*, and the nurse beats it *because* it cries. Thus with *blows*, *starving* and *putrid air*, with the aditions of *lice, itch, filthiness*, he soon receives his *quietus.*'[1]

Hanway's particular interest in infant mortality prevailing in London workhouses stemmed from his association with the Foundling Hospital, which had been opened in 1741 for destitute children, and which, for its time had a remarkably low death rate among its young children.

The circumstances of the foundation of the Foundling Hospital are an illuminating contrast to those in which Christ's Hospital was founded two hundred years before. Whereas the earlier foundation was the generous expression of the acceptance of community support for the deprived child, the Foundling Hospital was the result of the dedicated work of a group of private benefactors made effective by the zealous enthusiasm of one man in particular, Thomas Coram, who was forced to work for many years not merely against apathy but open hostility. From as far back as 1687,[2] there had been occasional expressions of concern for the welfare of the large numbers of very young

---

[1] Hanway, *An Earnest Appeal for Mercy to the Children of the Poor*. 1766. pp. 41–3.

[2] A Scheme for the Foundation of a Royal Hospital and Raising a Revenue of five or six-thousand Pounds a Year, by, and for the Maintenance of a Corporation of Skilful Midwives, and such Foundlings, or exposed Children, as shall be admitted therein. As it was proposed and addressed to his Majesty King James II. By Mrs. Elizabeth Cellier, in the Month of June 1687. Reprinted in the *Harleian Miscellany*, vol. IV (1745), pp. 136–40.

children found abandoned in the streets of London – a sad commentary on the ineffective use to which the existing poor laws were put. More particularly, attention had been drawn to the fate of unknown numbers of illegitimate children exposed to die or abandoned on the city's streets or actually done away with by their mothers for fear of shame or inability to support them. In July 1713, Addison was moved to write to the *Guardian* deploring the absence in England of 'a Piece of Charity which has not been yet exerted among us, and which deserves our Attention the more ... because it is practised by most of the Nations about us. I mean a Provision for Foundlings, or for those Children who for want of such a Provision are exposed to the Barbarity of cruel and unnatural Parents. One does not know how to speak on such a Subject without Horror. But what Multitudes of Infants have been made away by those that brought them into the World, and were afterwards either ashamed or unable to provide for them!'[1] At a time of mounting enthusiasm for schemes in which the poor were increasingly expected to contribute to their own support rather than look to public maintenance and when sexual misconduct, particularly among the poor, was increasingly condemned, the nature of the opposition to such a 'Provision' as Addison had in mind was predictable. Not only was it alleged that the very existence of a Foundling Hospital in London would encourage the parish officers to escape their duties and the poorer classes to shelve their responsibilities but also that 'in a Protestant Country like BRITAIN, where the Poor are so amply provided for' it would reflect 'dishonour, not only upon the State, but upon the whole community, as it tacitly implies, either a Want of Wholesome Laws, or a Want in the due execution of them. – A Foundling ... reflects the highest disgrace on Human Nature, and supposes a depravity in the Morals, and a degeneracy in the Affections of Rational Beings; such as sinks their characters *much* beneath the characters of Brutes; and to incourage such Depravity, must not only be offensive to God whose Image we bear, but destructive of all Social Order and Concord.'[2]

Undeterred, Thomas Coram, soliciting his cause 'with as much

---

[1] *Guardian*, no. CV.
[2] David Stansfield alias C. A., *A Rejoinder to Mr. Hanway's Reply to C. A.'s Candid Remarks*. 1760. p. 36.

ardour and anxiety as if every deserted child had been his own, and the cause of the unfounded Hospital that of his own family', began his agitation for it on his retirement from the sea in 1719. Long before the status of a legal charity had been granted to the project, Coram canvassed promises of benefactions against the day on which the desired Charter of Incorporation should be granted. To hasten this necessary step, he proceeded to organise several petitions to the Crown: the first signed by twenty-one 'Ladies of Quality and Distinction'; the second by 'Noblemen and Gentlemen' (which included Lord Derby and 51 others); and a third signed by many justices residing in and near London, as well as 'other Persons of Distinction'. Only after all these had been presented did Coram judge the time ripe to present his personal petition on 20 November 1739, as a result of which a Charter was finally granted for the establishment of a charitable foundling hospital in London. Thus, after nineteen years of persuasion, agitation and public debate, Coram's dream of establishing in England a Hospital similar to those already existing in Paris, Madrid, Lisbon, Rome and many other large towns in Europe for children abandoned by their parents, 'dropt in Church Yards or in the Streets, or left by Night at the Doors of Church Wardens, or Overseers of the Poor',[1] sometimes found more dead than alive, was made possible.

Coram's own explanation of this protracted and circuitous method of petitioning the Crown for a Charter reveals very clearly how little public support there was in the eighteenth century for a scheme which in many ways was to take up the work for which Christ's Hospital had partly been intended and which it had long since ceased to perform. There was no eighteenth-century counterpart of Nicholas Ridley to facilitate negotiation, for example, and 'without that round about way (of a number of petitions) I found it impossible to be done, for I could no more prevail on an Archbishop or Bishop or Nobleman Britain, or Foreigner or any Great Man, I tryed them all, to speake to the late King or his present Majesty on this affair than I could have prevailed with any of them, If I had tryed it, such was the unchristian shyness of all about the Court.'[2]

[1] *A Memorial concerning the Erecting in the City of London or the Suburbs thereof an Orphanotrophy or Hospital for the Reception of Poor Cast-Off Children or Foundlings:* ... Anon. *c.* 1728.

[2] *The History of the Foundling Hospital,* R. H. Nichols and E. A. Wray. 1935. p. 19.

'THE SUCCOURLESS POOR CHILD'

By 1756, however, the Governors of the Foundling Hospital found their resources inadequate to meet the demands of their work and presented a petition to the House of Commons asking that their Hospital, like similar institutions on the Continent, might have Government support. After a certain amount of delay, money was granted on the condition, *inter alia*, that the Hospital, contrary to its previous practice, admit indiscriminately all infants brought to it, whatever their physical condition.[1] From June 1756 to Lady Day 1760 this was in fact done, with the result that the death rate of infants in the Hospital's care rose markedly and the Hospital, besieged by children brought up from far outside London, as earlier Christ's Hospital had similarly been besieged, had to reorganise the basis of admission and relinquish the Government grant.

Hanway, himself a Governor of the Hospital, had been convinced by this experience that the Foundling Hospital could not be a substitute for parish care of poor children and therefore tried to get parish officers to do their statutory duty more efficiently. Between 1757 and 1763, Hanway visited every workhouse in London, collecting and publishing facts and figures concerning death rates among infants with the avowed object of shaming particular parishes and of encouraging a beneficial rivalry between workhouses in this particular aspect of their work. Hanway's figures, even on his own admission, were 'so melancholy that they were generally disbelieved'. Between 1750 and 1755, according to his information, all the 53 children under three years of age who had either been born or received in the workhouse at St. Luke's, Middlesex, had died. In the Union workhouse of St. Giles, 169 out of 415 children of the same age had died; 158 of the 312 children in the St. Martin in the Fields workhouse; and 137 of the 288 children in the workhouse of St. George's, Hanover Square, 'one of the best' Houses had also died. These figures become even more appalling when one notices that in all except St. Luke's workhouse, where none escaped at all, the infant death rate is masked by the withdrawal of substantial numbers of babies a few days or weeks after their birth in the House. When these withdrawals are added to the deaths of

---

[1] Previously, the Hospital had only accepted children under two years of age who, when examined by the Hospital's doctor, were declared free from contagion and disease.

infants, the numbers remaining alive in the St. Giles workhouse was 18; in the St. George's workhouse, 36; and in the House of the parish of St. Martin in the Fields, only 7.[1]

Although some might have had their doubts concerning the accuracy of Hanway's figures, their publication aroused a considerable amount of public interest and concern, Some parishes had made it difficult for Hanway to get anything like precise figures of the deaths of children in their workhouses, an obstructiveness which only added to the force of his appeal for parliamentary intervention to protect the lives of these innocent victims not merely of poverty but of the poor laws themselves. So successful was Hanway's campaign that, in 1762, an Act was passed by Parliament 'for the keeping regular, uniform and annual registers, of all parish poor infants under a certain age' within London and the Bills of Mortality.[2] 'Whereas the keeping regular, uniform and annual registers, of all parish poor infants under four years of age, within the bills of mortality, may be a means of preserving the lives of such infants', ran the Preamble to the Act, by July 1762, a register was to be kept in every parish within the Bills, of all infants under four years of age in the workhouse (where there was one), in any hospital in the parish, and of all children boarded out by the parish officers. Infants becoming a charge on the parish before they had been baptised, were to be baptised within fourteen days and their name and surname to be entered in the register 'and in case of a difficulty of distinguishing children, some proper mark shall be affixed to the child's cloaths, or hung round his or her neck'. A copy of the register was to be laid before the vestry every month 'And yearly delivered to the company of parish clerks, and be printed and six copies delivered to each parish'. Parishes which had established a workhouse for their poor had a slightly different schedule to complete from the parishes which had not done so. Parishes with a workhouse had to record information on:

1. Name
2. Age
3. Date of birth if in the House or of admission to the House
4. Name of the person by whom sent
5. If died or discharged, date

[1] Hanway, *An Earnest Appeal* . . ., p. 68.
[2] 2 Geo. III, c. 22.

'THE SUCCOURLESS POOR CHILD'

6. If removed or passed, to what place
7. When delivered to Father, Mother or other person
or
8. If put to nurse, name of nurse, place of residence, charges and date of removal.

Parishes without a workhouse had to return information on all save 3, 4 and 5. In addition they had to record, when a child was received into the parish's care, the name of the person by whom the child was received on the parish's account.

The penalty on churchwardens who failed to return the required information was to be 40s. payable to the informer. Compared with the very stringent regulations surrounding the acceptance and care of young children by the local authorities of our own day, the requirements of this piece of legislation were modest indeed. Even so, it did not pass without some opposition. 'Some persons of great note objected to it, as a thing unnecessary, presuming the duty to be already done; and that either there were no such evils existing as the act supposed, or, that it could not be a means to remedy them.' And although Hanway tells us that 'the common people called it an act for keeping children alive', since no particular authority was made responsible for supervising its execution, its implementation was very variable. This neither surprised nor daunted Hanway: 'it is true, that in our constitution every Member of the Legislature is supposed to observe what is passing in the world the same as other private men. But if an act is not of a nature to affect the revenue, nor concerns any private interest or convenience: if it creates no new office, nor affords occasion for any parade in the executive part of the law, there is room to suspect it will become a dead letter ... Nevertheless,' as Hanway shrewdly observed, '... to have attempted much in the compulsive strain, after so many years of relaxation of discipline might have failed ...'[1] His hope was that the willingness of some parishes to operate the Act would stimulate others to do so and, more especially, that the evidence of prevailing rates of infant mortality which might be collected by even an indifferent observation of the Act within the Bills of Mortality would prove an effective stimulus to greater parliamentary concern in this matter. How far Hanway's first aspiration was justified is far from clear, but he certainly left

[1] Hanway, *Letters*, vol. I, pp. 96, 101, 102-3, 110.

'THE SUCCOURLESS POOR CHILD'

no stone unturned to ensure the realisation of the second, since he deliberately used such registers as he could to further his campaign for infant life protection and in 1763, in an *Open Letter* to the vestries, exhorted them all to take care in their keeping of registers, the better to arm himself with statistical ammunition. That some parish officers continued to be reticent and that others should prefer to give out-relief to mothers in their own homes and thereby reduce the numbers of young children in their workhouse who might possibly swell the registers of the dead, was hardly surprising in view of the publicity given to comparative infant mortality statistics of the London workhouse by Hanway's campaign. It was generally considered, wrote Hanway, that even 'the best regulated parishes' did not preserve more than 47 per cent of their poor infants. Kindly disposed parish officers themselves realised that *'poor houses, or workhouses,* are in general *slaughter houses* to infants',[1] he asserted, and proceeded to illustrate his contention with detailed reference to the register of St. George's, Middlesex, where out of nineteen children under three years of age admitted to the workhouse during the year 1765–6, twelve died within 50 days; four died within nine months; and three were taken out. The St. Giles workhouse was supposed by its promoters to be so much a better way of providing for the care of small children than boarding them out with nurses: the statistics of infant mortality in the House for the year 1765 certainly do nothing to justify its sponsors' high hopes.[2]

1765	Died after about 1 month	53
	Discharged to mother after about 1 mo.	54
	Living	14
	Received at end of yr.	12
		133

Even if we allow for any exaggeration of the infant mortality prevailing in the London workhouses that Hanway's selection of his statistics may have introduced, either by his enthusiasm for his own cause or by the very inadequacy of the registers, it remains only too apparent that to choose to rear small children in the workhouse rather than to board them out was, in the eigh-

[1] *An Earnest Appeal* . . ., pp. 6 and 20.
[2] ibid., pp. 45–7.

'THE SUCCOURLESS POOR CHILD'

teenth century, to choose between two evils. Hanway chose the latter.

Having adduced the statistics of infant mortality in the St. Giles workhouse, he compared them with the experience of another vestry, St. Mary's, Whitechapel, where infants were boarded out at 2s. 6d. a week with a Mrs. Howe. Only two out of eighteen had died in the year 1764–5. 'One may see what wonderful things *may* be done by the regular payment of 2s. 6d. per week for children', he writes, although fully aware that such success was far from inevitable.[1] In contrast, of 23 children boarded with a Mrs. Poole by the vestry of St. Clement Dane for 2s. a week, 2 had been discharged, 3 remained alive at the end of the year and 18 died after 'a month or so'. In Hanway's judgement, the key to a successful boarding-out system was the careful choice of nurses by the parish officers (the Foundling Hospital, which had organised an extensive boarding-out system, had a strict rule that any nurse who had buried two children, was never to be allowed to imperil the life of a third) and also the regular inspection of children out at nurse by some responsible person or persons. This also the Foundling Hospital Governors had organised with marked success, and Hanway saw no reason why it should not be organised equally successfully for parish children.

Since Hanway's immediate interest was in the welfare of the infant poor of London, he adds a rider to his general advocacy of boarding out. The parish officers should board the children out some considerable distance from London, since they must know from their own experience that the villages around London were no more favourable places in which to rear children than London itself. Hanway's own evidence for this was that in some villages near to London, Edmonton, Kensington, Knightsbridge, Bow and Camberwell, over 80 per cent of children sent there by parishes between 1762 and 1767 had died as compared with an infant death rate of 30 to 40 per cent over the same period among children sent by the Foundling Hospital to villages forty miles away or more from London.[2] The advantage to the children was not however, merely to be measured in terms of physical well-

[1] ibid., p. 51.
[2] Hanway, *Letters to the Guardians of the Infant Poor; and to the Governors and Overseers of the Parish Poor.* 1767. pp. 65 and 76–8.

'THE SUCCOURLESS POOR CHILD'

being: children boarded at such a distance were less likely to be visited by parents, whose influence, since Hanway believed that only the very distressed among good parents would consent to give up their children in this way, would have been almost necessarily bad.

Even as Hanway, reinvigorated by the 1762 Act, was increasing the pressure of his campaign on behalf of the 'workhouse innocents', the parish of St. James, Westminster, was reorganising its administration of parish poor relief on what were hoped would be more efficient lines.[1] In 1763, 21 'gents' of the parish were appointed, with the churchwardens and overseers, who were corporately to be known as 'the Governors and Directors of the Poor'. Their very first attention was directed to the children 'who were mouldering away in the Workhouse, or with profligate and drunken Parents'. The regulations which the Governors and Directors laid down for the future relief of pauper children were very much on the lines which, five years later, Hanway advocated for all the London parishes. They also illustrate, by comparison with the evidence from other parishes we have quoted, how very variable the quality of parochial care for children was at this time, not merely from one part of the country to another, but from one London parish to another. In future, it was decided, the parish children should be billeted with carefully selected cottagers on Wimbledon Common. A nurse was to be allowed 3s. 0d. a week for each of the five or six children who were entrusted to her; and a local surgeon or apothecary was charged with the responsibility of attending to the children's health. To make sure that the children's health did in fact receive far more than the purely formal attention it received elsewhere, very particular directions were made for a nurse to be paid a bonus for any special contribution she herself made to the welfare and good health of any of her charges. Hence, she would be paid a guinea if a sick child recovered, or if a child under twelve months survived beyond its first birthday. For each child inoculated against smallpox, 10s. 6d. was paid to the nurse (and also the surgeon) if it survived; 5s. 0d. was to be given to a nurse for each child surviving whooping-cough or

---

[1] See *Sketch of the State of the Children of the Poor in the Year 1756 and of the present state and management of all the Poor in the Parish of St. James, Westminster, in January 1797*, pp. 2–8.

'THE SUCCOURLESS POOR CHILD'

measles; and extra expenses could be recouped, with a gratuity, where children had been successfully nursed through other kinds of illness. On the other hand, 'if two Children die with any Nurse in a Year, she is to be discontinued, as it seems to imply want of skill or attention, or both'. The Governors' anxiety to keep their charges alive was paralleled by an equal anxiety to keep them out of the workhouse for as long as the ratepayers would allow. Instead of bringing the children into their workhouse at three or four, they kept them out at Wimbledon Common until they were six or seven, and longer if they were at all sickly. During this time the Governors paid 3d. a child to a mistress who was to teach reading and sewing to any child old enough to walk to her school. At seven, however, the ratepayers insisted that the children should be brought to the parish workhouse, since it was less expensive to maintain them there than in the country.

The provision for the rearing of the poor children of St. James, Westminster, was a practical demonstration of what could be done. It was Hanway's belief that something similar should be done by all the London vestries. In 1766, a Parliamentary Committee was appointed 'to enquire into what was in fact being done for Parish Poor Infants under fourteen years of age within the Bills of Mortality with instructions to report from time to time to the House of Commons'. To this Committee were referred the *Abstracts of the Registers of the Parish Poor of and under four years of Age, from the 1st Day of July 1762 to the 31st Day of December 1765*. As regards the standard of care of the younger children in the workhouses, the Committee's report was substantially a vindication of Hanway's campaign for their protection. 'Taking Children born in workhouses, or received of and under 12 months in the year 1763, & following the same into 1764 and 1765, only 7 in a hundred appear to have survived this short period.'[1] Most of the children were kept either in the workhouse or nursed in the town, and not sent into the country and the boarding-out fee to the nurses, which in some cases appear to have started as high as 3s.0d. a week, got reduced over the years to 1s. 6d. and 1s. 0d. a week, 'an amount that cannot be presumed to be equal to the necessary Care of Infants'. The Committee also drew the attention of Parliament to the conduct of

[1] State Papers, *Journal of the House of Commons*, vol. XXXI, 1767, p. 248.

'THE SUCCOURLESS POOR CHILD'

parish nurses which, they claimed, had been criticised in Parliament as far back as 1715 and still called for proper regulation. The Committee therefore suggested that parish infants should be sent into the country to be nursed a number of miles from London itself; that parish officers should be required to give a minimum allowance to the nurses; that in each parish, a number of prominent citizens should be chosen as 'Guardians of the Parish Infant Poor' who would be responsible for inspecting the condition of children out at nurse; and that the parish officers should have the alternative of sending children to the Foundling Hospital (as Holborn had already started to do) and paying for them there, since it was not always easy for a parish to find suitable women to foster children. Parliament's response to their Committee's Report was to order that a Bill be introduced embodying these proposals and the result was *An Act for the better regulation of the parish poor children, of the several parishes therein mentioned, within the bills of mortality*,[1] – the first of a series of Acts of Parliament continuing to our own day, which seek to compel public authorities to provide adequately for the welfare of young children in their care.

The Act only related to children born in or received into workhouses of seventeen parishes outside the walls of London, twenty-three parishes in Middlesex and Surrey within the Bills of Mortality, ten parishes within the city and liberty of Westminster, and in the liberty of the Tower of London, but for these children, its regulations were very precise. Children under 6 years of age were to be sent into the country, 'not less than 3 miles off' to be boarded out there at the cost of their respective parishes. Children under two years, within fourteen days of their birth or reception into the House, were to be sent five miles into the country to be nursed. The weekly rates to be paid to the nurses until their charges were returned to the workhouse or put out as apprentices were set at not less than 2s. 6d. a week for children under six years of age and not less than 2s. a week for children above that age. In addition, the parishes were to pay every nurse at least 10s. for each child under nine months placed in her charge who was still alive and in good health after being in her care for a full twelve months 'as a reward for her pains and care taken in the nursing of such a child'.

[1] 7 Geo. III, c. 39,

'THE SUCCOURLESS POOR CHILD'

Furthermore, to 'guard against all dangerous consequences which may arise to the said children from false parsimony, negligence, inadvertency, or the annual charge of parish officers' the Act embodied the recommendation of the Committee concerning the election of Guardians of the parish poor children, 'five noblemen or gentlemen' or, failing these, five of 'the principal and most respectable inhabitants' of the parish. On them was to rest the statutory duty of inspecting the poor children out at nurse, scrutinising the registers, the books and accounts relating to the children, of reporting cases of neglect or maltreatment of the children to the vestry and the parish officers and, should these fail to take appropriate action in any case, of reporting the matter to one or two local justices of the peace, who would then rule in the matter. To guarantee the efficiency of the Guardians' supervision, they were to be summoned regularly every six weeks. The Act also provided that, where a parish found difficulty in boarding their poor children out with satisfactory nurses, they might arrange to board them in the Foundling Hospital, the charge for each child to be negotiated with the Hospital and to be honoured by the parish even if this meant the justices had to raise the money by distress and sale.

In 1778, reviewing the effectiveness of the Act, a Committee reported to the House of Commons that only in four parishes or unions had the Guardians met regularly; and that in some parishes, no Guardians had been appointed at all. They believed, nevertheless, that 'upon the whole, the said Act has produced very salutary effects in the preservation of the lives of great numbers of the Infant Parish Poor', even though they felt that the Act would have to be amended to make it more effectual.[1] Two years later, Hanway published in *The Citizen's Monitor* a comparison of pauper infant mortality figures before and after the passing of the Act and commented: 'And as to the advantage of the act of parliament respecting infants, which commenced in 1767, can there be any stronger evidence than this before us? – It still requires a vigilant inspection, that the lives of infants be not squandered ... The saving of forty-two and a half per cent infants under two years old, is an object of great importance, & not less of $53^{3/10}$ in 100 children past 2 years of age, viz. the

---

[1] Report from the Committe on the state of Parish Poor Children ... (within the Bills of Mortality), 1778. *B.P.P*, 1st series, vol. IX, p. 252.

difference of seven and a half and 4/5'.[1] In absolute figures, Hanway believed that the Act had saved the lives of 1,500 children annually, and there is no doubt that it did constitute a great contribution to the welfare of poor children in London. Like the earlier Act, however, its main deficiency was the absence of any provision for a central supervising agency; hence the variation in its use to which the Committee's report for 1778 refers, and regarding which Hanway had no illusions. In the course of the same article in *The Citizen's Monitor* in which he applauds the immediate effects of the Act, he also urges the necessity for 'vigilant inspection' of the nurses because of the number of children 'which the avarice of the nurse crowds into her hovel . . . This is an evil which happens much oftener near the town, than at a great distance; & although in general the number preserved in the country exceeds the most sanguine expectation of Parliament with regard to the 7th of his present Majesty; yet I am apprehensive, that the want of attention in this particular, hurries many an infant to his grave'.

If we have so far concentrated on the mortality of young children in the London workhouses, it is not because the children in workhouses in other parts of the country were not in similar need of protection, but merely because Hanway's campaign for the London children produced a far greater body of evidence concerning their welfare than exists for the welfare of workhouse children elsewhere. In 1776, a specially appointed House of Commons Committee[2] had produced tables of statistics relating to the death rates of children in workhouses throughout the country. Unfortunately these statistics are difficult to interpret for two principal reasons: they merely represent a crude death rate for children under eight years of age, not distinguishing between children under and above two years of age, with the result that infant mortality (even in the rather loose sense that Hanway used the term) is confused with child mortality. Moreover, although the numbers of children in particular workhouses is returned for each half-year for the years 1772–4, the number of deaths of children under eight years of age is merely recorded by a single figure for the entire year, although it is quite clear that the number of children in the Houses fluctuated over the

---

[1] *The Citizen's Monitor*, p. vii.
[2] *B.P.P.* 1st series, vol. IX, pp. 252–65, 266–71.

'THE SUCCOURLESS POOR CHILD'

twelve months. Far more important than the accuracy of the statistics, however, was the evident governmental interest in the high infant death rate of poor children throughout the country, and not in London alone, which these reports display. The previous year, the report of another Commons Committee which had been appointed 'to review & consider the several Laws relating to Vagrants; and also the several Houses of Correction'[1] had, among many other resolutions, advised the House of Commons 'that it is the opinion of this Committee, that such of the infant Poor under the age of four years, who have lost their parents or whose parents are unable to maintain them, and shall be willing to part with them, may by the direction of two or more of the . . . Guardians, be put out to nurse in that or some neighbouring parish until they shall be fit to receive instruction', when they should be sent to their local workhouse to be 'instructed in all necessary duties, & employed in such manner as shall be most suitable for their age & capacities'.[2] Over the age of four, the Committee were quite prepared for the children to be received into the workhouses immediately and maintained there until they could be put out as apprentices or as domestic servants. This was by no means the first time that a Commons Committee had expressed doubts concerning the wisdom of accepting children into the local workhouse indiscriminately. Both in 1735[3] and again in 1765,[4] Commons Committees on the operation of the poor laws of England and Wales had urged the desirability of providing 'in proper Places and under proper Regulations, in each County' separate institutions or 'Hospitals' for the care of poor children, foundlings, and the impotent and infirm poor, but their proposal was not embodied in either the abortive *Bill for the better Maintenance and Employment of Poor Children within that Part of Great Britain called England* (1751) nor in the equally abortive *Bill for the Relief and better Employment of the Poor, within that Part of Great Britain called England* (1765), both of which were more interested in the problem of workhouse economics than workhouse mortality. Even at the time when the second Bill was presented to Parliament, however, the importance of the latter problem had already been forced on to their

[1] *B.P.P.*, vol. 34.
[2] ibid., p. 7, Resolution I.
[3] See *Journals of the House of Commons*, 1735, vol. XXII, p. 483 et seq., 2 May.
[4] ibid., 22 January 1765, p. 38.

'THE SUCCOURLESS POOR CHILD'

attention and some limited action had already been set on foot, and it is of some importance to notice that the second of the two Reports presented to Parliament in 1776 on the rate of infant mortality prevailing in workhouses throughout the country was presented by Thomas Gilbert, the most famous eighteenth-century advocate of the workhouse system.

Gilbert's *Plan for the better Relief and Employment of the Poor; for Enforcing and amending the Law respecting the Houses of Correction, and Vagrants etc.*, published in 1781, in which he advocated easing the local poor rates by encouraging small parishes to unite to provide a workhouse, shows him to be anything but a blind workhouse enthusiast. Workhouses, he believed, ought to be reserved for the old and sickly; the able and willing should be hired out to work where this was possible; the idle and dissolute should be sent to the House of Correction; and children should be excluded from the workhouse altogether. 'I have long thought it a great defect in the Management of the common Workhouse; that all Descriptions of Poor Persons should be sent thither',[1] he wrote. Instead, 'the Infant Poor, in their tender Years, are to be placed out with Proper Persons, and under good Inspection, till they are of sufficient Age to be placed as Servants or Apprentices'. Gilbert's intention was that, as soon as any child was able to perform any small tasks, the 'Visitor', to whose appointment he attached a great importance, should see that they were properly employed in or near where they were boarded until they were fit to be placed out elsewhere 'some as Apprentices or Servants to Gentlemen, or to Persons in Trade or Husbandry: others may be sent to the Marine Society, or as Apprentices or Volunteers on Board of some of His Majesty's Ships of War'.

In the Poor Law Act of 1782[2], with which Gilbert's name has become so much associated, the original plan for children was very much vitiated by clause XXIX which, having stated that workhouses were only for the old, sick and the infirm, continued with the proviso, 'and except such Orphan Children as shall be sent thither by order of the Guardian or Guardians of the Poor with the Approbation of the Visitor; and except such Children as shall necessarily go with their mothers thither for Sustenance'.

---
[1] Gilbert, op. cit., pp. 6–7.
[2] 22 Geo. III, c. 83.

'THE SUCCOURLESS POOR CHILD'

Clause XXX goes on: 'And be it further enacted, that all infant children of tender years, and who, from accident or misfortune, shall become chargeable to the parish or place to which they belong, may either be sent to the poor house as aforesaid, or be placed by the guardian or guardians of the poor with the approbation of the Visitor, with some reputable person or persons . . .'. Gilbert's recommendation that a 'Visitor' should be responsible for inspecting the children boarded out was conspicuously dropped, despite the fact that he had believed that his precautions for the welfare of the parish children 'were not so ample and complete as I wish to see them'.

Disappointed though Gilbert may have been not to have achieved his object in excluding children from the workhouses in which he had otherwise such faith as a means of poor relief, it would have been even more surprising had his original plan been fully embodied in legislation. Even on his own showing, the main advantage of the workhouse over older systems of poor relief was that it was a better solution to the pressing problem of 'the grievous burden of the poor rate'. Such parishes as chose to establish a workhouse under Gilbert's or any other Act did so largely for economic reasons. From the beginning, there had been an inference that the parishes were interested in the welfare of the poor children of the parish, but in practice, where rate reduction and child welfare conflicted, it had been noticeable throughout the century that economy won the day. Gilbert's plan presented two supreme difficulties: it necessarily involved a great deal more administration and supervision than the simple expedient of collecting the children altogether in a workhouse; and there was absolutely no guarantee that it would be a cheaper form of relief for them than the workhouse.

There were, on the other hand, some signs of an appreciation that, if children were to be brought in to workhouses, then they should be specially provided for in terms of their accommodation. A plan had been canvassed at Sheffield in 1774, for example, for reorganising their workhouse on 'cottage home' lines both for families and for children who had been deserted, or were orphans or vagrants.[1] But the more popular solution was to provide for the children in a 'School of Industry', a much larger unit

[1] *Observations on the Present State of the Poor of Sheffield with Proposals for their Future Employment and Support.* Sheffield, 1774. pp. 29–30.

altogether, which was attached to the workhouse. St. James, Westminster, had adopted this scheme in 1781, despite 'Great Difficulties & Oppositions' from the more economically minded parishioners. Between 270 and 300 were accommodated in the school, where, in addition to being taught their duty as Christians, and learning to read, write and cypher, the girls were employed in mending their own clothes, doing needlework for sale, and making their own and the boys' stockings as well as the boys' linen. The boys were also taught to make their own clothes and clothes for sale, to mend their own and the girls' shoes and to head pins. At twelve to fourteen, after enquiry had been made as to the suitability of the prospective master or mistress the children were either apprenticed or put to service, beginning with a trial period of six weeks to ensure the suitability of the arrangement. The master of an apprentice was given a £2 premium at first with a further £2 at the end of two years if he had treated the child well. The financial basis of this particularly humane attempt to provide for parish children no doubt inspired yet more 'difficulties and oppositions', since the amount earned by the children came to £25 in a fortnight, whilst the cost of keeping them during such a period was £60, or rather more than twice what they earned![1]

Gilbert himself, in *A Plan of Police* (1786), was also to advocate a very similar arrangement for the children of parents who, in addition to being poor, were dissolute and abandoned. For such children, he wanted to see the creation on a county basis of 'Houses of Reception' for young children of an age to receive instruction and capable of any employment: 'the sooner they can conveniently be taken from their parents the better', he writes, 'that their minds may not be corrupted by evil habits and bad example'.

In most workhouses, however, children – orphaned or vagrant, the offspring of the deserving or of the dissolute, the illegitimate or the deserted – were forced to take their chance with such other adults as were in the House. In the Sunderland workhouse, of the 176 inmates, 36 were under twelve years of age and the remainder mainly old women and prostitutes. In the parish workhouse of Buckingham, the total fourteen paupers in the House were composed of a mixture of women, children and

[1] *Sketch of the State of Poor Children* . . ., pp. 5–18.

'THE SUCCOURLESS POOR CHILD'

old men, some of whom were insane. Of the 89 paupers in the Halifax workhouse, 'an old, small & inconvenient building', 42 were under twelve, and more than twenty under six years of age: 'one third of the whole number are lunatic'.[1]

Conditions within the workhouses differed as greatly as their size. Mr. Potter, the severe critic of the parish workhouse, in 1775 describes Bulcamp House, which was run by a board of incorporated guardians, as 'the scene of busy industry, whilst content smiles on every little countenance'. A similar account was given of the Shrewsbury House of Industry, opened in December 1783 by Isaac Wood, a local merchant. 'By habit, their daily employment soon ceases to become irksome,' Wood wrote. 'They see their little companions around them all engaged like themselves; & by their cheerful countenance & general vivacity, it is apparent that they are contented & happy. Their frequent amusement is to sing short moral songs, which they have learned by rote;...'[2] This last scrap of information is itself somewhat amusing in the light of Wood's own admission that, despite his claim that the children in the House were completely segregated from 'the abandoned and depraved', the older girls were allowed to associate with the prostitutes in the House during their leisure time! On the whole, however, this particular House was obviously extremely well run by contemporary standards, and was the subject of a letter written to Sir William Pulteney. It speaks of 'the pleasing spectacle of two hundred children & youth, well fed and clothed & taught; the young ones attending the schools established in the House; those of five years old & upwards, busy at the wheel, the jenny, & the loom: all of them early inured to habits of cleanliness, decency and virtue, & happily preserved from the misery and contagion of vice.'[3]

One aspect of the House's reputation on which Wood himself engaged in correspondence with the Revd. J. Howlett was its

---

[1] Frederic M. Eden, *The State of the Poor*. 1797. vol. II, pp. 172 and 26; also vol. III, p. 821.

[2] Isaac Wood, *Some Account of the Shrewsbury House of Industry*. 4th edn. 1795, p. 31.

[3] Isaac Wood, *A Letter to Sir Willian Pulteney, Bart.,... Containing some Observations on the Bill for the better Support and Maintenance of the Poor, presented to the House of Commons by the Right Honourable William Pitt.* Shrewsbury, 1797. p. 28.

infant mortality rate. In the 1780s, Howlett had been investigating the mortality rate of children under fifteen years of age in the large Houses of Industry set up in East Anglia under Incorporated Boards of Guardians. Whereas the local death rate among children of this age group was something between 1 in 39 and 1 in 41, Howlett had found that in Stow House, Suffolk, where 25 per cent of children under 4 died, 1 in 14; at Heckingham, Norfolk, the rate was 1 in 8, and so on. Howlett observed on these figures: 'We see that the houses on industry are in general almost five times as unhealthy for children as my but moderately healthy parish of Dunmow (1 in 24). ... Is it humane, is it politic, thus to poison & destroy our fellow creatures for the pitiful object of saving a few pounds! ... The Houses of Bulkingham (1777) Heckingham (1768) Shipmeadow (1767) & Gressinghall (1777) have saved between them, perhaps about 1,000l. a year since their institution; at the same time I am mistaken if they have not killed very nearly one thousand poor children.'[1] One can well understand Howlett's surprise, therefore, when he learned that of 91 children born in the Shrewsbury House of Industry between 1784 and 1791, not one of them had died during the first month of its existence.[2] (In London workhouses at this time, the equivalent mortality rate was 1 in 5.) On being informed by Wood that he had checked his figures and found them to be accurate, Howlett comments, not perhaps without a touch of cynicism, 'if this figure is right, I am ready to acknowledge it is a strong presumption that your house is not only more healthy than the rest of the town of Shrewsbury, & every other town of the same size, but than even the most healthy country villages in the kingdom; & that I cannot assign any other plausible reason for this peculiarity than the judicious care & management of those who have the superintendence of it ...'[3] On the quality and care of the management of the workhouses up and down the country a good deal more than the child mortality rates depended. Diet, discipline, employment and accommodation were all affected by the outlook of the workhouse masters and the local poor law officers. Eden's

---

[1] The Rev. J. Howlett, *The insufficiency of the Causes to which the Increase of our Poor, and of the Poor's Rates have been commonly ascribed* ... 1788. pp. 95–100.
[2] Wood, *Some Account* ..., p. 79.
[3] ibid., p. 85.

'THE SUCCOURLESS POOR CHILD'

State of the Poor gives scores of detailed accounts of contemporary workhouses, some of which, like those at Kendal, Halifax and Newark, reflect the same humanitarianism as distinguished the House at Shrewsbury. Many others give quite a different impression, among them the union workhouse at Oxford. A description of this, which Eden quotes at length, not only gives an interesting account of the gaol-like character which was common to many workhouses by the end of the eighteenth century, but also indicated very clearly the indiscriminate way in which children were herded together with the other inmates of the house, however undesirable these might be: 'The boundary walls were insufficient to confine the Paupers; the garden, yard and offices lay open, and in common with each other; the windows and doors of the house without proper bars or fastenings; no regular wards appropriated to the sick, aged or infirm; no nurseries for the children; the sexes strangely intermixed in their eating and sitting rooms, and also in their shops and exercise grounds; nor any separation between their wards and sleeping rooms ... The house in general dirty, unsweet, and in a miserable state of repair; without a single rule or order established for the regulation and government of its numerous family, who were in general idle, riotous and disorderly ....'.[1]

Of course, it is possible to counter the evidence of the Oxford house with that of the house at Shrewsbury, but there was quite sufficient evidence at the end of the eighteenth century to show that the Oxford conditions were far from unique and that the workhouse system in general had failed to fulfil for the children of the very poor the protective, educative and civilising role that men like Cary had dreamed it would. Writing at the end of the century, Sir Thomas Bernard asserted that: 'Children should on no account be put into workhouses if they have parents or relations who will take care of them; although it be requisite to give some allowance, & even to the full of what they would cost in the workhouse.'[2] Many of the children to be found in the workhouses, however, were in fact without parents who were able – or sometimes willing – to care for them. Eden gives a

---
[1] Eden, op. cit., vol. II, pp. 594–5. (Eden is quoting from the report of the local Guardians of the Poor on the conditions they found in the workhouse at the beginning of their year of office.)

[2] *The Reports of the Society for bettering the Condition and increasing the Comforts of the Poor*, ed. Sir Thomas Bernard, vol. I, p. 39.

'THE SUCCOURLESS POOR CHILD'

list of the children in the Epsom workhouse at this time which is very revealing:

BOYS

1. W. C. aged 10; his father was enlisted in the army
2. R. R. aged 10; a bastard
3. T. S. aged 9; his father dead and his mother married again
4. J. R. aged 11; his father a soldier
5. A. L. aged 10; a bastard
6. W. G. aged 8; a bastard
7. J. B. aged 8; parents dead

GIRLS

1. P. H. aged 10; } the father of these girls was a hairdresser;
2. M. H. aged 4; } but is now at sea, on board a man of war. The mother is an idle, worthless woman.
3. J. C. aged 12; sister to No. 1 of the boys
4. S. F. aged 10; a bastard
5. C. R. aged 8; a bastard
6. M. K. aged 10; a bastard
7. E. G. aged 12 }
8. S. G. aged 10 } daughters of a smuggler
9. M. L. aged 11; a bastard
10. A. B. aged 9 }
11. M. B. aged 6 } These three sisters, with a brother (see No. 7 among the boys) were all left destitute by their parents, who were always poor and died young.
12. S. B. aged 3 }
13. H. J. aged 14 } The father of these girls was a waiter at an inn, but is now a soldier; and their mother is dead.
14. M. J. aged 10 }
15. M. Y. aged 6; a bastard
16. S. C. aged 12; an orphan[1]

Here was a workhouse whose main function at the end of the century appears to have been to provide shelter for children otherwise without a home or parents to look after them. Whilst there is no means of knowing just how typical the Epsom workhouse was in this respect, the large number of illegitimate children amongst those for whom the house cared draws attention to the particular problems of this category of children of the poor for whom the community had also some responsibility

[1] Eden, op. cit., vol. III, p. 696.

under the existing poor laws. It had never been the intention of legislators that the care of bastard children should be readily or lightly assumed by the parish officers, and very special attention had been paid in the framing of statutes to the problems of the maintenance of the illegitimate child.

VIII

The Illegitimate Child

Prominent among those categories of children admitted by the charitable hospitals and swelling the numbers to be cared for under the Tudor poor laws were illegitimate children. Since, however, sexual conduct has never been a subject on which men and women have found it easy to reach rational views, it is worth remembering that there is little reason to believe that illegitimacy was more common in pre-industrial England than it is today. 'Nothing approaching promiscuity can be inferred from the evidence at any time or for any age group, and the whole issue seems peculiarly inappropriate to the study of life in the traditional world', writes Peter Laslett in *The World We Have Lost*. 'As far as we yet know, the illegitimacy rates of English people two centuries ago and more were rather lower than our own . . .'[1] Even so, sixteenth-century commentators on their moral scene, were no more than their twentieth-century successors disposed to view prevailing moral conduct with equanimity:

> So many maidens with child
> And wilfully begylde . . .
> So many women blamed
> And righteously defamed
> And so little ashamed,
> Sawe I never.[2]

---

[1] op. cit., p. 130.
[2] John Stretton, 1530, quoted in a letter to *The Times*, 14 October 1961.

THE ILLEGITIMATE CHILD

It would not be at all difficult to parallel such a statement from our own popular press and in both cases the allegations would be more significant of changing attitudes to extra-marital relations than they would be a reliable indicator of the prevalence of fornication and its natural consequences. Allegations such as these depend a great deal for their effect on the implication that moral standards have seriously deteriorated, yet there is little evidence to show that the picture of contemporary morals painted in such vivid colours by sixteenth and seventeenth century sermon writers and pamphleteers depicted a fall from an earlier state of innocence, and a great deal of evidence to show that the startling tones which these writers used in their work revealed a censoriousness and moral superiority towards sexual laxity which was not at all typical of their forebears. In previous generations, a more tolerant attitude to extra-marital relations had been the corollary, among the upper classes, of the essentially practical and unromantic matches which parents had contrived for their children: marriages which, as we have seen, often took place at too early an age for affection or love to be sure or sustained between the young couple. Hence, in early adulthood, the possibility of one or other developing a romantic attachment outside marriage – a possibility often made a probability by the cult of romantic love which, largely due to French and Italian influences, had developed as part of the elaborate system of mediaeval chivalry and had presented romantic love as possible only between lover and mistress, not husband and wife. Not till the sixteenth and seventeenth centuries was mature sexual satisfaction considered possible in married as much as in illicit love and although the troubadours might sing of the tragic consequences of such a love, practical here as in all things, society accepted the mistress, and the man owned responsibility for his offspring. Until the sixteenth century, bastardy had not been thought any great shame. Men took care of their bastards, were indeed often proud of them and in many cases brought them home to their wives or mothers to be brought up. Children born out of wedlock were thus to be found growing up in their father's house with their half-brothers and sisters without a hint of disgrace either to themselves or to their natural parents.

This is not to say that no distinction whatever was drawn between a man's illegitimate and legitimate offspring. An illegitimate child had no legal rights and owned no obligations to his parents; unless baptised in Church, he had no name. No action or subsequent marriage of his natural parents could alter this by one jot or tittle: the guiding principle of English law was 'once a bastard always a bastard'. Although this legal distinction did not convey the invidiousness of later social distinctions between the legitimate and the illegitimate, it nevertheless placed the illegitimate at a serious disadvantage. Only legitimate offspring were legally capable of succeeding to titles and estates and, at a time when admission to the Trade Gilds and Livery Companies was primarily by inheritance, the illegitimate were ineligible for admission to these fraternities, or to the corporation. Moreover, illegitimacy of any kind was established as a canonical impediment (admittedly one easily overcome by dispensation) to the holding of orders or preferment and so it remains in the Roman Catholic Church to this day. On the other hand, in the twelfth century, the Church had become committed to the principle that a marriage between two persons might legitimate any child born to them prior to the marriage, subject to the proviso that a child could not be legitimated if one or other of the parents was married to a third party at the time of birth or at some time during the period of ten calendar months preceding the birth. In this respect, Canon Law was at odds with the law of England and many attempts were made to incorporate the rule of Canon Law with regard to this particular matter in the law of the country. On the occasion of the Statute of Merton, 1235, 'all the Bishops instanted the Lords' that the ecclesiastical rule should be accepted. This prompted the famous response: 'All the Earls and Barons of England with one voice answered that they would not change the law of the Realm'. Until the Legitimacy Act of 1926, successive Parliaments were to agree with the Barons: not till then did it become possible for a child born illegitimate, to be legitimated by the subsequent marriage of his parents. For close on six hundred years the law of England on this remained unchanged.

It would not be true to suggest that society had been equally willing to condone sexual laxity in women as in men. So much is indicated, for example, in the account of how Rycharde Whytyngdon (Dick Whittington), a benefactor of St. Thomas's

Hospital, Southwark, 'made a new chambyre with viii beddys for young wemen that have done a-mysse, in trust for good mendement. And he commandyd that alle the thynges that had ben don in that chambyre shoulde be kepte secrete . . . for he wolde not shame no yonge woman in noo wyse'.[1] Nevertheless, there is little to suggest that, before the sixteenth century, it had been an overwhelming disaster for a girl to have an illegitimate baby and a great deal of evidence to show that until the sixteenth century, the illegitimate child itself, though legally underprivileged, was not socially stigmatised.

Indeed, in the households of the great, throughout the sixteenth century and for many years after, acceptance of a man's illegitimate children persisted. Ecclesiastical households, as is well known, were no exception as Wolsey's own life reveals. Indeed, it may very well be argued that the clerical celibacy of the pre-Reformation Church regrettably but inevitably contributed to a tacit acceptance of the human frailties of its ordained priests, which even in the mid-twentieth century might be thought remarkable. Wolsey's son 'by one Larck's daughter', for example, was made Dean of Wells and had numerous other preferments bestowed upon him in his father's lifetime and, although stripped of most of his preferments after Wolsey's downfall, was subsequently befriended by Cromwell and became Archdeacon of Cornwall – a history all the more significant since only in this century has illegitimacy ceased to be a legal bar to ordination in the Church of England. Successive monarchs continued to take their pleasures where they would and to provide for the inevitable children as they might. In the mid-seventeenth century, in his 1669 edition of the *Present State of England* E. Chamberlayne wrote: 'The Natural Illegitimate Son and Daughter of the King, after they are acknowledged by the King, take precedence of all other Nobles under those of the Blood Royal . . . They bear what surname the King pleaseth to give them, and for Arms, the Arms of England with a Band Sinister Gobionell or some other mark of illegitimisation.' He continued: 'Some Kings of England have acknowledged many and had more illegitimate Sons and Daughters . . . Henry VIII, amongst others had one by Elizabeth Blount named Henry Fitzroy, created him Duke of Somerset and Richmond, Earl of Nottingham and

[1] Quoted M. Hopkirk, *Nobody Wanted Sam*. 1949. p. 12.

Lord High Admiral of England, Ireland and Aquitain...'[1] Years later, another royal bastard, Charles Lennox, one of the fourteen illegitimate children of Charles II, was also to be created Duke of Richmond by his father who, having no ready money of his own to provide for his son, gave the nation the privilege of providing some by awarding to the Duke and his heirs a duty of a shilling a ton on all coals exported from the Tyne for use in England. The 'Richmond Shilling' continued till our own day, when it was redeemed for £633,333.

This royal acceptance of human frailty and regal solution of its consequences, which carried into the seventeenth century something of the ethos of the Middle Ages, stood in sharp contrast to a gradual but perceptible hardening of social attitudes regarding social misconduct which had been taking place since the mid-sixteenth century. Books of Domestic Relations had repeatedly laid stress on marital fidelity and had gradually helped to form public opinion on matters relating to the family and the home. One of the first, a translation of a French *Book of Good Manners*, was printed by Caxton in 1487, and in 1541 Miles Coverdale translated Heinrich Bullinger's *The Christen State of Matrimonye*, which summed up so well the essential points demanded of a contemporary treatise on domestic relations that its successors could do little more than amplify elements found in the earlier work, which itself had gone through nine separate printings by 1575. Notable among the proper duties of husband and wife which this book enumerates was sexual fidelity: 'how shameful and horrible a thing is whoredom and adultery' the author declares.[2]

The task of the moralist has never been an easy one: the remarkable thing about *The Christen State of Matrimonye* was its immediate and huge success. This was clearly a brand of literature which not only met a need, but met a need which was widely and consciously acknowledged. To no more powerful influence can this be so clearly attributed as to the growth of Puritanism both within and without the Church of England. 'After the break with Rome, with its conservative attitude to sexual relations, now no longer was virginity held to be the highest good, but a chastity of marriage was glorified by the Protestants... As

[1] op. cit., pp. 169–70.
[2] See L. B. Wright, op. cit., pp. 205–6.

Puritanism further modified Church beliefs, the insistence upon the sterling virtues of the home became louder. If the Puritan possessed some of the asceticism of his medieval forebears, he regarded marriage as a God given expedient for evading the damning sin of sexual indulgence. Thus he began to concentrate his interest upon preserving the purity of the married state rather than the physiological purity of the individual...'[1] For this reason, Puritan writers constantly protested against sexual laxity and indulgence and laid especial emphasis on the desirability of a single standard of morals for men and women alike – if for no other immediate reason than that, if husbands wanted virtuous wives, they must themselves first set an example of marital fidelity.

By the early seventeenth century men not necessarily inclined to excessively puritanical views, such as Alexander Nicholas and David Tuvil, were adding their voices to the growing demand for a single standard of sexual morality and thus testified to the growing influence of Puritanism on contemporary attitudes to sexual conduct.[2] But throughout all these many books, pamphlets and sermons, no concern is shown for the illegitimate child, the product of the sexual laxity they were concerned to condemn. Their sole concern was with morality, as they conceived it. In time, this moral myopia was to foster a censoriousness which sometimes manifested itself with a cruel ferocity. In 1585, for example, *Orders* were issued at Dedham then under strong Presbyterian influence, 'to be diligently observed by all persons dwelling in the said town'. One *Order* reads: 'If any be known to have known one another carnally before celebrating of their marriage, that none accompany them to the Church nor from the Church, nor dine with them that day, and that the pastor at the baptizing of the children of any such ... do publicly note and declare out the fault to all the congregation, to the humbling of the parties and the terrifying of others...'[3] Surely few aspects of English Puritanism are more distasteful than the unrelenting and uncharitable moral superiority it could display towards those who failed to live chastely. Nor could anything contrast so greatly with the mediaeval Catholic attitude which not only

---

[1] ibid., p. 203.
[2] ibid., pp. 216–18 passim.
[3] Quoted Hopkirk, op. cit., p. 15.

ignored premarital intercourse if the couple subsequently married but also allowed the marriage to legitimise their offspring.

It was inevitable that the growing conviction that a family based on the stable relationships of the parents was the *sine qua non* of a stable society, and the increasing censoriousness of conduct which ran counter to this view, should seek expression in the formal means of social control. Nowhere was this more clearly achieved than in sixteenth- and seventeenth-century poor law legislation in which the wanton production of children without families to incorporate them was conceived of as a hazard to internal peace and social organisation and therefore strenuously condemned.

We have already referred at some length to the local censuses of the poor carried out by many municipalities in the second half of the sixteenth century the better to devise policies with which to deal with them and, more especially, to safeguard the pockets of the citizens. Such a census was taken in Norwich in 1570, where it was revealed that one of the reasons for the increasing numbers who wandered from door to door, begging their bread 'the great complaint made by divers citizens' was that the poor 'when their bellies were filled, . . . fell to lust and concupisence, and moste shamefullie abused ther bodies, and broght forth basterdes in such quantitie that it passed belief'.[1] These enormities considered, 'The Mayor and whole assembly agreed to a reformation being made and a book of rules issued'.

The *Rules* were in fact issued the following year. In the event, they dealt mainly with the adult poor and laid down detailed rules for the local Bridewell. In any case, isolated municipal action was ineffective to deal with what was increasingly conceived of as a national problem and one closely associated with more general problems of the relief of the poor.

Hence, five years later, in the Poor Law Act of 1576, Parliament made the first legislative provision for illegitimate children so many of whom were abandoned by their parents and left to be maintained from charitable or public sources. The preamble of the Act indicates the spirit in which this problem was approached. 'Firste, concerning Bastards begotten and borne out of lawful Matrimony (an Offence againste Gods Lawe and Mans Lawe)

[1] *Records of Norwich*, ed. Hudson and Tingey, p. 344.

the said Bastards being now lefte to bee kepte at the chardge of the Parishe where They bee borne, to the greate Burden of the same Parishe and in defrauding of the Reliefe of the impotente and aged true Poore of the same Parishe, and to the evill Example and Encouradgement of lewde Lyef: It ys ordeyned and enacted . . .'

Under the Act, two local justices might both punish the mother and the putative father of an illegitimate child and also require them to support their child financially in so far as they were able. Failure to comply with the justices' *Order* was to entail imprisonment in the 'Warde' or 'Common Gayle', where defaulters were to 'remaine wthout Bayle or Maineprise, excepte hee or theye shall put in sufficient Suretye to *p*forme the said Order . . .' or else appear at the next Quarter Sessions and obey the Order made by the justices or, if no new Order made, obey the old one.[1]

It is significant that in this first legislation dealing with illegitimate children, no mention is made of their welfare. The main concern of Parliament was the relief of public expenditure and the exposure of the moral failure of those who were responsible for bringing the children into the world. Subsequent bastardy legislation until late in the nineteenth century continued to be obsessed by their moral guilt – a guilt which, with disastrous results, was transferred to the child. Hence the stigma of illegitimacy which has persisted from the sixteenth century until recent times.

Whilst the breeding of bastards was condemned in the Act of 1576 as contrary to the law of both God and man, it is noticeable that, under the latter, legal sanctions were only to be employed against men and women whose bastards became a charge on the community: there were no legal penalties for those who could afford to support the fruits of their own indiscretions. As with the Norwich Orders, so with this and subsequent legislation relating to illegitimate children, the laws of man were heavily weighted by economic considerations which at least imply the placing of some restriction on the overt exercise of Divine displeasure this side of the grave. 'And because great charge ariseth uppon many places wth in the Realm by reason of Bastardie, besides the greate Dishonor of Almightie God'; runs Clause

[1] 18 Eliz., c. 3.

VII of *An Acte for the due execucion of divers Laws and Statutes heretofore made against Rogues, Vagabonds and Sturdye Beggars and other lewde and idle persons* (1609). 'Be it therefore enacted by the authoritie aforesaid, that every lewde Woman wch after this *p*'sent Session of Parliament, shall have any Bastard wch may be chargeable to the Parish, the Justices of the Peace shall committ such lewde Women unto the House of Correction, ther to be punished and sett on worke during the terme of one whole yere; and if she shall eftsons offend againe, that then to be committed to the said House of Correction aforesaid, and ther to remain untill shee can put in good sureties for her good behavior not to offend so againe.'[1] A clause which must often have meant imprisonment for life if rigorously carried out!

Appeal to Divine displeasure, already relegated to second place in this Act, disappears entirely in the later statutes of 1662 and 1733 relating to bastardy and reveals the abiding interest of the State quite clearly as not merely wishing to discourage bastardy, but to fix parental responsibility, with an emphasis almost exclusively on financial considerations. Clause XIX of the 1662 Act 'for the better Reliefe of the Poore of this Kingdom' for example, is particularly directed to the situation where 'the putative Father and lewd Mothers of Bastard Children run away out of the parish and sometimes out of the County and leave the said Bastard Children upon the charge of the Parish where they are borne although such putative Father and Mother have Estates sufficient to discharge such Parishe . . .' It was thus enacted that churchwardens and overseers of the poor in such cases, had the power to seize the parents' goods and chattels and receive rents etc. sufficient to cover the cost of bringing up and providing for the child. The amount they seized and the size of the rent distraint depended on the orders of two justices at the Quarter Sessions. This same anxiety to repudiate public responsibility for the maintenance of bastards resulted in not merely property but persons being seized on the authority of the local justices by powers vested in them by the later Act passed some seventy years later, *An Act for the Relief of Parishes and other Places from such Charges as may arise from Bastard Children born within the same* (1733)[2]. Under this statute, a man charged on

[1] 7 Jac., I c. 4.
[2] 6 George II, c. 31.

THE ILLEGITIMATE CHILD

oath of being the father of her bastard child by a single woman, 'if the child was likely to be chargeable to the Parish' might be apprehended on warrant from the local justice and committed to gaol or House of Correction unless he gave security to appear at the next Quarter Sessions to be dealt with according to the law of 1576.

For a period of well-nigh two hundred years, successive bastardy laws, with only one exception, showed no concern for the illegitimate child itself. And then only for the preservation of its life. This exception was the Act of 1623, *to prevent the murthering of Bastard Children*, whose preamble indicates the effects of early Puritan censoriousness and harsh bastardy legislation and its obsession with guilt. 'Whereas many lewd women that have been delivered of Bastard Children to avoyd their shame and to escape punishment, doe secretlie bury or conceale the Death of their Children and after the Child be found dead the said Women doe alledge that the said Child was born dead, whereas it falleth out sometymes (although hardlie it is to be proved) that the said Child or Children were murdered by the said Women their Lewd Mothers, or by their assent or procurement.' The Act provided that: 'if any Woman . . . be delivered of any issue of her Body Male or Female, which being born alive should by the Lawes of the Realme be a Bastard, and that she endeavour privatelie either by drowning or secrett burying thereof, or any other way, by herself or the procuring of others, soe conceale the Death thereof . . . the Mother soe offending shall suffer Death as in the case of Murther, except such Mother can make proofe by one witness at the leest, that the child . . . was borne dead.'[1]

It is impossible to judge just how common infanticide from this particular cause actually was. Some held it to be essentially an urban phenomenon. One country gentleman, for example, avowed that 'as to the murdering of infants to conceal amours, we hardly hear of such a thing in the country; no such cruel delicacy prevails in my parishes . . . (whatever may be the case in London and larger towns) . . .' Illegitimate children fared as well as others in the country, he claimed. 'A child is always a stronghold on the man.'[2] It is not necessarily to question the

---

[1] 21 Jac. I, c. 27.
[2] *Genuine Sentiments of an English Country Gentleman*, p. 22.

sincerity of this opinion to wonder at its undoubted ingenuousness. Amongst a class where food was never very plentiful and at a time when individual life was not so highly regarded and the death of an infant no very remarkable thing, the temptation for a woman to escape ostracism and the penalties of the law and rid herself of a responsibility which, without a husband's support, might prove an impossible burden, was not always to be resisted in either town or country.

It is clear, however, that one feature of the Act itself which struck even contemporaries as unduly severe was that, contrary to normal English practice, it substituted a presumption of guilt for actual proof of guilt against the alleged culprit. Barrington, in his *Observations* wrote that this was rather to be accounted for because of the difficulty of proving the guilt of the mother 'rather than an intention to make the bare concealment occasioned by a mistaken shame amount to a capital felony'[1] – an explanation as irrelevant to the normal operation of English justice as the provision of the Act was itself foreign. Nevertheless, the Act remained on the statute book for a very long time, until 1803, when it was repealed by an Act in the preamble of which it was conceded that the earlier statute had been found 'in sundry cases difficult and inconvenient to be put into practice'. Henceforth, women accused of killing their illegitimate offspring were to be tried in the ordinary way as alleged murderers. If acquitted, they were still liable to imprisonment for up to two years for concealing burial of a still-born child.

How the more general legislation relating to bastard children had been operating meanwhile is amply recorded in the local records and in particular in the records of the Courts of Quarter Session to which hundreds of cases involving the maintenance of illegitimate children were referred. It is more than evident from these records of local practice that determination to protect the ratepayer frequently overbore a zeal for justice. The Mayor's Book of Chester, for instance, contains several entries of bonds entered into by the fathers of bastard children to provide for their maintenance. Such a bond was given by George Title to provide for his bastard child, Ellen, and also to marry the mother, Jane Davies. He was 'to take into his Custody the said Ellen, and her

---

[1] Daines Barrington, *Observations on the more ancient statutes*. 5th edn, 1796, p. 549.

at all times hereafter well and sufficiently Maintaine, provide for, norse, and kepe with all thinge as beseemeth' so that the Corporation 'shall not be in any wise Charged nor burthened with her Kepings'.¹ Title in fact admitted his fatherhood of the child, but there are scores of other maintenance orders made against men who strongly denied the child to be their own. In 1594, at 'Wedsfleide' Jon Nichols junior, the reputed father of the bastard child of Jane Reynolds, was ordered to pay £10 a year for seven years towards the child's upkeep, although he strongly denied paternity.² The same court, in the following year, ordered Michael Mole of Kingesley to contribute to the upkeep of the bastard child of Sara Heaton 'A most noteable Common vicious woman', although there seemed strong evidence that Mole was not in fact the father.³ Other Quarter Sessions placed an equally liberal interpretation on 'putative paternity'. By the mid-seventeenth century, when Puritan influence had become extensive throughout society, the Sussex Quarter Sessions had perfected a scheme whereby a putative father might pay a lump sum to be discharged of future liability for a bastard alleged to be his. Hence, in cases where there was a distinct doubt as to who actually was the father, the Court extracted sums varying between £5 and £14 as a kind of blackmail from men who wished to rid themselves of further trouble. In 1643, William Piggott's consent to pay £10 'for the salving of ... [his] Credit and reputation' is recorded in the Order Book. The receipt of the payment secured his complete discharge.⁴

The payment of a lump sum or composition fee to the parish which released the putative father from future liability was accepted practice, but more common, since these were cases concerned with the bastards of the poor, were magistrates' orders for a weekly payment to the parish by the father towards the maintenance of his child. Thus, in 1594, Richard Whiston of Wednesbury, the reputed father of a bastard by Katherine More, was ordered to give 4d. a week to Elizabeth and Humphrey More, who were rearing the child, until 'the child shalbe able to gett

---

¹ *Child Marriages, Divorces, and Ratifications etc. in the Diocese of Chester, A.D. 1561-66.* edit. F. J. Furnivall, 1897. p. 156.
² *The Staffordshire Quarter Sessions Rolls,* ed. S. A. H. Burne, vol. III, 1933. pp. 42-3.
³ ibid., pp. 81, 100 and 104 passim.
⁴ *Sussex Quarter Sessions Order Book, 1642-49,* pp. 34, 41, 85 and 121 passim.

her owne lyvyng'.[1] Similarly, at the suit of Alice Robin, an order was made against Stephen Taylor of Corpustey on 11 May 1615, for 1s. a week for the maintenance of his child and he was also required by the justice to enter into a bond of £10 to the churchwardens and overseers of the parish. The amounts stipulated in the orders naturally varied with the father's estimated ability to pay. Whilst Whiston was only required to pay 4d. a week by the Staffordshire Quarter Sessions, it was far more common for orders to be for 1s. and, occasionally, for 2s. a week.

Whilst the emphasis on the Orders we have so far considered is on defining the father's financial responsibility, the magistrates frequently availed themselves of their undoubted power to make a maintenance order against both parents on the child's behalf. Such an order was in fact made against Sara Heaton and Michael Mole, to whom we have alluded before, who were ordered to share the upkeep of their child 'until further agreement between the parties before the justices at the next Quarter Sessions'.

Where joint orders were made and enforced, it was usually because the mother herself either did not want, or could not afford, to look after the child herself. Thus the Warwick Quarter Sessions made several orders in 1684 in which the mother's contribution – usually substantially less than the father's – was contingent upon her 'not keeping and nourishing the child herself'. Where parents were unable to make cash contributions towards their child's upkeep, some parishes were only too anxious to put facilities in their way to enable them to do so: 'Item, that noe bastard be relieved by the Parish (of Illminster) but the supposed fathers and mothers if they be any of them founde to be able, and if there be found any that be not able to relieve theire owne bastards, such supposed father and mother to be sent to the House of Correction and by their worke there to relieve the same . . .'

From this and other similar records, it seems quite clear that commitment of the parents of illegitimate children was not merely punitive, although there were also many other cases where the mother and father – or either – were so committed until they gave security for the provision for their offspring.

If a father were not so much unable as unwilling to provide for

[1] *Staffordshire Quarter Sessions Roll*, p. 4.

15 The London Charity School Children in St. Paul's on the occasion of the National Thanksgiving for the Recovery of George III, 1787. From a drawing by E. Dayes

16 *The Graham Children*. William Hogarth

THE ILLEGITIMATE CHILD

his bastard and ran away from the parish, his flight engineered by some friend or relative, the Courts did not hesitate to transfer the father's liability to these misguided well-wishers until such time as the father himself could be produced in court, when he was promptly consigned to the House of Correction as punishment for his selfish behaviour. Not surprisingly, in many cases it was the man's own father who was supposed to have 'conveyed away' his son, and who was thus required to make either a weekly or a lump-sum payment to the overseers on his son's behalf.

The period for which the magistrates' orders were made, depended on local assessments of how long it would be before the child would cease to be a liability to the parish, an assessment commonly calculated in terms of the age at which the child might be apprenticed. According to the records of the Lancashire Quarter Sessions at the turn of the sixteenth century, the practice in that County was for the parents' responsibility to cease when the child was 10 or 12 years old. In a few cases the order terminated when the child was only 7 or 8 years old. In other parts of the country, orders were prolonged until the age of 14.

As we have already seen, the apprenticing of illegitimate children at a suitable age was a particular use of a more general permission accorded to overseers of the poor by the Act of 1597. Since binding a child apprentice always involved the payment of a fee to his prospective master, wherever possible, provision was made for this in the original maintenance order. Hence many orders stipulating a regular payment over a number of years towards the child's upkeep, terminate with a final payment – usually of £5 to £6 – towards the child's 'putting out'.[1]

Whilst these early attempts to legislate with respect to the illegitimate child were prompted by and largely related to the urgent need to solve contemporary economic problems, they were also, as we have seen from the statutes themselves, concerned even if at only one economic level to punish those whose behaviour offended puritan notions of sexual morality. To achieve this end, physical punishment and public disgrace were added to the economic penalties of the maintenance orders and committals to the Houses of Correction. Hence an order made by the

---

[1] See *Sussex Quarter Sessions Order Book*, pp. 38, 67, 109, 127, 132, 137, 160 passim.
Also *Warwick Quarter Sessions Records, 1682–90*, pp. 237, 244, 260 passim.

Lancashire Quarter Sessions in 1601 by which both the parents of an illegitimate child were to be publicly whipped and sat in the stocks during market time, naked from the middle up, with papers on their heads saying: 'These persons are punished for fornication'.[1] In 1588, the year of the Spanish Armada, a woman was brought before the Wardmote Court at Orford, Suffolk, and charged with the birth of a third illegitimate child. She was not only committed to the House of Correction but sentenced to be flogged through the streets as an example and warning to others. In this particular case, the father, though he was known, was not called in question.[2] Elsewhere, however, fathers did not escape so lightly. In 1601, the Lancashire justices made an order concerning the bastard daughter of Jane Sothworth of Wrightington and Richard Garstange, of Fazakerly. Jane was to have charge of their daughter Alice for two years 'so long as she does not beg' and then Richard was to have charge of the child until it was 12 years of age. The father was to give Jane a cow and 6s. in money. Both parents were to be publicly whipped at Ormskirk.[3]

Condemnations of sexual irregularity in the sixteenth and seventeenth centuries was, of course, no more dependent on, than it was derived from, the popular judgements of the market place. In the matter of the punishment of the parents of illegitimate children the laws of God were invoked to add awful reinforcement to the laws of man. For generations the Church had endeavoured to exert some control over sexual irregularities through the Archdeacon's Courts which, in the larger towns, met weekly. Various misdemeanours were dealt with by the Archdeacons but the most numerous cases with which they were concerned were those dealing with sex. After the Poor Law Act of 1576, the churchwardens and overseers who had been made responsible for the day-to-day administration of the laws in the parish, frequently brought the parents of illegitimate children before their Archdeacon for his judgement, which usually involved the imposition of a penance on one or both of the parties. Typical of such penances was that imposed in 1584 on John Gill, who got Mary Spencer with child. Gill was 'To come into Church

---

[1] *Lancashire Quarter Sessions Records*, vol. I (1590–1606), p. 74.

[2] R. A. Roberts, Borough Business of a Suffolk Town (Orford) 1559–1660, *Transactions of the Royal Historical Society*, 4th series, vol. XIV. 1931. p. 118.

[3] *Lancashire Quarter Sessions Records*, ed. James Tait, vol. I, p. 191.

on Sunday sennight next and there tarry the whole evening prayer and after evening prayer in some convenient place of the Church before Mr. Rawlins the vicar, the two churchwardens and four honest parishioners, confess his fault and there deliver 6s. 8d. to Mr. Rawlins for the use of the poor and undertake 6s. 8d. more to the same use on the feast of St. Michael next.'[1]

Sometimes previous penance in Church allowed avoidance of further punishment by the local Sessions whereas other Courts sometimes chose to impose some sort of penance themselves as a punishment for breeding bastards. Hence in 1598 the West Riding Sessions, adjudicating in the case of William Prince, a married man who had fathered a child on Isobel Hirst, first arranged to their satisfaction for the custody and maintenance of the child 'so as neither the said Isobel (being extreme poore) Nor the Town of Meathley shall hereafter be Chardged therwith', and concluded their judgement:

'And for the punyshment of the said pties for their said offence Yt is lastly ordered that the said willm Prynce shall stand in thr pishe Churche of Birkyn foresaid on a Saboth day in tyme of devyne service ther celebrated and said, appairaled in a white sheete duringe the tyme of the Celebracon of the said S'vice. and ther oppenly acknowledge his said offence: And the said Issabell shall in the same manner do the same in the pishe churche of Meathley: and either of them to appeare att the next Sessions and bring Certificate of their pformance hereof...'[2]

By no means all the punishments imposed bore so equally on both parties. As the influence of puritanism grew, there was a noticeable tendency for the sanctions upholding moral standards to be imposed more rigorously on women than on men. The Church itself seems to have paid a rather particular attention to the necessity of securing the penitence of the mother of an illegitimate child.

In the course of its constant and largely successful efforts to gain control of matrimonial causes, the Roman Church had come to attach importance to the mother's going to Church soon after the birth of her child to offer thanks for her safe delivery – to be

---

[1] E. R. Brinkworth, *The Archdeacon's Court: Liber Actorum 1584*, Oxford Record Society, vol. I, p. 11.
[2] *West Riding Sessions Rolls, 1597 – 1602*. Ed. John Lister. Yorkshire Archeological and Topographical Association, Record Series, vol. III, 1888, p. 121.

'Churched'. In this as in so many other ways, the Church of England continued Roman practice. For the unmarried mother, penance had always been the prerequisite of being Churched and, at the end of the sixteenth century, Bishops were at great pains, in their Visitation Articles, to make this clear. Most sets of Visitation Articles contained one setting out public penance as necessary for the mother of an illegitimate child. Typical is Article 12 of Bishop Aylmer's Visitation Articles for London, 1586:

'Whether any minister ... hath used the form of thanksgiving for a woman after childbirth being unlawfully begotten with child otherwise than in the form of a penitent person: viz. in a white sheet or other habit prescribed by the ordinary ... or before sufficient caution taken that she should not depart the parish till she should perform such penances as should be enjoined by the ordinary ...'[1]

In some measure it is possible to interpret this emphasis on the guilt of the mother as part of the traditional acceptance of a double moral standard which had been reinforced by an ambivalence in the Church's teaching with regard to women fostered by Pauline dualism. Again, it is possible to argue that the greater reliance of Puritanism on the teaching of the Old Testament served to re-emphasise the view of woman as the eternal temptress. But it is also possible to detect a particular argument for emphasising woman's greater moral responsibility in some of the very treatises which, as we have seen, advocated the general desirability of a single moral standard. For some at least, the greater culpability of women seems to have been related to the growing insistence on family stability as the basis of a stable society. William Gouge's *Domesticall Duties* (1622) and Matthew Griffeth's *Bethel* (1633), whilst disagreeing in their analysis of the relative importance of the sin of infidelity in man as compared with woman, both argued that faithlessness in a wife caused greater evils to the family. It is not difficult to see on this view why special attention should be called to sexual immorality in women and why its punishment should carry with it a marked element of publicity.

It would be surprising however, notwithstanding a twentieth-

[1] W. F. M. Kennedy, *Elizabethan Episcopal Administration*. 1924. vol. III, p. 224.

century concern for equity before the law, if the reader were not by now curious to know the fate of the children whose birth had aroused such public concern. Unfortunately, this is a curiosity more easy to arouse than satisfy. It is not by mere chance that so much space has been devoted to the treatment of the parents of illegitimate children for it was this, far more than the welfare of the children themselves which preoccupied our ancestors. Just occasionally one comes across instances where the local justices seem to have shown a real concern for the welfare of the child. In the Staffordshire Quarter Sessions rolls, for example, there are the details of the magistrates' ruling with regard to the bastard child of Robert Homersley and Katherine Bradbury. Homersley himself had died one and a half years before, in 1594, and his father, Thomas Homersley 'of the wood', in the parish of Chedham, had received 26s. 8d. from the child's mother in return for which Homersley was to have assumed responsibility and care for the child. But the grandfather had failed to keep his side of the bargain and the magistrates now write:

'And forasmuch as the reputed father is dead and the graundfather soe obstinate and ungodly disposed wee can doe noe other for the norrishment of the sayed childe but to commit it to the charge of the Parrishioners to be relieved by them in parte or in all as statute requireth. The Premisses considered, these bee to well and . . . straytly to charge and Commanunde you the wardens of the said church of Chedulton and Inhabitants of the sayde parishe to bee carefull and provideing for the education and norrishment of the sayde chile soe that it maye bee vertuously and godly brought up untill it come to conveny(ent) age. Herof fayle you not as yee favour your dueties and will answere to the Contrary at your perills . . .'[1]

But what we do not know is how the order was in fact carried out by the parish. Nor, from such other scant evidence as we possess on the practical organisation of parochial responsibility, is it at all easy to deduce how such children actually fared. Of the fate of the illegitimate child brought up in the home of one or other of its natural parents we know virtually nothing and we are little wiser concerning the fate of such children who were put out to nurse with strangers. The allowance usually paid to a nurse varied from 1s. to 5s.; hence, if we accept Alice Clark's calculation that the weekly

[1] *Staffordshire Quarter Sessions Rolls*, vol. III, pp. 172–7.

income of a labourer's family in the seventeenth century was 3s. 6d. a week for rent and clothing for all, and food for the mother and children,[1] the amount paid by the overseers for looking after a pauper child sometimes exceeded the total earnings of a labourer and his wife. For some, therefore, fostering a child was potentially a not unprofitable business, the more so when the nurse sought to benefit from economies of numbers by taking in several children and establishing a baby farm. Nevertheless, despite the modern bias against a social service being actually profitable for those who engage in it, it is not overwhelmingly clear that care for their charges was necessarily and in all cases hazarded by cupidity on the part of the foster-mothers. Dorothy Marshall's investigations of the *Poor Books* of Westbury over the period 1656 to 1698 led her to conclude of the boarding out of illegitimate parish children: 'The practice appears to have worked satisfactorily. The money paid for board and lodging, though not extravagant was slightly more than was paid to any parish pensioner, and probably fairly adequate when supplemented by clothes and any other incidental charges. In any case, the parish children so boarded out were probably as well lodged and fed as children of the same social class who lived at home on the family earnings. In the Westbury accounts there is nothing to indicate that the rate of mortality was higher among parish children than might ordinarily have been expected.' In this respect, however, she is careful to add that parishes would tend to differ.[2]

Any examination of evidence relating to the deaths of children who had been boarded out indicates, as one might expect, that a great deal depended on the efficiency and nature of the arrangements made for the payment of the nurses, whether by private agreement between parent and nurse or by agreement between the overseers and the nurses. Numerous complaints are recorded from nurses whose allowances for the children in their care were not forthcoming. In 1641 a case came before the York Quarter Sessions concerning a bastard which had been put to nurse by its father with a local baby farmer 'where itt is ready to starve for want of necessaryes'.[3] According to the nurse, the father had

[1] Alice Clark, *The Working Life of Women in the Seventeenth Century*. 1919. pp. 68–71.
[2] Dorothy Marshall, *The English Poor in the Eighteenth Century*. 1926. p. 97.
[3] *West Riding Sessions Rolls*, p. 328.

failed to make her an allowance for the child. Complaints on exactly the same grounds were made against the parish officers. In judging these cases, however, it is noticeable that the Court did not stop to enquire how the children had been maintained, it merely looked to the contract into which the parish had entered. Sometimes, as in the notorious case of Mary Compton in 1694, a nurse who had starved and murdered several infants placed in her care by the parish officers, the magistrates were forced to concern themselves with the welfare of such children. Whatever the trial may have proved concerning Mary Compton's character, it certainly demonstrated the folly of parish officers who put out children for whom they were responsible for a lump sum payment, thus providing an incentive for the unscrupulous to do away with their charge in whom the parish had no further interest and whose continued existence merely ate away the profit to the nurse. The Court therefore ordered that, at least in Middlesex where they had jurisdiction, the nurses should be paid weekly or monthly: that the churchwardens and overseers were to provide lists of children for whom they were responsible, noting where they were at nurse, how much the nurses were to be paid in each case, and how many died whilst in the care of the nurse. These lists were to be handed to the Clerk of Session every Easter and thus provide the basis for effective supervision of the boarding-out system. The immediate scandal having passed over, however, there is no evidence that the magistrates continued their vigilance.[1]

In the circumstances, it would be ingenuous to suppose that Mary Compton's could have been a unique case: how common such cases were we have no means of knowing yet a provision of a Bill introduced into Parliament in 1773 for *the Better Regulating the Settlement and Providing for the Maintenance of Bastard Children* might lead one to suppose that the children at Westbury had led a charmed existence. 'And whereas it appears that great Numbers of Children when boarded out or put out to nurse, usually die under the age of two years, for want of being properly taken Care of, and convenient Nurture had, or Account of an adequate Price for such Maintenance not being allowed or given by the Overseers of the Poor . . .', it was now proposed that no child should be separated from its mother without her

[1] E. G. Dowdell, *A Hundred Years of Quarter Session*. Cambridge, 1932. p. 54.

consent and that children boarded out should only be placed with someone approved of by the mother.[1] Both this and a similar Bill of 1802, though neither was successful, were striking attempts to achieve by statute what the magistrates of the Middlesex Quarter Sessions, with albeit fleeting enthusiasm, had tried to achieve. The earlier Bill called for a list of the names of children boarded out to be kept by the overseers together with details of the allowances made and the date from which the child had been in the nurse's care. The second Bill was rather more rigorous, requiring that no child be removed from its mother, even with her consent, without the agreement of the justices where the child was under seven years of age. Moreover, the Bill also sought to empower a magistrate to ask a nurse (or indeed the mother herself if she had custody of the child) to produce any illegitimate child she might have in her care 'and in case such Child shall appear to him to be ill-treated or neglected, can transfer the child to someone else's care in the neighbourhood'.[2] If the illegitimate child were to die in the care of a nurse, she was to report the death to one of the local justices or to a minister of religion who might, should he think it desirable, call for a postmortem examination at the expense of the parish. Failure to report such a death, it was recommended, should be punished by imprisonment.

Between them, these two Bills contained the seeds of any effective and responsible policy for the boarding out of children: careful recording of the circumstances under which a child was placed with a foster-parent and clear legal sanctions against abuse of the child by the nurse. The ground on which the seed fell, alas, was too hard for it to root. The only provision of either Bill to be enacted later, was the proposal to limit the length of time a mother of an illegitimate child might be committed to a House of Correction. The Act of James I, as we have seen, 'if rigorously inflicted, might be too severe' since it could lead to life imprisonment. Under the new Act of 1810, two justices might sentence such a woman for a limited term only to a House of Correction, varying between six weeks and twelve months. Were she to appear 'reformed' before the expiration of her sentence, she was to be released on the order of two justices.

[1] ibid., p. 11.
[2] ibid., p. 9.

THE ILLEGITIMATE CHILD

No woman was to be committed 'Until she have been delivered for the Space of One Calendar Month'.

Since no evidence was adduced or referred to which might show whether the Act of James I, had indeed been rigorously imposed, it would be difficult to claim this as a major contribution to the welfare of the illegitimate child in so far as it might possibly affect the length of time a child had to be boarded out. Indeed, when one compares the lack of success which attended Bills framed in 1773 and 1802 to promote the welfare of the illegitimate child with the success which attended Bills framed in 1773 and 1795 to protect the local ratepayers, it soon becomes clear that the continuing policy of the State with regard to the illegitimate child was largely the negative one of resisting by scrupulous limitation, the social liability for its support. A policy which, with the ruthless application of the powers given to overseers and justices by the 1795 Act,[1] in which 'every unmarried Woman with Child shall be deemed chargeable and taken to be a Person actually chargeable', and which allowed her removal to the place of her last settlement, was to add another dimension of misery to the life of the illegitimate child in a society where settlement was an increasingly irrelevant concept.

At this point, the inescapable fact that the State was only concerned with illegitimacy among the poor, and that the grounds of its concern were the economics of maintenance rather than the circumstances of conception becomes of critical importance. For whilst the inevitable and intended consequence of the laws concerning the illegitimate children of the poor was both to humiliate the mother and stigmatise the child so as to discourage others from the reckless procreation of children they were unable to support, in circles where the poor laws were an irrelevance, the illegitimate child remained largely untouched by the invidious consequences of its provisions. Throughout the seventeenth and eighteenth centuries, the natural children of the noble and the wealthy continued to be openly acknowledged and provided for by their parents without comment or indeed without criticism. It was not in the least remarkable that Joseph Banks, a Fellow of the Royal Society and, in 1735, High Sheriff of Lincolnshire, should make provision in his will 'against the birth of an illegitimate son'. Indeed, when his own father had died

[1] 35 George III, c. 101.

some years earlier, he had given John Norton £300 out of his father's personal property 'in consideration of his believing John to be the natural son of his late father, and that his late father intended to have given him this provision, but omitted it by mistake'. This matter-of-fact acceptance of sexual indulgence outside marriage was to continue among the aristocracy well into the nineteenth century. One of Victoria's early Prime Ministers, Lord Melbourne, was one of six children who were 'only doubtfully related' to the father whose name they bore. In his study of *The Young Melbourne*, Lord David Cecil makes some interesting observations concerning the aristocracy of the early nineteenth century, among whose married women the practice of having lovers was too common to stir comment. 'The historian grows quite giddy as he tries to disentangle the complications of heredity consequent on the free and easy habits of the English aristocracy. The Harley family, the children of the Countess of Oxford, were known as the "Harleian Miscellany", on account of the variety of fathers alleged to be responsible for their existence. The Duke of Devonshire had three children by the Duchess and two by Lady Elizabeth Foster; the Duchess one by Lord Grey. Most of them were brought up together in Devonshire House, each set of children with a surname of its own.'

Long before Victoria's accession, however, there were indications of a new and more restrictive attitude to the illegitimate child in some circles which called for special care when the child was being launched on a public career. Lord Chesterfield's illegitimate son, Philip Stanhope, for example, found that his illegitimate birth counted against him in his career as a diplomat, hence his father urged him to enter Parliament with the advice 'You must make a figure there if you would make a figure in your country'. 'I shall bring him into the next Parliament at my own (and probably no small) expense,' confided Chesterfield to Lord Newcastle, in 1753, 'I flatter myself that his seat there will be so far like the cloak of charity as to cover one sin at least, and upon my word I know of no other for which he wants a cover.'

Happy the child whose father's overt influence could provide him with such a cloak of charity. A hundred years later, society was not so disposed to withhold from the illegitimate scions of the eminent, the invidious status that Stanhope's contemporaries already accorded the bastards of the poor.

IX

The Twin Disciplines of Work and Worship

1. *Apprenticeship*

In considering the immediate implications and the later application of the Tudor legislation which formed the basis of statutory provision for the children of the poor for well over two centuries, it is essential to recognise that it was an integral part of a general social policy whose aim was to conserve a social order, hierarchical in character, sanctioned by Providence, and maintained by particular concepts of mutual responsibility. Among these, the duty of each to contribute according to his ability and station was emphasised as necessary to the social and spiritual well-being of State and citizen alike. In large measure, the achievement of such an end depended on the ability to instil habits of industry and the acceptance of Divine authority, and to this end therefore the Tudors and their imitators sought directly and indirectly to encourage the twin disciplines of work and worship.

The training of children in some kind of work and craft, so that they might learn habits of industry and have the ability to support themselves when they were grown up was a distinctive feature of sixteenth-century social policy. The alternative means devised to this end were the statutory system of apprenticeship and the many employment and training schemes for the children of the poor, particularly in the textile towns. The successful scheme at Norwich, where some nine hundred children were employed in the homes of 'select women' who supervised their work in the cloth industry has already been described. Similar schemes though on a smaller scale were established at London, York, Ipswich, Leicester and Bristol among others.[1] The municipal authorities responsible for these schemes either provided accommodation and heating and appointed a skilled worker to supervise the work of the adults and the technical training of the children, or, alternatively, granted an interest free loan to some established entrepreneur who was willing to teach and employ children. Leicester, for example, experimented with both methods in the second half of the century. A scheme for the technical training of the young in the cloth industry was set up under appointed clothiers in 1571, while in 1596 a loan of £20 was made to the wife of Thomas Clarke 'in respect shee doth keepe manye poor children in work in knittynge of jersye'. At Bristol, in 1589, the Common Council of the City set up a large school to instruct young children 'to knit worsted hosen'. Thus, where expanding industries provided opportunities for children to acquire a craft while still living at home, schemes such as these were a popular alternative to apprenticeship with individual masters.

The medieval system of apprenticeship evolved by the gilds was 'transformed into a national institution' by the Elizabethan Statute of Artificers in 1563,[2] which made a seven-year apprenticeship compulsory for all who wished to take up an industrial craft; and this, together with the compulsory system of poor law apprenticeship, envisaged what was virtually a national system of technical training for the industrial and labouring classes. The apprentice invariably lived with his master and was normally unpaid for his services; but in return for his work he received instruction in his craft; and board, lodging and clothing for the period of his apprenticeship. This system, the customary method of training for the children of the middle and artisan classes, came to be accepted by Tudor legislators as the favoured solution to more than one social problem. It will be remembered

---

[1] *Records of the Borough of Leicester*, ed. M. Bateson. 1905. vol. III, pp. XLVII, XLIX, 327.
[2] 5 Eliz., c. 4., For a general account of the history of apprenticeship, see Dunlop and Denman, *English Apprenticeship and Child Labour*. 1912.

how, in the time of Henry VIII and Edward VI, apprenticeship was a preventive remedy for vagrancy; since the vagrant normally had no trade, his child must be trained in one so that he might be kept from poverty and vagabondage. For the lessening of unemployment, the Statute of Artificers enacted that anyone under the age of twenty-one 'refusing to be an apprentice and to serve in husbandry or in any other kind of art, mystery, or science', might be imprisoned until he agreed to serve. And at the end of the century, by the Acts of 1597 and 1601, the justices were given further powers to apprentice the children of all parents thought unable to keep them. The dual purpose here was the relief of parents and the proper maintenance and training of their children.

In the distant as well as the more recent past, 'proper' training had relevance both to personal aptitude and local opportunity and social position. 'In choosing a profession he [the father] is directed by his child's disposition... Yet he humours not his child when he makes an unworthy choice beneath himself...'[1] In the sphere of industrial training, this social exclusiveness of certain crafts, long practised by the gilds, was now legally enforced by the Statute of Artificers, the intention of which was neither to promote the mobility of labour (as we have seen in the case of vagrancy, it was in fact used as an instrument to prevent it) nor to promote social mobility. In the countryside the Statute required that:

'All persons between twelve and sixty not otherwise lawfully employed, nor being a Gentleman borne... nor having Landes Rents or Hereditamentes of the clere yerely value of forty shilliges... nor being woorthe in Goodes and Cattelles to the value of Tenne poundes, nor being heir to the same... shall be compelled to be reteyned to serve in Husbandrye by the yere, withe any suche person so to serve within the same shire wher he shalbe so required.' Unmarried women between twelve and forty years of age, who were 'foorthe of service' could be compelled to serve 'by the yere or by the week or daye' and those who refused to serve were to be committed to 'warde'. 'And for the better advancement of Husbandrye and Tillage, and thinkent that such as are fit to be Apprentices to Husbandrye may be bounden thereto', any householder 'having and using half a

[1] Thomas Fuller, *The Holy State*. 1642. Section on the Good Parent, p. 13.

Ploughe Lande at the least in Tillage' was empowered to take on indenture as apprentice anyone between the ages of ten and eighteen until at least twenty-one or twenty-four 'as the parties can agree'.

The clauses intended to contain country folk were immediately followed by others devised to stratify entry into the employments of the town in terms of the existing social hierarchy; hence their very great detail. In general, except for their own sons, merchants and tradespeople might take as apprentice those whose parents possessed a forty shilling freehold. But in the market towns, traders overseas, mercers, drapers, goldsmiths, ironmongers, embroiderers, and clothyers who 'dothe or shall put Clothe to making and sale' might only accept the children of parents having a three pound freehold. Others might take as apprentice 'the Childe or Children of any other Artificer or Artificers not occupieng Husbandrye nor being a laborer'. Woollen cloth weavers everywhere were restricted to taking apprentices whose fathers held a three pound freehold, a stipulation, according to George Unwin, which closed the occupation of weaver 'to fully three-quarters of the rural population'.

Effectively excluded by the Statute from all the higher mysteries of the towns, the sons of men who were neither burgesses nor owners of a freehold were allowed to enter the inferior crafts, thus ensuring an adequate supply of fully trained tradespeople at this necessary, though humbler, level of occupation:

'yt shalbe laufull to any persone using and exercising tharte or Occupation of a Smithe Wheelewright Plowghwright Myllwright Carpenter Roughe Mason Playsterer Sawyer Lymeburner Brickmaker Bricklayer Tyler Slater Haelyer Tilemaker Lynnen weaver Turner Cowper Millers Earthen potters Wollen weavers weaving Housewiefs or Householde Clothe onely and none other, Clothe Fuller otherwise Tucker or Walker Burner of Ore and Woade Ashes Thatcher or Shingler' to be permitted to have apprentices even though their parents had no lands.

As far as the ordinary life of the apprentices was concerned, the Statute did not and did not intend to introduce any changes from the conditions which already obtained, largely devised and controlled by the gilds, nor would there have been the administrative machinery to effect any significant changes. Indeed, as Dunlop and Denman aptly remark: 'the want of administrative

THE TWIN DISCIPLINES OF WORK AND WORSHIP

machinery . . . led to the early ineffectiveness of the Act and the Government's dependence on the gilds . . . which gave an opportunity to the gilds to establish their monopolies, one result of which was that the Elizabethan apprenticeship system is not the apprenticeship system of the Statute of Artificiers but of the Statute as interpreted by the gilds,'[1] with all that implied in terms of the restriction of the numbers of apprentices a master might take; the custom of patrimony; and, after 1601, premiums for indentures, none of which was mentioned in the Statute, but all practised by the gilds as an important part of their system of control over the entry of labour into their crafts. Nevertheless, even had the Government itself been able to administer the Statute and benefit more children by the State regulation of labour (for the gild limitation of numbers must have closed the door of training and protection in the face of many who would thereby be relegated to inferior trades) just because their narrow apprenticeship rules were openly or tacitly sanctioned, the companies were willing to champion apprenticeship even to the extent of bearing the brunt of legal proceedings against unlawful work. From the child's point of view, their vigilance was important, for it meant that he did not serve his seven years only to find himself thrown aside, forestalled by men who had not undergone the burden of training. On the contrary, his after career was practically secure. Thus the narrow policy of the gilds was not without its value.

Of the day-to-day life of an apprentice there are few records either before or immediately after the passing of the Statute of Artificers. Such as there are frequently underline the harshness if not the brutality of the lives of our forebears. At the time of the passing of the Statute, in his indentures a boy promised good behaviour and civility to his master in whose house he lived and whose long hours of work were his own, although night work was forbidden on account of the poor quality of work done in a bad light. Usually, his work was only rewarded by instruction in his master's craft and board and lodging and clothing but sometimes an apprentice would enter an agreement for five or six years with small incremental earning, beginning at 40s. and ending at £3 6s. 8d. or £4 a year, the apprentice finding his own clothes and apparatus suitable to his work. At the end of his

[1] Dunlop and Denman, op. cit., p. 92.

THE TWIN DISCIPLINES OF WORK AND WORSHIP

agreement, an apprentice could expect to be given two complete sets of clothing: shoes, hose, shirt, breeches, doublet and hat, and often 40s. in ready money.[1]

The master's control over his apprentices was supervised by the gilds, who appointed two 'searchers' to look into the conditions of work and labour of its members and also, even before the passing of the Statute, by the municipal authority. At Norwich, for example, the Mayor held a weekly court at which, among other things, pleas from local apprentices were heard. Thus in 1556 the court pronounced in the case of John Palmer: 'Whereas one John Palmer was late bounden apprentyce to John Tompson sythens which time uppon certen occasion the seid John Tompson have gyven the seid John Palmer as it is thoghte by the courte unreasonable correctyon for his defaltes. Whereuppon the seid John Palmer hathe remayned w^t his mother Mrs Palmer. And now this day the partyes being present uppon examynacion hereof it is orderd that the seid John Palmer shall go home w^t the seid John Tompson and serue him as his apprentyce according to his indenture. And that the seid John Tompson shall entere bond for the peace against the seid John Palmer.'[2] Far more typically, however, it was the gild itself which intervened if a master exceeded his proper authority and abused his apprentice as was the case when the Wardens of the Merchant Taylors, some seven years later, heard in their Court of the illused Henry Bourefeld. Bourefeld's head had been broken open 'without any just cause' by his master, Thomas Palmer. The Court committed Palmer to prison and made him pay for the surgeon who attended to the hapless Bourefeld's head.

Even though the apprentice had certain avenues of appeal, however, the power of a master over his apprentice was very considerable. The services of an apprentice were looked upon as property which might be disposed of by its owner, the master, and from this arose the custom of 'sale or turnover'. Some masters occasionally sold some years of a boy's apprenticeship to another freeman; sometimes they sold back or gave some years to the apprentice himself. Obviously open to abuse on more than one count, the gilds tried to repress the custom by requiring their sanction for such trading and also some part of the

[1] R. A. Roberts, op. cit., pp. 110–11.
[2] *Records of Norwich*, p. 176, case CCCXIV.

A Collection of

On a fine LIBRARY.

WITH Eyes of Wonder the gay Shelves behold,
Poets, all Rags alive, now clad in Gold:
In Life and Death, one common Fate they share,
And on their Backs ftill all their Riches ware.

GILES

PRETTY POEMS.

GILES JOLT and his CART.

GILES JOLT, as sleeping in his Cart he lay,
Some pilf'ring Villains ftole his Team away:
Giles wakes and cries—What's here, a dickins what!
Why, how now—am I Giles, or am I not?
If he—I've loft fix Geldings to my Smart;
If not—Oddsbuddikin, I've found a Cart.

17 From, A Collection of Pretty Poems For The Amusement of Children Three Foot High

18 The Princess Sophia Matilda of Gloucester. Reynolds

profit for themselves, which was sometimes not inconsiderable. The early accounts of the Merchant Taylors' Company contains a reference to such a sale whereby Henry Whytethorne made 17s. 9d. profit of which 8s. 10d. had to be handed over to the gild.[1] Essentially, the Statute of Artificers was an endorsement, not a reformation, of an existing system of labour recruitment and organisation; extending its scope, not limiting its application. It was a legislative attempt, by compulsory and lengthy periods of training, to provide against the misuse of children's labour. Under its provisions, other methods of employment were forbidden to apprentices who were thus protected against temporary and odd-job work; from alternative spells of overwork and unemployment such as their adult relatives suffered from. Its intention was to make bonds of apprenticeship a supervised contract between the employer and the child, an intention which stands in marked contrast to the uncontrolled exploitation of child labour permitted by governments of later periods.

For the first twenty years, however, the enforcement of the Statute was uncertain. Technically its provisions were enforceable by three types of authority: the gilds themselves, the justices, and municipal authorities, to any of which an apprentice might appeal if abused. Of these, as we have already indicated, the gilds were by far the most important and effective force. By the second half of Elizabeth's reign they began to insist upon the *sine qua non* of effective supervision in this field, the enrolment of apprentices, as a check on whether indentures were actually being fulfilled. They continued, in their own bye-laws, to reiterate the obligation of a seven-year apprenticeship for all except sons working with their own fathers, just as they continued to appoint their own 'searchers' to see how and if the laws were being enforced. Since the municipal authorities nearly always supported the gilds' actions, there was only rarely a conflict between these two authorities. They were, after all, people of the same class with much the same interest in upholding the law. Nevertheless, despite the activities of town and gild, there were considerable evasions of the law, especially in the small towns where the gilds were weak or non-existent.

This is not to imply that the justices, with their very considerable powers of punishment and release from indentures can be

[1] Dunlop and Denman, op. cit., pp. 57-8.

entirely dismissed as an agency of the Statute's enforcement. In 1586, at Warwick, the local Sessions charged a jury with an enquiry into certain aspects of the Statute's application locally. The jury were to present the names of masters and servants in certain instances; either mercers, drapers or clothiers 'putting cloth to make or sale' who had as apprentices boys not their own sons or the sons of fathers with lands and rents of 40s. or, alternatively, men taking apprentices without proper indentures. This seems to have been part of a general checking-up operation on the apprentices and journeymen kept by local masters. It revealed, *inter alia*, that 'John Townesend kepith as Apprentice Thomas Sharples and Richard Egeworth neither bound nor enrolled' and that 'Richard Smyth weaver settith on work one John Lovett as a Journeyman wch Lovet is yet Aprentice to one Anthony Brigg'.[1]

Over the years, their authority to cancel indentures continued to be the means of releasing some unfortunate apprentices from the toils of a master who was either careless or vicious. The sermon of Henry Smith, *The Benefit of Contention*, first published in 1590 and constantly reprinted for the next half century, was a zealous attack on the excessive materialism of his day; the covetousness, which he describes as 'the Londoners sinne'; the lust for wealth that produces cut-throat competition; and 'the gready inhumanity that would make slaves of apprentices'.[2] Records of local Sessions and Courts of Assize during the first half of the seventeenth century only too amply testify both to the justice of, and the necessity for, such an admonition. In Wiltshire, an apprentice who had run away from his master, a glover at Warminster, was discharged from his apprenticeship on the grounds that his master had given him 'immodest' correction. (He had been often unmercifully whipped, sixty stripes at a time, although he was only nine years old.)[3] At the Chester Quarter Sessions, to whom it was reported that a master had broken an apprentice's head, 'threatening to hurt and kill him', the justices acknowledged that the boy did indeed have good cause to complain of his master and ruled that 'for asmuch as the said occasions and differences are so hainous that we

---
[1] *The Book of John Fisher*. (Warwick, n.d.) ed. Thos. Kemp, 1900. pp. 157–61.
[2] Quoted L. B. Wright, op. cit., p. 285.
[3] The Records of the Quarter Sessions in the County of Wilts., *Historical MSS Committee Report on MSS in Various Collections*, vol. I, 1901, p. 117.

cannot conceive any course to agree and reconcile the said Master and Apprentice wthout manifest danger to the Apprentice', the boy was to be discharged from his indentures and the master obliged to pay back fifty shillings of the four-pound premium to the apprentice's uncle.[1] In Suffolk, John Mobbes was released from his indentures to James Fokes, a tailor, who had beaten him 'overmuch' and had not supplied him 'with competent meat drink and clothing'. In addition to the loss of the boy's services, Fokes had to give the apprentice a doublet cloth and find him a 'quarter's scholarship in the art of writing' and return a covering which the boy's father had lent him.[2] What strikes one now in retrospect, is the mildness of the penalties usually imposed on the master in many cases. In 1655 a Nottinghamshire husband and wife were merely bound over by the justices 'for beating and abusing an apprentice inasmuch as he dyed upon itt wthin halfe a yere after as is affirmed by ye childs mother in Court'.[3]

In practice, however, the sentences and judgements of the local courts were only of academic interest to most apprentices for whom the courts of the gilds were a great deal more accessible and were thus far more likely in fact to be an effective protection against a bad master. To these courts the 'searchers' and other gild officers would report any offence they observed against the Statute's provisions or against their own bye-laws which empowered them to oblige a master to teach his apprentice his craft; allowed them to transfer an apprentice to a better master; and generally allowed the court to be arbiter in disputes between a master and his apprentices.

Of course, the apprentice was not by any means always the offended party; the behaviour of the boys themselves was often far from being above the reproaches either of the masters or of the general public. During the sixteenth century there is ample evidence that in London the apprentices were becoming increasingly turbulent and out of hand, not least (and in the mid-twentieth century this surely strikes a very familiar note) in the matter of their dress.[4] At a time when dress was distinctly associ-

[1] *Cheshire Quarter Sessions Records*, pp. 111–12.
[2] R. A. Roberts, op. cit., p. 111.
[3] *Nottinghamshire County Records, 1655*, p. 128.
[4] See Sir Walter Besant, *Survey of London: London in the Time of the Tudors*. 1904. p. 324.

THE TWIN DISCIPLINES OF WORK AND WORSHIP

ated with social status, very specific regulations existed concerning the appropriate dress for an apprentice. Much to the displeasure of the citizenry, however, the apprentices of the wealthier companies (by definition at this time the sons of wealthy fathers) could afford to deck themselves out in attire totally unsuitable to their present position. This particular source of conflict between the towns and the gilds had revealed itself long before the Statute of Artificers had been issued. The records of the Merchant Adventurers of Newcastle note a local order passed in 1554 'for the apparell of apryntyses' under which the Mayor and aldermen could make regulations laying down how apprentices might dress. Masters were to be fined if their apprentices were found attired contrary to the local bye-laws and – a shrewd way of striking an effective blow at these young peacocks – the apprentices themselves were to forfeit time they had already served.[1] In 1582, tried beyond measure by the behaviour of the apprentices, the Lord Mayor and Common Council of London passed an ordinance calculated to suppress the very extravagant apparel in which the apprentices of the wealthy London companies displayed themselves on the streets. For a first offence against sartorial discretion, the apprentice was to be punished by his master; for a second, he was to be given a public whipping; for a third, he was to serve an extra six months on his apprenticeship. At the same time, the master was to be fined for conniving at the offence.

The Common Council also made an attempt in this ordinance to restrict some of the other activities of the apprentices which had led to public disturbance, and forbade them to frequent dancing, fencing and music schools. From all appearances, however, the spirits of these Elizabethan juveniles (who were some of them as young as seven, although the better class trades would not accept a boy under twelve) were so little dampened by this kill-joy ordinance, that years later (1595) Elizabeth was forced to appoint a Provost Marshal whose particular duty it was to control the public behaviour of the London apprentices, 'especially such as were of base manual occupations and other riotous elements'.[2]

Jealous of their reputation, the gilds were far from leaving all

---

[1] See Dunlop and Denman, op. cit., pp. 190 and 191.
[2] Besant, op. cit., pp. 325–6.

control over their apprentices' social behavour to the public authorities. In fact they seem as a rule to have been even less disposed to look benignly on youthful high spirits than the local Mayors. The Shoemakers of Carlisle dourly declared in 1595: 'it is full condiscended and agreed upon by the fellowship of this gyld that no journeyman or apprentice shall make any foot balle to sell or play withal without consent and knowledge of his or their maisters and that they shall not play at football within the liberties of this cittie'. Equally repressively, the Merchant Adventurers of Newcastle forbade their apprentices to 'daunce dice cards mum or use any musick eyther by night or daye in the streetes' and pronounced against extravegence in dress and unduly long hair.[1] Determined to see its wishes observed, the Company went even further and in 1603 set up a special gaol, supervised by a specially appointed officer, to which their apprentices might be committed. 'And for the better orderinge & governing of such apprentices as shall misdemean themselves . . . thair shall-be one speciall gaioll or prison within this towne . . unto which all disobedyent apprentices . . . upon complainte, shalbe committed, ther to remaine untill oreder be gyven by thr . . . Governor [of the Company], his master or mistress . . . for his enlargement; and the said apprentice or apprentices to be relevyed at the charge of his master or mistress, in some stricte manner, having regard to the preservacion of his or their healthes.' The officer in charge of the prison was 'to see them saifflie kept accordinglie; not sufferinge them to plaie anie ghames whatsoever, or to have the companies of anie other person or persons, or to have anie conference with anie at all' without the leave of the Governor of the Company and of the apprentice's master or mistress. Firm in deed as well as purpose, the Company matched action to words. Three of nine apprentices brought before their Court for failing to conform to their regulations governing the cut of apprentices' hair and the quality of the dress remained 'obstinate', and were promptly clapped into the gaol under the supervision of the then keeper, Robert Sharpe, and given a daily ration of two penny worth of bread and a quarter of small beer and forbidden to see any of their friends. On another occasion, Allen Gilpin, who was said to have used abusive language to a woman, was brought before the Court where

[1] See Dunlop and Denman, op. cit., pp. 189–90 and footnote, p. 189.

'he was openly reproved for his lude carrage toward her, but he, not in the least shewing any remorse for his abuse, was by order of the courte sent to the apprentices' prison' there to be 'strictly kept' on the same diet as the other miscreants till further notice.[1] Few things so eloquently testify to the contemporary belief that the good workman was also a responsible citizen than these self-imposed attempts of the gilds to instil self-discipline and respect for the social code into those for whose industrial training they were responsible. In the context of present-day English society, so close a supervision of the daily lives of young workpeople would be considered by the employers themselves as an unwarranted interference. Doubtless even in the more disciplined days of the sixteenth and seventeenth centuries, the apprentices found it irksome, yet it was a small price to pay for the protection of their welfare and working conditions and technical training which the gilds' considerable powers over their workpeople gave and which certainly made this group of children better trained, less readily abused or overworked than the parish apprentices placed out under the Poor Law Act of 1597 and the Act of 1601.

The parish apprentice, for whom agreements were entered into with a master similar to those for industrial apprentices save that, in his indentures, where the overseers were parties to the bond, their names and not those of the child's parents appear, did not come under gild or company control. Though he might appeal to the justices, the authority of the law was less easily invoked than that of the gilds, as we have already seen. Action for ill-treatment was only taken after a complaint had been lodged; otherwise there was no regular supervision to see that parish apprentices were really learning a craft and not being overworked or ill-used.

Dunlop and Denman make a sharp distinction between industrial and parish apprenticeship on the ground that, whereas industrial apprentices were indentured to learn a trade, the object of apprenticing parish children was 'not so much to teach the child bound a trade as to remove him from injurious surroundings and provide him with maintenance. His position was, in fact, rather that of the "boarded out" child today. He might be

---

[1] See Extracts from the Records of the Merchant Adventurers of Newcastle-upon-Tyne, *Publications of the Surtees Society*, vol. I (S. Soc. XCIII), 1895, pp. 23, 169 and 154.

taught a trade if the master to whom he was bound apprentice happened to be a craftsman, but his apprenticeship in the usual sense of the term was not an essential part of his contract. What the overseers and justices had to do was to provide him with board, lodging and a guardian.'

As we shall see, this interpretation of the laws did in fact come to be used in many places and it is perfectly possible to cite evidence, such as these authors do, to show that this was a construction which was placed on the statutes by some people in the seventeenth century. In the 1630s, for instance, some of the Sheffield gentry tried to obtain immunity from taking parish apprentices on the plea that they had no trade to teach them. Their argument was dismissed on the grounds that 'ye meaning of ye statute was not for the education of boys in arts but for charity to keep ym and relieve ym from turning to roguery and idleness, so a man's house was, as it were, a Hospital, in yt case, rather than a shop of trade, for they might be brought up to husbandry, cookery, dayery and the like services in an house'.[1] Even in this account, however, it seems perfectly clear that the children were expected to learn something of practical use, and evidence from other sources only serves to emphasise that the whole intention of both the 1597 and the 1601 Acts was to ensure not merely maintenance for the children but a training which would enable them to support themselves in later life. The *Ease for Overseers*, first published in 1601, lays great emphasis on the importance of giving poor children 'some honest trade of life, when their parents for povertie cannot performe it', and lays down three principles for the guidance of overseers in placing parish children. First, they are to be put out young, 'for as a twigge will best bend when it is greene, so children are fittest to be bound when they are young, otherwise by reason of their idle and base educations, they will hardly hold service: but as they have wavering and straying mindes, so they will have wandering and unstaid bodies, which will sooner be disposed to vagrance than activitie, to idlenesse than to worke'. Second, the overseers are to give due regard to 'the facultie, honestie or abilitie of the masters', to teach the children a trade. If overseers fail in this duty, the author warns, unsuitable masters may provoke the children to run away, or the children will waste their

[1] Dunlop and Denman, op. cit., pp. 248, 250 and 251-2.

time without learning a craft and 'if they bee thus posted off it will nothing at all benefit'. In the third place, only those who were a burden to their parents, and not those already contributing to the family income, were to be placed out.[1] From such statements in the *Ease* and from similar remarks made later by Dalton, it is clear that the original intention of parish apprenticeship was not in fact merely to provide a type of boarding out for maintenance, but a system for instruction that would ensure a future means of livelihood.

The Act of 1597 allowed overseers to raise a rate to cover the cost of apprenticing poor children, and this, together with the Orders of the Privy Council to the justices issued in the following year reminding them of their duties in this respect, resulted in the immediate enforcement of the Act in the more populous parishes although, in the majority of small, rural parishes, a compulsory poor rate was probably not levied until a generation later. Thus Henry Arth, writing of the administration of the law in Wakefield, states: 'As for the younger sort, fitte to learne trades and occupations there is order taken to put them to apprenticeshippe or otherwise to service'. Early in the seventeenth century, the justices of Norfolk reported that they had apprenticed some five hundred poor children in the previous year; a little later, those of the West Riding had apprenticed two hundred; and those of Somerset four hundred. It is clear from the records that the total number of children who at the end of the sixteenth and in the early seventeenth centuries gained some kind of training and a start in life must have been very large.

The fees paid as premiums for parish apprentices – a system introduced by statute in 1601 – usually varied from two to three pounds. The parish sometimes augmented this by gifts of 'cloaths' to the child himself. The overseers of Westbury, having 'payd John Bramble ye Smith in money with Ned Hatter and expences' when Hatter was bound to him, the sum of £5 5s. 0d., also 'disburst for two suits of apparell, 4 shirts, A Hat, tow payre of shoes & 3 payre of stockings & other necessary for Ned Hatter when he was bound apprentice, the sum of £3/4/10, making a total of £8/9/10 in all'.[2] In some rural parishes, where there was as yet no compulsory poor rate, a special

[1] op. cit., p. 27.
[2] See Dorothy Marshall, *The English Poor in the Eighteenth Century*. 1926. p. 192.

THE TWIN DISCIPLINES OF WORK AND WORSHIP

'levie' was 'imposed for the putting forth of apprentices'.

Under the laws of 1597 and 1601, the churchwardens and the overseers were, like the justices themselves, authorised to apprentice not merely paupers and orphans, but also the children of such parents as were so overburdened by children that they were incapable of either maintaining them or of providing adequately for their training. In practice, they seem to have been reluctant to do so; nor, indeed, was there a great deal of incentive for them to exercise themselves on behalf of such children unless family allowances were being paid to the parents.

During the reign of Charles I, however, spurred on by the Privy Council, the justices appear to have devoted more attention to the apprenticing of poor children than to any other aspect of poor relief and the Privy Council both demanded and received more detailed reports on this subject than any other. Hence in Reading the Mayor requested the churchwardens and overseers of each parish 'to search their parishes and to finde what poore children there be whose parentes are not able to keepe them, & to take their names to the intent they may be placed and put apprentices to handicrafts forthwith'.[1] But for the increased activity, a price had to be paid other than money, since in some places, suitable masters were not always to be found. Local conditions naturally varied and in some parishes the justices seemed more sanguine of success than others. In 1644, at Lewes, the justices ruled that 'Whereas Thomas Okly and Alice Dotterell widow of the parish of Eastergate are lately deceased and have left seaven children upon the charge of the said parish It is ordered that foure of the said Children shalbe placed forth as apprentices by the Churchwardens and overseers of the poore upon foure of the most able men of the said parish And that the rest of the children be provided for by the Churchwardens and overseers of the poore at the common charge of the said parish'.[2] But for years past, from other parts of the country, it had been clear that it had been far from easy to find men both able and willing to whom parish apprentices might be bound.

According to Direction III of the *Orders* issued by the Privy Council in 1630, the justices possessed the power to compel any

---

[1] *Records of the Borough of Reading*, vol. III, 1896, p. 234.
[2] *Quarter Sessions Order Book, 1642–49.* ed. B. C. Redwood. Sussex Record Society, vol 54, 1954, p. 59.

person whom they deemed suitable to take an apprentice to do so: 'That the poore children in every Parish to put forth apprentices to husbandrey, and other handycrafts, and money to be raised in the Parishes for placing them, according to the Law; and if any party shall refuse to take the said Apprentice, being put out according to the Law, such party as shall refuse the said Apprentice, to be bound over to the next Quarter Sessions, or Assizes and there to be bound to his good behaviour, or otherwise ordered as shall be found fit'.[1] An elaboration on this was given in 1633 by one Assize Court whose justices in considered answers to particular questions on the operation of the law as it then obtained, were set out in a series of *Resolutions*. Among these, they held that 'Every man who is by calling or profession or manner of living, that entertaineth and must have the use of other servants of the like quality, must entertaine such apprentices, wherein discretion must bee given upon due consideration of the circumstances.' A wealthy man not needing a servant might be forced to contribute 'toward the putting forth of such an apprentice by a tax'. Further, they stated, the justices had the power to compel parishioners of another parish in the county to take a poor child as apprentice if its own parish were unable to provide for it.[2]

In some cases, the master on whom the local justices wished to impose an apprentice seems to have had genuine grounds for claiming that he was unable to accept him. George Ibbottson of Bradfield refused a parish apprentice alleging that 'he is not of sufficient abilitie to provide for the same apprentice, there being divers inhabitantes there of better abilitie than himselfe, who are eased by the said churchwardens and overseers and have not apprentices'. Noting this complaint, the West Riding Quarter Sessions asked Sir Francis Wortley (himself a member of the Sessions) to look into this matter and examine both Ibbottson and the churchwardens, whom they appeared to suspect since their order ends: '. . . if the said Ibbottsons allegacons be true then the said Churchwardens and overseers to pay such cost and charges unto him as the said Sir Francis shall thincke fitt, for the abuse therein'.[3]

[1] The *Orders* are better known, perhaps, as *The King's Book of Orders*.
[2] *Resolutions of the Judges of Assize*. 1633. pp. 26-7.
[3] *West Riding Sessions Rolls*, vol. II (1611-1642), ed. J. Lister, 1915. p. 271.

On the other hand, there were many instances, as in the case of the Sheffield gentry we have already quoted, where the distinction between inability and unwillingness was a fine one indeed, and it was unwillingness, rather than genuine inability, which proved the greatest obstacle to the efficient application of *The King's Orders*. Cases where one man made a private arrangement with another for transferring the responsibility of a parish orphan, as did a Sheffield mercer with a local cutler for the sum of 40s., were the least of the justices' worries. Many masters, having ostensibly accepted a parish apprentice, tried to default in their obligations towards him altogether. In Nottinghamshire, in 1632, it was claimed that 'Divers complaints are made in Court that many masters of apprentices with whom poor children were lately placed out by the Churchwardens and Overseers of the poor with the assent of two or more Justices of the Peace, a little after such placing out and abiding either dismissed the apprentices or allowed them to depart by which aforesaid liberty they also returned to their County and thereby the care and good interest of the Justices and the Overseers of the Poor were frustrated'. Time and again, justices' rulings in such cases punctuate the records of the Sessions. So frequently did complaints on this score reach the Nottinghamshire Quarter Sessions, that the justices made a general ruling as to the penalties which could be imposed so that the cases might be dealt with the more expeditiously: 'Ordered, that all such masters of apprentices from the time of the dismissal or departure of such their apprentices unless the case thereof be allowed by the Justices of the Peace should pay to the Churchwardens and Overseers of the aforesaid separate parishes and places where they inhabit 12^d per week for each week from the time of their departure until they shall again receive and keep the aforesaid apprentices again, which money shall be used towards the maintainence and relief of their poor and impotent poor and besides for raising a Stock for setting their poor to work and placing out apprentices.'[1]

The explanation the Wiltshire justices gave in 1633 of their difficulties in binding out parish apprentices makes interesting reading. Parish apprenticeship was opposed, they stated, 'partly by reason of the unwillingness of clothiers to take apprentices,

[1] *Nottinghamshire County Records.*, ed. H. Hampton Copnall, 1915, p. 129.

being, as they pretend, untrustworty and thievish, partly by the unwillingness of foolish parents to part with their children, and partly by the churchwardens neglecting the business or out of malice imposing apprentices upon such as are not of ability to keep them'.[1] As to the thievishness of apprentices and the maliciousness of churchwardens it is only possible to speculate – and only wise to moderate imagination with sympathetic allowances for the exasperation of much tried men. Nor is it any easier to estimate the degree of resistance to the apprenticing of their children on the part of parents. In 1641, in the West Riding of Yorkshire, Robert Savile, a butcher by trade, but at that time one of the poor of his parish, was threatened with committal to the House of Correction at Wakefield if he persisted in his refusal to allow the local overseers to put out as apprentice his ten-year-old son.[2] On the face of it, it seems unlikely that Savile persisted or that parents in his situation, dependent on the parish for support and liable to imprisonment if they defied the authority of the overseers, were in any position to put up any effective resistance to the enforcement of the law. Which is not to say that they couldn't, like Savile, make the putting out of their children a more troublesome matter to the parish officers than it might have been!

Opposition to the poor law apprentice was no new thing. The apprenticeship clauses of the 1601 Act had indeed from the outset encountered resistance. According to E. M. Hampson, 'the extreme youth and sometimes the weakly constitution of the children did not commend them to enterprising masters. It was, seemingly, in view of the earliest interpretations of the law that pauper children should be "put forth very timely" at the age of seven years, that practical difficulties led even the most energetic justice to enquire only concerning children above the age of ten years.'[3] Not all sixteenth-century commentators would have been prepared to take so charitable view. In his *English Law* Cook makes a very biting assessment of the situation: 'For the binding out of Apprentices, a good & wholesome Law, that the poor educated in better mens houses might be trained up to be fit for imployment, as Husbandmen and otherwayes; truly

[1] *State Papers Domestic, 1633–34*, p. 273.
[2] *West Riding Sessions Rolls, 1611–1642*, p. 259.
[3] E. M. Hampson, *The Treatment of Poverty in Cambridgeshire, 1597–1834.* 1934. pp. 49–50.

through the pettish wilfulness or niggardliness of some men in Authority, it was assumed to be against the liberty of the Subject, to impose a servant upon him; and few or none will take willingly, so that the Law requires it, but none looks at execution; if any do, the particular Justices must upon refusal binde them over to the Sessions, where he shall be plagued, and as he saith, malitiously vexed with attendance, and pay fees, & then nothing is done; 'Tis truth, the Law holds forth a way of raising stock to put forth Apprentices; but there is so much ado to make a Rate; if they will not do it, binde them over to the Sessions is all, & there Lawyers make such work for their Clients, as home they go without Fine or Punishment.'[1]

In the light of the evidence we have already quoted, one cannot help thinking Cook's innuendoes concerning the activities of the justices a little unfair. Certainly in the 1630s the evidence shows that the justices of assize did in fact attempt to comply with Lord Keeper Coventry's injunction that 'a straight course [was] to be held against those who oppose [the binding of the children of the poor] as apprentices'. Nevertheless, the justices of assize only dealt with cases referred to them and it is quite clear that both lack of local enthusiasm for the law and the absence of adequate administrative machinery to enforce it, meant that its operation was very variable. Whilst some Quarter Sessions insisted on an apprentice being accepted by the master to whom he had been assigned, others were prepared to accept a payment towards the binding of the poor apprentice to somebody else, a payment which sometimes discharged the master from the responsibility of accepting an apprentice at all.

The increased activity of the justices in the apprenticeship of poor children as shown by the actions of the parishes and the Privy Council in the 1630s could only exacerbate the problem of finding suitable masters in many places. Furthermore, it must be remembered that the Statute of Artificers, in line with the exclusive policies pursued by the gilds and with the hierarchical nature of the social structure, reserved the more lucrative crafts for the children of burgesses and owners of freehold. Hence the scope for placing the children of the poor was already limited to the poorer trades in which the general conditions of life were often so bad that even if the master did his best, the circum-

[1] *English Law.* 1651. p. 50.

stances of the appointee were unlikely to be very favourable. And where suitable masters could not be found, unwilling householders who had no trades to teach were compelled to take them or pay a fine in default. Thus in some places the emphasis laid in the *Ease for Overseers* on the importance of children learning a trade was already in the 1630s being ignored and parish apprenticeship, despite the high ideals of the progenitors of the legislation of 1597 and 1601, degenerated into a system of boarding out at minimum cost to the rates. Small boys apprenticed to husbandry and little girls to housewifery were frequently exploited as cheap labour on the land and in domestic drudgery. In such cases there must have been a good deal of friction and hardship involved on both sides. On the other hand, there is much to suggest that on the whole parish apprenticeship worked well up to the mid-seventeenth century. The numerous bequests left by philanthropists for the apprenticeship of poor children show that it was considered to be an excellent way of providing for their maintenance and training. 'Had abuses in parish apprenticeship been prominent during the sixteenth and first half of the seventeenth centuries,' observes Leonard, it is unlikely that 'the Privy Councillors in their private capacities would have taken so much trouble to extend its practice.'[1]

In fact, the Tudor system at its best had all the advantages of boarding out plus technical training. But success depended on good administration rather than on the system. As long as the central government exercised control through the Privy Council – the system originated by the Elizabethan administration – parish apprenticeship on the whole achieved its aims. Undoubtedly life must have been hard for many apprentices, but there was no spoon-feeding in that age for any class. Many poor children undoubtedly received a sound training in husbandry and housewifery, in weaving and other branches of the textile trades, and in small metal and hardware trades, while the alternatives to apprenticeship must, for many children, have been far worse. It was after the supervision of the central government ceased after the Civil War, and more particularly after the Settlement Act of 1662, under which serving an apprenticeship in a parish was authorised as one means of gaining a settlement, that the more serious and widespread abuses of parish apprenticeship devel-

[1] Leonard, op. cit., p. 217.

THE TWIN DISCIPLINES OF WORK AND WORSHIP

oped. Dorothy Marshall, commenting on the effects of the 1662 Act of Settlement, observes: 'Once the parishes discovered that they could rid themselves of the settlement of a pauper child by placing it out as an apprentice in another parish, they found in this expedient the chief uses of the apprenticeship clauses... Nothing so clearly marks the great gulf between Elizabethan conceptions of the functions of the Poor Law and those commonly held from the Restoration onwards though, in theory, on the statute book the law remained the same; if anything it was better defined in the latter period. But whereas in the first place its objective had been the prevention of poverty, its latter aim was to prevent a rise in the rates.'[1] The later Settlement Act of 1691 which, in clarification of the earlier Act, laid down that an apprentice gained settlement after serving the first forty days of his apprenticeship in another parish, at once magnified the importance and vitiated the purpose of this particular system of training, and only exacerbated the tendency to which Dorothy Marshall refers. Thereafter, it became a very general though not ubiquitous practice to bind 'town children' outside the parish, thus placing on their master's parish the liability of their future care if destitute. Whereas only thirty-eight of the two hundred and sixteen children apprenticed by the parish of Gnosall between 1691 and 1816, for whom apprenticeship bonds are still extant, were apprenticed outside the parish,[2] elsewhere the proportion was a good deal higher. In the parish of Doverage, Derbyshire, for example, twenty-two out of the ninety indentures of poor children apprenticed by the parish between 1699 and 1818 – or nearly one in four – show that the children were apprenticed to masters in other parishes.[3] In Bedfordshire the parish of Eaton Socon was exceptional in only apprenticing sixteen out of seventy-two poor children out of the parish during the period 1693 to 1731. In other parts of the county the proportion was higher, sometimes far higher, as in the case of Maulden where between 1658 and 1788 as many as forty-five out of sixty-six poor children were apprenticed out of their native parish.[4]

[1] Dorothy Marshall, op. cit., p. 183.
[2] S. A. Cutlack, The Gnosall Records, 1679–1837. Poor Law Administration, *Historical Collections, Staffordshire*, pt. I, 1936, pp. 34–5.
[3] W. E. Tate, *The Parish Chest*. 1946. p. 221.
[4] F. G. Emmison, The Relief of the poor at Eaton Socon, 1706–1834, *Publications of the Bedfordshire Historical Record Society*, vol. XV, Apsley Guise, 1933.

In Cambridgeshire, the determination of local overseers of the poor to reduce their own parish poor rate seems to have produced a situation in which it was far more common for a child to be apprenticed outside his parish than within it. According to E. M. Hampson's analysis of the indentures of parish apprentices in that county for the period 1691 to 1830, five hundred and eighty-two out of a total of eight hundred and forty parish apprentices were sent to serve masters in some other parish than their own; whereas in the previous sixty years only one in seven children appears to have been trained in this way.[1]

All too often, anxiety to apprentice children outside the parish so as to give them settlement there, meant that arrangements were made without much regard to the moral or technical suitability of a master. 'The master may be a Tiger in Cruelty; he may Beat, Abuse, Strip-naked, Starve, or do what he will to the poor innocent Lad, few People take much Notice, and the Officers who put him out least of Any Body: For, they rest satisfied with the Merit of having shifted him off to a neighbouring Parish... and the Duty they owe to every poor Child in the Parish, is no farther layd to Heart', wrote Goldsmith in 1738.[2] One of many cases of 'mock apprenticeship' known to him personally was that of an old weaver, poor and previously convicted several times for theft, who covenanted to take parish children for the usual indenture fee. As soon as the premium was spent, the weaver, together with his family and the luckless apprentice, went on to the parish. Obviously such a man was, from the beginning, quite incapable of fulfilling his obligations to the boy who was all too clearly liable to be corrupted by such a background. From time to time, one comes across references to children being released from their indentures to an unsuitable master by the local justices. Joseph Harris, a 'poor lame boy', was discharged by the Buckinghamshire justices of Quarter Sessions from his indentures to one Matthew of Ivinghoe parish, 'a person adjuged by this Court not capable to take such an apprentice'. The justices believed that the indenture was 'contrived by some fraudulent practices of the (Poor) Officers of Wooborne', in order to relieve them of the responsibility for Harris's lameness – which

[1] E. M. Hampson, Settlement and Removal in Cambridgeshire, 1662–1834, *Cambridge Historical Journal*, vol. II. no. 3, 1928, p. 283.

[2] *An Enquiry into the Causes of the Encrease and Miseries of the Poor of England.* 1738. p. 43.

might have made him a liability on their own poor rates.[1] (How far, one wonders, was this release a token of local concern for Harris or, rather, a powerful interest in protecting the Ivinghoe rate?) Occasionally, one reads of parishes which chose to pay the apprentice's premium by instalments as a means of assurance against the risk of the master turning off his ward after receiving his premium; losing him through cruelty; or otherwise failing to fulfil his contract.[2] But the overwhelming impression one gets from reading through the records of, and contemporary comment on, the practice of apprenticing children out of the parish of their birth is that it commonly led to the neglect of the children and the corruption of apprenticeship.

Yet, though the use of the Settlement Acts to rid a parish of its responsibilities towards a poor child was undoubtedly a major cause of the widespread neglect of both the moral and technical training of children, in the wider context of the general practice of parish apprenticeship it was only a symptom of changing social attitudes, a growing disregard for the basic ideals on which the Tudors had founded the original legislation which remained the statutory basis of parish apprenticeship. For this reason, to be apprenticed within the parish of his birth was no guarantee to a child of greater regard being paid to his training. Indeed, to compare the lot of the poor child apprenticed within his own parish with that of a poor child apprenticed out of it is, with few exceptions, to compare not the good with the bad but two evils of which it is sometimes difficult to discern the worse, since in either case the overseers' responsibility for parish 'economy' weighed heavily against their responsibility to the child. Of course, not every poor law authority chose to allow economy totally to outweigh responsibility. Perhaps one of the most remarkable examples of parish apprenticeship being continued in the light of Tudor principles of community responsibility was Bristol, where the parishes had combined to form a Corporation, the better to administer the law. Here, in consequence of the Act of 1696, under which parish children could enter indentures up to the age of sixteen, instead of up to fourteen as in the 1601 Poor Law, a committee was set up 'to consider of methods to put out the Boy Apprentices that are chargeable to

[1] *Buckinghamshire Sessions Records.* ed. Hardy and Reckitt, vol. I, 1933. p. 423.
[2] Emmison, op. cit., p. 69.

this Corporation'. Their report is a blue-print of the kind of sensible, sensitive and constructive care of its poor children a local authority could still take, if it chose to do so, at the end of the seventeenth century. First, they laid down guiding principles for action:

1. In respect of the Master to see that he be a man of ability and honesty also of some sort of employment or faculty lest otherwise the Child be ill treated and thereby tempted to forsake his service or else consume his time idly without learning anything whereby he may live hereafter.
2. In respect to the Children. That it be done early whilst they be young and tractable before idleness and the Effects of a bad education make them unfit for services.
3. In respect to the Parents that care may be taken to bind out the Children of such as are least able to relieve them.

The Committee then urge the Corporation to use their influence to persuade wealthy traders and citizens to take poor apprentices and also commend the idea that, when money is loaned to a local tradesman by the municipality, they should be asked to take some poor apprentices as part of the bargain. Captains of Bristol ships should be persuaded to take local boys on their ships instead of strangers, the Report continues. But perhaps its most important recommendation was that a register should be kept of all children bound apprentice by the Corporation; to whom they were apprenticed; and full details of the terms of their indentures.[1] Here as elsewhere, careful records were essential to the effective exercise of community responsibility: without them it was impossible to ensure the appropriate conditions of apprenticeship for the individual child and their conspicuous absence in most parishes is peculiar testimony to the assessment the local overseers had of their responsibilities to the poor children of their parish. Early in the following century, Caleb Parfect alleged of the manner in which most parish officers sought to rid themselves of parish children by apprenticing them too young, too cheap and to bad masters: ' 'Tis little better than murdering them'.[2] Lest the reader imagine this to be mere exaggeration to make a point, it is worth remembering that

[1] *Bristol Corporation for the Poor, selected records, 1696-1834.* ed. E. E. Butcher. Bristol, 1932, pp. 59-62.
[2] *Proposals*, p. 8.

THE TWIN DISCIPLINES OF WORK AND WORSHIP

apprentices were sometimes murdered by the masters to whom they had been bound by the parish. The Middlesex Sessions papers, for example, record that in 1736 James Durant, a ribbon weaver, beat his thirteen-year-old apprentice to death with a 'mop-stick', and that in 1748 Elizabeth Dickens murdered her girl apprentice by beating her and ill-using her.[1] Though there was no doubt of their guilt, both were acquitted – a judgement which is as revealing of contemporary attitudes to violence against child apprentices as the fact of their being apprenticed to such masters and mistresses is eloquent of the lack of care of the overseers for the welfare of poor children. At an earlier date, the North Riding Quarter Sessions had made an Order concerning an apprentice who had run away because of his master's brutality that he was 'to be received again as an apprentice by his said master, according to the form of his indentures, and the said master not to be too cruel with him, but use him accordingly as an apprentice ought to be'![2]

But the kind of 'murder' that Parfect had in mind was the reckless destruction of the talents of the young people apprenticed to unscrupulous masters by parish officers whose own integrity was not so great as to impel them to be over particular as to the character and competence of the masters to whom they entrusted the technical education of the pauper children. 'This barbarous Practice might indeed be in a good measure suppress'd', he declares, 'if His Majesty's Justices of the Peace would sign no Indentures, without enquiring into the Age of the Children, and the Character and Circumstances of their intended Masters; or at least not without an Order of Vestry, signed by the Minister of the Parish.'[3] There was, in principle, no objection to Parfect's suggested remedy. The fatal flaw lay in the absence of any central, supervisory body to ensure that it be carried out. Once, this had been the function of the Privy Council but, after the Restoration, no government sought or dared to seek to reinstate the Council's authority, thus there was no administrative machine left to convert Parfect's plan from an ideal to a reality. The operation of the parish apprenticeship system was thus left in the hands of men who, as parish officers, largely resented the

---

[1] See M. D. George, *London Life in the Eighteenth Century*. 1926. p. 231.
[2] E. Trotter, *Seventeenth Century Life in the Country Parish*. 1919. p. 155.
[3] *Proposals*, p. 8.

cost of the system to the ratepayers, and to the local justices who, ratepayers themselves and not over nice concerning the legal claims of the poor, contented themselves by taking merely the necessary minimum action when their authority was invoked, safe in the knowledge that their sins of omission would rarely find them out. Many children were therefore apprenticed to masters and mistresses only interested in laying their hands on such premiums as the parish officers would offer and throughout the eighteenth century complaints grew of masters driving out poor apprentices long before their indentures had been served. By some, it was believed that this sort of treatment was encouraged by the statutory sanction given in 1696 to the practice of allowing local justices to compel a householder to accept a parish apprentice, 'and if hee or she shall refuse so to doe Oath being thereof made by one of the Churchwardens or Overseers', the justices were to impose a penalty of £10. Where masters were thus compelled, 'the best of Usage cannot be expected', wrote one man and certainly it laid the poor child open not only to the abuse of a reluctant master but also of the irresponsible parish officer who, in some cases, would apprentice a child as young as seven rather than have the expense of maintaining it in the workhouse or in its own home until it was nine or more years of age.

When directly appealed to, the justices had the power to release a child from his indentures, as did the Hertfordshire Quarter Sessions who discharged William Spurr, 'a poor child of Hatfield', from his apprenticeship to William Andrews of Cheshunt, a cordwainer, on account of the latter ill-using his apprentice, and not teaching him his trade or providing him with 'convenient washing, cloathing and apparel'.[1] But how many cases of ill-treatment and neglect went unrecorded because the apprentice was too frightened of his master, too ignorant of his rights, or too fearful of the anger of the parish officers at the return of the poor child for whose responsibility they had believed themselves rid for good, we have no means of telling. Nor was it inevitable that an appeal to the justices regarding the cruelty of his master would necessarily result in their cancelling the apprentice's bonds to him. Sometimes the master was merely 'warned' and told by the Court 'to use him well in future'.

[1] *Hertfordshire Quarter Sessions Books*, ed. William le Hardy, vol. VII, p. 263.

THE TWIN DISCIPLINES OF WORK AND WORSHIP

What is clear from such records as exist of late seventeenth- and early eighteenth-century court actions affecting poor apprentices is that, either the justices did not have or did not always choose to exercise authority to punish masters for ill-treatment of apprentices, and that where they did elect to take some positive action to protect the apprentice it was usually in the form of cancellation of indentures. Sometimes, although not by any means always, they also required the return of the premium to the parish.

Ad hoc intervention of this kind was obviously a totally inadequate protection for the abused parish apprentice. Certainly it was no substitute for the expert and continuous regulation of the conditions of their apprentices which the gilds had operated within their own crafts with conspicuous success until the early eighteenth century, when changes in the structure both of the economy and of society weakened their organisation and undermined their authority. These facts did not escape notice in the eighteenth century – hence a series of attempts to provide greater and more effective protection for parish apprentices and ordinary apprentices bound out to masters in less well paid trades where the temptation to exploitation bore most heavily. In 1747 it was enacted that any parish apprentice or any other apprentice whose binding-out fee was less than £5 could complain to two local justices 'concerning any misusage, refusal of necessary provision, cruelty or ill-treatment' who could, upon satisfactory proof of the charge, discharge the apprentice from his indentures to that particular master.[1] The great defect of this piece of legislation was that, though it gave the justices general powers to free a child from a negligent or a cruel master, it did nothing to give them explicit authority either to punish the master or to require him to repay the premium he had acquired on taking the apprentice. Thus to some extent the Act itself could be used by the unscrupulous to rid themselves of their obligations to an apprentice with the minimum inconvenience and the maximum advantage to themselves. A further Act was therefore passed in 1792, whose preamble significantly refers to the instances of ill-treatment of apprentices which still 'frequently' occurred. Under this new statute the justices were empowered to order the guilty master or mistress to pay £10 to the parish towards putting the child

---
[1] 20 Geo. III, c. 19.

out to apprentice with another master, and fine them another £5 if they could not or would not deliver up to the parish such clothes as they had provided for the child on his apprenticeship.[1] Not content to leave things here, the following year, 1793, Parliament empowered the justices to fine masters or mistresses for 'ill-usage' of any apprentices bound to them with a premium of £10 or less. The fine, which was in no case to exceed 40s., was to be given to the apprentice as recompense for his harsh teatment.[2]

In theory, these three statutes afforded the apprentice at least minimal protection. In practice they did nothing of the kind, as those interested in the plight of apprentices knew all too well. In a letter to the *Monthly Magazine* in 1801, Mrs. Cappe, who had had personal experience of the consequences of apprenticing young girls from the Grey Coat Hospital, York, referred to a recent case in East London. One Jouveneaux, a tambourine-worker, had seventeen parish girl apprentices in his establishment whom he so ill-treated and under-fed that five died. All seventeen slept in one garret in three beds and were made to work at their embroidery from four or five o'clock in the morning until eleven or twelve o'clock at night, sometimes longer, all week and sometimes on Sundays as well. Mrs. Cappe remarks that such treatment 'was in the very nature of the contract itself' and continues: 'Children bound for their labour, and more especially girls, are always liable to be, and in fact generally are, in some respect or other unkindly if not cruelly treated'.[3] Elsewhere, Mrs. Cappe cites the case of another man, John Toms, who was accused in 1804 of having beaten and molested Ann Swinton, a fourteen-year-old girl apprenticed to him by her parish. Toms apparently kept a kind of 'black hole' in which he locked up his unfortunate parish apprentices, boys and girls alike, when they behaved badly. For this he was censured by the Chairman of the Middlesex Sessions, 'but to how much this censure would amount', comments Mrs. Cappe, 'it is not difficult to see'. Moreover, she demands, 'Whilst such instances continue to occur, what shall we say of the boasted privilege possessed by the poor apprentice Girl, of appealing against the profligacy

[1] 32 Geo. III, c. 57.
[2] 33 Geo. III, c. 55.
[3] Quoted M. D. George, op. cit., p. 255.

THE TWIN DISCIPLINES OF WORK AND WORSHIP

and cruelty of her tyrant?'[1] This particular case is all the more revealing of the defencelessness of the parish apprentice at the turn of the eighteenth century, since only four years earlier a special *Order* had been made by this same bench, after frequent complaints had been lodged before it of children being bound out to masters who didn't give the children decent conditions of work and maintenance. The *Order* instructed the justices when binding parish apprentices in future, to 'require the attendance of the master and apprentice before them at the same time', and to 'make a strict enquiry ... into the situation in life and circumstances of the person proposing to take such apprentice and that they satisfy themselves by proper enquiries of the fitness of such persons to provide for and maintain such apprentices with sufficient and proper meat, drink and clothing, and to teach and instruct such apprentices in his business and that such person is in all other respects fit and proper to be entrusted with the care and instruction of such apprentices'.[2] But there was in fact no defence against the irresponsible magistrate, as the Toms case shows.

It may well appear that the law would have been a good deal more effective had there been provision for the regular inspection of the conditons of work and training of the apprentices who had actually been bound out; had there been some sort of machinery to prevent the abuse of apprentices rather than a not very reliable method of redressing their wrongs. In fact a number of the London parishes did try to inspect the conditions of their apprentices fairly regularly. The vestry minutes of Walthamstow, for example, note that in 1764 it was 'order⁴ that Gallant do go twice a year to see after the Children that are put out apprentice. To go in the month of January and August and to give the children sixpence each to encourage them to be good'.[3] Unhappily, inspection on this scale was more likely to be testimony to the integrity of the parish in its acceptance of its responsibility to poor children than an effective protection to the children themselves as the Foundling Hospital, who organised a similar scheme of inspection, knew to their cost. Among a number of instances of the ill-treatment of poor apprentices quoted by the *Gentle-*

[1] Catherine Cappe, *Observations on charity schools, female friendly societies etc.* York, 1805, p. 45.
[2] Quoted M. D. George, op. cit., p. 248.
[3] *Walthamstow in the Eighteenth Century, being Extracts from the Vestry Minutes, Churchwardens' and Overseers' Accounts*, ed. Stephen J. Barnes. 1925-7. p. 46.

man's Magazine in 1767, was one involving a Mrs. Brownrigg, a successful midwife who had treated her three girl apprentices with such brutality that one had died and another fled back to the Foundling Hospital by whom she had been bound out. By the turn of the century the supervision of parish apprentices was recognised as clearly inadequate. The problem was to find some solution which was at once effective and acceptable. An attempt to find some solution to the problem is to be found in the *Health and Morals of Apprentices Act* of 1802, which affected only the Poor Law apprentices working in cotton mills.[1] The chief provisions of the Act were that the hours of work of such apprentices were to be limited to twelve a day and that night work was to be gradually discontinued and to cease by June of 1804. The apprentices were to be given some instruction in the three R's and provided with suitable clothing once a year. Apprentices of different sex were to be provided with separate sleeping accommodation, no more than two to share a bed. They were also to attend church at least once a month. To ensure that the Act was observed, the local justices were to appoint two of their number to inspect the factories in which the children were employed and were empowered to impose fines of two to five pounds for failure to observe the provisions of the Act. Only applying to the cotton mills, the Act's effectiveness was even there very variable. No protection whatever was given to apprentices in the silk or woollen and flax mills where conditions were equally bad – sometimes even worse. More significant for the protection of poor apprentices in cotton textile mills was the Act of the same year *to require Overseers and Guardians of the Poor, to keep a Register of the several Children who shall be bound or assigned by them as Apprentices* . . . This Act required each entry to be signed by the two justices making the indentures and imposed a fine of £5 for failure to comply on the overseers and guardians. The registers, which were open to public inspection for a fee of sixpence, were to include details as to the name, sex and age of the apprentice; the parents' name and address; the name, trade and address of the master; the term of apprenticeship; the amount of the premium paid to the master; and the names of the overseers and the two justices assenting to the indentures.[2] Within two years,

[1] 41 Geo. III, c. 73.
[2] 42 Geo. III, c. 46.

however, a number of Yorkshire justices were urging Wilberforce, well known for his championship of the oppressed and under-privileged, to introduce a new Bill in Parliament to protect children from the irresponsible, or unscrupulous use of parish apprenticeship. The magistrates represented to Wilberforce that 'as the law stood at present, they could not exercise that superintendence over parish apprentices, which the legislature intended'. They argued that registration without regular inspection and revision of entries was useless, and asked for powers to enforce the inspection of the apprentices by the overseers twice yearly, who would then furnish reports to the Quarter Sessions as to 'their Treatment, Condition, and Cloathing'. Essential though regular inspection and reports were to the responsible operation of parish apprenticeship, the Bill did not commend itself to parliamentarians who thought that it 'proposed to cast [upon the justices] an extraordinary degree of trouble', and who believed in exercising caution in 'granting authority upon the request of the men by whom it was exercised, as appeared to be the case in this instance'.[1] But although the Bill failed, the protection of a particular group of apprentices to whom its promoters made special reference, those apprenticed outside their own parish, was the focus of a later attempt at reform which proved successful.

The apprenticing of poor children not merely out of their native parish, but in parishes far distant from their own had become a serious problem by the end of the eighteenth century. Many years earlier Sir John Fielding had deplored the practice as almost certain to lead to abuse,[2] but the demands of the growing number of textile mills in the North of England provided an unprecedented market for the labour of poor apprentices whose numbers were an embarrassment to the officers of their own parishes. When, in 1811, a Bill was introduced to protect the poor children of the parishes within the London Bills of Mortality who were bound out in this way, it was in fact successfully resisted by these parishes 'as taking from them the means of disposing of the children of the Poor belonging to them'. The supporters of the Bill, however, argued that appren-

---

[1] See *Parliamentary Debates*, 2nd series, vol. 2 (8. V. 1804), cols. 398-9.

[2] *Extracts from such of the Penal Laws as particularly relate to the Peace and Order of the Metropolis, etc.*, pp. 414 and 415.

ticeship under these conditions inevitably led to abuse since both the children's parents and the parish officers 'are deprived of the opportunity of knowing the manner in which such Children are treated'. Moreover, where children were being bound out as far as three hundred miles from their homes, they were usually being bound to masters of textile mills, who could not possibly be expected to supervise with any degree of care the large numbers of apprentices entrusted to them. Sir Samuel Romilly, who in his diary records that he has known cases where factory apprentices had been murdered by their masters once the premium had been secured, declared in the House of Commons: 'There was no subject which has a more powerful claim on the interference of the House, nor any in which that interference was likely to be productive of more Good'. Not all his hearers agreed with him. Sir Robert Peel (the elder), himself a mill-owner, claimed that there was no great hardship in the children being 'torn', as had been alleged, from their parents, 'for, in fact, they had no parents who owned them but they were thrown on the parish'. Another member opposed the suggestion of the Bill that the numbers who might be apprenticed to any one manufacturer should be limited on the grounds that it would have bad economic results.[1] (A line of argument which was to appear in many guises throughout the long history of attempts to reform working conditions of children in the nineteenth century.) But the reformers persisted, and the House of Commons Committee, which had been appointed in 1811 'to examine into the Number and State of Parish Apprentices bound into the country from parishes within the Bills of Mortality', continued to collect evidence which was incorporated in a Report to the House in 1815.

According to this Report, between 1802 and 1811, 5,815 children had been apprenticed by the 50 parishes investigated, of whom 2,026 (1,018 boys and 1,008 girls) had been apprenticed to persons 'in the country'. More than half of them (1,066) were under eleven years of age; 58 being under eight years old. But most important of all, the Report revealed that of the total number of apprentices sent away from their home parishes, three out of every four had been bound to cotton manufacturers, a practice which its signatories condemned on a number of grounds.

[1] *Parliamentary Debates*, 2nd series, vol. 20 (7. VI. 811), cols. 517 and 518. See also Romilly's *Diary*, vol. II, p. 374.

These were that the children concerned were very young to be taken away from their parents; that their proper guardians, the poor law officers, were too far away to look after their interests; that conditions in the cotton factories were bad, both physically and morally, for children. Further, that as the annual number of children whom the parishes individually had to apprentice was only about 200, and in view of the fact that some of the parishes investigated had never had to resort to sending their children away, it should have been perfectly possible to apprentice poor children at least within occasional reach of their parents, who could then protect them if necessary. In the light of this evidence another Bill on much the same lines as that proposed in 1811 was introduced, this time with success. In July the following year, 1816, it was enacted that, with regard to the parishes within the London Bills of Mortality, every parish child whom the officers proposed to apprentice had to go before two local justices together with his parents. The justices were to study each case with care and see how far away the proposed master lived and enquire into the case of communication between the child and his parents. In no case whatsoever was any London apprentice to be bound out more than forty miles from his home and, in the case of an apprentice being bound outside the parish, not only had two justices of that parish to sign his indentures, but also two justices of the county to which the child was being sent – a precaution against overseers who might otherwise attempt to rid their parish of its responsibilities without due care for the child's future welfare and supervision. In its further provisions the Act stipulated that unless regulations were scrupulously observed, apprenticeship would not convey settlement, and overseers who attempted to evade the regulations would be liable to a fine of £10 for each apprentice they had tried to bind out irregularly. No child under nine years was to be apprenticed by the parish in any circumstances.[1]

There is no doubt that this Act virtually ended the wholesale apprenticeship of parish children from London to the North of England. But neither can there be any doubt that one of the major reasons for the Bill's success in Parliament was that by 1816 the increasing use of steam rather than water power, made it possible for cotton factories to be sited in towns rather than in

[1] 56 Geo. III, c. 139.

isolated valleys, and also made it easier for the manufacturers to recruit local labour, both adults and children, and thus rely less on the labour of parish apprentices. Hence the Act was in many ways only the formal death warrant of a practice already dying from natural causes and was unlikely to run into powerful opposition. It is interesting, however, that on this as on previous occasions, among the speeches in favour of reform a good deal of emphasis was placed on the unsuitability of child employment in factories at all. The Pontefract justices who had years before invoked Wilberforce's support for reform of conditions of parish apprenticeship had declared: '... we will not, on any account, allow of the apprenticing of Poor Children to the Masters and Owners of Cotton-Mills, or other works of the kind, where such Poor Children shall be obliged to work in the night time, or for any unreasonable number of hours in the day time'[1] and, as we have seen, the Select Committee investigating the condition of parish apprenticeship from the London parishes were firmly convinced that the cotton mills of Lancashire were no place for young people. We shall elsewhere examine in some detail the contemporary evidence on this particular aspect of child labour in the nineteenth century, and here we can only urge caution against the too ready acceptance of some allegations regarding early nineteenth-century factory conditions, which were often made on the scantiest of evidence and gained nothing in accuracy by their repetition by many who had never set foot in the North of England, let alone in a cotton mill. On analysis, however, allegations of neglect, overwork, cruelty, and of deliberate corruption in the cotton mills can in nearly every instance find their parallel in similar allegations regarding the treatment of apprentices in other textile mills, in the mines and also in the domestic industries. Certainly William Hutton's recollections of his seven years' apprenticeship, or 'servitude' as he himself remembers it, in the silk mill at Derby in the early eighteenth century show that working conditions in the cotton mills of a later generation, though perhaps better publicised, were no more disagreeable. Bound apprentice at the age of seven, 'I had now to rise at five every morning', he wrote, '... submit to the cane

[1] *Parliamentary Papers, Reports etc.* 1814–15 (304), vol. V, Report of the Committee appointed to examine into the Numbers and State of Parish Apprentices bound into the country from the parishes within the Bills of Mortality and to report the same to the House. Appendix A.

whenever convenient to the master; be the constant companion of the most rude and vulgar of the human race, never taught by nature, nor ever wishing to be taught. A lad, let his mind be in what state it would, must be as impudent as they or be hunted down.' Hutton goes on to recall the morning of 27 December 1731, when 'I did not awake, . . . till daylight seemed to appear. I rose in tears for fear of punishment, and went to my father's bedside, to ask what was o'clock? "He believed six"; I darted out in agonies, and from the bottom of Full street, to the top of Silkmill Lane, not 200 yards, I fell nine times! Observing no lights in the mill, I knew it was an early hour, and the reflection of the snow had deceived me. Returning, it struck two.'[1] But however harsh the condition of apprenticeship in such factories, in all probability they did not equal, they certainly could not have surpassed, the evils of apprenticeship to scattered masters and mistresses: conditions which it was almost impossible to control because of the very number of masters involved and the isolation of the children whom they employed in the privacy of their own homes and workshops. It was of apprenticeship under these conditions, not in either the silk mills of the eighteenth century or the cotton mills, that Mrs. Cappe wrote in 1800, 'Is it wise, is it human, is it Christian, to preserve in a measure, however sanctioned by custom, or by what may have been deemed sufficient authority, which has long been productive of, and is at this time daily productive of misery and ruin?'[2] Since the chief concern of the parish officers had become a concern to rid themselves of moral, and the ratepayers of financial, responsibility for the children of the poor, in the later seventeenth and in the eighteenth centuries the history of parish apprenticeship had become a history of neglect and exploitation. Moreover, if in some areas the system had become abused in terms of the method of its organisation, in others it had become equally abused by the very absence of local attempts to apprentice the children of the poor. In Cambridgeshire, from the records of the justices examining paupers, it is clear from the early eighteenth century onwards that many children were never apprenticed at all and that, of those actually bound out, the clause relating to their training was merely nominal, many of the

[1] *The Life of William Hutton . . . written by himself.* 1816. pp. 11–14 passim.
[2] *Observations*, p. 48.

children not completing their term of apprenticeship in fact. 'From the middle of the century', writes Hampson, 'the Industrial School, and the Workhouses, and from 1795 onwards the gravel pit and the "rounds", took the place of apprenticeship for many children.'[1] By the end of the century, accounts of the disuse of parish apprenticeship were common in rural areas. According to the Earl of Sheffield, farmers hired workhouse boys for a day or so when they needed them and paid them very little or nothing. 'Thus they constantly change their masters; no person is particularly interested about them; consequently they learn little or nothing . . .'[2] By the time of the Report of the 1834 Poor Law Commission, parish apprenticeship seems to have broken down in rural areas and in some places to have been abandoned altogether. In the towns, where parish apprenticeship was continued to any degree, its use as a system of technical training was usually minimal. Mr. Villiers, Assistant Commissioner for Warwickshire, Worcester and Gloucestershire, reported that children were frequently apprenticed to overstocked trades. In Coventry they were put to ribbon-weaving, although weavers were said to be starving through lack of employment. (How many of them had only accepted a poor law apprentice for the money to buy bread?) In Worcester, children were bound to glovemaking, although glove manufacturers were said to be leaving the town, trade was so bad. In Tewkesbury, where during the period when stocking weaving was thriving, 'cart loads' of poor children had been brought in from the surrounding country parishes to be apprenticed to the weavers, now, although hundreds were reported out of work in the trade, children were still being apprenticed to it.[3]

Never a system which had easily commanded local support, parish apprenticeship had from the outset required something more than merely local supervision if it was to be operated effectively. Had the supervision of the central government continued from the mid-seventeenth century onward, the whole history of parish apprenticeship might have been different. As

[1] E. M. Hampson, *The Treatment of Poverty in Cambridgeshire, 1597–1834*. 1934. pp. 163 and 164.

[2] John, Earl of Sheffield, *Remarks on the Bill of the Last Parliament for the Amendment of the Poor Laws*. 1819. p. 44.

[3] *Report of the Poor Law Commissioners*, 1834. appendix A, pt. II, B.P.P. 1834, XXIX, p. 6.

it was, the high hopes of Elizabethan paternalism to abolish the evils of poverty by securing the proper training of the poor child 'to some honest trade in life' were, after a brief period of success, unfulfilled. Nearly two centuries were to elapse before reformers in the nineteenth century once again focused attention upon the urgent need for the training and education of the children of the poor.

2. *The Religious Training of Children*

The technical education of children in the sixteenth and seventeenth centuries was expected to go hand in hand with their moral and spiritual education. As we have already seen, the courts of the great Companies and Gilds took an active interest in the good behaviour of their apprentices and sometimes went to considerable lengths to enforce it. But the individual masters were also expected to play their part and, though many may have failed in or neglected their duties in this respect, many others had regular systems of fines the better to emphasise the necessity of morality and piety to their young workpeople. One master imposed a twopenny fine on his apprentices if they absented themselves from family prayers; whilst 'toying with the maids' or teaching the master's children 'bawdy words' incurred a fourpenny fine:[1] and – contrary to later association between cleanliness and high moral tone – 'wearing a foul shirt on Sunday' rated a mere penny fine. Countless treatises were published for the edification of apprentices. *The Prentises Practise in Godliness* (1608), dedicated to the 'Religiously disposed and vertuous young men, the Apprentices of the City of London' – a dedication more remarkable for the optimism rather than the candour of its assessment of its intended readers – contained rebukes for Sabbath breaking, idleness, riotous behaviour and disobedience, together with exhortations to religious devotion. Successive generations produced their own guides to virtue. William Loe's *The Merchant's Manuell* (1628) was followed in 1646 by Abraham Jackson's *The Pious Prentice, Or, the Prentices Piety*, one of the most complete guides to the subject published, and which identified godliness with support for the established order, for in the ethics of the tradesman nothing was so vile as rebelliousness and a

---

[1] W. S. Davis, *Life in Elizabethan England*. 1930. p. 282.

forward spirit or imaginations yearning for change. Jackson urges the apprentices to observe particularly 'Sobriety, Chastity and Contentment', and holds out prosperity as the prize as did most pious handbooks, for this was a morality shaped to fit the particular needs of a rising capitalist nation in which faith supported property and the virtue of prudence.[1]

If nascent capitalism required the support of a moral system, there were also very particular, national, reasons why moral training associated with religious practice should play a much larger part in the everyday life of English households during this period. At the beginning of Elizabeth's reign, to ensure national unity in matters of religion and the maximum conformity to the new Church of England it was compulsory for everyone to attend his parish church on Sundays and Holy days on pain of a fine of twelve pence for every abstention. Legislation was also passed requiring all heads of families to instruct their children in the catechism and the principles of religion. The enforcement of this duty was the concern of the diocesan visitations, when the Bishop specifically enquired 'Whether all fathers, mothers, masters and dames of your parish cause their children, servants and apprentices, both mankind and womankind, being above six years of age and under twenty, which have not learned the Catechism; to come to church on Sundays and Holy days at the times appointed, . . . and then diligently and obediently to hear and be ordered by the minister until such time as they have learned the same Catechism'. Enquiries were also to be made as to how many children came for instruction; how many did not know the catechism; and of these, their names, ages and where they lived.[2] Municipal corporations sometimes made their own additional regulations, such as those of Leicester, where parents and masters who failed to teach their children 'the articles of there beleefe' were to receive the penalty of a fine or of 'iii days imprisonment at Mr. Mayors pleysure'.[3]

In these circumstances, it was scarcely surprising that Roman Catholics should try to send their children to be educated in the Roman Catholic seminaries on the Continent. Nowhere does the association between religious training and national unity appear

[1] See L. B. Wright, op. cit, pp. 259–67.
[2] W. P. M. Kennedy, op. cit., vol. II., p. 93.
[3] M. Bateson, *Leicester Borough Records*, Vol. III, 1905, p. 183.

more emphatically than with regard to the children of recusants in the sixteenth century, where determination to secure loyalty to the Crown, both of parents and children, inspired attempts at enforced indoctrination in the tenets of the Church of England by means which, in our own day, bear the familiar hallmark of the totalitarian state. Consider, for instance, the advice offered to his Queen by the Lord Treasurer, Burghley, in 1583. Burghley advised Elizabeth, in order to prevent the growth of papacy among the children of recusants, to 'use, therein, not only a pious and godly means, in making the parents, in every shire, to send their children to be virtuously brought up at a certain place for that end appointed; but you shall also, if it please your Majesty, . . . [choose] such fit and convenient places for the same, as may surely be at your devotion; and by this means you shall, under colour of education, have them as hostages of the parents' fidelities, that have any power in England and by this way their number will quickly be lessened.' Shrewdly he continued: 'That putting to death doth no ways lessen them; . . . persecution being accounted as the badge of the church . . .'[1]

In the event, the provisions of the Anti-Recusant Acts of 1585 and 1593[2] gave the Crown far more limited powers than Burghley had envisaged, although in making it illegal for recusants to send their children to the foreign seminaries to be educated, and empowering the Privy Council to lodge in the households of staunch members of the Church of England, at their parents' expense, both children discovered being smuggled out of the country and children of imprisoned recusants, they constituted a formidable limitation on religious liberty. Formidable, but not always successful, as the Privy Council's experience with the imprisoned John Fitzherbert's two unmarried daughters shows. After a whole year in the household of William and Richard Sale, rectors of Ashton on Trent and Weston on Trent – staunch conformists who had often had recusants' wives and children in their rectories – the two young women continued in their 'obstinacie' and could not 'be reduced into conformitie from their superstitious and erronious opinions'.[3]

The Church itself, increasingly dominated by bishops and

---

[1] *The Somers Collection of Tracts*, vol. I, 2nd edit., 1809, pp. 166-7.
[2] 27 Eliz., c. 2. and 35 Eliz., c. 2.
[3] J. C. Cox, op. cit., vol. I, p. 257.

Church dignitories who, during the Marian persecutions, had lived in the Calvinist atmosphere of Geneva, was no less anxious to reclaim recusant children, and included searching enquiries into their religious education in diocesan visitations. Even in 1638, nearly eighty years after Elizabeth's accession, the Norwich Visitation Articles contained some very particular questions on this point: 'Doth any recusant keep a schoolmaster in his house, who cometh not to church, nor receive the sacrament, or is refractory to the Church orders [i.e. of regular attendance at services]. Doth any public schoolmaster teach the children of recusants or sectaries? Doth the schoolmaster instruct his scholars in religion, in the points of the Catechism set forth in the communion book? Doth he orderly bring his scholars upon Sundays and holy-days, to Prayer and Sermons?'[1]

Whilst instruction on the catechism was considered a guaranty both of national stability and religious orthodoxy, it was also part of the essential religious training of children to teach that the reformed Church of England stood in the true tradition of Christian teaching; a teaching derived from historical record as elaborated in one book – the Bible. Only from a clear understanding of the Bible was it possible, not merely to refute the false and pernicious doctrines of Rome, but to come to appreciate fully and personally believe in the Christian faith, on which belief individual salvation was held exclusively to depend. Heads of families were constantly reminded of their duty to ensure their household's understanding of Scripture and many popular handbooks were published to provide them with guides to the efficient execution of their responsibility. Such a book was that of Josias Nichols – *An Order of Household Instruction; By which every master of a Familie may easily and in a short space, make his whole household to understand the principles and chief points of Christian religion, without the knowledge whereof, no man can be saved* (1596). Bible reading became the foundation of all religious teaching. The abundance and cheapness of printed Bibles placed them within the reach of every English citizen. The average preacher urged constant reading of Scripture as the instrument of salvation and the average citizen at least provided himself with the necessary means. In a well-known passage, the historian J. R. Green says of the Englishman of the sixteenth

[1] Foster Watson, *The Old Grammar Schools*. 1916. p. 79.

and seventeenth centuries 'he was a man of one book, and that book the Bible'.

It must be confessed that the immense popularity and influence of the Bible at this time was not entirely due to religious enthusiasm. In the absence of newspapers and scarcity of books of every kind, the books of the Bible presented a varied and new literature that had no rival, while the abundance and cheapness of printed Bibles made them available to almost every home. The exhortations from the pulpit made daily Bible reading a social custom among all classes from the manor house to the cottage. Soon after Elizabeth's accession, Roger Ascham could write: 'Blessed be Christ, in our city of London, commonly the Commandments of God be more diligently taught, and the service of God more reverently used and that daily in many private men's houses than they be in Italy once a week in their common churches.'[1] As the esteem of family Bible reading and prayer spread through the country, the religious households became the Protestant ideal, and it was largely due to Elizabethan emphasis on the religious training of children in the home based on Bible reading and the Prayer Book, that the new generation of Englishmen was weaned from the Roman Catholic Church and grew up staunch adherents of the new Church of England.

With the development of Puritanism in Elizabeth's reign, there came new and more urgent motives for the religious training of children in the minds of those who accepted Calvinist doctrine. The new attitudes were destined to have some extraordinary and often distressing effects on the lives and minds of children. Calvinism taught that children were born with an inheritance of sin and wickedness; consequently they were in the same danger of hell as the most hardened adult sinner. From this state they could only be saved by conviction of sin and personal conversion. We know today how difficult it is to convey religious concepts to the child and how different the normal religious responses of the child are from those of the adult, but the ignorance of developmental psychology, which is so striking a characteristic of the thinking of our forebears, resulted in religious pressures on the child which were wholly abnormal. Treated as little adults, they were subjected to the same religious pressures, disciplines and experiences as adults. For parents who accepted

[1] Quoted Earle, op. cit., p. 228.

THE TWIN DISCIPLINES OF WORK AND WORSHIP

Calvinist views there was the greatest incentive to start the religious instruction of their children at the first possible moment. As John Cotton advised, 'These Babes are flexible and easily bowed; it is far more easy to train them up to good things now, than in their youth and riper years.'[1] Moreover, godly parents were haunted by the unpalatable belief that 'children are not too little to die, they are not too little to go to hell'.[2] It is not surprising that they devoted as much thought to the spiritual upbringing of their children as conscientious parents spend today on health and general personality development.

Preachers advised that occasional instruction should begin with the child in the cradle, or while being dandled on the knees. 'So soon as the children be able to speak plainly', wrote Thomas Becon, 'let them even from their cradles be taught to utter not vain, foolish and wanton, but grave, sober, and godly words; as God, Jesus Christ, faith, love, hope, patience, goodness, peace, etc. And when they be able to pronounce whole sentences, let the parents teach their children such sentences as may kindle in them a love towards virtue, and a hate against vice and sin.' He suggested such sentences as: 'God alone saveth me'; 'There is no damnation to them that are in Christ Jesus'; 'Learn to die' etc. In this way Becon, himself the father of three 'Most sweet and dear children', believed that from infancy children might learn 'to die in godliness'.[3]

More formal instruction in the principles of religion was given by the catechetical method and for this purpose numerous catechisms were published during the sixteenth and seventeenth centuries by Puritan writers. Questions and answers alike were couched in language unintelligible to children, however, and Dean Nowell's *Catechism*, 1570, particularly in the middle and longer forms, was a serious undertaking even for the most studious; whilst the Westminster Catechism, 1647, assumed a comprehension of, or at least an acquaintance with, the whole range of Calvinistic dogmatic theology which it may be doubted their youthful intellects possessed. It was therefore the parent's duty to expound the catechism for his children 'at least labouring

---

[1] *A Practical Commentary*, p. 92.
[2] Janeway, A Token for Children, quoted Sandford Fleming, *Children and Puritanism*. 1933. p. 86.
[3] Thomas Becon, *Worckes*, pt. I. 1564. p. 348.

to drive into their heads the maine parts of the Christian Doctrine; and that in such familiar sort of questioning with them, that they may make them perceive they know what they speak'.[1] Similar expositions and questionings on the various catechisms used were a regular part of the religious instruction in the grammar and public schools of the period.

It was indeed no part of Puritan practice to make concessions to the immaturity of the young or to the exuberance of youth; rather it was their overwhelming anxiety that these diminutive brands be plucked from the fire of Hell into which young and old alike might be cast. Thus there were no Sunday Schools and no children's services – the catechism class was the only group organised for the young as such and was certainly no escape from the preacher and his hour glass.

Family worship, which the whole household, children, servants and apprentices were expected to attend was an important religious duty, and as soon as they could read, children were taught to study the Scriptures and other pious books – Baxter's *Call to the Unconverted*, Meads's *Almost Christian*, Vincent's *The Plain Man's Pathway to Heaven* – for themselves. As the fervour of Puritanism spread, the exhortations of the ministers to teach their children to read the Scriptures was a powerful incentive to all the classes to secure at least the rudiments of education for themselves and their children as a means to salvation. 'Oh the inexpressible wrong done to Children by their parents neglect to have them taught to read the Scriptures when they were young!' cries Thomas Cobbett. '... Better unborn [almost] than untaught...'[2] Since the parts of the Bible which were most attentively read in Puritan households and most frequently and vividly expounded by Puritan divines were conspiciously those which deal with sin, judgement and the torments of the damned, religious educationalists of our own day might have some reservations concerning the wisdom of Cobbett's appeal. There can be little doubt that the Puritan preoccupation with death and its attendant perils so frequently emphasised in the religious books written especially for children must have cruelly distorted their image of God. What impression of the Christian faith, one wonders, was conveyed to young minds by James Janeway's assurance

[1] William Whately, *The New Birth*. 1635 edn. pp. 178–9.
[2] *A Fruitful Discourse*. 1656. pp. 224–5.

to the young readers of his *A Token for Children* (a book which had wide circulation in the author's lifetime and went through very many editions, one as late as 1830) that 'Children who lye, play the truant and break the Sabbath – will go into everlasting burning . . . They which never pray, God will pour out his wrath upon them; and when they beg and pray in Hell Fire, God will not forgive them but there they must lye for ever . . . And are you willing to go to Hell to be burned with the Devil and his Angels? . . . O Hell is a terrible place, that's worse than a thousand whippings; God's anger is worse than your Father's anger. . . . How do you know but that you might be the next Child to die? and where are you then if you be not God's child?' Few admonitions to children so aptly illustrate contemporary inability to appreciate the fundamental differences between the nature of the religious experience of the child and that of the adult than when, in the same book 'written to deal with children as children', Janeway advises them to go into a chamber or garret and 'fall upon thy knees, and weep and mourn, and tell Christ that thou art afraid that he doth not love thee, but that thou would fain have his love; beg of him to give thee his Grace and pardon for thy sins, and that he would make thee his Child: tell God that thou dost not care who don't love thee, if God will but love thee; say to him Father, hast thou not a blessing for me, thy poor little Child? Father, hast thou not a blessing for me, even for me? O give a Christ; O give me a Christ: O let me not be undone for ever: thus beg, as for your lives, and be not contented till you have an answer; and do thus every day, with as much earnestness as you can twice a day at least'.[1]

As soon as children were considered old enough they were taken to Church for the more advanced instruction of the sermons in which the Puritans delighted. 'Bring them to Church,' wrote John Cotton, 'and help them to remember something, and tell them the meaning of it, and take a little in good part, and encourage them, and that will make them delight in it'.[2] But woe betide any child who should fall asleep during these delights: 'the devil rocks the cradle . . . and they that play . . . at sermons have the devil for a play-fellow'. Whether or not the children actually did 'delight' in the lengthy disquisitions on the proxi-

---

[1] op. cit., preface.
[2] *A Practical Commentary*, p. 102.

THE TWIN DISCIPLINES OF WORK AND WORSHIP

mity of Hell may seem open to doubt; but our more stalwart forebears spared no effort to ensure that children did in fact 'learn a little' from the sermons they heard. On the family's return from church, it was a common practice for parents to rehearse the children in the text and main points of the minister's disquisition. In the boarding schools it was often required of those able to write that they should take lengthy notes of the sermons as they were being delivered, – a practice which, it has been suggested, gave rise to note-taking in shorthand – so that the boys and girls might the more easily commit to memory those particular aspects of Christian teaching that the preacher had dealt with that morning. Thus the religious opinions of children were moulded and the stern, strong, irresistible features of Puritan indoctrination became ingrained deeper and deeper.

Not the least important feature of Puritan training was its insistence that theory and practice, theological principle and right action should be inextricably connected. 'Let parents be putting their Children betimes, upon actual exercise, and practice of religious principles, and rules, which have been taught, by their parents; what religious practices and precepts you would have them to attend, and not depart from them, when they are old, train them up practically, to those very godly exercises when they are young . . .'[1] It was thus the duty of the head of the household to point out duties, explain right conduct, control demeanour and himself afford an example of public and private practice. The insistence of Puritan teaching on duties, morals and manners as well as on doctrinal religion was part of their conscious and determined effort, directed rightly or wrongly, to build up character in the home.

It is impossible to overestimate the sense of human responsibility which pervaded the genuine Puritan home of the seventeenth century. One of the most popular of the Puritan manuals of household government was William Gouge's *Of Domesticall Duties* which makes the inculcation of good manners in the child a religious duty. 'Not only heathen men and other moralists who were not mere natural civil men, but also the Holy Ghost Himself hath prescribed many rules of good manners, and much urged and pressed the same . . . The Holy Ghost having urged

[1] Cobbett, *A Fruitfull . . . Discourse*, p. 225.

the point of good manners . . . it is not "a needless point", but a "bounden duty".'[1]

Household instruction of the members who, it will be remembered, often consisted of apprentices as well as children, was itself revised and re-directed by the ministers who recognised instruction as part of their work as well as preaching. Richard Baxter, Teacher of the Church at Kidderminster, in his *Reformed Pastor* (1656) shows how domestic education was directed by him in that town. 'We spend Monday and Tuesday from morning to almost night in the work, taking about 15 or 16 families in a week that we may do the parish (which hath above 800 families) in a year and I cannot say yet that one family has refused to come to me now, [and] but few persons excused and shifted it off. I find more outward signs of success with most that come, than of *all* my public preaching to them . . . At my delivery of the Catechisms, I take a catalogue of all the persons of understanding in the parish: and the clerk goeth a week before to every family to tell them when to come and at what hour (one family at 8 o'clock, the next at 9, and the next at 10, etc.). I am forced by the number to deal with the whole family at once but admit not any of another to be present, ordinarily.'[2]

One may well ask how children responded to religious appeal which did not differ to young or old; in which, the catechism class apart, no attempt was made to give a religious instruction that the child could understand. Some of the numerous references to contemporary children's religious experience undoubtedly tax the modern reader's credulity. One child, 'mightily awakened' between eight and nine years of age, 'spent a large part of the night in weeping and praying, and could scarce take any rest day or night for some time together, desiring with all her soul to escape from the everlasting flames'. She took her elder brother and sister into a room and told them of their condition by nature, and wept over them and prayed with them. Apparently no peace of soul came to her, for at fourteen years of age she took sick, and was in great distress. 'O mother,' she cried, 'pray, pray, pray for me, for Satan is so busy that I cannot pray for myself; I see that I am undone without Christ, and a pardon! O I am undone to all eternity!' Another little girl greatly

---
[1] See Watson, op. cit., p. 114.
[2] ibid., p. 117.

affected when between four and five years of age, 'became very solicitous about her soul and everlasting condition, weeping bitterly to think what would become of her in another world'. A boy, before he was six years old, 'prayed with such extraordinary meltings, that his eyes have looked red and sore with weeping by himself for his sins'.[1]

Nevertheless, there can be little doubt that the conviction of sin and the terror of Hell which Puritan teaching sought to convey to the young, did affect some children very profoundly. John Bunyan wrote in later life of his terrible childish visions of Hell, and of the conviction of sin given by a sermon denouncing dancing and games: 'When I was but a child of nine or ten years old these things did so distress my soul, that then in the midst of my merry sports and childish vanities, amidst my vain companions, I was often much cast down and afflicted in my mind therewith; yet could I not let go my sins.' Even in the midst of a game he was confronted with the subjective question, 'Wilt thou leave thy sins and go to Heaven, or have thy sins and go to Hell?' His conviction of divine displeasure and grievous punishment for these pleasurable and harmless pastimes was shared by many other children and must have been both oppressive and disturbing.[2]

This deep religious conviction and sense of sin in the young would nowadays be looked upon as not merely abnormal but fundamentally undesirable. In the seventeenth century, when parents lived in fear of infant damnation and thus made every effort to secure the earliest possible 'conversion' in their child, religious precocity, far from being unwelcome, was held up as an ideal of religious education: 'I further advise you,' writes John Norris in *Spiritual Counsel: A Father's Advice to his Children* (written when his eldest child cannot have been more than four years old) 'to be much in the Contemplation of the shortness and uncertainty of life, . . . Be much . . . in the Contemplation of the four last thyngs, Heaven, Hell, Death and Judgment. Place yourselves frequently on your death beds, in your Coffins, and in your Graves. Act over frequently in your Minds, the Solemnity of your own Funerals; and entertain your Imaginations with all the lively scenes of Mortality; Meditate much upon the places,

[1] See Fleming, op cit.. p. 87.
[2] Quoted J. R. Green, *Short History of the English People*. 1877. p. 454.

and upon the Days of Darkness, and upon the Fewness of those that shall be saved; and be always with your Hour-glass in your hands, measuring out your own little Span and comparing it with the endless Circle of Eternity.'[1] Writers other than Janeway devoted a great deal of space to descriptions of young religious prodigies. One widely read book was Thomas White's *A Little Book for Little Children*, 'Wherein are set down several directions for little children: and several remarkable stories both ancient and modern, of little children: divers whereof are of those who are lately deceased'.[2] Here, alas, was the rub, for it is a sad feature of many of these tales that those children who most nearly attained to the ideal of infant conversion seem soonest to have been claimed from the families whose adornment they might have been. Rarely can there have been in literature so formidable a number of vivid illustrations that 'those whom the Gods love die young'.

Some, at least, of those who were spared for some little while to their parents seem to have developed an almost unbelievable censoriousness. What would be our reaction today to a little girl of five years old who often prayed in secret and who, when hearing one of her brothers say he had been at prayer, 'rebuked him sharply, and told him how little such prayers were likely to profit him, and that there was little to his praise to pray like a hypocrite, and to be glad that any should know what he had been doing'?[4] Even in families where parents seem to have been less oppressed by the weight of sin and the imminence of Hell as was Norris, children developed religious attitudes which today, even in adults, we should view with some embarrassment. Gervase Holles, for example, relates how, when he himself was three years old, his four-year-old brother John sent for him as he lay dying 'and caused me to be brought to him, and layd downe by him, and kissing me prayed God to bless me, saying yt all yt was his he freely gave me . . .' Later in his *Memorials* of his family, Gervase describes his own son George, who died at the age of two, 'Full of life and spirit wch yet had a mixture of mildness and gravity, and he would many times suddainly step aside from the height of his litle sportes, and (kneeling against the wall) would

---
[1] John Norris, *Spiritual Counsel, a Father's Advice to his Children*. 1694. pp. 76–7.
[2] Fleming, op. cit., p. 89.
[3] Janeway, *A Token for Children*. 1709 edn., p. 28.

THE TWIN DISCIPLINES OF WORK AND WORSHIP

say his prayers.' Rather sadly, Gervase concludes: 'In short he was of so much forwardnes yt no man besides my selfe hoped for him a long life . . . for he was a miracle.'[1]

Horrifying, amusing or simply incredible though such tales seem to us now, it is as well to remember that the seventeenth century was an age in which precocity was fostered; a period when children, urged by parents all too mindful of the brevity of life and fearful that they themselves might die before their sons and daughters were equipped for the responsibilities of the adult world, sometimes achieved feats of learning which would now be remarkable in children more than twice their age. Moreover, it was not only the children of Puritan households who apparently displayed this formidable capacity. There is, for example, the well-known account of John Evelyn's son, Richard, who by the time he was two and a half years old could not merely read English, but Latin, French and 'Gottic' as well, speaking the first three 'exactly'. By the time he was five, he could 'not only read most written hands, but so decline all the Nounes, Conjugate the verbs, regular, & most of the irregular, . . . could make congruous Syntax, turne English into Lat: & vice versa, construe & prove what he read and did . . . began himself [to] wrote legibly, & had a strange passion for Greeke: . . . & when seeing a Plautus in ones hand, he asked what booke it was, & being told it was Comedy &c, & too difficult for him he wept for sorrow . . . As to his Piety, astonishing were his applications of Scripture upon occasion, & his sense of God, he had learn'd all his Catecisme early, & understood the historical part of the Bible & N. Test: to a wonder, how Christ came to Redeeme Mankind &c. & how comprehending these necessarys, himselfe, his Godfathers &c. were discharged of their promise: . . .'.[2]

Less well known, perhaps, but equally to the point, is Mrs. Lucy Hutchinson's account of her own childhood. Born in 1620, Mrs. Hutchinson recalls how, by the time she was four years old 'I read English perfectly, & having a great memory, I was carried to sermons; & while I was very young could remember & repeat them exactly, & being carressed the love of praise tickled me, & made me attend more heedfully. When I was about 7 yrs of age,

---

[1] Gervase Holles, *Memorials of the Holles Family*, Camden 3rd Series., vol. LV. pp. 195, 235-6.
[2] *Diary of John Evelyn*, ed. E. S. de Beer, 1955. p. 385.

THE TWIN DISCIPLINES OF WORK AND WORSHIP

I remember I had at one time eight tutors in several qualities, langages, music, dancing, writing, & needelwork; but my genius was quite averse from all but my book... After dinner & supper I still had an hour allowed me to play, & then I would steal into some hole or other to read. My father would have me learn Latin, & I was so apt that I outstripped my brothers who were at school,... As for music and dancing, I profited very little from them,... and for my needle I absolutely hated it. Play among other children I despised, & when I was forced to entertain such as came to visit me, I tired them with more grave instructions than their mothers, & plucked all their babies to pieces, & kept the children in such awe, that they were glad when I entertained myself with elder company;' – which is not, perhaps, surprising!

Both Richard and Lucy showed a piety commensurate with their astonishing academic gifts. During his fatal sickness, Richard 'would himself select the most pathetical Psalmes, & Chapters out of Jobe, to reade to his Mayde,... telling her (when she pitied him) that all God's Children must suffer affliction:...' The redoubtable Lucy 'was convinced that the knowledge of God was the most excellent study, & accordingly applied myself to it, & to practice as I was taught. I used to exhort my mother's maids much, & to turn their idle discourses to good subjects...'[1]

From the shelter of a materialist society where death is long postponed and the rich rewards of this life make speculation concerning those of the next seem both time wasting and irrelevant, and where the Church itself has long been reluctant to dwell on the pains and penalties of Hell, the desire and obvious ability of parents and ministers to instil in the young a sense of sin and an awareness of death appears grossly misconceived. The evidence of its immediate effects on children of Puritan and – to a less extent – non-Puritan households, suggests signs of considerable nervous strain. Nevertheless, it would be unwise to forget that many of these contemporary 'accounts' were undoubtedly exaggerated for effect and that, in actual fact, the Puritans both in their theology and in their practice interpreted the Christian faith in highly dramatic terms. Moreover, even if one concedes that such a characterisation of their faith led parents

---

[1] The Life of Mrs. Lucy Hutchinson written by herself. Prefixed to the 1908 edition of *The Memoirs of Colonel Hutchinson*. pp. 17–18.

to condemn as 'sinful' many of the innocent pleasures of childhood, in a period when life for many was nasty, brutish and short, the contemporary insistence on public worship and religious observance at home must have given both solace and security. Against the tales of the tears and torments of children in the course of their religious education should be set the assessment of its value to their later life which many contemporaries gave. Lady Halkett, recalling her childhood in the early seventeenth century, says: 'my mother's greatest care & for which I shall ever owne to her memory the highest gratitude, was the great care she tooke that even from our infancy, we were instructed never to forget to begin and end the day with Prayer, & ... every morning to read the Bible, & ever to keepe the church as often as there was occasion to meet there either for prayers or preaching. So that for many yeares together, I was seldome or never absent from divine service, at 5 a'clock in the morning in the summer & 6 a'clock in the winter till the usurped power putt a restraint to that publick worship so long owned & continued in the Church of England; where I bless God, I had my education, & the example of a good Mother who kept constantt to her owne parish church, & had allwayes great respect for the ministers under whose charge she was . . .'[1]

Later in the seventeenth century, however, there was an increasing disposition to preach a less rigorous gospel and to accommodate the will of God to the material, rather than the spiritual, comfort of men – particularly rich men. It was against precisely this relaxation in the Church's teaching and in public practice that John Wesley was to preach and to urge on his eighteenth-century contemporaries and adherents the prime necessity of bringing up children to understand that 'religion is nothing else than doing the will of God, and not our own: that the one grand impediment to our temporal and eternal happiness being . . . self-will, no indulgences of it can be trivial, no denial unprofitable. Heaven or hell depends on this alone . . .' Wesley's ideas on the religious and moral training of the young he got from his mother, Susannah Wesley, who, at his request, wrote of them to him in 1732. (The period to which she referred was about thirty years earlier.) All the children of her household were

---
[1] *The Autobiography of Lady Anne Halkett.* Camden Society. New series, no. 13. cited by Christina Hole, *English Home Life 1500–1800,* p. 80.

taught to read at the age of five years and were early introduced to Sabbath observance and family religious practices. 'They were very early made to distinguish the Sabbath from other days. They were as soon taught to be still at family prayers, and to ask a blessing immediately after, which they used to do by signs, before they could kneel or speak.' Susannah's household was to become the model for those of her son's followers, and it was conspicuously the Methodists who were to continue in the eighteenth century and on into the nineteenth century the tradition of family worship and religious and moral training in the home. Like the Puritans of the seventeenth century, Susannah's discipline, though stern, was even and just and leavened with kindliness. Here are some of her rules about punishment:

'That whoever was charged with a fault, of which they were guilty, if they would ingenuously confess it, and promise to amend should not be beaten . . .

'That no sinful action . . . should ever pass unpunished.

'That no child should ever be chid, or beat twice for the same fault; and that if they amended they should never be upbraided with it afterwards.

'That every signal act of obedience, especially when it crossed upon their own inclinations, should always be commended, and frequently rewarded, according to the merits of the case.

'That if ever any child performed an act of obedience, or did anything with intention to please, though the performance was not well, yet the obedience and intention should be kindly accepted; and the child with sweetness directed how to do better for the future.'

In this régime there was, of course, little room for infant self-expression. 'In order to form the minds of children, the first thing to be done is to conquer their will, and to bring them to obedient temper. To inform the understanding is the work of time, and must with children proceed by slow degrees as they are able to bear it; but the subjecting the will is a thing which must be done at once; and the sooner the better.' For Susannah, as for her Puritan forebears, it was necessary to 'bend the twig'. 'As self-will is the root of all sin and misery, so whatever cherishes this in children insures their after-wretchedness and irreligion; whatever checks and mortifies it promotes their future happiness and piety.'[1]

It may seem to us now that such a religious training as this must have been oppressive to those for whom it was designed, but in the eighteenth, as in the sixteenth and seventeenth centuries, religion was not intended to 'lift the spirits' but to concentrate the heart and mind on the nature of man's relationship to God. It may appear to have placed excessive emphasis on the negative aspects of the relationship, yet the positive advantages of contemporary religious training – of building up character and of instilling a profound sense of social and moral obligation should not be lightly dismissed. It may well be asked whether more recent generations have yet devised as effective a system of moral training for the young.

[1] Quoted D. R. Miller and G. E. Swanson, *The Changing American Parent*. 1958. pp. 9–11.

X

The Schoolchild

In the recognition of the importance of religion, both the family and the school education of our forebears were at one. It is often supposed that the schools founded at the time of the Renascence, and later under post-Renascence impulse, were predominantly permeated with classical aims. The Italian Renascence was not specifically or essentially connected with any other aim than 'the Revival of Letters'. But it is an unwarranted conclusion to suppose that the same statement may be applied to the English Grammar Schools, founded in the period immediately following on the Renascence, and still less in the latter part of the sixteenth and the whole of the seventeenth centuries. The English grammar schools were, indeed, classical in aim. The curriculum and text-books dealt with classical authors, Latin and Greek speech, Latin and Greek composition. Nevertheless, the main stimulus, the outstanding motive of the whole grammar school system, seen both in the statutes of foundation, in the curriculum and in the text-books employed, is distinctly religious.

The Renascence grammar schools in England may be said to be those founded between 1509 (Colet's St. Paul's School) and 1558 (the accession of Queen Elizabeth). The key-note of these schools is struck in Dean Colet's Statutes, dated 1518, when he says: 'My intent is by this school specially to increase knowledge and worshipping God and Our Lord Jesus Christ and good Christian life and Manners in the children.' It is true that a writer on education speaks of the 'reading of Isocrates, Demosthenes, and the most revered author and orator Christ Jesus, with the apostles'. But he adds, with regard to the last-named 'orators',' whose writings I allow ever first and last'. It is doubtful whether any statutes of a school could be produced in the period 1518–59 which do not explicitly name some aspect of religion as the cause which led the founder to establish his school.

Nevertheless, still more emphatic is the religious motive in the establishment and conduct of schools in the later period 1559–1660 – the period of the Puritan influence on schools. The return of the Protestant exiles to England from Strasburg, Frankfurt, and Geneva, after their flight to escape the Marian Persecution, brought into England the keenest desire to educate the children of this country in the tenets of Protestantism and to arouse the fiercest aversion against, and even terror of, the Roman Catholic régime. In the schools, actual religious instruction was severely enjoined. It was thought to be a matter of life and death – literally after the experience of Queen Mary's reign, when nearly three hundred Protestants had been burnt to death for their refusal to recant – that all persons should be trained to adopt the religious views of Elizabeth's Government, which stood for the impossibility of ever allowing Roman Catholics to regain their old domination and, moreover, that all children should be brought up to give a reason for the faith that was in them. Elizabethan fathers and mothers, with their régime of family prayers and readiness of mind and soul for long religious services and sermons, would have insisted on school religious exercises, even if the ecclesiastical and civil authorities had not just as determinedly prescribed them. Everyone was agreed that it was a national duty, indeed one of the most pressing of all national duties, that children should be trained in the grounds of their faith in the school, equally as in their homes. Only in this way, it was believed, could national unity and stability be maintained.

That schools should be used to further the ends of the Church was nothing new in English tradition. From medieval times, the Church had had a monopoly control of education since no one was allowed to teach without the licence of the Bishop of the diocese. At the Reformation, the Church of England had assumed the control previously exercised by the Church of Rome and took good care that, even in schools established by private munificence, provision was made for direct instruction in the tenets of the recognised national Church. Thus religious instruction became as much a part of the school curriculum after the Reformation as before; an instruction which, with the growing influence of Puritanism in Elizabeth's reign, became increasingly theological in character.

The content of the instruction appropriate to be given in schools was the subject of as much concern in the sixteenth and seventeenth centuries as it now is to those to whose lot it has fallen to revise the Agreed Syllabuses for the religious education in the State schools. But whereas in the twentieth century Loukes and Gouldman argue that anything approaching formal instruction on Christian theology is only suitable for the older schoolchildren, in the seventeenth century Brinsley and Hoole advocated its introduction at a much earlier age. Hoole's *New Discovery in the old Art of Teaching School*, although published in 1660, was based on the writer's experience stretching over the previous thirty years. It makes astonishing reading for the religious education specialist of the nineteen-sixties. Hoole suggested, for example, that children should buy copies of Gerard's *Meditations*, Thomas à Kempis's *Imitation*, and St. Augustine's *Soliloquies* or *Meditations*, in Latin and in English, 'or the like pious and profitable books' and continually bear them about in their pockets to read at spare times in Latin or English. It is true that this exercise was primarily with a view to the acquisition of Latin, but he chose these particular books because they were religious. The Assembly's Catechism had to be known in English and in Latin in the third form. Morever, he adds: 'If out of every lesson as they pass this little Catechism [i.e. the Assembly's] you extract the doctrinal points by way of propositions and annex the proofs of scriptures to them, which are quoted in the margent, as you see Mr. Perkins hath done in the beginning of the book, and cause your scholars to write them out fair and large, as they find them in the Bible; it will be a profitable way of exercising them on the Lord's day, and a good means to improve them in the real knowledge of Christianity.' (Children in this form were supposed to be between nine and ten years of age!) Mr. Perkins's book to which Hoole refers is entitled: *The Foundation of Christian Religion gathered into Six Principles. And it is to be learned of ignorant people that they may be fit to hear Sermons with Profit and to receive the Lord's Supper with Comfort.* (1591.)

Later in the grammar school, the pupil continued his lessons in morality with such aphoristic wisdom as was to be extracted from Cicero, Seneca, Plutarch, Demosthenes, Aesop, Erasmus, Corderius, and a host of other moral teachers, both ancient and modern. Even though a few parents might believe that too many boys wasted their time with such classical languages, the average middle-class parent did not think to question the practical quality of such instruction that obviously sought to inculcate such good morality. To be sure, he sometimes suggested that Christian authors were better than pagan Greeks and Romans, and he would have liked to see more utilitarian courses substituted for a few of the classic authors, but in general he believed that even the boy who left the grammar school early to begin an apprenticeship would receive valuable training which would help him to become a godly and successful man.

Over and above the inculcation of practical Christianity, however, grammar school syllabuses represented a response to the Puritan insistence, to a degree unknown before, on the need for a learned ministry. Latin, Greek, and, in the upper forms, Hebrew were the 'holy' languages which especially enabled the pupil to get a closer acquaintance with the Bible, and with the early times of the Christian Church. Latin and Greek New Testaments were commonly the first text-books in the reading of 'the holy tongues'.

Religious instruction in the school, just as religious education in the home, was regularly associated with religious observance and instruction in church. Hence Hoole would have the schoolmaster meet his pupils at school an hour before the church service was due to begin in the morning so that he could instruct his pupils in their catechism after which the children went off to church, sitting in seats specially reserved for them. From Hoole the suggestion also comes that, after attending a service, the children should return to school, there to be rehearsed in the main points of the sermon. Some schools, in fact, required their pupils to take notes on the sermons to which they listened, which then had to be handed in to their schoolmaster for correction, to ensure that the children had not only heard but had intelligently noted the points of doctrine to which the minister had devoted his eloquence that day, and were thereby the better informed of the full doctrine of the national church.[1]

The long working hours in the schools of the sixteenth and seventeenth centuries have already been detailed.[2] By contrast, the holidays were short. The school year was divided into four quarters, but the usual number of vacations was three. Their length varied, but averaged about three weeks at Christmas, and a fortnight at Easter and Whitsun. At Shrewsbury, eighteen days were allowed at Christmas, twelve days at Easter and nine days at Whitsun. At Winchester, where the young Edmund Verney was a pupil in the early seventeenth century, it was also possible for the boys to have a three-week summer holiday, but for this, special permission had to be given. Anxious that his father should write to his schoolmaster to obtain it, Edmund writes home in August 1643: 'The commoners custome and the childrens are not alike . . . the children cannot go home without the consent of the Warden and Schoolmaster, and the commoners only of theire parents. The cause which makes me so desirous to goe home is, because all the commoners do go home at that time and most of the children (though they are compelled to make great sure before they can obtain leave).' According to Edmund, the boys who remained at the College during this three weeks 'have not soe much taske imposed upon them, that can take up one dayes labour' – a piece of information which he hopes his mother will pass on to his father. 'I feare that the earnestness of my sute hath made my father mistrust that I neglect my time, but I am sorry if it be soe . . . protesting that I never desired anything so much as learning, which I make noe question but I shall obtaine.'

Shrewsbury and Winchester, of course, were two of the great boarding schools. In the local grammar schools, the holidays were more often like those at Alford, where it was stated in the Orders of 1590, the masters 'shall not break up the school at any times of the year, but from the even of St. Thoam the Apostle before the Feast of the Nativity until the next day after the Epiphany, and again from the Tuesday before Easter Day until the Sunday next after Easter Day, except sickness shall enforce thereunto' (i.e. the holidays were twice a year, sixteen and twelve days

---

[1] See Watson, op. cit., p. 44.
[2] See also ibid., p. 119.

respectively). The holy-days not spent in school lessons were often mortgaged to outside work. For example, writing and 'devout and virtuous endeavours and exercises' – whatever these were – as the statutes at Kirkby Stephen prescribe, and they might be required in the school or the church. Half-holidays might be granted at the pleasure 'of some honourable or worshipful person', such as the Mayor.[1]

The time spent in school work was therefore vastly greater than it is today, and in this fact lies the explanation of how it was possible to attempt the different sides of classical discipline already outlined. A boy stayed in the grammar school six, sometimes seven years. If he came under a really erudite scholar and capable teacher, the authors read and the method of training in Latin composition and style produced a good classicist, and a man in touch with the knowledge of his age. The subject matter studied in the schools was much wider in scope than is often supposed, for the simple reason that wise schoolmasters chose topics which could be illustrated by examples from the arts and sciences, from history and literature. During a period when, as we have already seen, the association between knowledge and power, both political and commercial, was increasingly appreciated not merely by those who had traditionally held the former but also by the middle and merchant classes who increasingly aspired to both, the attraction of schools giving such an education is very obvious. It manifested itself both in the generosity of Tudor merchants and the great Companies towards the founding of grammar schools both in London and in other urban centres, and also in the determination of middle-class parents that their children should be amongst those to benefit by them, hence Richard Mulcaster's comment: 'everyone desireth to have his child learned'.[2]

The size of grammar schools varied a good deal. St. Saviour's Grammar School, Southwark (1562), was to have no more than a hundred boys; St. Alban's Grammar School (1570), a hundred and twenty, and Blundell's School, Tiverton, a hundred and fifty. Some were much smaller. For instance, Queen Elizabeth endowed a grammar school at Penryn, in Cornwall, for a master to teach three boys. Bath Grammar School was founded in 1553

[1] ibid., p. 58.
[2] Quoted L. B. Wright, op. cit., p. 7.

for the education of ten poor boys, whilst Dedham Grammar School (1571), in Essex, provided for twenty boys. On the other hand, Merchant Taylors' School, London, was planned for two hundred and fifty boys, whilst at Shrewsbury the numbers at one time reached three hundred and sixty and indeed later are said to have reached six hundred. It is described by William Camden as 'the best filled school in England', but Shrewsbury had no greater distinction than that of numbering Sir Philip Sydney amongst its pupils.

Large or small, public or private, the education of the classical type supplied in these schools was popular. According to one authority, at the time of the Reformation, to take two counties, Herefordshire with an estimated population of 30,000 had seventeen grammar schools, and Essex with an estimated population of 11,000 had at least sixteen. The number of schools in the latter county in the sixteenth and seventeenth centuries was still greater. The admission registers of St. John's College, Cambridge, and Gonville and Caius College show that in these two colleges students were entered from schools in Essex established at such little known places as Bumpstead, Moreton, Heydon, Chishull, Mareshall, Horkesley, Stanstead, Foxworth, Ramsey, Hulton. Investigation into other counties confirms that Essex was not unusual in its enthusiam for grammar school education.

Many of these grammar schools were founded as 'free' schools, or if not, were often free to the poor. Hence Watson, in his history of *The Old Grammar Schools* writes of them that there was no institution which did so much to aid the humbler classes to rise in the social scale when they had the ability to profit by school education as the grammar schools founded in Elizabeth's reign. But the extent to which they did so, as Watson himself concludes, was a good deal more limited than the terms of their foundation statutes might seem to suggest. The types of parents who sent their boys to the local grammar school may be seen by an analysis of the list of Colchester Grammar School in 1643. In the list of 177 boys who had entered the school during the previous five years, a large proportion were sons of gentlemen or clergy together with tradespeople's children: tanners, grocers, tailors, linen-drapers, an ironmonger, a goldsmith, a dyer and a chemist.[1] In practice, the grammar schools catered for the sons

[1] Watson, op. cit., pp. 530–1.

of the more cultured or the more ambitious parent: the children of the working classes, although technically eligible under the statutes of many of the grammar schools, had neither the background nor, in an essentially unegalitarian society, the incentive to avail themselves of the education the schools had to offer.

From the Restoration, however, there were indications that the education the old grammar schools had to offer was becoming less attractive even to the very social groups for whose sons' edification they had been founded a hundred years before. The endowed grammar schools, restricted by their statutes to a curriculum devoted to the teaching of the Latin and Greek languages and to religious instruction, became increasingly less relevant to the training of children whose adult years were to be spent in a society where command of contemporary foreign languages and literature, rather than an intimate knowledge of classical Greek and Latin, was of growing importance. In *Some Thoughts concerning Education* (1693), John Locke showed how important foreign learned works, especially French, had become, so that in many branches it was clear, in a way that it was not clear, say to Milton, in the preceding generation, that modern text-books were better adapted to modern needs than the treatises of ancient classical writers on the same subjects. Defoe pointed out that not one seafaring man in twenty understood Latin, yet a man could be a good navigator without it. Going further than Locke, Defoe boldly affirmed that 'you can be a gentleman of learning, and yet reading in English may do all that you want'. In other words, utilitarianism had become the watchword of the new age, and to meet this want other kinds of school were instituted, following examples in France and Germany. Thus in the latter part of the seventeenth century and throughout the eighteenth, a new type of private venture school began to emerge alongside the old grammar schools. These schools sometimes provided Latin, mathematics, and French, or one or other of them. If they taught Latin, they were called 'private grammar schools'. Yet another set of schools developed for the teaching of modern languages, particularly French and Italian. Pupils of grammar schools had frequented these schools as supplementary to classical education, but in the latter part of the seventeenth and in the eighteenth centuries, schools which had begun as modern language schools sometimes also chose to add Latin to their curriculum and thus themselves became substantially private grammar schools.

Most of the private grammar schools supplied exactly what was wanted: they were practical and commercial. Teaching became a good business when well managed and the advertisements in the newly rising periodicals show in many cases the flashy pretensions of some of the private schools, whilst the wages paid to the drudges of ushers whom they employed to save the expense of educated teachers, reveal unconsciously the shallowness of the new type of school. Still the Bishops refrained from interfering with these private venture schools, reserving their vigilance for dealing with the Nonconformists on account of their refusal to conform, rather than interesting themselves in any proved pedagogic disqualifications.

Just as the repressive legislation of Elizabeth had driven Roman Catholics to seek education on the Continent, so the policy towards Nonconformists after the Restoration drove Protestant Nonconformists to devise separatist schools and colleges. The Act of Uniformity and the Five Mile Act were aimed at Protestant Dissenters who carried on the profession of schoolmaster. At the same time, Nonconformist tutors at the universities were expelled. Far from suppressing the activities of these teachers and tutors, many of them proceeded to open colleges and schools – the 'Academies' – for the express purpose of training candidates for the Nonconformist ministry although other pupils were accepted as well. It was in one of these academies, the Newington Green Academy, kept by Charles Morton, a former fellow of Wadham College, Oxford, that Samuel Wesley, father of the evangelist, and Daniel Defoe were educated. From these two men we learn a good deal about the curriculum followed. Wesley wrote: 'This Academy were indeed the most considerable, having annext a fine Garden, Bowling Green, Fish Pond, and within a laboratory and some not inconsiderable rarities with air-pump, thermometer and all sorts of mathematical instruments.' From Defoe we learn that in addition to the classical languages, the pupils studied French, Italian, and Spanish, mathematics, natural science, history, geography, logic and politics.

Never secure from prosecution under the laws of both Church and State, the Academies led a precarious existence and were carried on – certainly during the later seventeenth and early eighteenth centuries – more or less under conditions of secrecy. Thus the Academy at Rathmell, near Settle, in Yorkshire, the earliest institution of its kind in the North of England, had to move several times during its short existence, 1669–98. The consequence was that the Nonconformist schools and Academies learned that the only way even to go on existing was to have a full belief in the task of education, and to maintain the highest aims of scholarship, so as to produce that type of mind in their pupils which would be able to hold its own on a high level in controversy and the practice of life. Their schools and Academies were, accordingly, probably the soundest educational establishments of the eighteenth century, and as they could not easily become settled institutions, each individual school had to think out for itself afresh its methods and even its curriculum. Yet the classics, though in a modified form, were taught intensively and extensively, sufficiently to entitle the Academies to rank essentially as grammar schools and as classical colleges.

With such competition, the clientele from which the old endowed grammar schools could draw became more and more limited. The wide-awake, practical parents sent their children to schools which laid claim, rightly or wrongly, to move with the times. The Dissenters, of conscientious conviction, wished their children to be taught be their own ministers, or at least by teachers who were not out of sympathy with their point of view. Many held that an elementary education was sufficient and the sooner that the children went into apprenticeship the better. When the nation was united in religion, or at least where religious conformity was enforced by laws supervised by the Church, the grammar school had attracted the best 'wits' amongst the boys. In the eighteenth century the grammar schools got only the leavings. Many parents, for one reason or another, preferred to send children to the private schools where they paid fees, rather than to the old grammar schools even where they were free. Without doubt, the loosening bonds of the old puritanical rigour of religion and life at the Restoration was partly the cause. The rebound of the secular side of life naturally told against the 'schools of learning', since learning had actually been allied to religion of the Puritan type. And so another small but important class of the community preferred to send their children away from all the English schools with their increasingly conflicting interests, and settled them either in foreign schools, or more frequently with learned Huguenot pastors or foreign scholars.

The diminished enthusiasm of parents to send their sons to schools whose curriculum was thought too restricted, or too biassed, to meet the needs of post-Restoration society, was matched by the diminished enthusiasm of public and private philanthropists to contribute to the maintenance and extension of the education which the old grammar schools provided. Harassed by the failure of funds during the Civil Wars, after the Restoration the old grammar schools found themselves deprived of support because they were thought to have undermined the loyalty of the King's subjects. No less a man than Thomas Hobbes paid the schools the dubious compliment of protesting against them, on the ground that the boys became so impressed by the studies of civil conflicts which had taken place in the pursuit of liberty in ancient Greece and Rome, that when they became men they sought to emulate the ancients by a civil war against their king. As an advocate of absolute power in the monarch he boldly declared against classics being taught for that reason. It was felt, unconsciously or consciously, by the Royalists that Hobbes was not entirely wrong in thinking that the grammar schools had helped to produce the doughty champions of the Parliamentarians, men like Selden (Chichester Grammar School), John Milton (St. Paul's), John Hampden (Thame Grammar School), and the redoubtable Oliver Cromwell himself (Huntingdon Grammar School). All of them were men who argued about legal precedents, and appealed to documents of old English rights and liberties with an antiquarian zeal and readiness, evidently due to the scholarly methods of enquiry of which the grammar schools had sown the seeds. For they had provided the foundations of severe classical studies, which pupils afterwards developed in the universities. The later Stuart kings and their advisors accordingly felt no desire to go out of their way to encourage the old schools. Charles II, in so far as he showed interest in schools, did so by imitation of French models, and turned his royal attention to the foundation of the mathematical department in Christ's Hospital which, by this time, had long ceased to function as a foundling hospital and had become well known as a grammar school. Thus, suspected on the one hand of doing their work only too well in the past, the old grammar schools lost support on the other for failing to provide an education appropriate to the present. In part, as we have seem, this criticism was founded on the restriction on the academic subjects which could be taught in their curriculum. It also stemmed from an awareness, stimulated by the needs of the increased population of the country, for an increased provision for elementary education in reading and writing, which the grammar schools had so determinedly refused to admit as part of their work. In some quarters, this became connected with the problem of educating the poor child.

In the sixteenth century, aptitude and ability, and not merely parentage and wealth, had been recognised as validating the individual child's claim to be educated. To commissioners who wished to exclude the 'ploughman's son' from the Cathedral School at Canterbury, Archbishop Cranmer replied by insisting that ability should be the basis of choice: '. . . if the gentleman's son is apt to learning, let him be admitted; if not apt to learning, let the poor man's Child, being apt, enter in his room'. This point of view, which was very much that of Starkey and of Forrest, was long to prevail and was to make the grammar schools and the universities the stepping stones to preferment for a poor child.[1] Hence the foundations of free grammar schools by the merchant classes which gave to the lowborn opportunities 'that by virtue of learning even the meanest man of all may attain to honour high'. The history of how the ploughman's son was in the end virtually excluded from the grammar schools both by the rising cost of maintaining the schools, and by the deepening social divisions in English society, themselves increasingly related to the type of education given by a man to his son, has been too well documented by others for its rehearsal here to be necessary. In any case, not every ploughman's son was 'apt' for the type of education the grammar schools provided: for many, such teaching would have been irrelevant alike both to their capacities and to their ambitions. During the latter half of the seventeenth century, however, whilst the numbers of poor children to be found in the grammar schools dwindled, the anxiety that the poor child should not be altogether illiterate grew. The reason for this renewed interest in the education of the poor

[1] See pp. 23-4, 128 ante.

child the enthusiasts make abundantly clear: the schools would provide an essential form of social control and an agency for social discipline amongst a social class conspicuously in need of both. Of children's behaviour at the time of the Interregnum, Samuel Harmar had written in 1642: 'they curse and swear, drawing the vengeance of God upon the Land: and besides neither Man nor Beast can passe by them quietly: for some are so unhappy like those children that mocked the old prophet Elisha, that neither Men, Women nor Children upon their business can passe by them without a mocke or it may be a stone at them . . .' Harmar goes on to complain that when the fathers of these children are told of their faults all they do is chide them 'and there is all the correction they give, and this will be a means to encourage Children more in their wickednesse . . .' A schoolmaster, he believes, would strike terror into the badly behaved boys, 'being like a magistrate, to try offences'. Harmar's faith in the social effects of school discipline was complemented by the belief that school uniform might also teach children their right 'place' in society. 'The very garments that in some places are given them to wear, and their maintenance in all of them by charity, are the constant badges and proofs of their dependence and poverty; and should therefore teach *them humility* and *their parents* thankfulness; the frequent contributions made for their support shows them their obligations to their benefactors and friends, and naturally leads them into gratitude and submission; and must, if anything, inspire them with a desire to please, by their faithfulness, diligence, and industry, that they may not forfeit the protection and assistance they need in any future station in life.'[1] In brief, whereas the old grammar schools had been clearly seen as a vehicle of social mobility for such poor children as were educated in them, the schools for the poor for which subscriptions were now being canvassed were seen as a means of educating them – and keeping them – 'in that station of life wherein Providence hath placed them'.

The Charity School movement proper began in 1699 with the foundation of the Society for the Propagation of Christian Knowledge, the oldest Anglican Missionary Society. Its aim was to co-ordinate scattered, local efforts and to 'weld together the separate and occasional charity of the benevolent into an or-

[1] Vox Populi, *Thomason Tracts*, E 146, no. 2.

ganised movement for the education of the poor'. It is important to notice that, in effect, their work was to establish the idea of elementary education, not as in earlier ages, as a stage preliminary to the grammar schools, by which boys of parts might climb to the universities, but as a system complete in itself. Unlike the Incorporated Societies set up with similar aims in Scotland and Ireland, the London S.P.C.K. did not manage, and only rarely financed, the schools. Local control was the basis of its scheme. Its policy was to excite the interest and support of the parish clergy and laymen in the work. It advertised and encouraged new methods of subscription, because it allowed men of moderate means to contribute to the schools, but it did not thereby exclude from its membership the managers and trustees of schools supported wholly, or in the main, by endowment. Its aim was to make religious instruction the backbone of education in all sorts and conditions of schools. The value of its work may be measured in the decline of the Charity School movement in England when the Society's interest was diverted from the schools to the foreign mission field and to the development of a great publishing connection. From 1699, great numbers of schools were founded in London and its environs under S.P.C.K. influence. In 1704, there were 54 schools with over 2,000 pupils: a quarter of a century later, 132, with 5,225 pupils. By this time, support of the charity schools was the favourite form of practical piety in London, and it was clear that the schools were objects of pride to its citizens. Popular support was encouraged by royal patronage. Queen Anne urged both the Archbishop of Canterbury and the Archbishop of York 'by all proper Ways, to encourage and promote so excellent a Work, and to countenance and assist the Persons principally concerned in it, as they shall always be sure of Our Protection and Favour'. In 1713, at the public thanksgiving for peace, the London charity children, some four thousand of them were placed in tiered seats in the Strand to see the processions pass on their way to St. Paul's 'whereby all the Children appear'd in full View of both Houses of Parliament, in the solemn Procession they made to St. Paul's upon that joyful Occasion, and who, by their singing Hymns of Praise to God and her Majesty, as well by their appearance, contributed very much to adorn so welcome a Festival; and gave great Satisfaction to all the Spectators, not without some surprise to Foreigners who never had beheld such a glorious Sight'. One hymn, which the children had specially rehearsed for the occasion, was to be sung as the Queen's procession wound its way down to St. Paul's:

> Lord give the Queen Thy saving Health,
> Whose Hope on Thee depends:
> Grant Her Increase of Fame and Wealth,
> With bliss that never ends!
> Allelujah, Allelujah, Allelujah, Allelujah!
> Allelujah, Allelujah, Allelujah, Allelujah![1]

It must have been a great disappointment to them that, due to an indisposition, the Queen herself did not pass by to hear their tuneful invocations on her behalf.

The generosity with which wealthy Londoners contributed to their charity schools and the pride with which the charity children were produced to line the streets on great occasions such as this was to continue throughout the century. In the provinces, neither in the towns nor in the country districts did the efforts of the S.P.C.K. meet with such enthusiastic support. In the country, the schools were mainly dependent on the interest of the local incumbents. They initiated the movement and managed and inspected the schools which were set up. But the absence of a large and prosperous middle class outside London and the overt hostility of many of the well-to-do-farmers to the education of the poor made for serious difficulties in the advancement of the work. Even where there was no particular opposition to a local charity school, many parishes were too small and too poor to support a school for their own children. Moreover, at certain times of the year, at harvest for example, parents were unwilling to spare their children from the fields. In these circumstances, *A Proposal for Teaching Poor Children to Read* (1708), which was probably issued by the S.P.C.K. itself, suggested that 'discreet & sober Persons' should be selected in each parish who might be paid by results: 2s. 6d. for each child knowing its alphabet, 2s. 6d. when it could spell, and 5s. when it could read and say its catechism. On this reckoning, the cost of the 'education' of each child would be only 10s., with a small extra sum for books. According to the pamphlet, this method of teaching the poor was already being put into practice with success in two Wiltshire parishes, although we are not told who was responsible for

[1] Ashton, op. cit., p. 16.

providing such money as even this restricted method required. The difficulty of getting parents to send their children to school regularly also inhibited the work of charity school enthusiasts in the mining and industrial towns, where the value of the children's wages to their parents was weighed against the value of education to the child, and where wages won the day. Nor was it altogether unreasonable that they should. In London, knowledge of the three 'R's' had a certain practical value to a child as an asset in life, which might pay relatively high dividends in a large, expanding commercial centre: whereas in these small towns and in the country, where most children of the poorer classes went into agriculture or domestic industries, the potential value of learning was much lower.

By 1729, the S.P.C.K. had helped establish over 1,600 schools with 34,000 pupils. Addison described the charity schools as 'the glory of the age'. Not everyone agreed with him. In 1723, de Mandeville appended to the second edition of his *Fable of the Bees*, *An Essay on Charity and Charity Schools*, in which he made a scurrilous attack not merely on the work of the schools but on the motives of the Governors, who 'are made of middling People, and many inferior to that Class . . . There is a Melodious Sound in the word Governor that is charming to mean People: Every Body admires Sway and Superiority . . . there is a Pleasure in Ruling over any thing, and it is this chiefly that supports Human Nature in the Tedious Slavery of School-masters. But if there be the least satisfaction in governing children, it must be ravishing to govern the Schoolmaster himself.' The delight his contemporaries so obviously took in London in the sight of files of charity school children winding their way through the streets, de Mandeville dismisses as either analogous to popular enthusiasm for military parades or as an opportunity for men to display their own wealth: 'There is a natural Beauty in Uniformity which most People delight in. It is diverting to the Eye to see Children well match'd, either Boys or Girls, march two and two in good Order; and to have there all whole and tight in the same Cloaths and Trimming must add to the comeliness of the Sight; and what makes it still more generally entertaining is the imaginary Share which even the Servants and the meanest in the Parish have in it, to whom it costs nothing: our Parish Church, our Charity Children. In all this there is a shadow of property that tickles every body that has a Right to make use of the Words, but more especially those who actually contribute and had a great hand in advancing the pious work . . .'[1] But in addition to denigrating the characters of those who applauded the work of the schools, de Mandeville also denied that the education of the poor was either useful or socially desirable. Parents, not schools, were the most important agents for inculcating good and right behaviour in the young. And where, he demanded, was there evidence to show that literacy was consonant with honesty? Schools merely kept children from working and 'are more Accessory to the growth of Villainy, than the want of Reading & Writing, or even the grossest Ignorance & Stupidity'. More particularly, and more typical of contemporary criticism of the work of the schools, de Mandeville argued that not only a large number of poor but also a large number of ignorant people were necessary for the smooth functioning of society. 'Knowledge both enlarges & multiplies our Desires', thus education can only make the working class more reluctant to work. The three 'R's' might be necessary to some 'but where People's Livelihood has no dependence on those Arts, they are very pernicious to the Poor, who are forc'd to get their Daily Bread by their Daily Labour . . . Going to School in Comparison to Working is Idleness, & the longer Boys continue in this easy sort of Life, the more unfit they'll be when grown up for downright Labour . . . Men who are to remain & end their Days in a Laborious, Tiresome & Painful Station of Life, the sooner they are put upon it at first, the more patiently they'll submit to it ever after.'[2]

Even at a time when abuse was no uncommon feature of public debate, the tone of de Mandeville's pamphlet ensured it a wide circulation. The barbed criticisms of the author of the *Fable of the Bees* stung some of the charity school enthusiasts into eloquent reply, among them the supporters of the Foundling Hospital, then being canvassed, since they themselves planned to give the children in their charge an education on the same lines as that given in the charity schools. From a pamphlet issued about 1728, appealing for interest in the Hospital, there comes a spirited defence of the work of the schools. Arguing that 'any wise Person' would sooner look for a servant from the charity

[1] de Mandeville, op. cit., pp. 318–21 passim.
[2] ibid., pp. 328–9 passim.

THE SCHOOLCHILD

school than from the homes of the poor, the most biassed opponents of the schools are asked to examine why this should be the case: 'let any such a one go to the Habitations of such Children before taken into a Charity School, and he shall find them without Shoes and Stockings, perhaps half Naked, or in tattered raggs, Cursing and Swearing at one another, almost before they can speak; or he shall find them with the like Black-Guard to themselves, rolling in the Dirt and Kennels, or Pilfering on the Wharffs and Keys, or when grown up to any Bigness Crying of Oysters, or the like Employments, and where he finds them, devoid of all Breeding, and good manners. But let him view the very same Children either in or come out of the Charity Schools, He or She shall find the very same Children not the same; but as much distinguished from what they were before as is a tamed from a wild Beast.'[1]

Nevertheless, de Mandeville's argument that the work of the charity schools was a threat to established social order was well taken by a society in which the relationship between education and social advancement was increasingly appreciated. Let the middle and upper classes be taught what they may; the working classes were on no account to be educated beyond their station. Public opinion thus turned once again to the problem of how to educate the working classes to work, but not to think. Thus one writer wished to see schools set up in every parish of the land which would teach poor children the rudiments of education – 'provided that their learning it did not interfere with their being brought up to Industry & Work'.[2] Jonas Hanway, who saw education of the poor as 'the only method for us to establish a solid police', called for the establishment of schools on the model of Christ's Hospital ('except the learned part'), which were to be maintained from 'a tax on our diversions, & profuse unnecessary expence'.[3] The S.P.C.K. itself, after several years of promoting the establishment of charity schools, was becoming disillusioned with literary instruction of the poor as a satisfactory method of reformation. The reformed manners and morals so confidently promised by the Society in the early years still tarried, and in 1722 the Secretary of the Society, Henry Newmann, wrote that

---

[1] *A Memorial concerning the Erecting . . . Orphanotrophy*, c. 1728, pp. 17–18.
[2] *Enquiry into the Causes of Encrease of Poor.* 1738. (Anon).
[3] *Citizen's Monitor*, p. 256.

'twenty four years of experience had shewn that a working school is in all respects preferable to one without labour & more in keeping with the present trend of public opinion'.[1] Financially dependent on public support, the Society inevitably was influenced by public opinion. Moreover, the Society was anxious to find some means of making its schools more financially self-sufficient so that the funds at its disposal might be more extensively employed. In addition, the provision of employment, from which profits might accrue both to the school and the children, was seen as having the double advantage of adding to the resources of the schools and of encouraging parents to support them by allowing their children to attend regularly instead of withdrawing them from time to time as economic necessity dictated. To achieve this end, some charity schools, such as those at Stroud and Stockport, were now united to the local workhouse. Others were housed in the workhouse itself, as was the case at St. Dunstan's in the East. But in the majority of cases the same end was achieved by adding work for profit to the curriculum of an existing school. At the Burlington School, London, for example, which had originally been founded in 1699 as a day school, becoming a boarding school for forty girls in 1725, this development is particularly well documented.[2] Training for industry had always been one of the principal objects of the school, hence the girls were taught simple arithmetic and domestic training, leading to service or apprenticeship in one of the needlework trades. By 1708, writing was taught and in 1711 a writing master appointed, so that 'the Children Shall be taught to write and Cast Accounts one Afternoon in a Week'. Even in the early days of this school, however, the tenor of the children's twelve-hour day was influenced by orders being placed for their work, thus 'if at any time linning Shall be brought in to be made, . . . the Mistress shall Order from the . . . girls so many as may be Necessary to do the same . . .' The mistress had to keep accounts of the work done and the profit made, any profits being put back in support of the school. In 1727, spinning wheels were purchased for the girls, together with a supply of flax, on which they were not merely to be taught to spin but to add to their

[1] Quoted M. G. Jones, *The Charity School Movement in the XVIIIth Century.* 1938, p. 92.
[2] See M. A. Burgess, *The History of Burlington School.* 1936.

wares for sale in support of the school. In the early 1740s, the industrial nature of the school intensified, the Trustees beginning a system of taking in needlework for profit, a system which proved so satisfactory financially that it was not given up until a century later, although it proved to be an almost intolerable burden for both staff – a Housekeeper and a schoolmistress – and pupils, who continued to be responsible, under the direction of the Housekeeper, for all the cleaning, washing, ironing, cooking and spinning that their household required.

In general, however, the introduction of work for profit in the charity schools was no more successful than it had been in the workhouse schools. Only in girls' schools such as Burlington School, where domestic labour could be combined with rudimentary education, did school labour prove to be an effective way of self support. The five essentials for the success of such a scheme were seldom to be found in isolation, and never in combination. Raw materials cheap enough to minimise the wastage of experimentation and unskilled labour; work which could be adapted to the strength and capacity of the learners 'all weak, some sickly, all young'; a market for the defective work which the children commonly turned out; regular attendance of the children at the school; and last, trustees with sufficient leisure to supervise, and teachers competent to teach, not only the catechism and the three 'R's', but the technical employments followed by the children. In all, these requirements proved too heavy for the majority of schools to sustain. In the result, the struggle between the discipline of labour and the discipline of literature for the control of the charity school curriculum ended in the defeat of labour. It also ended, for many generations, any widespread attempt to provide full-time liberal education for the lowest ranks of the children of the poor. By the end of the eighteenth century, the pupils of the older charity school were no longer the poorest of the parish, for the poor who could afford to send their children to a day school in which no remuneration was offered for labour and no training given to fit them for manual work, were the superior poor. The education their children received was an education which fitted them for work of a superior character, work offered by artisans and tradesmen who were demanding boys who could read and write and cast accounts. These could only be supplied by the charity schools.

Such attempts as were made to educate the children of the poorer working classes depended on either the desultory attempts of philanthropists to establish industrial schools to train the less able child for manual employments (attempts which were rarely more successful than the similar exercises of the old charity schools or indeed workhouses of the Bristol pattern) or on the energies of Robert Raikes and his supporters who, in the 1780s, sought to revive and expand the facilities of the Church Sunday Schools. The Sunday School movement was, in fact, something of a continuation on a very attenuated scale of the original charity school movement. It was financed by the voluntary subscriptions of the middle classes, and aimed like the original charity schools themselves at rescuing the very poor child from vice and ungodliness by instructing him in a curriculum based on the Bible and the catechism. By limiting the instruction given in the Sunday Schools to one day a week, the Sunday Schools were not seen as a threat to employment, but rather as an appropriately timed exercise which at once both protected the peace of the Sabbath from the disturbance of 'wild ignorant children' who might otherwise roam the streets, and also provided a bulwark against the insidious growth of radicalism and non-conformity. 'The points aimed at are to furnish opportunities of instruction for the poorer parts of the parish without interfering with any industry on the week day, & to inure children to early habits of going to Church & of spending the leisure hours of Sunday decently & virtuously. The children should be taught to read, & be instructed in the plain duties of the Christian Religion with a particular view to their future character as labourers and servants.'[1] In practice, the Sunday Schools did rather more than this, since they were sometimes used to sift out the more intelligent who might still profit by attendance at an industrial school. Hence by the end of the eighteenth century, there had been created *ad hoc* a hierarchy of schools exclusively for the working classes, which though inadequate as to their number, was yet seen as being appropriate to their condition and to the economic requirements of society.

Neither the inadequacy of educational provision for the working classes, nor the limited efficiency of the schools for the

[1] From a Sermon preached at St. Nicholas Church, Rochester on the occasion of the introduction of Sunday Schools. 1785. Quoted M. G. Jones, op. cit., pp. 146–7.

upper and middle classes, should be allowed to detract from the underlying significance of this growing consciousness of the importance of education for self-fulfilment and social order. Whatever else may be said of the schools of the seventeenth and eighteenth centuries, the argument and discussion which surrounded their foundation and expansion were testimony to a growing awareness of the desirability of 'moulding the man', not by precipitating him at the early age of seven into the adult world, but by withholding him from it till such time as he might have acquired some elementary skills which would enable him the better to acquit himself in later life. The world of the school is the world of the child, dependent on a wider, adult society but apart from it; a world which by its very existence asserts the difference in the natures of the child and the man. With their long hours of work, few holidays and harsh discipline, neither the schools of the rich nor the schools of the poor of our forebears appear to us now to show any understanding of the nature of the child at all. On the other hand, every society selects its own criteria for the socialisation of its children and uses its own methods of inculcating the values of its adult world. The abiding importance of the school is that, in providing a separate institution for children, it gives to childhood an independent and recognisable status.

XI

The Child in a Changing Society

1

For the vast majority of children in the seventeenth and eighteenth centuries, the sociological significance of the increasing emphasis on formal education in the sense we ourselves know it was more potential than immediate. Not only was formal education largely the prerogative of such of the middle and upper classes as chose to avail themselves of it, but even amongst these classes the old attitudes and expectations regarding the young were too deeply rooted to be changed quickly. Just as the schoolboy's appearance was that of a small-size adult – special dress for children only began to appear at the end of the eighteenth century and even then was thought eccentric – so also children were expected to think and behave as mature people at an age when our own children are only recently embarked on their primary education. In 1741 Lord Chesterfield writes to his son: 'This is the last letter I shall write to you as a little boy, for tomorrow you will attain your ninth year, so that for the future I shall treat you as a youth. You must now commence a different course of life, a different course of studies. No more levity. Childish toys and playthings must be thrown aside, and your mind directed to serious objects. What was not unbecoming to a child would be disgraceful to a youth ...'[1] Over-zealous for the future success of their children, Chesterfield and the many parents like him urged their children to the study of subjects which today

---

[1] Quoted Earle, op. cit., p. 178.

would only be deemed suitable for children many years older. Thus they became older than their years and sometimes unbelievably precocious. Parental anxiety and ignorance of developmental psychology, together or independently, both contributed to the perpetuation of the idea that childhood was but a brief introduction to the heavy responsibilities of the adult world. John Evelyn was by any standards a man of great good sense and not the sort of father to force his child unduly – indeed, he averred that he abhorred precocity in children. Yet the extraordinary record of his son's intellectual attainments, it may be remembered, shows very clearly how a parent would permit his child's mind to be crowded with the intellectual problems of the adult even before the minimum age at which we believe it advisable to begin the most elementary instruction of the child.

The continued projection of the hopes and fears of the adult world into that of the child was not only confined to matters of dress and formal education but also found expression in countless other ways, not least in the almost complete absence of books written to divert and entertain children as compared with the scores of works, short and long, intended to improve and edify them. There was no counterpart to the vast, commercial production of children's books of our own day. Up to the end of the seventeenth century, children's leisure-time reading was limited to the Bible and to religious treatises. *Pilgrim's Progress* (1688), *Robinson Crusoe* (1714) and *Gulliver's Travels* (1726), though appropriated by later generations of children as story books, were originally religious, political and satirical works written for adults. Not till 1780 did professional authors turn their attention to writing juvenile literature, although since 1744, certain publishers had begun to interest themselves in publishing books specially for children's reading. The pioneer in this field appears to have been John Newbery, a London publisher, who published upwards of two hundred titles, including one announced in 1744 as 'a pretty little pocket book' which contained the story of Jack the Giant Killer. The texts of Newbery's books were either written by himself or by authors, amongst whom was Oliver Goldsmith, whom he managed to commission. It must be confessed, however, that the tone and sometimes content of the children's books which began to appear at the end of the eighteenth century – Mrs. Sherwood's *History of the Fairchild Family* (1788), Thomas Day's *Sandford and Merton* (1783), Maria Edgeworth's *The Parents' Assistant* (1792) – were not strikingly different from the unadorned moral treatises of earlier authors. James Janeway's painfully religious tales were not the only ones to familiarise death to the reading child. *The Fairchild Family*, once deemed 'a most charming' book for children, has countless death-bed scenes scattered over its earnest pages, some of them no ordinary death-beds either. As an object lesson, the little Fairchilds are taken to see the body of a man hanging in chains on a gibbet. The horror of their progress through a gloomy wood to this revolting sight; the father's unsparing comments; the hideous account of 'the thing', rattling, swinging and turning its horrible countenance while Mr. Fairchild describes and gloats over it, and finally kneels and prays, covers several pages which few parents, even today, would wish their child to read. Mr. Fairchild's purpose was to 'show them something which I think they will remember as long as they live, that they may love one another with perfect and heavenly love'. One may well imagine that at least the first of these hopes was amply fulfilled.

2

The preoccupation with death and sin which is so much a feature of these children's books, though shocking to us today, has to be seen in the context of a society where premature death, especially infant death, was still a common and accepted feature of family life. According to the London Bills of Mortality, of 1,178,346 deaths between 1730 and 1779, 526,973 were those of children under five years of age.[1] In the middle of the century it had been claimed that, in London, 75% of all children christened were dead before they were five years of age: many of them died before they were one year old.[2] Comparisons made at the time with other parts of the country suggest that outside London and the large cities the rates of mortality were far lower – according to one account for the period 1756–60 the mortality of children under two years of age was 13% as com-

[1] T. R. Edmonds, On the Mortality of Infants in England, *Lancet*, 30 January 1836, p. 692.
[2] E. Caulfield, *The Infant Welfare Movement in the Eighteenth Century*. 1931. p. 7.

pared with a rate of 30–40% in London and the large cities. Even so, by our own standards these rates remain enormous and in any particular family they could and did have spectacular effects. John Wesley, for example, was one of nineteen children only six of whom reached maturity. So usual was the reduction of effective family size by the premature death of its youngest members, that Gibbon (five of whose brothers and one sister died in early infancy) writes in his *Autobiography:* 'The death of a new-born child before that of its parents may seem an unnatural, but it is a strictly probable event'.[1] The reasons for this continuing waste of infant life are not far to seek: indeed, they are almost identical with the reasons for the high infant and child mortality rates which had prevailed for generations past. Obstetrics remained an undeveloped science and was in the hands of the untrained midwife. As the person who delivered the child was supposed to take care of it after its birth, the care and diseases of infancy were left to the so-called nurses and old women. Walter Harris, in the course of his *Treatise of the Acute Diseases of Infants* (1742) has some harsh words to say on this score: 'There are some wicked Nurses, reckoned more skilful than the rest, who commonly attend lying-in Women during the Month, & are not afraid to give Wine and Brandy, sweetened perhaps with Sugar, to new-born Infants, with great Secrecy, as often as they can conveniently, to still their crying, & procure Ease to themselves; whence dreadful Symptoms arise from hidden Causes...'[2] The carelessness of the nurses was often matched by an indifference on the part of parents, an attitude almost inevitably induced at a time when parents had so many children that they ceased to take an interest in them individually. 'Mrs. Thrale,' we are told, 'regarded the death of various daughters at school with great equanimity'; and Sir John Verney cheerfully remarked when two of his fifteen children died that he still had left a baker's dozen. On such occasions as parents were not merely indifferent, they were often fatalistic, seeing in the death of their little ones the mysterious ways of God. 'It is a wonderful Part of the Providence of God that so many little creatures seem to be born only to die ... God, who does nothing in vain, has wise ends no doubt, & Purposes worthy of Himself to serve in

[1] Gibbon, op. cit., p. 4.
[2] Harris, op. cit., pp. 18–19.

and by the Birth of Infants who seem born only to die.'[1] Praiseworthy though this attitude might seem to some, it is unlikely to have contributed much to the advance of either obstetrics or pediatrics. To the consequences of fatalism concerning the deaths of infants there was added in the eighteenth century the consequences of the growing fashion among fashionable and wealthy women of refusing to nurse their children lest their figures should suffer – a revival of sixteenth-century practice. In these circumstances, the alternative means of rearing the child, by hand or by wet nurse, each had its own hazards. It was the custom to send for a number of wet nurses of whom the most suitable was chosen to suckle the child, but the ignorance and carelessness of these women, whose consequences for the children of the poor we have referred to elsewhere, also took its toll of the children of the well-to-do. As to rearing the child by hand, at a time when little was known of infant dietetics and when patent baby foods had yet to be invented, the consequences were often even more disastrous. A comparison between the death rate of infants reared by hand, as compared with that at wet nurse, revealed that the former was more than twice the latter.

Ignorance, indifference and fatalism, however, are only a partial even though substantial explanation of the many deaths occurring among children in the seventeenth and eighteenth centuries. An unknown proportion were undoubtedly the result of culpable neglect and cruelty. Today it is impossible for a parent voluntarily to relinquish his rights and responsibilities in respect of his children except in the manner prescribed by the Adoption Acts. But until the end of the eighteenth century, and to a less extent even in the nineteenth century, it was a common practice to expose unwanted children, either the children of unmarried mothers, or of those who considered their family already overlarge, in the streets and lanes of the cities or in the country. Frequently these children died before being discovered. Sometimes they were discovered by beggars who would mutilate them to excite pity and hire them out to other beggars for fourpence a night. Understandably, few of these children lived to reach maturity. In their own homes, children were not always better treated. *The Covent Garden Journal* for 3 March 1752, contains a particularly gruesome account of a child which was

[1] *The Gentleman's Magazine*, vol. X, February 1740.

virtually tortured to death by its step-mother: 'A Man and Wife are committed to Malden Gaol for threatening to kill their Neighbours for upbraiding them with Cruelty. It seems, the woman used frequently to stick Pins in a Child (to which she was Mother-in-law) and stir up the Fire with its Feet, so that its toes rotted off; on which the Parish took it from her on the Neighbour's Complaint, and put it in the Workhouse, where it is since dead; But', continues the account laconically, 'we don't hear that there are any Proceedings against her yet on this Score.' The uncertainty of the prosecution of parents in cases of cruelty to children was to continue not merely throughout the eighteenth century, but until the last quarter of the nineteenth century when the first *Act for the Prevention of Cruelty to Children* was passed. In large measure, this was a reflection of the continuing social acceptance of violence which, as far as children were concerned, was as much a feature of their treatment by their parents as it was of their treatment by their teachers. William Blundell, a member of a Lancashire recusant family, was not an especially harsh father. Indeed, he seems to have had some genuine sympathy for children. Yet for minor misdemeanours such as faulty deportment and boisterous behaviour, his little daughters of about seven or eight were often 'whipped and penanced' and after failing to keep their promise of better behaviour, were whipped again. When on one occasion one of the girls was not whipped for her bad and unladylike deportment, but escaped with the injunction to 'Pray & mend', she commented: 'I never came off thus in all my life when my father was so angry. I expected no less than to have been shut up in a dark room for a week or a fortnight together & to have dined & supped upon birchen rods . . .'[1] So accustomed were our forebears to such discipline that when the author of an essay on 'Flogging', published in the *Gentleman's Magazine* in 1735, stated that he had often wondered that 'neither in the present age or the last one no learned Dissertator had treated professedly of the Art', 'Britannus' was moved to write to the editor, 'Is not this sort of Correction common in almost every Family, as well as every School in Great Britain? What great Wonder that no learned Dissertator has told us what everyone knows'. Warming to his theme,

[1] Margaret Blundell, *Cavalier; Letters of William Blundell to his friends, 1620–98.* 1933. pp. 304–8 passim.

'Britannus' goes on to declare that the author appeared to make 'very unhandsome Returns for the Care of his Youth instead of thanking his Superiors for Seasonable Correction' and, for good measure, to assert that he was clearly a dull fellow, brought up probably by 'an old Woman or Country Paidegogue', who in the next edition would undoubtedly add to his present folly by showing his 'indignation against the Whipping Post, the Pillory, & the Gallows...'[1]

3

There was no novelty in 'Britannus's' explicit assumption of the natural superiority of the old over the young. Nor was there any novelty in its contemporary expression in family life and discipline. A married man, writing to his father in 1715, signs himself as being: 'honoured Sir, your most dutifull son & obliged humble servant...' and his wife, writing to her father-in-law, 'I beg my dughty may be made ecceptable to my mother & best serveses to my Sister. I am, honoured Sir, your obedient & dughtyfull daughter,...'[2] After the Restoration, parents were being admonished not to make 'thy family the frequent subject of thy talk'[3] so as not to give them a false sense of their own importance; and well into the eighteenth century parents were being warned of the lamentable consequences of the indulgence of the young. 'Common people are said to express more fondness for their children than persons of rank; the good sense of the latter preventing their affection being troublesome, whereas the other lack consideration & plague company with details of beauty, wit & spirit of their child, are affronted if its impertinences are not liked. In consequence of the fondness, children are much indulged by servants not allowed to check them, they do not consider that such children will prove headstrong & disobedient in mature age.'[4] Not all persons of rank, however, attempted to disguise their fondness for their children nor prevent them from becoming troublesome. Lord Holland – Henry Fox – described his son, Charles, with the utmost satis-

[1] *The Gentleman's Magazine*, vol. V, February 1735, pp. 89–90.
[2] *Letters and Papers of the Banks Family of Revesby Abbey*, ed. J. W. F. Hill. 1952. pp. 26, 20 and 27.
[3] Thos. Fuller, *The Holy State*.
[4] *The Gentleman's Magazine*, vol. II, January 1732, p. 556.

faction as being 'very well, very pert and very argumentative'.[1] Charles James was in fact the original of the almost legendary story of the spoilt child who was allowed to ride to table on the saddle of mutton with his feet splashing in the gravy, a story which is more than adequate testimony to the determination of his doting parent that the child's 'spirit shall not be broken . . . the world will do that business fast enough'. Progressive child psychology of the twentieth century could hardly go further, and most eighteenth century parents did not go anywhere near as far. Even though towards the end of the century, the old formality was beginning to break down in some families, children no longer kneeling to ask their parents' blessing or standing in their presence, in many households the old, more formal usage remained so that Mrs. Sherwood, for example, was to write in later life: 'I never sat in a chair in my mother's presence'.[2] In many ways, this retention of old ways was supported by the rise of Wesleyanism and the Evangelicals. The Wesley family itself was to set the pattern for many of the English young for nearly a hundred years and descriptions of the Wesley household stand in marked contrast to those of Lord Holland. Susannah Wesley records how her children were kept largely on 'spoon meat' and made to eat sparingly till the age of six, a regimen which was supposed to allay the angry passions. 'When turned a year old (and some before), they were taught to fear the rod, and to cry softly; by which means they escaped abundance of correction they might otherwise have had; and that most odious noise of the crying of children was rarely heard in the house, but the family usually lived in as much quietness as if there had not been a child among them.'[3] Thus whilst, *pace* the *Gentleman's Magazine*, among some upper-class households a more permissive attitude to children was beginning to manifest itself by the end of the eighteenth century, in very many others, the old, harsh attitudes to children prevailed without much comment. Men like Mary Wollstonecraft's father regularly flogged their children for no apparent reason but to satisfy their own brutality;[4] and the new children's literature, such as the

[1] See Lynd, op. cit., p. 36.
[2] See Bayne-Powell, *The English Child in the Eighteenth Century*. 1939. pp. 3 and 7.
[3] Quoted Miller and Swanson, op. cit. p. 10.
[4] Bayne-Powell, op. cit., p. 5.

monthly *Juvenile Magazine: or an instructive & entertaining Miscellany for Youth of Both Sexes* continued to teach the old duty of the respect of a child for its parents.

4

Yet though the old ways persisted, the context of family life was changing, and changing in a way which inevitably, though gradually, was to affect the nature of parent–child relationships. As we have seen, in pre-Restoration England the numerical size of many middle and upper-class households, including as it did not only parents and young children but elderly relatives, cousins and in-laws, together with the servants to all the inhabitants, as well as apprentices of various kinds, was far larger than even the largest household with which we are familiar today. In the mid-seventeenth century, 'families' of between thirty and forty were not unusual. Mrs. Isham complained in 1643 of having soldiers quartered in her house, 'there is one hundred men in our House, which my thinkes is very harde to be put in one house, & we being allmost 50 in family . . .'[1]

In the later seventeenth century and in the eighteenth century, however, the increasing wealth of certain sections of the middle and upper classes began to encourage a more comfortable way of living. One of the practical evidences of this was the separation of the servants' living quarters from those of the family, with the result that the family itself, no longer submerged by numbers of household servants and apprentices, was free to develop more intimate family relationships and a degree of family self-consciousness in a way hitherto impossible. This was a development which was not restricted to the houses of the wealthy in the towns, but also was beginning to influence family life in the countryside. Arthur Young, describing the houses of well-to-do farmers, draws special attention to the new bell-pull in the farmhouse living-room for the farmer's wife to summon her domestic servants, just as he also comments on another feature of eighteenth-century farmhouse life – the declining habit of boarding and feeding large numbers of servants in husbandry in the farmhouse itself.

Just as the institutional development and acceptance of formal

[1] *Verney Memoirs*, vol. II, p. 191.

education in schools with the consequent isolation of the child from adult society, was a prerequisite of the emergence of modern sociological and psychological concepts of childhood, so also the gradual isolation and individualisation of the family as a social and psychological entity ultimately contributed to the same end. The ties between parent and child were necessarily strengthened in a family reduced to parents and children, a family from which servants, clients and friends were excluded. Greater familiarity of parents with their own children was to contribute to less formality between them, and to an increasing concern of parents for the welfare of their children, which manifested itself both in the use of terms of endearment between parents and children and as an increasing anxiety of parents to have details of their children, of their health and behaviour, when members of the family were apart for some reason or another.

In the main, these influences were far more observable among the middle classes of eighteenth-century England than among any other section of contemporary society. Among the upper classes, a continuing regard for lineage, rather than nuclear family, contributed to the perpetuation of an attitude towards children which still viewed and indeed used them, as a means of extending the material and social status of the larger kin group; as a form of family property to be exploited rather than as immature but individual personalities to be carefully developed. If this was reflected in a continuing formality in the relationships of parents and children in many upper-class households, it was also illustrated by the continuation into the eighteenth century of the traditional attitude to their marriages. As late as 1729, a little girl of some wealth but of only nine years of age, was taken from her boarding school by her guardian and married to his own son, an apprentice. It is of some importance to remember that such practices persisted because of successful opposition to a number of attempts during the last twenty years of the seventeenth century to introduce changes in the marriage laws of England, relating to the legal age of consent of minors and the powers of guardians over the marriage of their wards. Had attempts to raise the one and limit the other succeeded, the pressures which were exerted on the children of old and wealthy families would necessarily have been diminished and one of the most inhibiting factors to the development of modern attitudes to children and childhood removed. As it was, the triumph of vested family interest as regards the rights of children concerning marriage continued throughout the eighteenth century and into the next so that John Cordy Jeaffreson could write in 1872; 'and to this day it is within the power of English parents to couple in most unholy wedlock a pair of reluctant children who lack the courage and knowledge requisite for the protection of their natural rights'.[1]

5

The same energy which was directed to upholding the old marriage laws during the latter half of the seventeenth century and thoughout the eighteenth century, was notably absent as regards maintaining the old, Tudor paternalistic policies for the children of the poor and propertyless. Perhaps it is unreasonable to expect that it could have been otherwise. Underlying the complex structure of Tudor policy was the belief that poverty, vagrancy and delinquency could be virtually wiped out in one generation by the introduction of training schemes and the imposition of penalties on those who deviated, or caused others to deviate, from the Tudor ideal of self-support. Time had shown, however, that neither human inadequacy nor economic inefficiency was to be so quickly eradicated from human society. Nor was contemporary administration adequate for the tasks laid on it by statute. As the years passed, the enthusiasm for the old policies thus waned. Locally, as we have seen, support for the various schemes had been very variable before the Interregnum: after it, determination to restrict the power of the Crown had destroyed such administrative machinery as had endeavoured to secure efficient local operation of the laws. The chaos which resulted in the breakdown of administration of the Elizabethan statutes when the individual parishes and masters of poor apprentices were left unsupervised, thus enabling them to ignore their statutory duties, provided the fertile soil for many of the problems of the nineteenth century. Moreover, the assertions, first of the Puritans and later of the Evangelicals, that poverty and wickedness were inextricably connected, reinforced the general conviction that statutory provision for the poor and their children should be both minimal in amount and, where possible, punitive in character. Thus the

[1] *Brides and Bridals*, vol. I. 1872.

positive and constructive aspects of the social policies of the Tudors in which children figured so largely were mainly lost.

As we have already seen, from the late seventeenth century onwards, the local schemes for the provision for the poor child which aroused the most enthusiastic public support were those in which children were expected to help support themselves. It may be argued that 'by setting the poor on work', these policies were a continuation in essence of the Elizabethan poor laws themselves. But in their emphasis on the work, not the welfare of the child, in their concern for economic profitability rather than educational content, they reflect a society in which the Tudor notion of the 'common weal' had become coloured by materialism and where the promotion of national wealth, rather than the promotion of national stability, had become the current ideal.

These fundamental shifts in emphasis are very well illustrated in a *Report for the Reform of the Poor Law* presented to the Board of Trade in 1697 by the philosopher John Locke, then Commissioner of the Board of Trade:

'The children of the labouring people are an ordinary burden to the parish, and are usually maintained in idleness, so that their labour is also generally lost to the public, till they are twelve or fourteen years old . . . The most effectual remedy for this, that we are able to conceive, and which we therefore humbly propose, is, that working schools be set up in each parish, to which the children of all such as demand relief of the parish, above three and under fourteen years of age, whilst they live at home with their parents, and are not otherwise employed for their livelihood, by the allowance of the overseers of the poor, shall be obliged to come. By this means,' explains Locke, 'the mother will be eased of a great part of her trouble in looking after and providing for them at home, and so be at more liberty to work: the children will be kept in much better order, be better provided for, and from their infancy be inured to work which is of no small consequence to making them sober and industrious all their lives after.' Had this been the total explanation of the virtues of Locke's proposals and the main ground for their acceptance, Locke's scheme would have already appeared as a corruption of the Tudor policy of 'bending the twig' and inculcating habits of sobriety and industry in the young. In fact, Locke commends his proposals very largely on the explicit ground that, if adopted, they would make possible the withdrawal of the allowances payable to the parents of large families which, as we have seen, was an accepted feature of Tudor poor law provision. Instead of family allowances, parents unable to support their numerous offspring were to send them to the working school where, in time, they would contribute substantially to their own upkeep and hence be no charge on the community at all. 'Whereas it may reasonably be concluded,' wrote Locke, 'that computing all the earnings of a child from three to fourteen years of age, the nourishment and teaching of such a child during the whole time would cost the parish nothing, whereas there is no child now which is maintained by the parish, but before the age of fourteen, costs the parish fifty or sixty pounds.'[1] It was precisely this whittling down of the area of accepted community responsibility for the poor; this undiscriminating attempt to make the poor keep the poor which so typifies the operation of the poor law after the Interregnum and makes it markedly different in spirit and in practice from the operation of the earlier period. Moreover, Locke's scheme for putting to work children of three years old and above which virtually denied them the chance of any formal education, stands in sharp contrast to the generosity of the sixteenth-century proposals of the citizens of London when founding Christ's Hospital, and others who, like Starkey, advocated a school for the poor in every parish. That Locke, himself a man of broad humanity and a pioneer in educational ideas, could propose such a scheme as official policy for the reform of the Poor Law is eloquent testimony to the change in the climate of opinion by the end of the seventeenth century.

Child labour for the poor, instead of education, was however to become the pattern and the ideal that was accepted throughout the eighteenth century. In 1724, according to Defoe, 'there was not in all the Eastern and middle part of Norfolk, any Hand, unemploy'd, if they would Work; and the very Children after four or five years of Age, could every one earn their own Bread'. At Taunton, he found 'there was not a Child in the Town, or in the Villages round it, of above Five Years old, but, if it was not neglected by its Parents, and untaught, could earn its own

---

[1] Locke, op. cit., quoted in the Report of the Select Committee appointed to consider of the POOR LAWS and to report their Observations thereupon from time to time to the House, *B.P.P. 1817*. p. 14.

Bread'; whilst in Yorkshire, he declared, there was 'hardly anything above four Years old but its Hands are sufficient to itself'. The extent to which the domestic industries depended on the labour of children has already been described elsewhere. 'The exploitation of child labour in the early factories has probably caused more horror and indignation, and rightly so, than any other feature of the industrial revolution; but it is not so often realised that the same sort of thing was equally characteristic of the older domestic industries. Hidden away in cottages, where they attracted no attention, thousands of children in rural areas worked factory hours every day, under conditions which were often no better than those which aroused so much feeling in the industrial centres.'[1] This pattern was continued at least until the mid-nineteenth century. In the lace-making areas, children were taught to handle bobbins as mere infants of three or four years old, and were often working regular hours in the lace schools at five. In straw plaiting, children were sorting straws at four, plaiting at five and earning a regular wage at six or seven, and not infrequently before. The majority of children employed in such industries worked in cottage schools owned either by the mistress herself, or by a dealer who provided materials and employed a teacher or overlooker to supervise for him. In some schools, reading was taught once a day – generally verses from the Bible – but in actual practice the schools were nothing but workshops in which children were commonly taxed beyond their strength by parents or mistress. In agriculture also, where from the mid-eighteenth century onwards wages had fallen rapidly in relation to prices, children were sent out to work at what must now seem an incredibly early age to add their pittance to the support of themselves and their family. The same was true of the mining areas, where children worked from infancy in the coal and metal mines under incredibly harsh conditions.

Yet the eighteenth century also saw slowly developing a challenging ideal of philanthropy and humanitarianism which, in relation to children, was devoted to securing them from greed and abuse; to providing institutions for the unwanted child; to training schemes for waifs and delinquents; and to providing some sort of education for the poor child that, at the last, he might

[1] Ivy Pinchbeck, *Women Workers and the Industrial Revolution*. 1930. p. 232.

not be damned through ignorance of the Christian religion.

If the objectives of some of these schemes bear some resemblance to Tudor attempts to provide for children in English society, the social context in which they were to be realised underlines marked differences in contemporary attitudes to communal responsibility and the function of private philanthropy.[1] In the sixteenth century, private philanthropy was often regarded not as an alternative to, but as an expression of, communal responsibility, as the scheme for the Royal Hospitals well illustrates. Even more important to recognise, however, is that the founders of Christ's Hospital, just as those who framed Tudor legislation affecting the child, had a far less restricted view of the nature of the provision to be made: seeking not the immediately cheapest, but the most enduring methods of assisting the deprived child. Hence they attempted to elaborate comprehensive policies in which relevant training and appropriate education played a significant part. Later generations, as we have seen, were to erode these policies and transmogrify them into mere rate-reducing exercises, in which economy to the public purse was the paramount concern. It was left to private individuals, should they so wish, to make more positive provision. If the initiation of philanthropic schemes in the eighteenth century was erratic, and their results variable, they nevertheless represented the vestigial remains of a concept of positive community support which Tudor administrators had seen fit to embody in statute, and their eighteenth-century successors conceived of as the proper concern of private individuals.

With growing industrialism and urbanisation, there developed in the nineteenth century a fierce conflict of opinion between *laisser faire* philosophers and philanthropic reformers. The ultimate victory of the latter led to a new awakening of the national conscience, and the gradual recognition that for the State to abrogate all but minimal responsibilities for children was both wasteful and wrong. The outcome was a community concern embodied in a network of social legislation which has now given all children a new status based on their own legal rights. The analysis and growth of these developments will be the subject of a subsequent volume.

---

[1] See W. K. Jordan, *Philanthropy in England, 1480–1660.* 1959. p. 151.

Bibliography

Parliamentary Debates (Hansard)
1st series, vol. 32.
2nd series, vols. 2, 19, 20.

Parliamentary Papers
Journals of the House of Commons, vols. I, III, IV, VII, VIII, IX, X, XI, XII, XVIII, XXI, XXII, XXVI, XVII, XXXI.
Journals of the House of Lords, vol. XIII.

Parliamentary Reports
First and second reports from the committee appointed to enquire how far the orders of the last session, respecting the poor, had been complied with (1776), 1st series, vol. IX.
Report from the committee on the state of parish poor children, etc. (i.e. within Bills of Mortality) (1778), 1st series, vol. IX.
Report from the Committee who were appointed to consider the several returns which have been made to the order of this House of the 16th day of December 1778, 'that there be laid before this House, an Account of Persons convicted of felonies or misdemeanors', etc., vol. 35, no. 37.
Abstract, presented to the House of Commons, of returns relative to the expence and maintenance of the poor (1804), 1803–4, XIII.
Report from Committee on the State of Mendicity in the Metropolis (1814), 1814–15, III.
Report from the committee on parish apprentices (i.e. within Bills of Mortality) (1814) 1814–15, V.
Report from the Select Committee on the State of Mendicity in the Metropolis, etc., 1816, V.
Second Report from the Committee on the State of the Police of the Metropolis, 1817, VII.
Report from the Committee on the Prisons within the City of London and Borough of Southwark, 1818, VIII.
Report from the Select Committee on the State of the Gaols, etc., 1819, VII.
Returns from parishes within the Bills of Mortality of Male and Female Pauper Children (1819), 1819–20, IV.

BIBLIOGRAPHY

Report from the Select Committee on the Police of the Metropolis, 1828, VI.

Report from His Majesty's Commissioners for inquiry into the Administration and practical operation of the poor laws, 1834: Report XXVII Appendices XXVIII, XXIX, XXXV, XXXVII.

Contemporary Books, Pamphlets and Local Records

An account of the General Nursery of Colledge of Infants, set up by the Justices of the Peace for the County of Middlesex, with the Constitutions and Ends thereof. 1686–7.

An Account of the Corporation of the Poor of London . . . 1713.

An account of several Work-Houses for Employing and Maintaining the Poor, 1725 (1st edn.), 1732 (2nd edn.).

An account of the Rise, Progress and Present State, of the School and Work-House maintained by the People called Quakers, at Clerkenwell, London. 1746.

An account of the hospital for the maintenance and education of exposed and deserted young children. 1749.

An account of the Marine Society. . . 1758.

Account of the Receipts (sic) and payments of the hospital for the maintenance and education of exposed and deserted young children. 1759.

An account of the receipts and disbursements relating to Sir John Fielding's plan, for the preserving of distressed boys, by sending them to sea, as apprentices in the Merchants Service. 1770.

An account of the asylum, or home of refuge (situated on the Surrey side of Westminster Bridge) for the Reception of Orphan Girls etc. (App. to Gregory Sharpe's Charity Sermon, *The Advantage of a Religious Education.* 1770).

An Account of the Origin and Progress of the Society for the Promotion of Industry, in the Hundreds of Ongar and Harlow, and the Half Hundred of Waltham, in the County of Essex. 1797.

Acts of the Privy Council of England, 1619–21, ed. C. H. Firth and R. S. Rait, 1930.

Acts of Ordinances and the Interregnum, 1642–1660, ed. C. H. Firth and R. S. Rait, 2 vols. 1911.

At a Court held by the Right Honourable the Lord President, and the rest of the Governors of the Corporation for the Poor of London. 1655.

An address to the Public from the Philanthropic Society, 1790 and 1791.

AIKIA J., *A description of the country from thirty to forty miles round Manchester.* 1795.

ANDREWS J. P., *An Appeal to the Humane, on behalf of the most deplorable class of society, the climbing-boys, employed by the chimney sweepers,* 1788.

BIBLIOGRAPHY

ARTH(INGTON) HENRY, *Provision for the Poore, now in Penurie, out of the storehouse of God's plentie.* 1597.

Articles to be enquired of within the Diocese of Exeter, in the Generall and Trienniall Visitation of the Reverend Father in God, Joseph, Lord Bishop of Exeter. London, 1638.

ASCHAM ROGER, The Scholemaster (1570) in *English Works*, ed. W. A. Wright. Cambridge, 1904.

BACON NATHANIEL, *The Annalls of Ipswich.* 1654 (1884 edn.).

BAILEY WILLIAM, *A treatise on the better employment and more comfortable support of the poor in workhouses, etc.*, 1758.

BARRINGTON DAINES, *Observations on the more ancient statutes.* 5th edn., 1796.

BATTUS BARTHELEMY, *The Christian Man's Closet* (trans. by William Lowth). 1581.

BECON THOS., *Worckes*, pt. I. 1564.

The Catechism of Thomas Becon, ed. John Ayre, Parker Society, Cambridge, 1844.

BENTHAM JEREMY, *Observations on the Poor Law Bill.* 1797.

BERNARD SIR THOMAS, *An account of the Hospital for the Maintenance and Education of exposed and deserted young children.* 2nd edn., 1799.

Beverley Borough Records, 1575–1821, ed. J. Dennett. *Yorkshire Archeological Society Records Series*, vol. LXXXIV, 1933.

BOUYER R. G., *An account of the origin, proceedings and intentions of the society for the promotion of Industry, in the southern district of the parts of Lindsey in the County of Lincoln.* 1789 (3rd edn.)

BOWEN THOMAS, *Extracts from the Records and Court Books of Bridewell Hospital.* 1798.

BRADDON LAURENCE, *The Miseries of the Poor are a National Sin.* 1717.

BRINKELOW HENRY, *Complaynt of Roderyck Mors.* E.E.T.S., ed. J. M. Cowper. 1874.

BRINKWORTH E. R., *The Archdeacon's Court: Liber Actorum.* 1584. vol. I.

BRINSLEY JOHN, *The Grammar Schoole.* 1612.

Bristol Charters, 1155–1373, ed. N. Dermott Harding, *Bristol Record Society Publications*, vol. I, 1930.

Bristol Corporation for the Poor, selected records, 1696–1834. ed. A. Ruth Fry, 1935.

Buckinghamshire Sessions Records. ed. William J. Hardy and Geoffrey L. Reckitt. 2 vols., 1933.

The Bye-Laws and Regulations of the Marine Society. 1792 (4th edn.)

CARY JOHN, *An account of the proceedings of the Corporation of Bristol, in execution of the Act of Parliament for the better employing and*

BIBLIOGRAPHY

maintaining the poor of that City. 1700.
The case of the distressed orphans of London. 1691.
The case of the City of London, in reference to the debt of the orphans, and others. 1693.
The case of the parish of St. Giles Cripplegate. (n.d.)
The case of the parish of St. Giles in the Fields, as to their poor, And a workhouse designed for employing them. (n.d.)
Certayne Sermons, or Homilies etc. 1547.
CHAMBERLAYNE EDWARD, *Reflections on the present state of England.* 1669.
CHANDLER SAMUEL, *Doing good recommended from the example of Christ.* 1728.
Cheshire Quarter Sessions Records, ed. J. H. E. Bennett and J. C. Dewhurst. vol. I, 1940.
CHILD, SIR JOSIAH, *A new discourse of trade.* 1693.
Child Marriages, Divorces and Ratifications etc. in the Diocese of Chester, 1561–66. E.E.T.S., ed. F. J. Furnivall, 1897.
Church wardens of the Paryshe of St. Christopher's in London, 1575–1662. ed. Edwin Freshfield,
The City-Law, or the course and practice in all manner of juridicall proceedings in the Hustings in Guild-Hall, London. 1647.
COBBETT THOMAS, *A Fruitfull and Usefull Discourse touching on the Honour due from Children to Parents and the Duty of Parents towards their Children.* 1656.
A collection of pamphlets concerning the poor. 1787. (Including Thomas Firmin's *Some proposals for the employing of the poor*).
COOK CHARLES GEORGE, *English Law: or a summary survey of the household of God.* 1651.
CORNELIS-SON PETER, *A way propounded to make the poor in these and other nations happy.* 1659.
Corporation of London Records (MSS), including the Courts of the President and Governors of the Poor of London. 1702–5.
COTTON JOHN, *A practical commentary . . . upon the first epistle generall of John.* 1656.
The Covent Garden Journal. 1752.
DALTON MICHAEL, *The Countrey justice.* 1630 edn.
DEFOE DANIEL, *The Family Instructor.* 1715.
DEFOE DANIEL, *A plan of English commerce.* 1728.
The Genuine Works of Mr. Daniel Defoe . . . 1710.
DEFOE DANIEL, *Giving alms no charity and employing the poor a grievance to the nation.* 1704.
DEKKER THOMAS, *The Belman of London.* 1608.
DINGLEY ROBERT, *Proposals for establishing a public place of reception for penitent prostitutes etc.* 1758.

BIBLIOGRAPHY

The Municipal Records of the Borough of Dorchester, Dorset. ed. C. H. Mayo, Exeter, 1908.

DYER GEORGE, *The complaints of the poor people of England.* 1793.

DYER GEORGE, *A dissertation on the theory and practice of benevolence.* 1795.

An ease for overseers of the Poore. 1601.

EDEN SIR FREDERIC M., *The State of the Poor.* 3 vols. 1797.

An enquiry into the caues of the encrease and miseries of the Poor of England. 1738.

The Diary of John Evelyn, ed. E. S. de Beer, 1955.

FIELDING JOHN, *Extracts from such of the penal laws as particularly relate to the peace and order of the Metropolis, etc.* 1768 edn.

The first minute book of the Gainsborough Monthly Meeting of the Society of Friends, 1669–1719. ed. Harold W. Brace, *Lincoln Record Society,* vols. 38, 40, and 44, 1949–51.

The book of John Fisher, Town Clerk and Deputy Recorder of Warwick, 1580–1588. ed. Thos. Kemp, 1900.

FOLEY ROBERT, *Laws relating to the poor ... with several cases adjudged in the Court of Kings' Bench, upon the several clauses of them.* 1751 (3rd edn.)

The Journal of George Fox, ed. John L. Nicholls, 1952.

FRANCKE A. H., *Pietas Hallensis* (trans. from German). 1705.

FULLER THOMAS, *The Holy State.* 1642.

Mr William Fuller's Trip to Bridewell... Written by his own hand. 1703

FURLEY J. S. *Quarter Sessions Government in Hampshire in the Seventeenth Century.* n.d.

GEE JOSHUA, *The trade and navigation of Great Britain considered.* 1729.

A general account of the dispensary for the relief of the infant poor, instituted by Dr. George Armstrong. 1772.

The genuine sentiments of an English Country Gentleman, upon the present plan of the foundling hospital. – Appended to Hanway's *Candid Historical Account* ... 1759.

GIBBON CHARLES, *A work worth reading.* 1591.

GILBERT SIR HUMPHREY, *Queen Elizabethes Achademy.* E.E.T.S., ed. F. J. Furnivall and J. M. Cowper. 1871.

GILBERT THOMAS, *Plan for the better relief and employment of the poor, etc.* 1781.

GILBERT THOMAS, *A plan of police: exhibiting the causes of the present increase of the poor etc.* 1786.

GILLINGWATER EDMUND, *An essay on parish work-houses.* 1786.

GOUGE WILLIAM, *Of domesticall duties.* 1622.

GRAUNT JOHN, *Natural and political observations mentioned in a following index and made upon the Bills of Mortality.* 1662.

BIBLIOGRAPHY

HAINES RICHARD, *Provisions for the poor: or reasons for the erecting of a working hospital in every county.* 1678.
HAINES RICHARD, *A model of government for the good of the poor and the wealth of the nation.* 1678.
HALE SIR MATTHEW, *A discourse touching provision for the poor.* 1659.
HANWAY JONAS, *A letter from a member of the Marine Society.* 1757 edn.
— *Motives for the establishment of the Marine Society. By a merchant.* 1757.
— *Three letters on the subject of the Marine Society.* 1758.
— *Plan for the Magdalen House.* 1758.
— *An account of the Marine Society, etc.*, 1759 ed.
— *A candid historical account of the hospital for the reception of exposed and deserted young children.* 1759.
— *Serious consideration on the salutary design of the Act of Parliament for a regular uniform register of the parish-poor in all the parishes within the Bills of Mortality.* 1762.
— *An earnest appeal for mercy to the children of the poor.* 1766.
— *Letters on the importance of the rising generation of the laboring part of our fellow-subjects.* 2 vols. 1767.
— *Letters to the guardians of the infant poor: and to the Governors and overseers of the parish poor.* 1767.
— *The citizen's monitor.* 1780.
— *A sentimental history of chimney sweepers, in London and Westminster etc.* 1785.
HARMAN THOMAS, *A caveat or warning for common cursitors, vulgarly called vagabonds.* 1566.
HARMAR SAMUEL, *Vox Populi*, 1642.
Harrison's description of England, 1577–1587, ed. F. J. Furnivall, pt. I. 1877.
HARRISON G. B. *The Elizabethan Journals. 1591–1603.* 1938.
HARTLIB SAMUEL, *The Parliaments Reformation.* 1646.
HARTLIB SAMUEL, *London Charitie, stilling the Poore Orphans Cry.* 1649.
HATTON EDWARD, *A new view of London,* vol. II, 1708.
(HAY WILLIAM, M.P.), *Remarks on the laws relating to the poor,* 1751 edn.
Herts County Records; Quarter Session Book. VII (1700–52).
Hert County Record; Session Rolls. vols. I, V, VI, ed. William J. Hardy, Herts.
Hints and Cautions for the information of the churchwardens and overseers of the poor of the parishes of St. Giles in the fields and St. George, Bloomsbury, in the county of Middlesex (1781), 1797 edn.
The Reports of ... Sir Henry Hobart, 1641.
Diary of Lady Margaret Hoby, 1599–1605, ed. D. M. Meads, 1930.

BIBLIOGRAPHY

HOLLES GERVASE, *Memorials of the Holles Family, 1493–1656*, ed. by A. C. Wood. *Camden Third Series*, vol. LV, 1937.

HOOKER JOHN, alias VOWELL, *Orders enacted for orphans and for their portions within the citie of Excester, with sundry other instructions incident to the same*, London, 1575.

John Howes' MS, 1582, ed. William Lempriere, 1904.

HOWLETT REV. J., *The insufficiency of the causes to which the increase of our poor, and of the poor's rates have been commonly ascribed.* 1788.

HOWLETT REV. J., *Examination of Mr. Pitt's speech, in the House of Commons, on Friday, February 12, 1796, relative to the condition of the poor.* 1796.

'HUMANUS', *Considerations on the present state of the poor in Great Britain, etc.*, 1773.

The infant's lawyer: or, the law (ancient and modern) relating to infants. 2nd edn., 1712.

Instructions to the apprentices in the City of London (n.d.)

JANEWAY JAMES, *A Token for Children*. 1709 edn.

Journals of the Common Council, vol. 55 (MS. Corporation of London Records Office).

KENNETT WHITE, *The charity of schools for poor children recommended in a sermon.* 1706.

KING GEOFFREY, *Natural and Political Observations and Conclusions upon the State and Condition of England*, 1696. 1810 edn.

LAMBARD WILLIAM, *Eirenarcha, or of the Office of the Justices of the Peace.* 1602 edn.

LAMBARD WILLIAM, *The Duties of Constables, Borsholders, Tythingmen etc.* 1602.

Lambeth Churchwardens' Accounts 1504–1645, edit. Charles Drew, vol. I, 1940; vol. II, 1950.

LAWSON THOMAS, *An appeal to the Parliament concerning the poor, that there may not be a beggar in England.* 1660.

LEVER THOMAS, *Sermons*, 1550, edit. Edward Arber, 1895.

LOCKE JOHN, Report of the Board of Trade to the Lords Justices, in in the year 1697, respecting the relief and employment of the poor – in *An Account . . . of the Society for the Promotion of Industry in . . . Lindsey etc.*, Louth 1789.

LYSONS DANIEL, *The environs of London*, vol. III, 1795 edn.

MADDOX ISAAC, *The expediency of preventive wisdom.* 1750.

MADDOX ISAAC, Bishop of Worcester, *The Wisdom and duty of preserving destitute infants, a sermon, etc.*, 1753.

MCFARLAN JOHN, *Inquiries concerning the poor*. Edinburgh, 1782.

MALTHUS T. R., *An essay on the principle of population as it affects the future improvement of society.* 1789.

BIBLIOGRAPHY

MANDEVILLE B. DE, *An essay on charity and charity schools*, 1723. Appended to 2nd edn. of his *The Fable of the Bees*.

MAITLAND W., *The history of London from its foundation to the present time*. 1756.

MASSIE J., *A plan for the establishment of Charity Houses for exposed or deserted women and girls and for penitent prostitutes, etc.* 1758.

MASSIE J., *Farther observations concerning the foundling hopital*. 1759.

A memorial concerning the erecting in the City of London or the suburbs thereof of an orphanotrophy or hospital for the reception of poor cast-off children or foundlings. Anon. c. 1728.

Middlesex County Records, vols. II–IV.

Middlesex County Records: Calendar of the Sessions Books, 1689–1709. edit. W. J. Hardy, 1905.

Minutes of the Norwich Court of Mayorality, 1630–31. edit. William L. Sachse, 1942.

M. Missons memoirs and observations on his travels over England. Trans. Ozell, 1719.

NELSON ROBERT, *An address to persons of quality and estate*. 1715.

Newes from Guild-Hall. 1650.

NORRIS JOHN of Benston, *Spiritual Counsel, a father's advice to his children*. 1694.

Nottinghamshire County Records. ed. H. Hampton Copnall. 1915.

Nottinghamshire County Records of the Eighteenth Century. ed. K. Tweedale Meaby, 1947.

Observations upon a paper intitled reasons humbly offered etc. (n.d.)

Observations on the present state of the poor of Sheffield with proposals for their future employment and support. 1774.

Orders taken and enacted for orphans and their porcions. 1551. (1557 edn.)

Orders and directions etc. 1630–31.

Orders appointed to be executed in the Cittie of London, for setting roges and idle persons to worke, and for releef of the poore. 1587. (1793 edn.).

The origin, progress and present state of the Marine Society. 1770.

PARFECT CALEB, *Proposals made in the year 1720, to the parishioners of Stroud, near Rochester in Kent, for building a work-house there, etc.* 1725.

PHAIRE THOMAS, *The Boke of Chyldren*. 1957 reprinted of 1553 edn.

PICKARD EDWARD, *Charity to orphans and other necessitous children*. 1760.

The plan of the Magdalen House for the reception of penitent prostitutes. 1758.

The plan of the charity for the maintenance, instruction, and employment of orphans and other poor children, erected at Hoxton in the year 1760, etc. 1769 edn.

Poor outcast childrens song and cry. 1653.

BIBLIOGRAPHY

PORTER DAVID, *Considerations on the present state of chimney sweepers, etc.*, 1792.
POTTER R. *Obervations on the poor laws, on the present state of the poor, and on Houses of Industry.* 1775.
Proposals for the better maintaining and imploying the poor of the City of Bristoll. Bristol 1696.
A proposal for teaching poor children to read, etc. 1708.
The Rambler, 26 III 1751.
Reasons humbly offered, for setling a yearly incom from Hackney-coachmen, and by a duty on coals, towards the relief of the orphans of the City of London. 1691.
Reasons humbly offered to this honourable house, why a bill pretended to give further powers to the corporation for setting the poor of the city of London and liberties thereof to work, should not pass into law. 1700.
Reasons for passing the bill for relieving and employing the poor of this Kingdom humbly offered. 1700.
The Report of the Governors of the Corporation for imploying and relieving the poor of this City of London, and Liberties thereof. 1655.
The Report of the general committee for directing, managing, and transacting the business, affairs, estate and effects of the corporation of the governors and guardians of the hospital for the maintenance and education of exposed and deserted young children. 1740.
Records of St. Alphage, London Wall. ed. G. B. Hall. n.d.
The Records of Dunwick, *Hist. MSS. Comm.*, Report on MSS in various collections, vol. VII, 1914.
Records of the Borough of Leicester, Cambridge, vol. III (1905) ed. Mary Bateson; vol. IV (1923), ed. Helen Stocks.
Records of Maidstone. 1926.
The Records of the Borough of Northampton. ed. C. A. Markham and J. C. Cox, vols. I and II, 1898.
The records of the City of Norwich, ed. W. Hudson and J. C. Tingey, vol. II, 1910.
Records of the Borough of Nottingham. vol. IV, 1889.
Records of the Borough of Reading, vol. II, 1895; vol. III, 1896; vol. IV, 1896.
The records of Quarter Sessions in the County of Wiltshire. *Hist. MSS. Comm. Reports on MSS in various collections*, vols. I and II.
Remembrances of the City of London, 1579–1664. 1878.
Resolutions of the Judges of Assize. 1633.
RIDLEY GLOCESTER, *The Life of Dr. Nicholas Ridley, sometime Bishop of London.* 1763.
North Riding Quarter Sessions Records, ed. J. C. Atkinson, vol. II, 1884.
The rise and progress of the foundling hospital considered. 1761.

BIBLIOGRAPHY

ROGERS DANIEL, *Matrimoniall Honour*. 1642.
The royal charter, establishing an hospital for the maintenance and education of exposed and deserted young children, etc. 1745.
RUGGLES THOMAS, *The history of the poor*. 1797 edn.
Rules and orders to be observed by the officers and servants in St. Giles's workhouse, and by the poor therein. 1726.
SABATIER WILLIAM, *A treatise on poverty, its consequences and remedy* 1797.
SAUNDERS ROBERT, *Observations on the present state and influence of the poor laws*. 1799.
Quarter Sessions Order Book, 1642–1649. ed. B. C. Redwood. *Sussex Record Society*, vol. 54, 1954.
A short state and representation of the proceedings of the President and Governors for the poor of the City of London for the year 1701. 1702.
A short account of the workhouse belonging to the President and Governors for the poor, in Bishopsgate Street, London. 1702.
A sketch of the general plan for executing the purposes of the Royal Charter, establishing an hospital for the maintenance and education of exposed and deserted young children. 1740.
Sketch of the state of the children of the poor in the year 1756, and of the present state and management of all the poor in the parish of St. James, Westminster, in January 1797.
SMITH SIR THOMAS, *De Republica Anglorum*. 1583. (1906 edn.)
Some early tracts on poor relief. ed. F. R. Salter. 1926.
Some considerations offer'd to the citizens of Bristol, relating to the Corporation for the poor in the said City. 1711.
Some considerations on the necessity and usefulness of the Royal Charter establishing an hospital for the maintenance and education of exposed and deserted young children. 1740.
Some objections to the foundling hospital, considered by a person in the country to whom they were sent. 1761.
Some observations on the Bill now pending in Parliament, for the better support and maintenance of the poor, prepared for the use of the trustees of the poor of the parish of Kensington, and published by their direction. 1797.
The Assembly Books of Southampton. ed. J. W. Horrocks. 3 vols. 1917–25.
Staffordshire Quarter Sessions Rolls. ed. S. A. H. Burne, vol. III, 1933.
Staffordshire Quarter Sessions Rolls. ed. D. H. G. Salt, vol. VI, 1950.
STANSFIELD DAVID, alias C. A., *Candid remarks on Mr. Hanway's candid historical account of the foundling hospital, etc.* 1760 (2nd edn.).
STANSFIELD DAVID alias C. A., *A rejoinder to Mr. Hanway's reply to C.A.'s candid remarks*. 1760.
STARKEY THOMAS, *Dialogue*, ed. K. M. Burton, 1948.

BIBLIOGRAPHY

STARKEY THOMAS, *England in the reign of King Henry VIII.* E.E.T.S., ed. S. J. Heritage and J. M. Cowper.
STOCKWOOD JOHN, *A Bartholomew Fairing for Parents.* 1589.
STOW JOHN, *A Survey of London,* ed. C. L. Kingsford, 2 vols., 1908.
STOW JOHN, *A survey of the cities of Lsndon and Westminster.* ed. John Strype, vol. II, 1720.
STRYPE JOHN, *Ecclesiastical memorials, relating chiefly to religion and the reformation of it, and the emergencies of the Church of England, under King Henry VIII, King Edward VI and Queen Mary, etc.,* vol. II, pt. II. 1822 edn.
STUBBES PHILLIP, *The Anatomie of Abuses,* 1583. ed. F. J. Furnivall, 1879.
Surrey Records, vol. VII (Sessional Order Books and Rolls, 1661–1663), edit. D. L. Powell and H. Jenkinson, 1935.
Four Supplications, 1529–1553. E.E.T.S., edit. F. J. Furnivall and J. M. Cowper, 1871.
SWINBURNE HENRY, *A treatise of testaments and last wills.* 1590. (1803 edn.)
TALLACK WILLIAM, *Reasons for the boarding out of pauper children.* (n.d.)
THORESBY RALPH, *Diary* (1677–1724), ed. J. Hunter, 2 vols., 1830.
Thoughts on the present state of the poor, and the intended Bill for their better relief and employment. By a Kentishman. 1776.
TILLOTSON ARCHBISHOP JOHN, *Of the Education of Children, Six Sermons.* 1694.
A true report on the poor maintained and imployed in the Work-House, Easter, 1703.
Letters and Papers of the Verney Family. ed. John Bruce, Camden Society, 1853.
Memoirs of the Verney family during the seventeenth century. ed. F. P. and M. M. Verney, vol. I, 1925 edn.
Vox Populi, Thomason Tracts, e. 146.
Walthamstow in the eighteenth century, being extracts from the vestry minutes, Churchwardens and Overseers Accounts. edit. S. J. Barnes, 1925–7.
Warwick County Records, ed. S. C. Ratcliff and H. C. Johnson, vol. I, 1935; vol. III, 1937; vol. VIII, 1953.
West Riding Sessions Rolls, 1597–1602. ed. John Lister, 1888.
West Riding Sessions Rolls, 1611–1642. ed. John Lister, 1915.
WHATELY WILLIAM, *The New Birth.* 1635 edn.
WHETSTONE GEORGE, *An Heptameron of Ciuill Discourses.* 1582.
WILSON THOMAS, *The state of England,* 1600. ed. F. J. Fisher, *Camden Miscellany,* vol. XVI, 1936.
WOOD ISAAC, *Some account of the Shrewbury House of Industry.* 1795. (4th edn.).

BIBLIOGRAPHY

WOOD ISAAC, *A letter to Sir William Pulteney, Bart., . . . containing some observations on the Bill for the better support and maintenance of the poor, presented to the House of Commons by the Right Honourable William Pitt.* 1797.
The Workhouse Cruelty, Workhouses turn'd gaols, and gaolers executioners. (n.d.)
York Civic Records, ed. Angelo Raine, vol. VII, 1950; vol. VIII, 1953.
YOUNG ROBERT, *The undertaking for the reform of the poor.* 1792.
YOUNG SIR WILLIAM, M.P., *Considerations on the subject of poor-houses and workhouses, etc.,* 1796.
ZOUCH HENRY, *Copy of remarks upon the resolutions of the House of Commons on the poor, etc. in 1775.* 1797.

Nineteenth Century Publications

An account of the Gifts and Legacies . . . in the Town of Ipswich. 1819.
ACKERMANN R., The History of Christ's Hospital. *The History of the Colleges of Winchester, Eton and Westminster; with the Charterhouse, the Schools of St. Paul's, Merchant Taylors', Harrow and Rugby, and the Free-School of Christ's Hospital,* by William Combe. 1816.
ASHLEY SIR WILLIAM JAMES, *An Introduction to English Economic History and Theory.* 1888.
ASHTON JOHN, *Social Life in the Reign of Queen Anne.* 1882.
The Autobiography of Edward, Lord Cherbury, ed. Sidney L. Lee, 1886.
BLOMEFIELD FRANCIS, *An essay towards a topographical history of the county of Norfolk.* vol. IV, 1806.
BRENTON CAPT. E. P., *Letters to His Majesty, etc. on population, agriculture, poor laws and juvenile vagrancy.* 1832.
BRENTON CAPT. E. P., *Observations on the training and education of children in Great Britain.* 1834.
BRENTON CAPT. E. P., *The Bible and the Spade.* 1837.
BRENTON VICE-ADMIRAL SIR J., *Memoir of Captain Edward Pelham Brenton.* 1842.
BROWN JOHN, *A memoir of Robert Blincoe, an orphan boy.* Manchester, 1832.
BROWNLOW J. HANS SLOANE, *The History of the Foundling Hospital in London.* 1831.
Callendar of Wills in the Court of Hustings, London. ed. Reginald R. R. Sharpe, vol. I, 1889.
CAPPE CATHERINE, *An account of two charity schools for the education of girls.* 1800.
CAPPE CATHERINE, *Observations on charity schools, female friendly societies, etc.* 1805.
Charity Commisioners' Reports, vol. 32, pt. VI, 1840.

BIBLIOGRAPHY

Children's Friend Society, Fourth Annual Report, 1834.
COATES CHARLES, *The history and antiquities of Reading.* 1802.
COLQUHOUN P., *A new and appropriate system of education for the labouring people.* 1806.
COPELAND A. J., *Bridewell Royal Hospital, past and present.* 1888.
COX J. CHARLES, *Three centuries of Derbyshire Annals.* vol. I, 1890.
The select works of Robert Crowley. E.E.T.S., ed. J. M. Cowper, 1872.
DAVIES J. SILVESTER, *A history of Southampton.* 1883.
The autobiography and correspondence of Sir Simonds D'Ewes, ed. J. O. Halliwell, vol. I, 1845.
EARLE A. M., *Child Life in Colonial Days.* 1899.
Extracts from the information received by His Majesty's Commissioners as to the administration and operation of the poor laws. 1833.
EDMONDS T. R., On the Mortality of Infants in England. *The Lancet,* 30 January 1836.
Extracts from the records of the Merchant Adventurers of Newcastle-upon-Tyne. *Publications of the Surtees Society,* vol. XCIII, 1895.
FURNIVALL F. J., *Early English Meals and Manners.* E.E.T.S., 1818.
HAMILTON A. H. A., *Quarter Sessions from Queen Elizabeth to Queen Anne.* 1878.
HERBERT WILLIAM, *The twelve great livery companies of London,* 1837.
HUTCHINS JOHN, *The history and antiquities of the county of Dorset.* vol. II, 1863 (3rd edn.)
JERRAM CHARLES, *Considerations on the impolicy and pernicious tendency of the poor laws.* 1818.
JOHNSON JAMES, *Transactions of the Corporation of the Poor in the City of Bristol.* 1826.
The works of Hugh Latimer. ed. G. E. Corrie, vol. I, 1844, vol. II, 1845.
LATIMER JOHN, *the Annals of Bristol in the 18th century.* 1893.
MAITLAND F. W. and POLLOCK SIR F., *The history of English law before the time of Edward I.* vol. II, 1898.
Memoranda, References and Documents relating to the royal hospitals of the City of London. ed. J. F. Firth, 1836.
NICHOLLS SIR G., *A history of the English poor law.* vols. I and II, 1898 edn.
Notes or abstracts of the wills in the great orphan book of wills in the council house at Bristol. ed. T.P. Wadley, 1886.
Of the Education of the Poor. 1809.
OLIVER E., *History and Antiquities of Beverley.* 1829.
PULLING ALEXANDER, *A practical treatise on the laws, customs, usages and regulations of the City and Port of London.* 1849 edn.
The reports of the society for bettering the condition and increasing the

comforts of the poor. ed. Sir Thomas Bernard. 5 vols., 1798, 1800, 1802, 1805 and 1808. Also the 37th Report, 1815.

Report of the committee for investigation of the causes of the alarming increase in juvenile delinquency in the metropolis. 1816.

RIBTON-TURNER C. J., *A history of vagrants and vagrancy and beggars and begging.* 1887.

RIGBY EDWARD, *Further facts relating to the care of the poor, and the management of the workhouse in the City of Norwich.* 1812.

Rules for the government of Ackworth School, etc. 1816.

Rules and regulations for the government of the workhouse, of the parish of St. Martin in the Fields, and of the infant poor house at Highwood-Hill. 1828.

ROBINSON WILLIAM, *The history and antiquities of the parish of Hackney in the county of Middlesex.* vol. I, 1842.

ROLFE W. J., *Shakespeare the Boy.* 1897.

SELLERS MAUD, The City of York in the sixteenth century. *Eng. Hist. Rev.,* vol. IX, April 1894.

SHEFFIELD, JOHN, EARL OF, *Remarks on the bill of the last Parliament for the amendment of the poor laws.* 1819.

The Somers Collection of Tracts. vol. I, 1809 (2nd edn.).

STRYPE JOHN, *Ecclesiastical Memorials, relating chiefly to religion, and the reformation of it, and the emergencies of the Church of England, under King Henry VIII, King Edward VI and Queen Mary,* etc. Oxford, 1822. vol. II, pt. II.

TOWNSHEND DOROTHEA, *Life and Letters of Mr. Endymion Porter.* 1897.

TRIMMER SARAH, *The Economy of charity.* 1801.

Liber Famelicus of Sir James Whitelocke, ed. John Bruce. 1858.

Twentieth Century Publications

ARIÈS PHILIPPE, *Centuries of Childhood.* 1962 edn.

BAYNE-POWELL R., *The English Child in the Eighteenth Century.* 1939.

BELL H. E. *An introduction to the history and records of the Court of Wards and Liveries.* 1953.

BESANT SIR WALTER, *London in the Eighteenth Century, Survey of London.* 1902.

BLUNDEL MARGARET, (ed.) *Cavalier: Letters of William Blundell to his friends, 1620–1698.* 1933.

BOLAM DAVID W., *Unbroken community.* 1952.

BROWN J. HOWARD and WILLIAM GUEST, *A History of Thame.* 1935.

BURGESS M. A., *The history of Burlington School.* 1936.

BIBLIOGRAPHY

BYRNE M. ST. CLARE, *Elizabethan Life in Town and Country*. 1947 edn.
CAULFIELD ERNEST, *The infant welfare movement in the 18th century*. 1931.
CHAMBERS J. D., *Nottinghamshire in the 18th Century*. 1932.
CLARK ALICE, *Working Life of Women in the 17th Century*. 1919.
COMPSTON H. F. B., *The Magdalen Hospital*. 1917.
COPELAND A. J., *Bridewell Royal Hospital and King Edward's Schools*. 1912.
CUTLACK S. A., The Gnosall Records, 1679–1837. Poor Law Administration. *Historical Collections, Staffordshire*, pt. I, 1936.
DAVIS WILLIAM STEARNS, *Life in Elizabethan England*. 1930.
DUNLOP O. J. and DENMAN R. D. *English apprenticeship and child labour*. 1912.
DOWDELL E. G., *A hundred years of quarter sessions*. 1932
The Elizabethan Underworld, ed. A. V. Judges. 1930.
Elizabethan Churchwardens' Accounts, edit. J. E. Farmiloe and Rosita Nixseaman. *Bedfordshire Historical Records Society*, vol. XXXIII, 1953.
ELTON G. R., An early Tudor poor law. *Economic History Review*, 2nd series, vol. VI, August 1953.
EMMISON F. G., Poor relief accounts of two rural parishes in Bedfordshire, 1563–1598. *Economic History Review*, vol. III, January 1931.
EMMISON F. G., The relief of the poor at Eaton Socon, 1706–1834. *Publications of the Bedfordshire Historical Records Society*, vol XV, 1933.
The English Reports, vol. XXIV (Chancery, IV), 1903.
FLEMING SANDFORD, *Children and Puritanism*, 1933.
GEORGE DOROTHY, *London Life in the 18th century*. 1926.
GEORGE DOROTHY, *England in Transition*. 1953 edn.
HAMPSON E. M., Settlement and removal in Cambridgeshire, 1662–1834. *Cambridge Historical Journal*, vol. II, No. 3, 1928.
HAMPSON E. M., *The treatment of poverty in Cambridgeshire, 1597–1834*. 1934.
HARRISON DAVID, *Tudor England*. 2 vols., 1953.
GODFREY ELIZABETH, *Home Life under the Stuarts, 1603–1649*. 1925.
HOLDSWORTH SIR WILLIAM, *A history of English law*. vol. III, 1909 (1st edn.), vols. IV, V & VI, 1937 (2nd edn.).
HOLE CHRISTINA, *The English Housewife in the seventeenth century*. 1953.
HOPKIRK M., *Nobody wanted Sam, the story of an unclaimed child, 1530–1948*. 1949.

BIBLIOGRAPHY

HURSTFIELD J., Lord Burghley as Master of the Court of Wards, 1561–98. *Transactions of the Royal Historical Society*, 4th series, vol. XXXI, 1949.

HURSTFIELD J., The Revival of Feudalism in early Tudor England. *History*, New Series, vol. XXXVI, June 1952.

HURSTFIELD J., Corruption and Reform under Edward VI and Mary: The example of Wardship. *English Historical Review*, vol. LXVIII; January 1953.

HURSTFIELD J., The Profits of Fiscal Feudalism, 1541–1602. *Economic History Review*, August 1955.

HURSTFIELD J., *The Queen's Wards*. 1958.

Memoirs of Colonel Hutchinson. 1908 edn.

JAMES MARGARET, *Social Problems and Policy during the Puritan Revolution, 1640–1660*. 1930.

JONES M. G., *The Charity School Movement in the XVIIIth Century*. 1938.

JONES PHILIP E. and RAYMOND SMITH, *A guide to the records at Guildhall, London*. 1950.

JORDON W. K., *Philanthropy in England, 1480–1660*. 1959

KENNEDY W. P. M., *Elizabethan Episcopal Administration*. 3 vols., 1924.

KIRKMAN GRAY B., *A History of English Philanthropy*. 1905.

LASLETT T. P. R., *The World we have lost*. 1965.

LATIMER JOHN, *The Annals of Bristol in the 17th century*. 1900.

LATIMER JOHN, *Sixteenth century Bristol*. 1908.

LEONARD E. M., *The Early History of English Poor Relief*. 1900.

LESLIE-MELVILLE R., *The life and work of Sir John Fielding*. 1934.

Letters and Papers of the Banks Family of Revesby Abbey, edit. J. W. F. Hill, 1952.

LIPSON E., *The economic history of England*. vol. III, 1934.

LYND SYLVIA, *English Children*. 1942.

MARSHALL DOROTHY, *The English Poor in the 18th century*. 1926.

MEYER A. O., *England and the Catholic Church under Queen Elizabeth*, trans. J. R. McKee. 1916.

MORGAN EDMUND S., *The Puritan Family, essays on religion and domestic relations in 17th century New England*. 1944.

O'DONOGHUE E. G., *Bridewell Hospital, Palace, Prison, Schools, from the earliest times to the end of the reign of Elizabeth*. 1923.

OGG DAVID, *England in the reigns of James II and William III*. 1955.

OXLEY J. E., *Barking Vestry Minutes and other parish documents*. 1955

PEARCE E. H., *Annals of Christ's Hospital*. 1908 (2nd edn.)

POWELL CHILTON LATHAM, *English domestic relations, 1487–1653*. 1917.

BIBLIOGRAPHY

SMITH CHARLOTTE FELL, *Mary Rich, Countess of Warwick (1625–1678): Her Family and Friends*. 1901.
SMITH ABBOT E., *Colonists in Bondage*. 1947.
STONE L., Marriage among the English Nobility. *Comparative Studies in Society and History*, vol. III, 1961.
TATE W. E., *The Parish Chest*. 1946.
TAWNEY R. H., *The Agrarian Revolution of the Sixteenth Century*. 1912.
Tudor Economic Documents, ed. R. H. Tawney and Eileen Power, vol. III, 1924.
THOMSON GLADYS SCOTT, *Life in a Noble Household, 1641–1700*. 1937.
Transcription of the Poor Book of the Tithings of Westbury-on-Trym, Stoke Bishop and Shirehampton from A.D. 1656–1698. ed. H. J. Wilkins, 1910.
TROTTER ELEANOR, *Seventeenth century life in the country parish*. 1919.
WATSON FOSTER, *The English Grammar Schools to 1660*. 1908.
WATSON FOSTER, *The old grammar schools*. 1916.
WEBB S. and B., *English Prisons under Local Government*. 1922.
WEBB SIDNEY and BEATRICE, *English Local Government: English Poor Law History:* Pt. I. The Old Poor Law, 1927.
WILSON VIOLET A., *Queen Elizabeth's Maids of Honour and Ladies of the Privy Chamber*. 1922.
WREN MELVIN C., The Chamber of London in 1633, *Economic History Review.*, 2nd series, vol. I., 1948, No. 1.
WRIGHT LOUIS B., *Middle-class culture in Elizabethan England*. Chapel Hill, 1935.

Index

Abdy, Anthony, 107
Act for reducing the Laws relating to Rogues, Vagabonds, Sturdy Beggars and Vagrants into one Act of Parliament ... (1713), 122
Act for the better regulation of the parish poor children (1767), 188–9; and election of Guardians, 189
Act for the due execution of divers Laws and Statutes heretofore made against Rogues, Vagabonds and Sturdy Beggars (1609), 207–8
Act for the increase of seamen and better encouragement of navigation ... (1703), 108
Act for the Relief of Parishes ... from such charges as may arise from Bastard Children ... (1733), 208–9
Act for the Relief of the Orphans and Creditors of the City of London (1694), 85–6
Act for the Relief and Imployment of the Poor ... (1647), 146
Act for the setting of the poore on worke ... (1576), 97, 138
Act of Settlement (1662), *see* Settlement Act
Act to prevent the Murthering of Bastard Children (1623), 209–10
Act to require Overseers and Guardians of the Poor to Keep a Register ... of Apprentices (1802), 252–3
Addison, Joseph: on charity schools, 291; on provision for foundlings, 179
Address to Persons of Quality and Estate (R. Nelson), 109
Age of children: and lawsuits, 7; Committees of Wards, 7; early entry into adult world, 8–13; inexact registration, 7; proof by reference to other events, 7–8; sixteenth-century uncertainties and indifference, 7
Agricultural labourers' children, restraints in their education and apprenticeship, 22–3
Aldersgate: Firmin's linen manufacturing workhouse, 161–2; St. Anne's workhouse, 174
Alford Grammar School, holidays, 280–1
Almost Christian (Meads), 265
Anatomie of Abuses (Stubbes), 46
Anatomy of a Woman's Tongue (1638), 14
Anne, Queen, 290: supports charity schools, 289
Anti-Recusant Acts (1585 and 1593), 261
Apologie for Women, An (Heale), 14
'Apostume of the brayne', 5, 6
Apprenticeship, 22–3, 25–7, 42, 43, 76, 86, 122, 123, 133, 223–59: Statute of Artificers (1563), 98, 224–32, 241, Act of 1597, 236; Privy Council *Orders* of 1630, 237–8; Act of 1696, 245, 248; Acts of 1747 and 1792, 249–50; Act of 1816, 255–6

alleged murder of apprentices, 247; and attempts to transport children, 105–6; and sea service, 108–9; apprentices sent to North of England textile mills, 253–8; attempts at restraint, 232–4; attempts to carry out inspection, 251–2; avenues of appeal, 228; cancellation of indentures, 230–1, 248–9; cases of brutality, 250–2; complaints about dress, 231–2; compulsion in suitable persons to

INDEX

Apprenticeship—*contd.*
  take apprentices, 237–9; compulsory apprenticeship of vagrants, 96–7; control by gilds, 224, 226–9, 232–4, 249; control by Municipal authority, 228, 229; control by the Courts, 229–31; daily life, 228–9; early nineteenth-century legislation, 252–6; effects of Settlement Acts, 242–5; eighteenth-century attempts at protection, 249–51; establishment of registers (1802), 253–4; gifts from parish and special levies, 236–7; illegitimate children, 213; increasing turbulence in London, 231–2; industrial and parish apprentices, 234–7; master's power, 228–9; moral and religious training, 259; opposition to poor law apprenticeship, 240–1; premiums for parish apprentices, 236; rates to cover cost of apprenticing poor children, 236
Archery, children's training in, 10
Ariès, P., 26
Arth, Henry, 236
Arundell, Earl of, 27–8
Ascham, Roger, 16, 31, 39, 67, 263; his education, 34–5, 43; on education of the nobility, 34
Ashley, Sir William, 91
Aylmer, Bishop John, 216

Baby farms, 218
Bacon, Sir Nicholas, and Royal Wards, 35–6, 64, 66
Banks, Joseph, 221–2
Baptism of infants, 5
Barrington, Daines, 210
Bartholomew Fairing for Parentes, A (Stockwood), 48
Bath Grammar School, 281–2
Bawdy-house Keepers, and Act of 1752, 116–17
Baxter, Richard, 265; directs domestic education in Kidderminster, 268

Becon, Thomas, 13–15; on child marriage, 47, 52; on religious teaching of children, 264
Bedford, Earls and Dukes of, 28, 55
Bedford, Lucy, Countess of, 89
Bedfordshire: parish apprentices, 243; payment of family allowances, 142
Bell, H. E., 62
Benefit of Contention, The (Henry Smith), 230
Bernard, Sir Thomas, 197
Bethel (Griffeth), 216
Beverley, borough orphans, 81–2, 141
Bibles and Bible reading, 262–3
Binns, Sir Richard, 109
Bishopsgate workhouse, 153–60: and poor rate, 157; benefactors' rights to recommend children, 157; children's earnings, 159–60; daily life, 154–5; discipline, 155–6; finances, 156–60; older persons admitted separately, 156; staff, 154; uniform and food, 154
Blount, Elizabeth, 203
Blundell, William, 303
Blundell's School, Tiverton, 281
Boarding out, 175–7, 184–93: advantages of boarding at distance from London, 185–6; baby farms, 218; foster-parents' complaints of irregular payment, 176; importance of choice and inspection of nurses, 185; of illegitimate children, 217–21; scandals of system, smallness of payments to nurses, 176–7
Boarding-out (1870), 141
Boke of Chyldren, The (Phaire), 5–6
Boke of Matrimony (Becon), 13–14
Boleyn, Anne, 32, 92
Book of Good Manners (1487), 204
Books of Domestic Relations, 13–14, 18, 20, 40, 48, 204
Borough orphans, 75–90: appointment of guardians, 75–6; care of orphans' rights, 88–90; City of

332

INDEX

Borough orphans—*contd.*
London model for Courts, 76, 78–80; City of London's financial difficulties, 82–5; Courts of Orphans, 76–81; Courts' functions and Crown's authority, 77–8; local opposition to Courts, 87–8; wardship and apprenticeship, 76
Brevity of life in pre-Restoration England, 4–8, 12–13
Bridewell Hospital, 103, 127, 128, 132–4, 144, 147: and technical training of children, 133
Bridewells, committal of children to, 102–4
Brinkelow, Henry on selling of wards for marriage, 71, 72
Brinsley, John, on grammar schools, 10, 37–8, 40, 278
Bristol: and destitute children, 133, 141; boarding out of children, 175; borough orphans, 76, 78, 87, 160, 296; boys' workhouse, *see* Mint, the; Cary's workhouse scheme, 162–3, 172, 173; Charter of Edward III (1331), 76; Corporation of the Poor, 160, 163–4, 171–2, 245–6; girls' workhouse, 163–4; report of committee on apprentices, 245–6; shipping of children to plantations, 107; training for young in cloth industry, 224
Buckingham parish workhouse, 194–5
Bulcamp House, 195
Bullinger, Heinrich, 204
Bunyan, John: his childish visions of Hell and conviction of sin, 269
Burghley, Lord, 27, 28, 36: and education of recusants' children, 261; care for his wards, 65; Master of the Wards, 35; 58, 60–2, 64–7, 70, 74, 75; memorandum on university education, 34; profits from traffic in wardships, 61, 65; 'school' for wards at Cecil House, 66–7

Burlington School, London, training for industry and work for profit, 294–5

Caesar, Sir Julius, Master of the Rolls, 143
Call to the Unconverted (Baxter), 265
Calvinism, 263–4
Cambridgeshire, parish apprentices, 244, 257–8
Cambridge University: admissions from Essex grammar schools, 282; entry of precocious children, 9
Camden, William, on Shrewsbury School, 282
Campbell, Sir Thomas, Lord Mayor of London, 89
Canon Law and illegitimacy, 202
Canterbury: Cathedral School, 287; criticism of workhouse, 173
Cappe, Mrs., on ill-treatment of apprentices, 250–1, 257
Carew, Sir Peter, 14–15
Carlisle, Shoemakers' Gild, 233
Cary, John, 197; introduces workhouse scheme in Bristol, 162–3, 172, 173; urges adoption of scheme throughout kingdom, 165
Case of the Distressed Orphans of London, The (1691), 83
Castiglione, Baldassare, 40
Catechism: instruction in, 262; Puritan catechisms, 263–4
Catechism (Becon), 15, 47
Catechism (Nowell), 264
Caxton, William, 204
Cecil, Lord David, 222
Cecil, Sir Edward, 10
Cecil, Thomas, 61
Cecil, Sir William, *see* Burghley, Lord
Centuries of Childhood (Ariès), 26
Chamberlayne, E., 8, 203
Charity Schools, 288–95: in the country, 290–1; introduction of work for profit, 294–5; Mandeville's criticisms, 291–3; Queen

INDEX

Charity Schools—*contd.*
Anne's support, 289; schools united to workhouses, 294; S.P.C.K., 288–91, 293–4
Charles I, City of London's loan to, 83
Charles II, 10: and Christ's Hospital mathematical department, 286; and City of London's finances, 83; his illegitimate children, 204
Chester: borough orphans, 75; Queen's Letters Patent (1574), 76
Chesterfield, Lord, and his illegitimate son, 222, 298
Chichester Grammar School, 286
Child labour, 310–11: cottage schools, 311
Child marriage, 44–57, 307–8: advancement of merchant's business interests, 50; and poverty, 46–7; businesslike arrangement of marriages, 49–50; children's feelings 51–2; consent and consumation, 44–5, 52–3; incidence, 46; legal position, 44–6, 52–3; parental authority over marriage, 47–8; parents' duty to achieve "good marriage", 48–9; repudiation of precontracts, 44; rights of veto, 55–6; separations and divorces, 53–4; views of Puritans, 54
Child Marriages (Furnivall), 44–6
Children's books, 299–300
Children's workhouses, 146–99: beliefs in their virtue, 147–8; Act of Settlement (1662), 148, 149; Clerkenwell Scheme, 149–53; Bishopsgate workhouse, 153–60; Firmin's scheme, 161–2; Bristol scheme, 162–5, 171–3; private Acts of incorporation, 163, 165; small parish workhouses, 166–9, 171, 173, 174; Poor Relief Act (1722), 166; unions of parishes in urban areas, 168–71, 177; infant mortality in London workhouses, 177–8, 181–5; Foundling Hospital, 178–81;

Act of 1762 for registration of poor parish infants, 182–3, 186; keeping of registers, 184; provisions of St. James, Westminster, 186–7; proposals of Parliamentray Committee (1766), 187–8; Act of 1767, 188–9; election of Guardians, 189; infant mortality throughout country, 190–2; Gilbert's plans, 192–4; Poor Law Act (1782), 192–3; Schools of Industry, 193–4; children not segregated from adults, 194–5; large Houses of Industry in East Anglia, 196
Cholmley, Sir Hugh, on his wife's virtues in training girls, 30
Christen State of Matrimonye, The (Bullinger), 204
Christ's College, Cambridge, 9
Christ's Hospital (London), 92, 127–33, 141, 178, 180, 181, 286, 293, 310, 312: campaign for funds, 129; disorganisation in Civil Wars, 144; education, 130–1; equipment and staffing, 130; foundation of mathematical department, 286; humane concept, 128; numbers admitted, 132; receipt of poor rates, 137–8; reopening to accommodate 500 poor orphans, 129; restricted to children born in wedlock, 131; restricted to children of citizens and freemen, 131–2
Church attendance, 260
Citizen's Monitor, The, 189–90
City of London and deprived children: compulsory poor rate, 137–8; disorganisation in Civil Wars, 144–6; outdoor relief, 136; survey of wards, 126; use of Hospitals, 127–33, 312, *see also* London Corporation of the Poor
City of London Court of Orphans: model for Courts, 76, 78–80; nature and function of Court, 78–80; extent of jurisdiction, 79;

INDEX

City of London Court—*contd.*
deposit of orphans' portions in City Chamber, 79-80; City's debts and orphans' monies, 82-4; criticisms of handling of orphans' money, 83-4; attempts at legislation, 84-5; Act of 1694, 85-6; establishment of Orphans' Fund, 85; the Court in the eighteenth century, 86; freemen given right of free disposition of their estate (1724), 87

Civil Wars: dislocation of poor law, 144; disorganisation of charities, 144-6

Clapham, John, secretary to Burghley, 65

Clarke Hall, Sir William, 1

Class-consciousness in Elizabethan England, 21

Classical studies, 39, 276, 279

Classification of prisoners, 123-4: recommendations of 1778 Committee, 124

Clerkenwell workhouse, 149-53: established (1663), 149; taken over by Middlesex justices (1685), 149; objectives, 149-50; College of Infants, 150-3; transfer of College to Hornsey, 152; opposition to scheme, 152

Clifford, Lady Anne, 28, 32

Cobbett, Thomas, on parents and children, 18-20, 265

Coke, Lord, 61, 143

Colchester, and workhouse provision, 165

Colchester Grammar School, analysis of entries, 282

Colet, John, Statutes for St. Paul's School, 276-7

College of Infants, Clerkenwell, 150-4, 156, 157

Colonists in Bondage (Abbot Smith), 107

Committees of Wards, 7

Compton, Mary, murders foster-children, 219

Contagious diseases, 4

Cook, Charles George, on apprenticeship, 240-1

Cooke, Sir Antony, erudition of his daughters, 31-3

Coram, Thomas, 178-80: agitation for Foundling Hospital, 179-80

Corporal punishment, 15-18, 20, 135, 303-5; and Puritanism, 20; by parents, 15-16; by tutors, 16; divergent attitudes, 17-18; in grammar schools, 38-9; in Houses of Correction, 102; in workhouses, 155; of apprentices, 230, 232; of girls, 16, 33; of parents of illegitimate children, 213-14; of vagrants, 94, 95, 97, 122

Cottage schools and child labour, 311

Cotton, John, 264, 266

Courtesy books, 40

Court of Wards, *see* Royal Wards

Courtyer, The (Castiglione), 40

Covent Garden Journal, 302-3

Coverdale, Miles, 204

Cranmer, Archbishop Thomas, on education of poor men's children, 24-5, 287

Cromwell, Oliver, 286

Cromwell, Thomas, 92, 203

Dakins, Margaret (Lady Hoby): education and matrimonial history, 28-30, 32-3, 48, 49; trains girls in own service, 30

Dalton, Michael, 236

Day, Thomas, 300

De Civilitate Morem Puerilium (1532), 40

Dedham, Essex; Grammar School, 282; *Orders* of 1585, 205

Defoe, Daniel, 105, 283, 284: on child labour, 310-11

Dekker, Thomas, on young delinquents, 99-100

Delinquent children, 98-125: and vagrancy, 98-101; apprentices taken into sea service, 108-9; at-

INDEX

Delinquent children—*contd.*
tempts to transport children, 105–7, 109; committed to Bridewells, 102–4; delinquent girls, 116–21; equipment of boys for Navy, 111; Fielding's analysis of causes and attempts at prevention, 110–12; gangs of children in towns, 104; hanging of children, 110; Marine Society, 111–16; need for classification, 123–4; proposals for prevention, 109–12; prostitution, 117–21

Denman, R. D., 226–7, 234

Derbyshire, parish apprentices, 243

De Republica Anglorum (Sir Thomas Smith), 64, 72

Description of England (Harrison), 31

Desertion of unwanted children, 22

Dialogue (Starkey), 23–4, 128

Dingley, Charles and Robert, 119

Discourse Touching Provision for the Poor (Hale), 147

Diseases of children and their remedies, 5–6

Disobedient Child, The (Ingeland), 39

Divorces, 53–4

Dobbs, Sir Richard, Lord Mayor of London, 129

Domesticall Duties, of (Gouge), 216, 267

Dorchester Hospital, 145

Dunbar, Clemens, on prevention of delinquency, 110

Dunlop, O. J., 226–7, 234

Dyer, George, 120

Early entry of children into adult world, 8–13: accompanying their lords to battle, 10; entry to universities, 9–10; maids of honour, 10–12; pages, 10; premature deaths of parents, 12; remarriages of parents, 12–13; training in archery, 10

Early History of Poor Relief (Leonard), 143

Ease for Overseers, The (1601), 139–43, 176, 235–6, 242

East Anglia, Houses of Industry, 196

Ecclesiastical Memorials (Strype), 53–4

Eden, Sir Frederic M.: accounts of contemporary workhouses, 196–8; list of children in Epsom workhouse, 198; on gaol-like conditions at Oxford, 197

Edgeworth, Maria, 300

Education in pre-Reformation England, 22–43: agricultural labourers' children, 22–3; appeal to Scripture, 39; apprenticeship, 25–7, 42, 43; boarding at school, 43; classical studies, 39; elementary and free schools, 23–4, 41–2; girls' education, 28–34, 41–2; grammar schools, 23, 36–41; importance to merchants, 36–7; increased contact between parents and child, 43; middle-class enthusiasm, 42–3; Royal Wards, 35–6, 58–75, 89, 90; sending children from home, 26–32, 43, sociological significance, 42; upbringing of poor children, 22–5

Edward VI, 31: and agreement for use of London Hospitals, 127–8

Elementaire (Mulcaster), 35

Elizabeth I, 34: children as her maids of honour, 11–12; her Court, 31; intellect and attainments, 31; revenue from wardships, 60, 65; uses violence against maids of honour, 17

Elizabethan social structure, 21–3: children of the poor, 22–3; consciousness of social hierarchy, 21–2; major divisions, 22

English Law (Cook), 240–1

Epsom workhouse, list of children in, 198

Erasmus, 40

INDEX

Essay on the State of England ... An (Cary), 162
Essays (Montaigne), 17-18
Essex, Earl of, as ward of Burghley, 27, 28, 65, 66
Essex grammar schools, 282
Evelyn, John, and his son Richard, 271, 272, 299
Exeter: and workhouse provision, 165; orphans, 75-7, 80-1, 133, 141; report on destitute children, 126-7

Fable of the Bees (Mandeville), 291-2
Fairchild Family, History of the (Sherwood), 300
Family, pre-Reformation ideas of, 13-22: as essential unit of social organisation, 13; Books of Domestic Relations, 13-14, 18, 21; corporal punishment, 15-18, 20; duties of husband and wife, 13-14; household organisation, 20-1; obedience and respect to parents, 18-20; parent-child relationships, 14-22; personal affections of minor concern, 13
Family allowances, 142-3
Family worship and household instruction, 268
Female Orphan Asylum, 118-19
Fielding, Henry, 116
Fielding, Sir John, Bow Street magistrate, 114, 122-3; analysis of causes of delinquency and attempts at prevention, 110-12; and Marine Society, 111-12, 116; and prostitution, 117-19; equips boys for Navy and merchant navy, 111, 116; Female Orphan Asylum and Magdalen Hospital, 118-19; on sending of apprentices to distant parishes, 253; on smallness of payments to nurses, 176-7
Firmin, Thomas, 104: advocate of workhouses, 161-2; sets up linen manufacturing workhouse in Aldersgate, 161-2
Fitzroy, Henry, illegitimate son of Henry VIII, 203-4
Florio's version of Montaigne's *Essays*, 17-18
Forrest, William, 23, 287
Foster-parents, 176, 218, 220
Foundation of Christian Religion gathered into six Principles, The (Perkins), 278-9
Foundling Hospital, 178-81, 188, 251, 252, 292-3: Coram's agitation for Hospital (1719-39), 179-80; opposition to proposal, 179; granting of Charter (1739), 180; boarding out system, 185
Fox, Charles James, 304-5
Free schools, 41-2, 282, 287
Fruitfull Discourse touching the Honor due from Children to Parents, or the duty of Parents towards their Children (Thomas Cobbett), 18-20
Furnivall, F. J., 16, 24, 68: on child marriage, 44-6

Garrick, David, 118
Gentlemen's Magazine, 110, 117, 251-2, 303-5
Gibbon, Charles, on child marriage, 52
Gibbon, Edward, 301
Gilbert, Sir Humphrey: and royal wards, 35, 64, 66; scheme for *Achademy* in London, 35
Gilbert, Thomas: and Poor Law Act of 1782, 192-3; proposals to exclude children from workhouses, 192-3; proposes county Houses of Reception, 194; proposes Visitors to inspect boarded out children, 193
Gilds, and apprentices, 224, 226-9, 232-4, 249: appointment of 'searchers', 228; interpretation of Statute of Artificers, 227

INDEX

Gillingwater, Edmund, 174

Girls' education in pre-Reformation England, 28–34; at Queen Elizabeth's Court, 31; 'co-educational' households, 28; intellectual studies, 31–3; upbringing at home, 32–3; upbringing in households away from home, 28–30

Gloucester, and workhouse provision, 165

Goldsmith, Oliver, 299

Gouge, William, 216, 267

Grammar Schoole, The (Brinsley), 40

Grammar Schools, 23, 36–41, 276–84: classical studies, 276, 279, 286; competition from Nonconformist Academies and private schools, 285; corporal punishment 38–9; courtesy books, 40; holidays, 280–1; leading Parliamentarians as pupils, 286; Puritan influence, 277–9; regimen, 37–8; religious teaching, 276–80; restricted curriculum, 283, 286; size, 281–2; syllabus, 39, 279; types of parents, 282–3

Grand Magazine, 114

Grey, Lady Jane, 16, 18, 32

Griffeth, Matthew, 216

Guardians, election under Act of 1767, 189

Gulliver's Travels (Swift), 299

Hale, Sir Matthew, on value of children's workhouses, 147–8, 160–1

Half-Moon Alley, *see* Bishopsgate

Halifax workhouse, 195, 197

Halkett, Lady, account of her childhood, 273

Hamblyn, Mistress, 33

Hampden, John, 286

Hampson, E. M., 240, 244, 258

Hanway, Jonas, 152, 186, 187, 293: and Act of 1762, 183, 186; and infant mortality in London workhouses, 177–8, 181–5, 189–90; and keeping of registers, 184; founder of Marine Society, 111–13, 119; Governor of Foundling Hospital, 178, 181; on boarding-out system, 184–6; *Open Letter* to vestries, 184

Harman, Thomas, on young delinquents, 99–100

Harmar, Samuel, on bad behaviour of children (1642), 288

Harris, Walter, 301

Harrison, William: on education at Elizabeth's Court, 31; on grammar schools, 37

Harte, John, 67

Hartlib, Samuel, 147

Harvey, Sir James, 88

Hatton, Edward, on Bishopsgate workhouse, 154–5

Heale, William, 14

Health and Morals of Apprentices Act (1802), 252

Henry VII, and wardships, 59

Henry VIII: and use of London Hospitals, 127; establishing Court of Wards, 59; his illegitimate children, 203

Herbert of Cherbury, Lord, 9

Herbert, Thomas, 10

Hereford, and workhouse provision, 165

Herefordshire grammar schools, 282

Hobbes, Thomas, criticises grammar schools, 286

Hoby, Edward, 66

Hoby, Lady, *see* Dakins, Margaret

Hoby, Sir Thomas, 40

Holinshed, Ralph, 129

Holland, Lord (Henry Fox), 304–5

Holles, Gervase, 270–1

Holles, John (Earl of Clare), 9

Holles, Sir William, 43

Hooker, John (John Vowell), Chamberlain of Exeter, 77

Hoole, Charles, on religious teaching in grammar schools, 278, 279

INDEX

Hoskins, Dr. W. G., 41
Houses of Correction: committal of children to, 102–4; Suffolk justices' rules, 102–3
Howard, John: on classification of delinquents, 123–4; on state of prisons, 123–4
Howes, John, 126: on Christ's Hospital, 130, 132
Howlett, Rev. J., investigation of infant morality in workhouses, 195–6
Huntingdon, Countess of, as instructress to upper-class girls, 28, 33
Huntingdon, Earl of, 28
Huntingdon Grammar School, 286
Hurstfield, J., 59, 65
Hussey, Sir John, 59
Hutchinson, Lucy, account of her childhood, 271–2
Hutton, William, on his experiences of apprenticeship, 256–7

Illegitimate children, 200–22: legal and commercial impediments, 202; legitimation, 202; in households of the great, 202–3; hardening of social attitudes, 204; Puritans and sexual morality, 204–6, 213–16; Poor Law Act (1576), 206–7, 209, 214; sanctions against parents whose bastards became charges on community, 207–8; later legislation, 208–9; infanticide, 209–10; enforcement of legislation, 210–13, 220–1; payment of lump composition to the parish, 211; orders against parents for maintenance payments to parish, 211–13; apprenticeship, 213; physical punishment and public disgrace of parents, 213–14; Church penances, 214–16; emphasis on guilt of women, 215–16; lack of evidence on fate of children, 217; boarding out, 217–21; case of Mary Compton (1694), 219; attempts to regulate boarding out, 219–20; Acts of 1795 and 1810, 220–1; aristocratic acceptance of sexual indulgence, 221–2
Infanticide, 209–10
Infant mortality, 5, 7, 196, 300–3; and Act of 1762, 182–3; before and after Act of 1767, 189–90; carelessness of nurses, 301–2; culpable neglect and cruelty, 302–3; detached attitude to deaths of children, 7, 301–2; Hanway's enquiry and statistics, 177–8, 181–5; Howlett's investigations in East Anglia, 196; ignorance of obstetrics, 301; in London workhouses, 177–8, 181–5; throughout country, 190–2
Ingeland, Thomas, 39
In Reference to the Debt of the Orphans and Others (1693), 84
Ipswich: and destitute children, 136; Christ's Hospital, 133, 134, 141; compulsory poor rate, 137; training for young, 224

Jackson, Abraham, 259–60
James I: and child marriage, 55; and transportation of children to Virginia, 106; negotiation with Parliament on rights of wardship, 73
Janeway, James, 265–6, 270, 300
Jeaffreson, John Cordy, 308
Juvenile Magazine, 306

Kendal workhouse, 197
King's Lynn, and workhouse provision, 165
Kingston, and workhouse provision, 165
Kirkby Stephen Grammar School, 281

Lacock Abbey, 33
Laslett, Peter, 46, 200

INDEX

Latimer, Bishop Hugh, 9, 10: on corporal punishment, 15–16; on marriage of wards, 68, 72; proposes school for royal wards, 64

Leach, A. F., 41

Legitimacy Act (1926), 202

Leicester: borough orphans, 75: training for young in cloth industry, 224

Leicester, Earl of, 67

Lennox, Countess of, 66

Leonard, E. M., 143, 147, 148, 242

Lewes, parish apprentices, 237

Little Book for Little Children, A (White), 270

Liverpool, shipping of children to plantations, 107

Locke, John, 283: proposals for reform of poor law, 309–10

Loe, William, 259

London, *see* City of London

London Corporation of the Poor, 145–7, 153–60: established (1647), 145, 146; lack of funds during Commonwealth, 145; powers under 1647 Act, 146–7; new Corporation elected (1698), 153; and Bishopsgate workhouse, 153–60; and poor rate, 157; friction with parishes, 157–9

Lord Williams' School, Thame, 38

Magdalen Hospital, 119–21: foundation, 119; girls' employment, 119–20; records, 120–1; rules, 119–20

Maids of honour, 17: children as, 10–12

Maitland, William, on the London Court of Orphans, 86

Mandeville, Bernard de, criticisms of Charity schools, 291–3

Manners, Lady Bridget, 11–12

Manners, Roger, 11

Marine Society, 111–16, 119, 192: foundation (1756), 111; number of boys assisted, 112–13; public support, 112; qualifications, 113–14; regimen and instructions for treatment, 114; treatment on ships, 114–15

Marshall, Dorothy: on boarding out of illegitimate parish children, 218; on settlement Acts and apprenticeship, 243

Marshall, William, translator of Ypres poor relief regulations, 92, 94, 126, 142

Massie, J., proposals for reclamation of prostitutes, 121

Melbourne, Lord, 222

Merchant's Manuell, The (Loe), 259

Merchant Taylors' Company, 229

Merchant Taylors' School, 36, 282

Milton, John, 283, 286

Mint, the (boys' workhouse at Bristol), 164–5, 171–3: criticisms of quality of education, 172–3; failure of attempts to teach skilled trades, 171–3; financial difficulties of Corporation, 172; local opposition, 171; motives of economy, 171–3; recourse to unskilled employment, 171–2

Miseries of Enforced Marriage, The (Wilkins), 49

Montaigne, 7: on his upbringing, 17–18

Monthly Magazine, 250

More, Sir Thomas, 35: erudition of his daughters, 31

Morgan, E. S., 20

Morgan, Francis, Judge of Sheriffs' Court, 89

Morton, Charles, 284

Mulcaster, Richard, first headmaster of Merchant Taylors' School, 35, 36, 281; and education of girls, 41–2

Nelson, R., 109

Nettleton, Robert, 119

INDEX

Newark workhouse, 197
Newbury, John, publisher of children's books, 299
Newcastle: Merchant Adventurers' company and restraints on apprentices, 232–4; special gaol for apprentices, 233–4
New Discovery in the old Art of Teaching School (Hoole), 278
Newes from the Guildhall (1650), 84
Newington Green Academy, 284
Newmann, Henry, 293–4
Nicholas, Alexander, 205
Nichols, Josias, 262
Noncomformist Academies, 284–5: competition with grammar schools, 285; curriculum, 284; precarious existence, 284–5
Norfolk, apprenticeship in, 236
Norris, John, 269–70
North, Lord, on child marriage (1638), 55
Northampton, borough orphans, 77–8, 87
North Riding of Yorkshire: and treatment of apprentices, 247; payment of family allowances (1618), 142–3
Norwich, 148; and destitute children, 133, 135–6, 141; and workhouse provision, 165; census of poor persons, 126, 206; compulsory poor rate, 137; Hospital of St. Giles, 135; Mayor's Court hears pleas from apprentices, 228; outdoor relief, 136; *Rules* concerning illegitimate children and the poor (1571), 206, 207; training for young in cloth industry, 135–6, 224
Norwich Visitation Articles (1638), and education of recusants' children, 262
Nottingham: St. John's Hospital, 133, 141; weekly allowances, 141
Nottinghamshire, and defaulting masters of apprentices, 239

Nowell, Lawrence, Dean of Lichfield, 67, 264
Nurses and boarding-out system, 175–7, 185

Observations on the more recent Statutes (Barrington), 210
Observations on the Poor Laws... (Potter), 173
Old Grammar Schools, The (Watson), 282
On the Relief of the Poor (Vives), 91
Order of Household Instruction, An (Nichols), 262
Orders enacted for Orphans and their portions within the Citie of Excester (Vowell (Hooker)), 77
Osborne, Dorothy, 56
Osborne, Sir Peter, 56
Outdoor relief, 136
Overseers, 139–40; 213: and apprentices, 236–7, 245
Oxford, Lord, as ward of Burghley, 66
Oxford union workhouse, gaol-like conditions, 197
Oxford University, entry of precocious children, 9

Page of Plymouth, murdered by his child-wife, 52
Pages, children as, 10
Parent-child relationships, 304–7; consciousness of social hierarchy, 21–2; in pre-Restoration England 14–20
Parents' Assistant, The (Edgeworth), 300
Parfect, Rev. Caleb, 174: and abuses of apprenticeship, 246–7; *Proposals* for children's treatment in Stroud workhouse, 167; survey of other workhouses, 168
Parish apprentices: boarding children outside parish, 243–5; breakdown in rural areas, 258; compulsion on suitable persons

341

INDEX

Parish apprentices—*contd.*
to take apprentices, 237–9; difficulties in boarding them out, 239–42; effects of Settlement Acts, 242–5; eighteenth-century attempts at protection, 249–51; gifts and special levies, 236–7; minimal technical training in towns, 258; overstocked trades, 258; premiums, 236; sent to North of England textile mills, 253–8

Parish Registers of birth, 7

Parish workhouses, 166–71, 173, 174; and Poor Relief Act (1722), 166; unions of parishes in urban areas, 168–71, 177; returns of details of children's employment, 174; infant mortality, 177–8, 181–5; Act of 1762 for registration of poor infants, 182–3, 186; proposals of Parliamentary Committee (1766), 187–8

Parker, Archbishop Matthew, 136

Paston, Agnes, and punishment of her children, 16

Paston, Margaret, 53

Paulet, Lord Harry, and equipment of boys for Navy, 111

Peacham, Henry, 38–9

Peel, Sir Robert (the elder), 254

Peel, Sir Robert (the younger), 124

Penryn Grammar School, 281

Phaire, Thomas, on children's diseases and their remedies, 5–6

Pilgrim's Progress (Bunyan), 299

Pious Prentice, The (Jackson), 259–60

'Plague', the, 4

Plain Man's Pathway to Heaven, The (Vincent), 265

Plan for Preserving Deserted Girls, A (Sir John Fielding), 116–19

Plan for the Better Relief and Employment of the Poor. . . . (Thomas Gilbert), 192

Plan of Police, A (Thomas Gilbert), 194

Plymouth: and destitute children, 133, 141; and workhouse provision, 165

Pontefract justices, and apprentices in cotton mills, 256

Poor Law Act (1572) and amending Act of 1576, 97–8, 138, 139, 209, 214; and illegitimate children, 206–7; and poor rate, 138; Census of aged and impotent poor, 138

Poor Law Act (1597), 98, 138–9, 141, 142, 146, 149; and apprenticeship, 213, 225, 234–7; Privy Council Orders, 98, 138–9, 143, 236

Poor Law Act (1782), 192–3

Poor Law Act (1834), 98, 121, 138, 143

Poor Law Act (1899), 100

Poor Man's Plea, The (Defoe), 105

Poor rates, 137–8, 157, 160, 169

Poor Relief Act (1722), and parish workhouses, 166

Popham, Sir John, Lord Chief Justice, *Resolutions* for use of justices on treatment of vagrant children, 100–1

Potter, R., 195: on parish workhouses, 173–4

Prentises Practice in Godliness, The (1608), 259

Preparation to Marriage, A (Henry Smith), 14

Present State of England (Chamberlayne), 8, 203

Proposal for Teaching Poor Children to Read, A (1708), 290

Prostitution, 117–21: Female Orphan Asylum, 118–19; Magdalen Hospital, 119–21

Pulteney, Sir William, 195

Puritans, 146: and child marriage, 54; and punishment of children, 20; and religious training of children, 263–73; and sexual morality, 204–6, 213–16; catechisms, 263–4; influence on gram-

INDEX

Puritans—*contd.*
mar schools, 277–9; sense of human responsibility, 267; sense of sin and fear of Hell, 268–9; sermons, 266–7

Queen Elizabeth's Maids of Honour (Wilson), 31

Raikes, Robert, 296
Rambler, The, 117
Ramsden, Robert, Archdeacon of York, 67
Rathmell Academy, Yorkshire, 285
Reading (Berkshire): and apprentices, 237; Hospital, 133, 134, 141
Reformed Pastor (Baxter), 268
Registration of Births Act (1836), 7
Religious training of children, 259–80: Bible reading, 262–3; Calvinist views, 263–4; Catechisms, 262, 264–5; church attendance, 260; family worship and household instruction, 265–6, 268; in schools, 276–80; precocious piety, 271–2; Puritanism, 263–73; recusants, 260–2; sense of sin and fear of Hell, 268–9; sermons, 266–7; treatises for apprentices, 259–60
Remedies for children's diseases, 5–6
Report for the Reform of the Poor Law (Locke), 309–10
Rich, Sir Richard (Lord Rich), 69
Richmond, Duke of (Charles Lennox), illegitimate son of Charles II, 204
Ridley, Bishop Nicholas, 127, 180
Robinson Crusoe (Defoe), 299
Rogers, Daniel, 70
Roman Catholic recusants, 260–2; Anti-Recusant Acts, 261; children sent to Continental seminaries 260, 261
Romilly, Sir Samuel, on murder of apprentices, 254

Rowe, Sir Thomas, and College of Infants, 150, 152
Rowse, Dr. A. L., 21–2, 42
Royal Wards, the, 35–6, 58–75, 89, 90: establishment of Court, 59; as source of revenue, 59, 60; Bacon's scheme of studies, 39; Burghley's 'school' at Cecil House, 66–7; competition for wardships, 62; criticism of guardians' conduct, 64–5, 69, 72, 73; disregard of family relationships, 62–3; family interests, 62–3, forced marriages, 70; guardians' care of estates, 67–8; intermediaries, 60; marriage of wards, 68–72; numbers of wardships, 60; official valuation and real price of wardships, 61; Parliament's negotiations with James I, 73; profits to officers of Court, 61; abolition (1646), 72
Royal Wards, The (Hurstfield), 59, 65
Russell, Lady, 66: on her daughter's dowry, 49–50
Rutland, Countess of, 11
Rutland, Earl of, 49

St. Albans Grammar School, 281
St. Bartholomew's Hospital, 127, 144
St. Clement Dane vestry and boarding out, 185
St. Dunstan in the East, charity school in workhouse, 294
St. George, Hanover Square, incidence of mortality in workhouse, 181, 182
St. George's Middlesex, incidence of mortality in workhouse, 178, 184
St. Giles workhouse, London, 168–70, 177–8: alarming rumours about it, 170; harsh régime, 169–70; incidence of mortality, 178, 181, 182, 184; motives of economy, 169; united parishes of St.

INDEX

St. Giles workhouse—*contd.*
Giles in the Fields and St. George, Bloomsbury, 168, 177
St. James, Westminster: billeting of younger children with cottagers on Wimbledon Common, 186; establishment of School of Industry, 194; older children brought into workhouse, 187
St. Luke's, Middlesex, incidence of mortality in workhouse, 181
St. Martin in the Fields, incidence of mortality in workhouse. 181, 182
St. Mary's, Whitechapel, vestry and boarding out, 185
St. Paul's School, 37, 38, 276–7, 286: Dean Colet's Statutes, 276–7
St. Saviour's Grammar School, Southwark, 281
St. Thomas's Hospital, 127
Sandford and Merton (Day), 300
Sandys, Lord, 70
Scholemaster, The (Ascham), 34
Schoole of Virtue (Seager), 40
Schools of Industry attached to workhouses, 193–4
Selden, John, 286
Select Committee on the Police of the Metropolis (1828), 109
Settlement Act (1662), 100, 148, 149, 157, 160: effect on apprentices, 242–3
Settlement Act (1691), 243
Shaftesbury, and workhouse provision, 165
Sheffield, and parish apprentices, 235, 239
Sheffield, Earl of, 258
Sherrington, Grace, 33
Sherrington, Sir Henry, 33
Sherwood, Mrs. Mary Martha, 300, 305
Shrewsbury House of Industry, 195–7; absence of infant mortality, 196; humanitarian management, 195–7
Shrewsbury School, 282: holidays, 280

Smith, Abbot, 107
Smith, Henry, 14, 230
Smith, Sir John, Governor of Virginia, 106
Smith, Sir Thomas, on wardships, 64, 68, 72–3
Society for the Propagation of Christian Knowledge, *see* S.P.C.K.
Some Proposals for the Employment of the Poor (Firmin), 104
Somerset, apprenticeship in, 236
Some Thoughts concerning Education (Locke), 283
Southampton, Earl of, ward of Burghley, 70
Span of life in sixteenth century, 4–5
S.P.C.K., 288–91, 293–4: foundation and aims, 288–9; promotion of charity schools, 288-291
Speenhamland system, 143
Spelman, Sir Henry, 63
Spiritual Counsel: A Father's Advice to his Children (Norris), 269–70
Stanhope, Philip, 222
Starkey, Thomas, 23–4, 72, 128, 287: on beggars, 93, 94
State of the Poor (Eden), 197
State of the Prisons of England and Wales (Howard), 123
Statute of Artificers (1563), 98, 224–32, 241: application to country folk, 225–6; detailed application in towns, 226; enforcement of Statute, 229–30; interpretation of Statute by gilds, 227; judgments of the Courts, 229–31; seven-year craft apprenticeship, 224
Statute of Merton (1235), 202
Stockport, charity school united to workhouse, 294
Stockwood, John, on child marriage, 48, 52
Stone, Lawrence, 46
Strangeways, Sir Giles, 68–9
Stroud parish workhouse, 166–8, 170: charity school attached to workhouse, 168, 294; emphasis

INDEX

Stroud parish workhouse—*contd.*
on formal education, 167–8; Orders for children's treatment, 167–8; outstanding example of humanitarian concept, 167–8; Parfect's *Proposels*, 167

Strype, John, on frequency of divorce, 53–4

Stubbes, Philip, on child marriage, 46–7

Sudbury, and workhouse provision, 165

Suffolk, Duke of, 35

Suffolk justices' rules for treatment of offenders (1589), 102–3

Sunday Schools, 296

Sunderland workhouse, 194

Supplication of the Poore Commons, A (1546), 96

Swinburne, Henry, 73

Sydney, Sir Philip, 282

Sydney, Thomas, 28

Sylvius Frisius, 67

Tanfield, Elizabeth (Lady Falkland), 18

'Teething in infants', 5–6

Temple, Sir William, 56

Tewkesbury, apprenticeship in, 258

Thame Grammar School, 286

Thornton, John, 119

Thrale, Mrs., 301

Tiverton, and workhouse provision, 165

Token for Children, A (Janeway), 266

Transportation of children overseas, 105–7: Transportation Act, (1717), 109, 122

Treatise of the Acute Disorders of Children (Willis), 301

Tring workhouse and reduction of poor rate, 169

Tudor policies for the deprived child, 126–46: family allowances, 142–3; function of overseers, 139–40; legislation, 138–9; London schemes, 127–33; outdoor relief, 136; Privy Council's attempts to enforce laws, 143–4; responsibility of justices, 143; schemes in provincial towns, 133–7; surveys of categories of poor, 126, 138; use of Hospitals in London, 127–33; weekly allowances, 141–2

Tuvil, David, 205

Universities, 34: entry at early age, 9–10

University College, Oxford, 9

Vagrancy Act (1744), 123

Vagrant children, 91–101: Vives' poor law plan, 91–2; Ypres scheme, 92, 94; increase in vagrancy and vagabondage, 93–4; sixteenth-century classification of the poor, 93–4; assumption that vagrants were avoiding work, 94; Acts of 1536, 1547 and 1549, 94–7; compulsory apprenticeship, 96–7; Poor Law Act (1572) and amending Act of 1576, 97–8; distinction between adolescents and younger children, 97; Act for the Relief of the Poor (1597), 98; Privy Council Orders, 98; maintenance and training placed on systematic basis, 98, and delinquency, 98–101; separation of parents and children, 100–1; Popham's *Resolutions*, 100–1; principle of Settlement, 100–1; attempts at transportation, 105–7, 122, apprentices taken into sea service, 108–9; Act of 1713, 122; Act of 1744, 123

Verney family, 12–13, 55, 71–2, 280, 301: and corporal punishment, 18

Vives, Johannes Ludovicus, 104, 126, 131: lecturer in rhetoric at Oxford, 92; plans for poor law policy, 91–2; resident at Henry VIII's Court, 91

Vowell, John, *see* Hooker, John

INDEX

Wakefield, administration of apprenticeship in, 236
Walthamstow vestry and inspection of apprentices, 251
Watson, Foster, 282
Weekly allowances, 141-2
Welch, Saunders, 111, 119
Wesley, John, 301: ideas on religious and moral training of young, 273; rules of his mother's household, 273-4
Wesley, Samuel, 284
Wesley, Susannah, 273-4, 305
Westbury, Wiltshire, gifts to apprentices, 236
Westminster Catechism, 264
West Riding of Yorkshire, apprentices in, 236, 238, 240
Whetstone, George, on forced marriages of wards, 70
White, Thomas, 270
Whitelocke, Sir James, 80
Whitford, Richard, 17
Wife-beating, 14, 17
Wilberforce, William, 253, 256
Wilkins, George, 49
Wilson, Thomas, 65
Wilson, Violet, 31

Wiltshire justices and difficulties of boarding out apprentices, 239-40
Winchester College, holidays, 280
Wingfield, Sir Anthony, 35, 43
Wollstonecraft, Mary, 305
Wolsey, Thomas, preferment of his illegitimate son, 203
Wood, Isaac: and Shrewsbury House of Industry, 195-6; on infant mortality rate, 196
Worcester: and workhouse provision, 165; apprenticeships, 258
Worke for Householders, A (Whitford), 17
Workhouses for children, 146-99
World We Have Lost, The (Laslett), 46, 200

York: and destitute children, 133-6; St. Thomas's Hospital, 133-5, 141; training schemes for young, 224
Young, Arthur, 306
Young Melbourne, The (Cecil), 222
Ypres scheme of poor relief, 92, 94, 142

www.ingramcontent.com/pod-product-compliance
Lightning Source LLC
Chambersburg PA
CBHW020239030426
42336CB00010B/548